OFFICE ORGANISATION AND SECRETARIAL PROCEDURES

GW00374073

Helen Harding

To Dad and to the memory of my Mother

PITMAN PUBLISHING
128 Long Acre, London WC2E 9AN

A Division of Longman Group UK Limited

First published in Great Britain 1988
Reprinted 1989, 1990 (twice), 1992 (twice), 1994

© Helen Harding 1988

British Library Cataloguing in Publication Data
Harding, Helen
Office organization and secretarial procedures.
1. Office work - Manuals - For secretaries
I. Title.
651

ISBN 0 273 02872 3

Printed and bound in Singapore

CONTENTS

7 Office communication systems 130

8 Office equipment 182

9 Office environment 228

10 Office personnel 247

PREFACE

Like most textbook users I always feel that there tend to be gaps –
even in those texts designed to cater for a particular syllabus – or that
I should have liked a bit more on certain aspects covered.

Being conscious of the fact that it is virtually impossible to produce
the definitive text on any subject area, far less one that is experiencing
continual change, I have, nonetheless, attempted to encompass within
one book essential information for anyone preparing to work in an
office in a secretarial capacity.

While the content is geared specifically toward the LCCI's Private
Secretary's Certificate in respect of the Office Organisation and
Secretarial Procedures syllabus in particular, it is equally suitable for
students undertaking the more advanced LCCI Diploma examinations
and for students studying for a wide range of RSA, PEI or BTEC
qualifications.

The book is comprehensive in scope but selective in detail. It is
divided into two units. The first comprises nine sections which deal
with the office, its related systems, procedures, personnel, accommodation and equipment. The second unit, split into five sections,
considers the secretary's role and function by examining the skills
needed and the sort of organisational abilities sought by employers.
Each section begins by listing a series of objectives.

The format I have chosen to adopt favours a fairly detailed treatment of topics, supported by lists of concise points as an aid to recall.
The aim is to be informative and to widen the reader's appreciation
and awareness of the subject by introducing more than the bare
essentials.

Each section concludes with a checklist summarising the main
points covered and this is followed by a selection of quick revision
questions to test the understanding of the section and where
difficulties are experienced it will be essential to study the relevant
portion again.

While topics are arranged in a particular way, all sections are totally
free-standing so may be read in any order. Cross-referencing is
included where mention is made of something elsewhere in the text.
Glossaries are also incorporated in the hope that they will prove
helpful, not only in deciphering any unfamiliar terms during reading,

but in providing a general backcloth for the more technical areas as well as a useful source of reference.

When structuring Unit 2 it occurred to me that readers might gain an added dimension by reading what practising secretaries actually do in the work situation. Consequently I contacted four former students who very kindly agreed to supply synopses which reflect the typical content of their jobs and these are included in the introduction to the unit.

Appendix 3 deals specifically with examination preparation. Rather than feature selected examination questions throughout the book I felt it would be more useful to include two complete papers, together with the Background Notes which are supplied by the examining body in advance. These should help provide students with a real feel for the examination and I have added some advice which I hope will be useful.

HH

Throughout the book I have referred to a secretary as 'she' and a manager as 'he'. This is simply for fluency and is in no way meant to infer that the roles may not be reversed. Similarly I have adopted the term 'chairman' rather than 'chair' or 'chairperson' but here again the holder may be male or female.

ACKNOWLEDGEMENTS

The author and publishers wish to acknowledge the following for permission to reproduce material:
Apricot Computers plc
British Telecom
Building Design Partnership
Canon
Kardex
Philips Electronics
Project Office Furniture plc
Rexel
Roneo Alcatel Ltd
Rotadex Systems Ltd
Sony
Twinlock UK Ltd

I should like to express my gratitude to the London Chamber of Commerce and Industry for permission to use specimen question papers and Background Notes from past examinations.

I should also like to express my gratitude to my colleague Joanna Gaukroger, who is Joint Chief Examiner for the LCCI Office Organisation and Secretarial Procedures examination, for her constructive comments and general support throughout the project.

My thanks are extended to Karen Alexander of Fulwood Executive Travel in Preston and to Neil Maynard, Head of the Lancashire–China Centre attached to Lancashire Polytechnic for their advice on the travel section.

Also thanks to Helen, Janet, Libby and Mandy for their willingness to contribute and for their ability to meet my deadline!

Last, and by no means least, my warm thanks to my husband Peter, for supporting me, *yet again*, through what has been another seemingly mammoth task.

HH

ABBREVIATIONS AND ACRONYMS

ABTA (Association of British Travel Agents) 309
ADC (Advise Duration and Charge) 154
AGM (Annual General Meeting) 139, 353
ASC (Accounting Standards Committee) 114
ATM (Automated Teller Machine) 76
BA (British Airways) 311
BACS (Bankers' Automated Clearing Services) 76
BIM (British Institute of Management) 266, 376
BSI (British Standards Institution) 377
BT (British Telecom) services 154
CAD (Computer Aided Design) 201, 206, 238, 239
CAR (Computer Assisted Retrieval) 46
CCITT (Comité Consultatif International des Télégraphes et Téléphones) 159, 172
CCTV (Closed Circuit Television) 244
CHAPS (Clearing House Automated Payments System) 76
CIM (Computer Input Microfilm) 41
CIPFA (Chartered Institute of Public Finance and Accountancy) 376
COD (Cash On Delivery) 138
COM (Computer Output Microfilm) 44, 208
CPU (Central Processing Unit) 191, 195
CV (Curriculum Vitae) 253–259
DBMS (Database Management System) 168, 199
DE (Department of Employment) 15
DEC (Digital Equipment Corporation) 197
DHSS (Department of Health and Social Security) 15
DTI (Department of Trade and Industry) 376
DTP (Desk Top Publishing) 201, 202, 203
EEC (European Economic Community) 15, 113, 117
EFT (Electronic Funds Transfer) 4
EFTPOS (Electronic Funds Transfer at Point Of Sale) 77
FDD (Franc de Droits) 138
FIFO (First In First Out) 125
GBS (Guardian Business Services) 266
HMSO (Her Majesty's Stationery Office) 375
IAM (Institute of Administrative Management) 242, 376
IATA (International Air Transport Association) 317
ICSA (Institute of Chartered Secretaries and Administrators) 376
ID (Identification) 64

UNIT 1
The Office

Everyone has an idea of what is meant by an office but few can offer a comprehensive definition, most tending to perceive of an office merely in terms of what it looks like, eg a room with desks, typewriters, filing cabinets and telephones, or a series of such rooms or even an entire building given over to the transaction of business functions of some kind. It is more accurate to consider the actual work undertaken and the methods, systems and procedures used to ensure effective and efficient performance.

This unit explores different aspects of the office and its work and brings into focus topics such as systems, equipment, environment and personnel.

1 Office work

To appreciate the nature of office work it is necessary to have some idea of the context in which it operates and of the changes which have taken place. There has been a substantial growth in office work and many new techniques, procedures and items of equipment have been introduced which have literally changed the entire concept of the office as well as the roles of those who work there. These changes came gradually at first but have increased in momentum during the last quarter of this century.

At the end of this section you should be able to:

- briefly outline the development since the Industrial Revolution;
- highlight the major changes which have taken place in that time;
- explain the nature of office work;
- describe the different departments found within organisations;
- understand the nature of the work undertaken by these departments;
- appreciate the hierarchical structure of organisations;
- provide diagrammatical representations of departmental structures;
- describe the functions of an office;
- appreciate that external factors can affect office work;
- list the services provided by a typical office;
- compare and contrast centralised and decentralised provision of services;
- appreciate the role of the office as the information centre of the organisation.

A brief historical perspective

While offices have been around for a long time, office work played a relatively minor part in people's lives prior to the Industrial Revolution. Since then there have been tremendous developments in terms of the work undertaken, the systems, procedures and equipment used and in the environment itself.

It is difficult to appreciate that less than 150 years ago clerks worked an 11-hour day, often supplied their own wood or coal for the office stove, cleaned their own offices, were forbidden to talk to one another during office hours and could not leave the room without the office manager's permission – and all for a few shillings a week! Yet this was very much the order of the day.

Initially offices were very much the domain of poorly paid clerks, seated at large desks, on high stools, painstakingly copying out letters in fine copperplate writing or poring over musty ledgers and accounts. However, with the growth in manufacturing came the need to process increasing quantities of information of all kinds and to maintain accurate records.

In the 1870s the first commercial typewriter was introduced, while Alexander Graham Bell invented the telephone and predicted the future of the telephone network. Clerical personnel began to occupy more significant positions within organisations as companies grew and prospered in the new industrial era, and the demand for clerical, professional and managerial workers to process the growing volume of paperwork increased. The office began to adopt its present day role as the central cog in the working environment.

During the 1930s 'scientific management' took the first rational look at business practices and we had the basis for 'systems analysis' as we understand it today. Important machine developments were also taking place and by the 1950s there were electric typewriters (first introduced as early as 1920), calculators, the first computers and copying machines, all of which greatly contributed to the ease with which routine office tasks could be performed.

Since the 1960s the pace has accelerated even more. The single element typewriter was patented by IBM in 1961, followed by the Selectric memory typewriter in 1964 (the real forerunner to word processing equipment). In the 1970s word processing really took off and the introduction of digital networks made faster and better communication possible between computers, particularly across great distance, while local area networks improved internal communication systems.

During this period Management Information Systems (MIS) emerged to bring with them better organisational efficiency and effectiveness via improved information provision and decision-making support. Emphasis was also placed on the use of behavioural science as a management tool to facilitate organisational change. This meant

3

that increasing attention was given to human factors which are so vital when sophisticated technology is introduced into the working environment.

Current and future trends

In the early 1980s considerable developments took place in the area of telecommunications with the introduction of computerised telephone networks. Information technology generally developed continually with a boom in personal computers, increased power and potential for microprocessing equipment, success with networking and electronic mail and continued experimental work with fibre optics and voice recognition. There have also been substantial advances in business applications such as Electronic Funds Transfer (EFT) while the City of London experienced the 'Big Bang' in October 1986 when all dealing on the Stock Exchange went over to computer.

What the year 2000 and beyond has in store is difficult to predict, such is the pace of change, but one thing is certain and that is that office work is evolving with a continual move towards integrated or 'convergent' systems. How near we are to achieving the 'paperless office' which has been talked about for a number of years now is still difficult to specify. The technology undoubtedly exists but there remain hurdles to overcome in terms of cost, compatibility and acceptability by workers.

The nature of office work

Office work is by its very nature **secondary** to the principal raison d'être of the organisation it supports, irrespective of the process involved, ie whether it be the manufacture of goods or the provision of a service of some kind. The office is but a subsystem of the organisation as a whole, just as the organisation itself is a subsystem of a

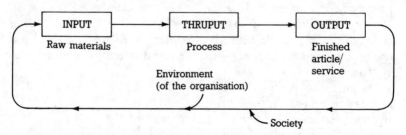

Fig. 1.1 Systems model: the organisation as a system

greater system or suprasystem, ie the total environment in which it interacts. This is illustrated by a simple systems model (see Fig. 1.1).

Similarly any individual aspect of office work, eg the distribution of incoming mail, can be illustrated by applying the same type of simple systems model. (Draw one up for yourself for distributing incoming mail.)

The 'complementary' role

Just as office work is secondary to the principal function of the organisation so too is it complementary in that without the essential support and information provided by office staff no materials would be ordered, no bills or wages paid, no invoices sent out or payments collected, no returns submitted. Also many of the statutory obligations which organisations require to meet would be left unattended. In other words, essential paperwork would literally grind to a halt.

The 'control' element

The other vital element exercised by the office is that of control. The office controls activities undertaken via a series of checks and balances. For example, it controls expenditure by administering strict budgets; it controls staff by implementing appropriate policies for clocking on and off and operating flexitime agreements; it controls the issue of supplies and establishes essential procedures for the efficient operation of the office-based side of the organisation's activities, such as the control of forms.

The departments of an organisation

Offices perform those functions within the framework of an organisation's structure and in the majority of instances this is made up of a number of departments. Table 1.1 provides a summary of eight principal departments found within most manufacturing companies, together with the functions they perform and the business documents and forms which would be associated with their systems and procedures.

Organisational structure

While presenting the different departments within a manufacturing organisation and detailing, in a tabulated form, the sorts of tasks undertaken by their functionaries does help general understanding, the fact remains that organisations are very complex and require further consideration.

Table 1.1 Breakdown of departmental functions and responsibilities

Department	Special observations	Functions and responsibilities	Associated documents and forms
Purchasing	Frequently a centralised function.	Securing the best prices; checking quality and sources of supply; ensuring reliability of suppliers; matching deliveries to production schedules; negotiating discounts; monitoring goods received; checking against invoices; stock control; devising distribution and requisition procedures.	Requisitions; price lists; quotations; estimates; orders; advice notes; delivery notes; invoices; debit notes; credit notes; stock control cards; stock lists.
Administration	The principal paperwork department dealing with all day-to-day running of office type activities. Often headed by a Company Secretary or Chief Administrative Officer (CAO).	Provision of central administrative and secretarial support; handling and processing of mail; telephone service; forms design and control; stationery and stock control; printing and reprographic services; maintenance of official company records; share registration matters; all legal and insurance matters; registering of patents and copyright; public and press relations;	Variety of standard business forms and documents.

Table 1.1 (*cont'd*)

Department	Special observations	Functions and responsibilities	Associated documents and forms
Administration (cont.)		maintenance of technical library; publication of house journals.	
Production	Usually a mix of engineering, planning and control sections.	Balancing requirements against resources, ie orders and sales forecasts against men, materials and machines; balancing work schedules to ensure production economies; working to specified standards, eg EEC regulations, BSI specifications; ensuring safety standards; carrying out work study; designing special tools; performing quality control tests; controlling stock levels; monitoring machine breakdowns; rescheduling as necessary; diversifying in response to innovation and change.	Production schedules; stores requisitions; specifications; time sheets.
Research and Development (R & D)	The centre of innovation and change but often underfunded and subject to	Design, develop and test new products and prototypes; make short-term, low-cost	Bills of quantity; specifications; quotations; proposal forms.

Table 1.1 (*cont'd*)

Department	Special observations	Functions and responsibilities	Associated documents and forms
R & D (cont.)	cutbacks because investment is very expensive. A company's failure to invest often means losing out to fierce foreign competition.	improvements; establish long-term projects; engage in pure and applied research; suggest ways of diversifying, eg extending product range, going off in a new direction.	
Marketing	Central to any organisation. Conveniently divided into three principal areas of activity viz, research, sales (home & export) distribution.	Market research; advertising and publicity; attending exhibitions and trade fairs; customer relations; after sales service; customer liaison; document processing; sales analysis; specialist packaging; communicating with overseas agents; liaising with sales representatives; franchising; warehousing; distributing goods; liaising with wholesalers; dealing with currency regulations; dealing with export formalities; promoting the company image.	Inquiries; estimates; quotations; price lists; catalogues; sales orders; advice notes; invoices; debit notes; credit notes; dispatch notes; delivery notes; bills of lading; bills of exchange; certificates of origin; consignment notes; customs declarations; questionnaires.
Management Services	A range of specialist services which may include: Computing and DP; MIS; O & M.	Analysing work patterns; improving procedures; improving facilities and working environment;	Policy documents; plans; progress charts; reports; legal documents; pro formas;

Table 1.1 (*cont'd*)

Department	Special observations	Functions and responsibilities	Associated documents and forms
Management Services (cont.)	Facilities Management; Security Services. This department provides expertise which may be called upon by any other individual or department.	reviewing office layout; designing computer systems; programming computers; processing information; solving problems; standardising procedures; enhancing decision-making capacity of management; introducing checks and control mechanisms; improving the use of resources; improving security.	Government forms; confidential designs; specifications; flow charts; standard business documents; agendas; minutes.
Personnel	Four main areas of activity: recruitment and selection; training; welfare; industrial relations.	Manpower planning – assessing future needs against present staffing; appointment, promotion and distribution of staff; implementation of employment legislation; designing incentive schemes; operating suggestion schemes; staff development and training; designing job specifications; job analysis; job evaluation; staff appraisal; salary and wage matters;	Contracts of employment; job descriptions; job specifications; interview assessment forms; suggestion scheme forms; safety reports; accident report forms; job evaluation forms;

Table 1.1 (*cont'd*)

Department	Special observations	Functions and responsibilities	Associated documents and forms
Personnel (cont)		redundancy and dismissal procedures; attendance at Industrial Tribunals; Health and safety; environmental factors; welfare; social and recreational matters.	person specifications; Staff Handbook insertions.
Finance and Accounting	A mix of financial accounting, funding and control activities	Preparation of final accounts; maintenance of accounting records for submission to Registrar and HM Inspector of Taxes; compilation of financial reports; internal audits; analysis of capital and revenue expenditure; preparation of budgets; credit control; cost accounting; payment of wages and salaries; tax matters; ascertaining sources of funds; comparing and contrasting alternative investments; performing different analytical techniques to	Trial balance; trading and profit and loss accounts; balance sheet; flow of funds statement; bank reconciliation statement; petty cash book; wages records; cash analysis; P45, P60, P2; tax tables; NI deduction cards; clock cards; tax returns.

Table 1.1 (*cont'd*)

Department	Special observations	Functions and responsibilities	Associated documents and forms
Finance and Accounting (cont.)		control finance, eg cash flow analysis cost benefit analysis; introducing computerised methods.	

All organisations, even though they are quite unique in themselves, exhibit similar arrangements when it comes to making sure that the work gets done. For example, most, if not all, organisations have an overall boss, different levels of managers and supervisors and a general workforce. This is usually expressed in the form of a pyramid as shown in Fig. 1.2.

At the top of the pyramid is the boss, managing director or chairman, who presides over the whole organisation, whatever its size. The overall success or failure of the organisation is his ultimate

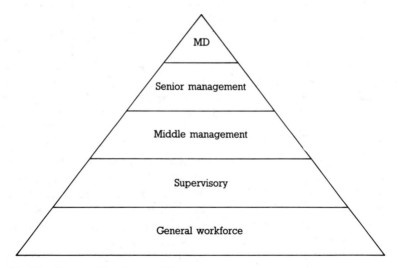

Fig. 1.2 Organisational pyramid

responsibility, even though he may not be directly involved in day-to-day management decisions. Depending on the nature of the company the boss will be responsible and accountable to a board of directors, or board of governors (as, for example with the British Broadcasting Corporation) and to shareholders in the case of a publicly owned company.

Senior management comprises a team of executive managers who are responsible for determining policy for the organisation as a whole, as well as for specific sections or divisions falling within their area of specialisation, eg Marketing. They report directly to the Managing Director while exercising control over their subordinates, viz middle managers and supervisors.

Middle managers have no executive decision- or policy-making power. Their primary function is to ensure the smooth operation of day-to-day, often routine, activities. Their jobs involve co-ordinating the different functions taking place across and within the different departments.

Supervisors tend to undertake trouble-shooting roles, eg when a machine is down, when someone is ill, or where there is a backlog of work in a particular area, and will need to resolve the problems.

Finally the workers at the bottom of the pyramid represent the prime functionaries within the organisation since they fulfil the raison d'être of the enterprise. In industry the shop floor workers **make** the products, in hospitals the nurses **look after** the patients, while in banks or shops the counter clerks or shop assistants **serve** the customers. In other words, the further up the pyramid you go the more removed are the roles from the day-to-day functions of the organisation and this is one of the principal reasons for misunderstanding between workers and management.

Horizontal and vertical communication

Organisations are, therefore, structured on hierarchical lines and in most situations communications are issued one way, viz 'top down' rather than 'bottom up'. This can be a mistake since many of the 'workers' have original ideas as well. Therefore, effective management systems encourage the development of a variety of systems by introducing appropriate channels of communication which operate both vertically and horizontally throughout the organisation. For example they may establish Joint Consultative Committees (see also Section 7 page 140) and generally encourage wider worker participation at meetings in general. Another technique may be to develop quality circles, (ie small groups of between say six and ten individuals with a common interest in either· a product or process) which will ensure quality control.

Organisation charts

Organisation charts supply the traditional means of illustrating the design of an organisation together with the patterns of interrelationships which exist between divisions, departments, sections and individuals. At a glance they are able to show the distribution of authority in an organisation and indicate individual responsibility, specialisms and spans of control.

Fig. 1.3 shows a typical organisation chart indicating the vertical 'top down' command network and the lateral distribution of labour across the organisation as a whole.

It should be noted that while this is the most common layout for organisation charts it is also possible to prepare them horizontally or as a circle (concentric charts).

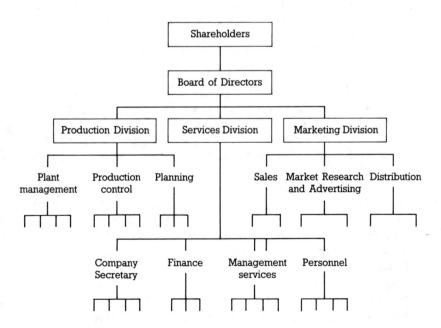

Fig. 1.3 Organisation chart

The functions of an office

Most standard texts on office administration or office management would state that the office basically performs five types of activity. These are as follows:

Receiving information of all kinds in all its various forms via all possible channels of communication, eg the written word, the telephone, word of mouth, computer printout, facsimile transmission, etc.

Recording information of all kinds via the maintenance of appropriate record systems whereby the information may be stored in an appropriate format and retrieved at a later date. This may necessitate keeping a verbatim record or a synopsis, making a statistical breakdown or visual record or transferring the data to some form of computer storage. It may also entail a high level of confidentiality.

Preparing and arranging information of all kinds so that it is available in the manner in which it will be of most use in the future. For example, information may be assembled, calculated, summarised, classified, arranged, interpreted, edited, duplicated or reproduced in some totally different format for subsequent use by management.

Communicating information of all kinds to those who need it both within and outside the organisation. Such communication may be via any medium which is appropriate to the accurate dissemination of the information, eg by letter or report, by telephone, at a meeting, by visual or graphical representation, via computer link or in person.

Safeguarding assets This represents the role of the office in accounting for all the assets of an organisation and warning management of any apparent irregularities. It involves such procedures as the recording and monitoring of capital equipment, the reporting of bad or doubtful debts and the general care of the organisation's financial interests.

Such broad office functions require to be undertaken by any organisation irrespective of its size and nature, although within the one-man business or the small partnership many of these responsibilities will fall to the owner or partners rather than to a specific administration department.

The information processing centre of the organisation

Whatever an organisation's activities might be, the office acts as the nerve centre and focal point in respect of the processing and dissemination of information. Never before has information been so plentiful and covering such a wide area of interest. The problem rests in identifying what is required for different purposes and then making the best use of it.

An increasing number of external agencies now influence organisations in one way or another and these make additional demands in terms of paperwork and returns. Examples are government departments, eg Department of Health and Social Security (DHSS), Department of Employment (DE), the Inland Revenue and the EEC. Also social, political and economic factors generally have a bearing on the world in which we live and work and these, too, bring pressures to bear together with the attendant paperwork. Consequently, the problem is not so much collecting data, but determining precisely what is needed and handling it appropriately.

Office services

The type of services which any office provides will be to a certain extent dependent upon the organisation, its function, scale, ownership and design, ie whether it is product-producing, people-processing, international, national or local in flavour, whether it is nationalised or privatised, whether it is a company, a partnership or a co-operative and whether it is run on departmental or some other lines – not to mention where it stands in relation to the wider environment as referred to above.

However, irrespective of those features the range of services provided by the office will be similar and are likely to include:

- secretarial support, ie typing, shorthand, audio and word processing;
- maintenance of records, ie filing and indexing;
- distribution of incoming mail;
- circulation of internal mail;
- collection and despatch of outgoing mail;
- control of stationery;
- reception of visitors;
- operation of the switchboard and routing of calls;
- duplicating and copying.

Centralisation versus decentralisation

Prior to the arrival of new technology many of these services tended to be centralised, particularly within larger organisations, in order that general clerical support would be provided for a range of management functions, such as personnel, accounting and marketing. The idea behind centralisation was to benefit from standardisation of procedures, better supervision and improved management control whilst reducing peaks and troughs in the workloads of individual departments and generally making economies in terms of staff, facilities and equipment.

However, with technology the tendency has been to return to a decentralised provision of office services where departments can now benefit from the convergence of data and word processing and the ability to provide a range of clerical, secretarial and management information services in one location thanks to local area networks and management work stations. Although managers may now be responsible for their own office systems they still need to conform to certain standards laid down within the organisation as a whole in order that there is compatibility to enable them to communicate with other systems in the company and possibly outside. (See also Section 7.)

CHECKLIST

1 Office work is undergoing an evolutionary process.

2 Technology is changing the face of office work.

3 Office work still remains secondary to the primary function of any organisation.

4 Offices perform a complementary role, providing an essential control element over personnel and activities.

5 Offices also have a strong financial role to perform.

6 Organisations are frequently divided into a number of departments and office work is an integral part of the work of all departments.

7 Organisational structures tend to be hierarchical in nature and are commonly represented as pyramids with the chief at the top and the workforce at the bottom.

8 Communication takes place both vertically and horizontally within the pyramid.

9 An organisation's position in relation to the wider environment is also significant in determining the support services it needs.

10 Sometimes services are centralised in large organisations in an attempt to enhance efficiency, reduce costs and increase productivity.

QUICK REVISION QUESTIONS

1 State four principal office developments since the Industrial Revolution.
2 State the primary functions of:
   a a textile factory;
   b a hospital;
   c a travel agency.
3 State three ways in which an office can exercise control over the activities of an organisation.
4 List the four principal areas of activity in a personnel department.
5 Describe six functions you would expect a management services department to perform.
6 Name five documents you would associate with exporting goods.
7 List the five principal functions of any office.
8 Name six typical office services.
9 Suggest three advantages to be gained by centralising an office service.
10 Name three external factors/agencies which affect the volume and nature of office work.

2 Office systems

The systems approach

Systems are introduced to assist organisations to operate efficiently and effectively. All well-managed organisations have good systems and many operate through a network of systems. Such an integrated or 'systems' approach is best described diagrammatically (see Fig. 2.1) where the organisation itself is a system, operating within a suprasystem as expressed by the total environment. The functional areas operate as subsystems, each with its own set of procedures which in turn have their own methods.

At the end of this section you should be able to:

- appreciate the systems approach to organisational effectiveness;
- differentiate between systems, procedures and methods;
- define the component parts of an office system;

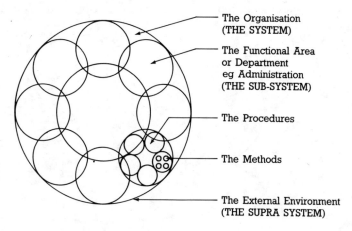

The Organisation
(THE SYSTEM)

The Functional Area
or Department
eg Administration
(THE SUB-SYSTEM)

The Procedures

The Methods

The External Environment
(THE SUPRA SYSTEM)

Fig. 2.1   An integrated office system

18

- suggest the sort of factors which would contribute to an effective office system;
- identify techniques used by systems analysts in designing or improving existing office systems;
- devise simple procedures;
- draw simple flow charts;
- identify the essential elements of a good management information system.

Systems, procedures and methods

A system is a group of interrelated and interdependent parts which operate in sequence according to a predetermined plan which has been established to achieve a goal or series of objectives. The sequential steps are referred to as **procedures**. This is really the working level of a system and provides guidelines to employees in terms of who should do what, how and when. Procedures are then broken down into a series of specific operations which are performed by using particular **methods**.

The concept of a system

Systems may be manual, mechanical, computerised or automated, but will be designed to best accommodate the office function or service concerned. To appreciate the concept it is necessary to view it as a combination of people, equipment and procedures (see Fig. 2.2 below). Hence it is absolutely vital that individuals with responsibility for analysing, designing, implementing and controlling office systems have a sound appreciation of these joint needs.

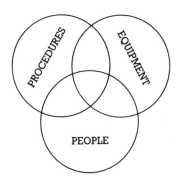

Fig. 2.2 The concept of an office system

Analysing office work

Systems analysis studies the interrelationships between the component parts of a system, ie people, equipment and procedures, in an attempt to simplify work processes and provide a firm basis for managerial decision-making to take place. The term is associated primarily with the application of computer techniques in creating and designing appropriate methods. Persons performing an analysis are referred to as systems analysts. They may be members of the organisation's full-time staff or they may be outside consultants.

Whenever analysis of office work is taking place with a view to establishing appropriate systems, certain questions must always be asked, viz. What is done? Why? Where? When? How? and By whom?

Management will tend to be concerned with the overall function or task of particular sections or departments, eg to produce accounts, to investigate complaints, to maintain personnel records or to market a product, rather than the detail of the specific processes which take place within the office to support these functions. Therefore, managerial concern is with the objectives of the system, with how systems are prioritised within departments, with the ways in which system performance is measured, with whether improvements are called for, with security measures in force to ensure against, loss, damage or theft rather than the details which make up the systems themselves.

It will fall to the supervisory and operational levels, ie those responsible for the setting up and day-to-day running and using of appropriate systems to analyse the detail and give thought to the following:
- degree of simplicity;
- logic of operation;
- ease of supervision;
- training necessary to operate the system;
- equipment factors;
- flexibility of techniques used;
- adaptability to change;
- ease of introduction of changes;
- keeping rules to a minimum;
- avoiding unnecessary duplication;
- user satisfaction;
- monitoring of the system;
- reliability;
- speed with which breakdowns can be dealt with.

Techniques and tools used in systems analysis

A range of possible techniques and support tools are used by systems analysts and these include:

Procedure narratives where the steps in a procedure are presented in narrative form (see Table 2.1). Sometimes the form may be more detailed than the example given.

Table 2.1 Procedure Narrative

Procedures	Operations/methods	Functional areas involved
1	*Requisitioning* a) Complete Requisition Form b) Acquire authorisation c) Transmit to Purchasing Dept	Personnel
2	*Obtaining quotes* a) Telephone selected suppliers b) Reduce to three possibles c) Prepare requests for written quotes d) Send out requests e) Log quotations received	Purchasing
3	*Ordering* a) Complete official order form b) Send to supplier c) Notify Personnel Dept	Purchasing
4	*Receiving Goods* a) Sign delivery note b) Check invoice against order c) Deliver item to Personnel Dept d) Check for damage e) Submit invoice to Accounts Dept	Purchasing Personnel Purchasing
5	*Paying for goods* a) Calculate any special discounts due b) Draw up appropriate cheque c) Send cheque with invoice d) Log payment in appropriate ledger	Accounts

Work distribution charts which identify the units of work performed (it is usual to allocate activity codes to the various activities, eg A = Typing, B = Telephoning, C = Filing, D = Photocopying and so on), together with those performing the activities and the times taken.

Such charts would be prepared over a representative work period, eg two weeks, and would be based on information provided in activity time logs maintained by workers. They would highlight inefficiencies in existing systems, help analyse productivity and assist in improving the efficiency of work flow.

Block flow charts which are really diagrammatical representations of information contained in narrative statements. Therefore, the procedure narrative for the purchase of a typewriter for the Personnel Department might be presented as shown in Fig. 2.3.

Procedural flow charts incorporate symbols and conventions to identify each step in a process. These standard symbols are as follows:

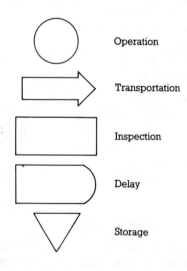

Operation

Transportation

Inspection

Delay

Storage

Once the procedure has been determined, the symbols are used to represent each step and are joined together by lines to indicate the flow. Basically any procedure can be described by using some combination of these five symbols. A completed chart will provide a summary of the procedure and will enable the analyst to question, for example, why any one symbol is used more frequently than others. Proposed improvements to the procedure can then be put forward by drawing up an alternative route side by side with the existing procedure.

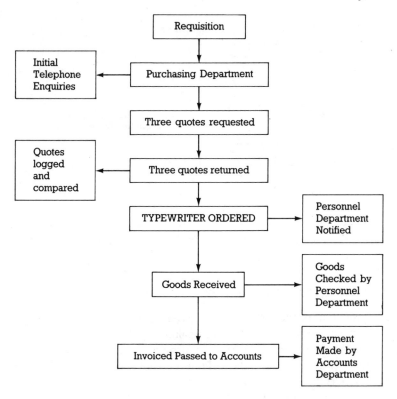

Fig. 2.3 Specimen block flow chart

Office layout charts are frequently used with procedural flow charts to help visualise actual work flow. A scale drawing of the office layout would be supplied and lines would be drawn on it depicting work flow between the various work stations. This simple device can frequently illustrate a lot of repeated movement between certain work stations and may suggest the need to review layout or eliminate certain 'journeys', by modifying the procedure, eg reducing or eliminating certain checking mechanisms.

Symbolic flow charts are variations of the other flow charts already described and are used to discuss, develop and design computer-based programmes, rather than those for manually-processed information. They use different symbols, and the principal ones are as follows:

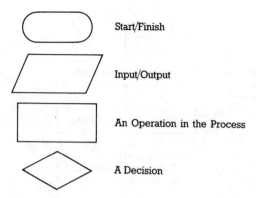

An example of a symbolic flow chart representing the recruitment and shortlisting process within a personnel department is given as Fig. 2.4.

Management information systems (MIS)

The growth of paperwork already referred to brought with it problems for managers in terms of decision-making in that it became increasingly difficult to obtain the right information, in the right format at the right time, such was the volume of paperwork to sort through. Although computers did help to some extent, their very existence often generated even more information!

Consequently many organisations developed management information systems to overcome these difficulties. The computer was the linchpin of the system providing a sort of clearing house for all the information input by the organisation's various functional areas. What was really being developed with these systems was an enormous database providing all managers with a wide variety of information to facilitate decision-making.

Managers need not only internal information, eg personnel data and productivity figures but information from external agencies, eg details of other companies in the same line of business, if they are to remain competitive. Without information, management is hampered and will very likely make inappropriate financial decisions, the repercussions of which could be disastrous.

What constitutes a good management information system?

A properly conceived, well-developed MIS will be likely to possess the following characteristics:

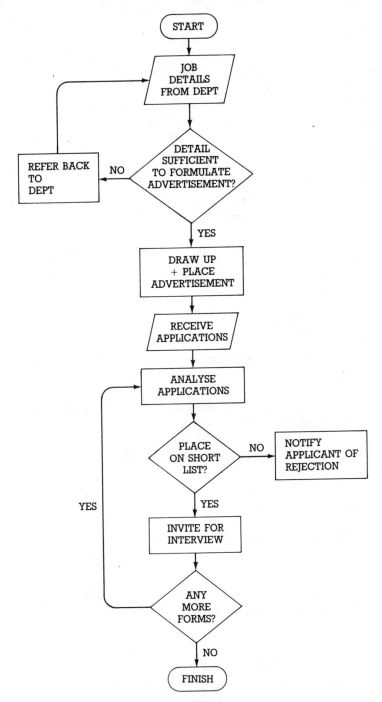

Fig. 2.4 Recruitment and shortlisting process

- total organisational involvement;
- a sense of purpose and focus on end results;
- a framework determined by the functional areas of the organisation, ie purchasing, production, marketing, personnel, finance, administration, research and development etc.;
- maximum integration between the functional areas;
- automation of routine procedures;
- the reduction of uncertainties by the allocation of specific responsibilities;
- built-in control mechanisms to ensure essential feedback in order that adjustments and modifications may be made as and when necessary;
- the capacity to relieve managers of time-consuming, routine research activities, so enabling them to do what they ought to be doing, viz planning, innovating, decision-making and evaluating performance.

A successful management information system will need to achieve the following objectives:

- provide information in the format desired, where and when needed;
- supply accurate, up-to-date information at high speed;
- be cost-effective in producing information;
- be capable of introducing essential security controls and checks for the processing of confidential data;
- be flexible and adaptable to changing needs and circumstances;
- generally provide for more efficient administration.

CHECKLIST

1 An organisation can usefully be viewed as a system.

2 Functional areas of activity, eg finance, administration, personnel, represent subsystems.

3 To function effectively these subsystems are made up of inter-dependent areas which have their own procedures, eg accounting procedures.

4 Procedures in turn are broken down into methods.

5 Methods may be manual, mechanical or automated.

6 Individual office systems are made up of the interrelationship of procedures, equipment and people.

7 The study of interrelationships is known as systems analysis.

8 A wide range of systems analysis techniques is used to design workable office systems.

9 The growth in paperwork and the increasingly important role in organisations played by computers gave rise to the introduction of what are termed management information systems (MIS).

10 Management information systems, often computerised, are designed to provide management with the key information it requires for decision-making.

QUICK REVISION QUESTIONS

1 If an organisation represents the system what represents the suprasystem?
2 What is the difference between a procedure and a method?
3 What are the three component parts of any office system?
4 Suggest six essentials of a good office system.
5 Name three techniques used in systems analysis.
6 Draft a procedure narrative for filling a vacancy for a clerk in the sales department.
7 Devise a block flow chart for issuing office stationery.
8 Devise a symbolic flow chart for dealing with incoming mail.
9 Describe a management information system.
10 What are the advantages of MIS?

3 Office record systems

Accurate records form an essential element of all business information systems. The setting up and monitoring of appropriate systems frequently presents problems for many organisations with filing and indexing rarely rating among the most popular office tasks. Why is this the case? As already commented today's office is literally swamped with paperwork and the volume of paper retained by each office worker is still growing steadily every year. While there have been considerable advances in recent years with the introduction of mechanised and electronic storage systems to replace familiar 4-drawer vertical cabinets (still present in many offices), the fundamental record management problems do not disappear with these introductions. Whether records are held on paper, film, tape or disk the information still needs to be organised, and organised well, if it is to be retrieved with ease.

At the end of this section you should be able to:

- explain the different stages in the life cycle of records within an organisation;
- identify the principal features of a good records management programme;
- describe the main filing classifications;
- appreciate the Dewey Decimal Classification system;
- describe different types of filing and indexing equipment;
- appreciate the concept of electronic filing;
- describe different types of microform storage;
- explain the main features of the principal types of microfilm equipment;
- outline a procedure for filing;
- suggest reasons for inefficiency in filing systems;
- appreciate the need for effective retention and destruction policies for records.

The records cycle

Records, whatever their form, pass through a cycle (see Fig. 3.1) and sound procedures and methods are required at each stage of that cycle. For example, it is at the **creation stage** that decisions need to be made with regard to the length of time records need to be stored before they can be destroyed.

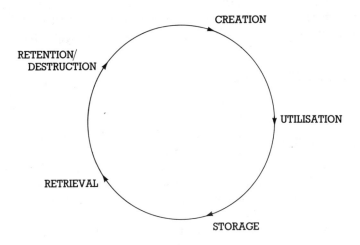

Fig. 3.1   The records cycle

At the **utilisation stage** it is important that records are kept in such a way that information can be retrieved quickly and efficiently by whoever needs it and that efficient procedures exist to ensure good work-flow. Much of this will depend upon the appropriateness of classifications, the quality of the initial indexing and the existence of adequate cross-referencing systems which should be incorporated into filing procedures at the creation stage.

The actual **storage stage** is concerned with the selection of suitable equipment and the utilisation of space together with convenience and accessibility for those who need the information. It is at this point in the cycle that the desirability of introducing some form of centralised record management will be considered. The physical safety of documents in storage and security aspects such as confidentiality and unauthorised access need to be taken into account also.

The **retrieval stage** is largely concerned with the speed and ease with which documents can be located on request. This will depend again on aspects such as suitability of classification, equipment and authorised access, but will also involve the setting up of appropriate tracer systems or 'signing out' procedures in order that documents may be followed up when they have been absent from the system for an unreasonable length of time.

The **retention/destruction stage** determines the format in which records should be stored, eg in original hard copy form, in some type of microform storage, translated onto computerised storage or transferred to archival storage. Decisions will also have to be taken in relation to methods of destruction, eg shredding or incineration.

Records management

The supervision of the records cycle is referred to as records management. Some organisations select a centralised system where the supervision is confined to a group of specialist staff, but it will be rare to find a system which is totally centralised and consequently everyone within an organisation should have an awareness of filing and indexing procedures. After all, they are the users of the information and their appreciation of the operational aspects of a records system should help with its smooth running.

Try to imagine a situation where no records management system exists, where everyone does his own thing, where there is no standardisation of any kind and no formal procedures and methods. The result would inevitably be chaos.

The objectives of a records management programme

The following are characteristics of any typical programme:

- provision of accurate information throughout the organisation;
- control of records through each step of the records cycle;
- recognition of the responsibility for operating the programme;
- development of sound systems and procedures;
- standardisation of procedures and equipment;
- staff appreciation and awareness of procedures via essential training and the provision of necessary procedure manuals;
- safety and security of information;
- establishment of appropriate retention/destruction policies;
- elimination of unnecessary duplication of records;
- adaptability to future developments, including expansion or contraction;
- on-going monitoring and evaluation of existing procedures;

- economies in terms of the cost of providing the service;
- increased efficiency of information storage and retrieval.

Filing and indexing systems

There is always a problem of determining the precise use of the word 'system' in terms of filing and indexing as it could refer to the method of classification, the type of equipment used, whether storage is centralised or decentralised, to the procedures used to physically store and access information or even to all of these aspects taken together. In this section 'system' is taken to refer to the types of classification and these are briefly as follows:

Alphabetical

This is used to describe the filing of documents under a proper name, ie a person's name or the name of a company or organisation, according to the first letter. This is probably still the most common type of classification and it does have the advantages of being directly accessible, in that it does not require an index, and it is easy to understand given that everybody knows the alphabet. However, other than in very small systems it can become difficult to manage in that it is not easy to estimate space requirements for active files and there can be problems when there are many files with the same or similar names.

Numerical

This type of classification is also popular in that it too can be simple to operate on the basis of allocating consecutive numbers to new files. All files will possess a unique number which can also be usefully used for reference purposes. It is unnecessary to estimate space requirements other than in overall terms, and expansion potential is limitless. It is, however, vital to maintain an accurate index in order that files may be easily located. This indirect access not only slows down the location time but requires the acquisition, setting up and maintenance of a separate indexing system. This does, however, provide an element of confidentiality in the files and the index can prove useful in its own right. An obvious example for the application of a numerical classification would be where a number already exist, eg an order number or numbered minutes.

Subject

Here files are stored according to subject, eg Electricity, Gas, Rates, allowing again for direct access and making simple provision for the inclusion of miscellaneous files. Such systems are frequently arranged in alphabetical order although this is not a prerequisite.

Geographical

This is where files are maintained according to their geographical or district location. While this may appear to have a somewhat limited application it can be particularly useful in certain types of organisation, eg local authorities, firms dealing with sales territories, either on an international or national level. Once again access will be direct, probably with an element of alphabetic arrangement present in the breakdown of sub-files, eg the American continent may be broken initially into states and then into cities/towns within the state and finally to districts within the city/town. Possible problems which can be experienced with geographical systems arise out of poor knowledge of geography on the part of users together with difficulties experienced when boundaries change or when countries change name. This element can be minimised by incorporating appropriate cross-referencing, eg 'Sri Lanka see also Ceylon'.

Chronological

Here filing is done according to date. While the system is rarely the sole classification criterion or the main one in operation, a chronological element will exist within all other systems with the most recent communication/information always appearing on top of the file. Where chronological systems are useful is when the date has major significance, eg a departure date for a business trip, and is the key factor in triggering off some necessary action. Hence the importance of maintaining follow-up files in date order (see also Unit 2 p 371).

These are the five main types of classification system but there are many other specialist applications and variations. For example, alphanumeric systems may be adopted in an attempt to overcome the limitations of any individual system. Similarly organisations may opt for a specialised numerical system such as **terminal digit** which comes into its own where records are held on a particularly large scale, eg by building societies, insurance companies, hospitals. The idea is to divide large numbers, ie six digits or more (smaller numbers can be made up to six by adding noughts to the left of the number) into groups of two or more digits which have individual significance. For example, take the number 925614. Here the terminal digits would be 14 and this number would represent a location indicator, eg the fourteenth drawer, while 56 would represent the guide card within the drawer and 92 would be the folder number. When a new folder is added it would be 935614.

Such systems are complex and require training on the part of filing clerks but they do have the advantage of enabling a better distribution of folders throughout a system, of easing the addition or removal of folders, of minimising error, in that the clerk need only remember two digits at any one time, and of spotting misfiled folders. Very large numbers can be read three digits at a time.

A word about the Dewey Decimal Classification system

Just as files within an organisation need to be stored in a readily accessible order so, too, do books in libraries. While fiction books will be arranged on the shelves in alphabetical order according to the surname of the author, non-fiction books are arranged according to their subjects. Several classification and cataloguing systems exist throughout different libraries but the Dewey Decimal system is very common. It takes its name from Melvil Dewey an American who invented his system when working in a library in the 1870s. The system is based on dividing knowledge areas into ten main sections, identified by a three digit code as follows:

000.	General	500.	Science
100.	Philosophy	600.	Technology
200.	Religion	700.	The Arts
300.	Social Sciences	800.	Literature
400.	Language	900.	Geography, History

Each of these areas is subdivided further into ten more divisions, eg 600–610, 611–620 and so on. Each book within an area has its own number. For example, 651.HAR could refer to a book on the Office by Harding and this would fall within the 650 division which is allocated to Business Practice. Obviously it is unnecessary to memorise all subdivisions but useful to recall the ones which you need to consult frequently.

Colour coding Another useful aid to classifying materials is to introduce colour coding to simplify the location process. This can be particularly useful in indexing systems where different coloured cards or strips will indicate different classes of information. Colours are also useful as general identifiers, eg the use of different coloured folders to denote filing from different departments. Similarly, colours are frequently incorporated into multiple copy documents. For example, the top copy on an invoice set may be white, the office copy pink, the salesman's personal copy blue, the stores copy yellow and the delivery note green. Such divisions greatly facilitate paper handling and substantially reduce error.

Filing equipment

The range of equipment available is varied offering a wide selection of system, design, material, colour, facility and price. Broadly speaking equipment falls into the following general categories:

Vertical filing

This refers to the storage of documents in upright cabinets which may be between two and six drawers in capacity, although the most common is the four-drawer variety. Papers may be stored within these cabinets in either folders which stand upright, one behind the other, on the base of the drawer, or within files or folders suspended in pockets within the drawers. These pockets may in turn be free-standing from the metal frame which is fitted into the drawer or linked together. The former has the advantage of enabling very swift insertion of new files but has two principal disadvantages, viz the labelling tends to stand proud of the folder and so frequently becomes damaged with the opening and closing of drawers, and there is a strong likelihood that papers and slim files may be inserted between the pockets, so ending up on the base of the drawer.

In terms of vertical storage generally the cabinets are somewhat bulky occupying a lot of floor space (space must also be allowed for the extent of the open drawers). Also there is a tendency to over-fill drawers, possibly because of the difficulty of inserting large quantities of new material. This often means a total rearrangement of the original drawer allocation given the knock-on effect of inserting material into the first drawer of the system. These cabinets also used to have a bad safety record in that they readily toppled forward when more than one drawer was opened at a time. However, this hazard has been overcome with modern cabinets which have an in-built safety feature whereby it is impossible to open more than one drawer at a time. On the positive side, one possible plus for vertical cabinets is their tidiness. There will never need to be unsightly papers visible as can be the case with other forms of storage where doors are frequently left open, exposing the entire contents of the system to view.

Lateral filing

This type of filing is particularly practical where floor space is at a premium but where there is a need to retain hard copy information. Files are basically stored side by side in rows with the ends of the files visible. They may either be stored on shelves or suspended in pockets as described above. Where lateral cabinets extend virtually from floor to ceiling the labelling of the pockets is particularly important. Ideally the labels should be attached in such a manner that they may be adjusted according to the location of the files within the cabinet, ie angled downwards for high shelf location, angled straight for eye-level storage and angled upwards for low-level storage. It is also helpful if the file detail is protected by a plastic strip which magnifies the information.

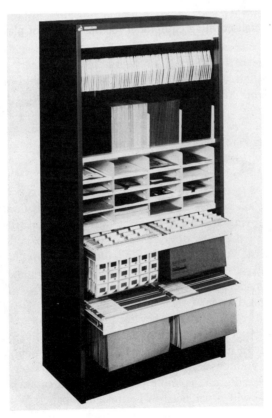

Fig. 3.2   Multi-purpose adapted lateral filing

Adapted lateral filing

It is useful to consider this form of lateral filing separately as many manufacturers now produce a multi-purpose type of cabinet which is capable of incorporating a selection of filed material (see Fig. 3.2). In such a cabinet it is possible to include, for example, a vertical arrangement which pulls forward on rails (see bottom sections of Fig. 3.2), as well as an element of traditional lateral storage and sections for stationery or whatever. These multi-purpose cabinets can be fitted out to user specification and may, for example, incorporate space for computer print-out, plans, card indexing, floppy disk storage and so on. It is also useful to remember that lateral filing cabinets can conveniently be used in open plan offices to section off work areas and introduce an element of privacy where required.

Horizontal filing

This is specialised filing equipment for the storage of plans, maps and

Fig. 3.3   Chest plan filing

drawings. It consists of shallow drawers of considerable depth in which materials can be laid out flat, one on top of the other. Not only does this sort of system take up a lot of floor space but the contents can soon become damaged along the edges through frequent handling. Also the cabinets cannot serve a useful dual purpose, eg operate as a desk top as there is no space for knees.

Chest plan filing

A more popular method of storing plans and drawings is in a chest plan file (see Fig. 3.3). Here plans are separated by upright dividers and are either suspended from some form of rail/clip arrangement or allowed to stand freely between the dividers. Such files are usually mobile and fireproof and are capable of holding a vast number of drawings.

Fig. 3.4   Rotary filing

Rotary filing

Sometimes referred to as carousels these files (see Fig. 3.4) as the name suggests rotate on a central axis. They can have several tiers of different depths suitable for holding either lever arch files or index cards, each tier capable of revolving independently of the others, and can be used for random access from a number of suitably located workstations. Some systems are even motorised so that at the press of a button the carousel will revolve until the desired section is beside the appropriate workstation.

Mobile filing

This term can be used to describe simple mobile file units which consist of single drawers placed on trolleys which can be easily moved between workstations. They are particularly useful in open plan layouts where they may form part of the total systems furniture concept (see p 236). Alternatively it can refer to rows of filing with aisles in between which can be brought together on rails, either manually or by electric motor. At the end of the day, the aisles are closed up for protection and security purposes. All such systems have safety devices which prevent the rows of shelves from moving together while someone is still in the aisle!

Automated filing

In addition to the more standard type of system described above many forms of automated system exist. The intention with such systems, which are largely centralised, is to reduce operator fatigue and speed up the location process by automating many of the filing and retrieval functions. The filing clerk simply keys in the name or code number of the file or file space required and the machine will activate and deliver the appropriate file or space to the operator who will have remained seated throughout the entire operation. Such systems reduce a lot of the drudgery associated with large filing systems in that the filing clerks no longer need to stretch or bend to reach files. An example of automated filing is given as Fig. 3.5.

Indexing equipment

When considering filing equipment it is also essential to give thought to the selection of appropriate indexing equipment, as not only do many classification systems demand a separate index but indexing equipment is useful in its own right. Once again the selection varies from card indexing systems stored in boxes, drawers, on rotary stands

Fig. 3.5 Automated filing

or shelves, to strip indexing systems in book form or on desk-top rotary stands. A selection of indexing equipment is given as Fig. 3.6.

Electronic filing

While all the filing systems already described have been concerned with the storage of some tangible object, whether it be correspondence in a file or folder, bulky advertising brochures, computer print-out, plans, drawings, cards, floppy disks or any other physical objects, a considerable amount of storage is now undertaken by electronic means. Here the documents themselves are not stored, merely the information contained in them. This is done by computer technique where the data is passed in the form of electronic pulses into computer or word processor for storage on magnetic tape or disk. At the creation stage data generation will tend still to be via the keyboard, but where data already exists in hard copy form it may be capable of

Fig. 3.6 Indexing equipment (a) index card drawers, (b) Rotadex card index, (c) rotary card index, (d) visible card index, (e) visible strip index.

being read by machine for transfer onto computer. This would involve Optical Character Recognition (OCR) (see also p 205) or Computer Input Microfilm (CIM) techniques. Where initially such text generation facilities were few and far between, and very expensive, they are becoming more common and costs are decreasing.

The volume of material capable of being stored electronically is dependent on the storage medium used, eg magnetic tape, floppy disks, micro-floppies, or hard 'Winchester' disks (see also p 209). The latter has a much greater capacity and is at less risk from contamination in that it is hermetically sealed which means that, in theory at least, the data should be perfectly safe on disk. However, whatever the medium it is always advisable to make back-up copies and this, of course, adds to the cost, the time element in terms of preparation and the need to provide extra storage space for the disks.

So much for the input storage element of electronic filing. But how is the information retrieved? Here the answer is even easier. The operator simply keys in the code for the desired information, the system scans the file, locates the data and displays it on the VDU screen – all in a matter of seconds. Another major bonus is that more than one person at a time may consult the data held on file. Therefore a member of staff located in Accounts may wish to consult a file for certain information while, at the same time, someone in Personnel may wish to consult the file for different information. In a traditional hard copy system only one person could have the complete file at a time and so considerable time could be wasted going to a central filing department only to find that the file had already been taken out by someone else. Where the need was urgent this would mean tracking the file down or, where the need was less vital, waiting for it to be returned before the task could be completed. With an electronic system simultaneous interrogation of a database or file presents no such problems.

The problem of keeping track of files is virtually eliminated as the system does all the work. What is important is that the indexing is logical and easily understood by those operating the system. Additionally there is the need to ensure that only those entitled to access certain information have clearance to do so. In all large computerised filing systems there are built-in security checks to handle this. Also precautions are built-in to the system to ensure that data cannot be altered or deleted either deliberately or in error. Computer fraud is a growing area of criminal activity and systems need to be well managed and monitored in order that any irregularities are quickly detected.

Optical disks

With the movement towards office automation there have been increasing demands to handle vast quantities of files, quickly and inexpensively while occupying the minimum of space. One positive answer appears to be the optical or laser disk. A 12-inch disk is said to be capable of storing 500,000 pages of word-processed material.

Disks are unaffected by fingermarks and dust and so are well suited to typical office conditions. In appearance the disk is similar to an LP record but it is read not by contact with a stylus but by shining a thin laser beam of light onto the disk. However, there is one major disadvantage and that is that like LP records the disks are incapable of being amended or updated, hence you may sometimes come across the term 'write once, read often' to describe these disks. Therefore their main use is in terms of archival storage.

Microform storage

Microfilm was first used as early as 1870 during the Franco-Prussian war when the French used the technique to smuggle messages from Paris via carrier pigeon. Its popular application to the storage and retrieval of office records arises out of the immense savings it can bring about in floor space at a time when office rates and rental charges are at a premium. Microfilmed documents need only about two per cent of the space required to file paper documents. The principle of microform storage is, therefore, one of reduction and this can be anything from 24 to 150 times, dependent on the type of storage and the particular application.

Types of microforms

Strictly speaking 'microform' is the generic term for the different types of storage media available, eg roll film, fiche, jackets and aperture cards, although most people will use microfilm to describe any of the forms which are still viewed as the modern substitutes to paper filing.

Roll film is exactly what it sounds like, viz a roll of film (100 or even 200 feet long) on which documents have been filmed one after the other. Completed rolls are stored on reel, cartridges or cassettes to protect them from dust and fingermarks. Film can be 16-mm or 35-

mm. The former is commonly used for filming routine business correspondence and has a reduction ratio of about 24×, while the latter would be applied to plans, technical drawings and the like and has a reduction ratio of about 18×. The principal advantages of roll film are that it provides maximum storage capacity, it is relatively inexpensive to prepare; the continuous roll format ensures minimal misfiling and maintains file integrity. On the other hand it has the disadvantages of being difficult and costly to update, of being difficult to use in terms of locating individual frames quickly and the readers are of the most expensive variety.

Jackets provide the answer in terms of the ability to update roll film in that a jacket is a thin plastic carrier of about 6 × 4 inches, into which strips of 16-mm roll film can be inserted. Each microfilm strip normally contains up to 12 frames and a jacket would normally accept 5 or 6 strips into a channel so that the total capacity of a jacket could be 72 frames. This technique has the advantages that the film is protected by the jacket, images can be simply and speedily reproduced and updates and deletions are easy. The principal disadvantage is that the preparation of the jackets can be time-consuming, although where there are large volumes it can be done by machine.

Aperture cards measure $3\frac{1}{8} \times 7\frac{1}{8}$ inches and within this card one single 35-mm frame (it is possible to include more than one per card) is inserted into a rectangular hole (aperture). This is a somewhat specialised form of storage and is used principally by architects and engineers to store drawings, plans, etc. The blank space around the film image can be used for written information, or where a lot of cards are prepared it may incorporate a punched hole system to facilitate retrieval. Aperture cards have the advantage in that large documents can secure the benefits of microfilm reduction but still be handled on an individual basis. Also duplicate copies can be relatively easily and inexpensively prepared.

Microfiche, commonly referred to as 'fiche' looks similar to a jacket in that it is a rectangular sheet of film measuring 6 × 4 inches. However, the likeness stops there in that preparation is different. Fiche is not prepared from roll film and it requires a different type of camera. The result is the formation of a grid pattern of 98 frames made up of seven horizontal rows each containing 14 frames. The reduction ratio is 24×. Space is retained at the top of the fiche for an eye-readable descriptive index. Preparation is quick and inexpensive, but the majority of fiche cannot be updated. Nonetheless, it has the advantage of being extremely durable, convenient to post and usable with very inexpensive readers. The principal disadvantage is the inability to easily update, coupled with the fact that quality is inferior to high quality roll film.

Com fiche is a special type of fiche used in conjunction with computer technology. COM stands for 'Computer Output Microfilm' and is concerned with printing directly from computer onto microfilm by bypassing the paper stage. Digital information from a computer is sent to a VDU screen from which it is photographed onto film. The big advantage is the speed with which the Com fiche is produced and the fact that a greater reduction ratio enables greater quantities of data to be handled, stored and moved around. Low cost fiche readers combined with sending Com fiche data by post can work out cheaper than transmitting data direct via computer terminals.

Micrographics equipment

Equipment is required to create, duplicate, retrieve and reference microforms and will fall into the following categories:

Cameras While many microform users do not invest in their own cameras, depending rather on the services of an outside bureau, three principal types of camera are used, viz rotary (or flow), flat bed (or planetary) and step and repeat.

Briefly, **rotary** cameras which are the cheapest and fastest to use (capable of up to 20,000 exposures per hour) are used to photograph correspondence, particularly large batches of uniform-size paper. Material is photographed as it moves or flows with the film. **Flat bed**, on the other hand, is more expensive and slower but more versatile, enabling books, magazines etc. to be filmed. Also the quality is superior, particularly where originals may not be particularly sharp. **Step and repeat** cameras are used to photograph images directly onto microfiche.

Duplicators These refer to special machines designed to reproduce additional copies from original microforms. There are different machines for the different types, ie roll to roll, fiche to fiche, card to card. Machines come in a vast price range governed primarily by speed factors.

Readers Irrespective of the extent to which any organisation opts for microfilm a reader will always be required. This is the one piece of hardware which is indispensable in any micrographics system (the others can be supplied by bureaux engaged to do the filming). Readers are designed to meet the requirements of different types of microform and are available in abundance and across a wide price range. Selection criteria will be based on the following:

- type of film to be read;
- ability to accept more than one type of microform;
- screen size;
- picture quality and clarity;
- ease of searching;
- cost factors, eg number of readers required, manual or motorised film drive;
- ease of use, eg location of controls;
- service arrangements;
- special features.

Readers/printers (See Fig. 3.7) These possess all the qualities of straightforward readers plus the additional capacity to print out hard

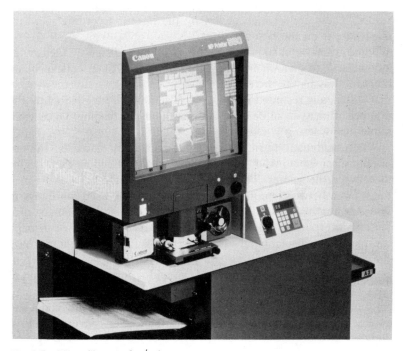

Fig. 3.7   Microfilm reader/printer
(*By courtesy of Canon Business Machines Ltd*)

copy copies at the press of a button. Hard copies will be enlarged by the same amount as the copy seen on the screen. Special consideration will need to be given to the size of the machines, the speed with which copies are produced, the quality of copies and the cost.

Indexing techniques for micrographics systems

One of the problems with microfilming techniques rests with the choice of indexing system. Any filing system needs an efficient index for ease and speed of retrieval. Various methods exist – some manual, others mechanical and some computer-assisted. The simplest type of index is that incorporated in the margin of fiche, jacket or aperture card or even on the first few frames of a film roll. Such indexing is eye-readable. Another technique which can be incorporated into systems and which makes it possible for material to be read by the unaided eye involves the use of blank white areas on the film, sometimes marked with an identifying symbol, letter or number. These 'flash' index marks, as they are termed, enable the reader to locate material more easily. Its use is really limited to material filed in alphabetical or numerical order. Code lines also act as a guide to the reader. These are set high or low on the screen, according to where the reader is on the film sequence.

Some cameras and readers have inbuilt distance meters or 'odometers', to give them their technical name. These work in much the same way as the meter on an audio or video-cassette recorder, so that distance is recorded at the time of filming and consequently the number of images can be offset against the meter reading. Once again sequential ordering is essential.

Where automatic retrieval is sought, reliance is placed on the use of optical sensors to read 'blips' or other marks placed on the margins or between the frames. The sensor either counts the blips or a match takes place between information requested by the user, who keys in an index number into an image control keyboard, and the binary code pattern incorporated on the film, which is read as it passes through the reader. Such computer-assisted retrieval (CAR) techniques have the advantage of capitalising still further on the space-saving economies of microfilming by ensuring fast and accurate manipulation of data. Fully automated systems are capable of identifying desired information from the simple keying of an appropriate code and producing it on screen from where it may be read or converted to hard copy.

Filing procedures

Whatever type of filing is undertaken within an office system, ie whether manual, electronic or micrographic, sound procedures and methods will require to be devised and implemented if the system is to operate efficiently and effectively. Basically this will require an analysis of current practice, with a view to establishing future needs and this will be done by undertaking the following:

- conducting an inventory into the number of records kept;
- classifying the types of records kept;
- identifying users;
- reviewing methods and equipment;
- identifying current problems;
- highlighting inefficiencies;
- considering retention policies.

Once this has been concluded, it will be practical to give due consideration to the actual processes of filing. Dependent on the type of systems in operation these should incorporate the following steps:

1 Collection The assembly of all papers ready for filing in baskets, trays, etc. These would be collected periodically (possibly by specialist filing clerks, where a centralised system operates) and taken off for filing.

2 Inspection Documents should all be checked prior to filing to ensure that they are in fact ready to be filed. Inspection should throw up a release symbol or identifier of some kind which is readily recognised by the filing clerk. This could, for example, be a tick, the word 'file' or someone's initials.

3 Indexing This involves the selection of the appropriate caption or name under which the document is to be filed, or the allocation of a number in a numerical system, together with the simultaneous preparation of an index card or reference. While this will depend primarily on the classification system in operation, consideration should be given to the manner in which the document is likely to be described when referred to for future retrieval purposes.

4 Coding Once the indexing is determined the document is coded. This means that the relevant name, number, subject, date, or whatever, is highlighted, underlined or added to the document.

5 Cross-referencing It is at this point that any necessary cross-reference cards should be prepared.

6 Sorting and preparing Finally documents are sorted in readiness for filing. Sorting should be done at a desk, away from the filing cabinets, with the help of trays, sorters or dividers. Documents should also be prepared appropriately in terms of having holes punched in readiness for insertion in files, having paper clips removed where necessary, and being generally squared up, ready for insertion in files.

A word about indexing with electronic systems

Just as indexing is important for manual systems so, too, is it vital for electronic systems. Speed of retrieval can only be guaranteed where disks are well labelled, where the contents of a disk are logically indexed, where old material is transferred or deleted and where regular housekeeping is carried out. It is also important to have the appropriate facilities for storing disks safely and securely.

Confidentiality and security

Certain records systems will always need to be not only physically secure from fire, water, dirt and dust, but will be set up to minimise the risk of loss, misplacement and theft. Some types of record are more valuable than others, with some being difficult if not impossible to replace. It is not necessarily the document itself which is valuable (this would rest mainly in the province of archive material) but rather the nature of the material in it which is intrinsically valuable in its original form. Take something like Title Deeds as an example, or your examination certificates!

Additionally there is the responsibility of keeping records confidential and free from scrutiny by those who should not have access. Sometimes it may be sufficient to introduce some sort of code system for naming the documents held and this technique may be used in either manual or computerised systems. However, where the information may be of particular interest or value to someone else, eg a competitor, it may be necessary to establish a very complex code that makes illegal access all the more difficult. In such instances it will also be vital to keep a key to the code. In terms of access to central computer storage this will normally be controlled via passwords which may be changed as often as considered necessary for security purposes.

Where a floppy disk storage system is used as well as using code names for all the documents held on disk, the disks themselves should be carefully labelled and kept under lock and key. Incidentally, when labelling disks the labels are best prepared on a typewriter for clarity, but where a pen is used the label should be prepared before it is stuck on the disk or, where it is placed on a disk sleeve, the disk should not be in the sleeve while the label is being written, otherwise there is a risk of damaging the disk. It is inadvisable to leave disks lying around loose and a range of lockable storage boxes is readily available to ensure security and general protection.

What about data protection?

These days we hear a lot of talk about data protection and, rather than referring to the protection of data as referred to above, viz in the interests of the organisation, it refers to the safeguarding of the interests of individuals where information about them is held on computer. Legislation, in the form of the Data Protection Act, 1984, is having far-reaching effects on many aspects of business today, notably credit control and employee records. (See Appendix 2, p 390)

Retention and destruction

It would be remiss in a section on records systems not to refer to the importance of clearly defined retention and destruction policies. Any retention policy should be developed at executive level and should carry full management support. All records pass through different stages in their lives, from 'Active' to 'Dead', but some records can never be destroyed and consequently some satisfactory solution has to be reached for their retention. Records can be classified according to their value, importance and uniqueness and this will provide some guidance in terms of how they might best be stored.

Records may be vital to the essential functioning of an organisation in that they may be impossible to replace. Their retention may be a statutory requirement, eg certificates of incorporation, memorandum and articles of association, share registers, patents, property documents, accounting records, auditors' reports, tax returns, etc. have to be stored permanently. Whether documents need to be retained in original form varies according to legal requirements, but this will be one of the issues which requires consideration. It may, for instance, be possible to retain microfilm copies and lodge originals with a bank for safe keeping.

At the other end of the spectrum documents may be of little or no importance and, once read and dealt with as necessary, may be relegated immediately to the waste-paper basket. Each document will require an independent judgement and that judgement needs to be based on solid guidelines issued from well up the organisation's hierarchy. Essentially judgements will be made on the following criteria:

- relative value, ie uniqueness, historical significance, etc.;
- existence/availability of other copies;
- the format in which the information must be retained;
- legal requirement;
- frequency of reference;
- speed of retrieval;
- space availability;
- cost implications of converting to some alternative storage.

'Housekeeping'

It is worth remembering that just as physical storage can become cluttered with the result that it will invariably take longer to find something, so, too, can floppy disk or mainframe computer storage and it is important that regular 'housekeeping' is undertaken to 'weed out' unwanted material by either transferring or destroying files.

In floppy disk terms this will mean transferring documents to back-up disks or deleting them altogether. Where mainframe computer storage is used it will be the province of the system manager. There will be guidelines for computer users in respect of the length of time files are retained and once again it will be up to individuals to consult their index of files on a regular basis and delete unwanted materials before the extent of their disk space quota is reached. Otherwise there may be the danger of material being deleted by default.

Long-term physical storage

Where actual documents are transferred to some form of archival or long-term storage, care should still be taken to ensure that the storage is safe from fire, dirt, dust, damp and temperature changes.

Frequently, alternative storage will mean the transfer of files to basements or to locations in less expensive buildings. Papers can be conveniently transferred to strong fibreboard boxes, available in various sizes to accommodate A4 paper, computer print-out, punched cards, etc. These boxes, which when empty can be stored flat for transportation purposes, are easily assembled and very durable. They can be well labelled to denote contents and are then easily stacked to form the equivalent of a solid bank of filing drawers. Reports would suggest that such arrangements offer remarkably good protection against all kinds of hazards – even fire and water – such is the strength of the cartons and the tightness with which they may be packed.

The popular alternative to long-term archival storage is, of course, microfilming, which is particularly useful for providing access to certain source documents which might otherwise be difficult to consult, eg back copies of old newspapers and journals.

Destruction methods

When it comes to actual destruction, shredding or incineration are the most likely methods, although from the point of view of environmental protection and the potential in recycling paper, shredding is likely to be preferred.

Great care needs to be exercised to ensure that confidential records are adequately disfigured in the destruction process prior to any recycling. As far as the shredding of general documentation is

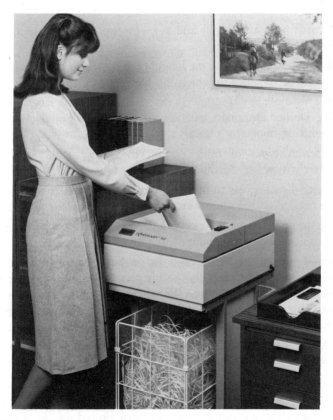

Fig. 3.8 Shredding machine

concerned staff need to appreciate the capabilities of the shredding equipment. All paper clips and, where possible, staples, should be removed prior to shredding and care should be taken not to over-tax smaller machines by feeding too many sheets through at one time.

There are many different models of shredder on the market, ranging from the hand operated desk top variety to large industrial models capable of handling vast quantities of paper at a time. A typical office shredder is shown as Fig. 3.8.

One other thing worthy of note in terms of shredding is the value of waste paper for recycling purposes. Where a company has a lot of shredded paper it will be worth its while contacting a waste-paper merchant to collect the paper. Payment is usually by the ton and dependent on quality.

CHECKLIST

1 Records have a life cycle and at each stage of that cycle there are procedures and methods.

2 One system involved in the handling of records is the classification system, ie the way in which the files are arranged, eg alphabetically or numerically.

3 The Dewey Decimal Classification system is a popular means of organising books in a library.

4 Different types of filing equipment are available for storing different types of document.

5 Where direct access to files is not possible, eg where a client's file has been allocated a number, a separate index needs to be set up.

6 Electronic filing refers to a computer-based system for information storage, cataloguing, manipulating and retrieval of documents.

7 Sound security systems need to be built in to any electronic system to prevent unauthorised access, to reduce the effects of computer failure, minimise the potential for computer fraud and take into account data protection legislation.

8 Microphotography is a great space-saving technique for record storage, particularly for archival materials which can easily be stored in a permanent sequence.

9 Filing procedures include the following stages: collection, inspection, indexing, coding, cross-referencing and sorting.

10 Sound retention policies together with procedures in respect of

destruction techniques are essential aspects of any records management system.

QUICK REVISION QUESTIONS

1 What are the different stages in the life cycle of a document?
2 Give six reasons for establishing a proper records management programme.
3 Provide three possible interpretations of the word 'system' in connection with filing and record management.
4 Name five filing classification systems.
5 Describe or make sketches to illustrate vertical, lateral and horizontal filing equipment.
6 What are the principal advantages of electronic filing?
7 What is the difference between microfiche and jacket microfilm?
8 How might the confidentiality of records be ensured in both manual and electronic systems?
9 Suggest five considerations an organisation might make in establishing a retention policy.
10 Describe two alternative forms of archival storage.

4 Office reprographic systems

Reprographics is taken to refer to the reproduction and handling of all copy documents at all stages from creation, through to finishing and distribution. For many years after the Industrial Revolution the most common way of reproducing copy documents was to use carbon paper, but as the paper explosion grew the demand increased for a variety of new duplicating and copying processes to be developed. Organisations began to find it extremely difficult to operate effectively without reliable copying facilities and consequently reprographics now forms a vital link in the communications network of the modern office.

At the end of this section you should be able to:

- distinguish between different types of reprographic process;
- describe different duplication processes;
- describe different types of copier;
- suggest appropriate reprographic equipment for different tasks;
- discuss the pros and cons of establishing an in-house print facility;
- identify other items of equipment which support a complete reprographics system;
- list suitable selection criteria in choosing equipment.

The distinction between duplicating and copying

One important point to clarify before exploring the reprographics area in more detail is the difference between duplicating and copying, as this is fundamental to a sound appreciation of equipment, supplies, operating skills and procedures as well as the end product achieved.

Where a duplicating process is being used it is always necessary to prepare a 'master' first of all, before the duplicated image can be run off on the appropriate machine. The type of 'master' prepared will depend on the nature of the process to be used, eg it would be a stencil of some kind for ink duplicating and a plate for offset duplicating. Stencils and plates come in different forms and are prepared in a variety of ways according to the purpose they are required to serve. At their simplest they may be prepared by hand or on a typewriter, while more specialised applications can be secured by preparing a facsimile stencil on an electronic scanner or an aluminium or plastic plate on a special plate-making machine.

Duplicating methods

Essentially, there are three methods of duplication, viz spirit, stencil and offset.

Spirit duplicating

This is the simplest and least expensive method but is less frequently found in business situations today. Master copies can be prepared on any plain paper, although art paper with a shiny surface produces the best and most easily corrected masters. The plain paper is placed on hectographic carbon paper (carbon side uppermost) and the material for duplication handwritten, drawn or typewritten on the plain paper. The result is a mirror image carbon deposit on the reverse side of the plain paper. This plain paper then becomes the spirit master and is placed round the roller of a spirit duplicating machine. When the copy paper, having been moistened with spirit fluid, is fed through the machine by rollers and comes into contact with the master copy, the spirit dissolves a small amount of the carbon deposit and produces a copy. The quality of the copy achieved will depend on the colour of the carbon used (purple is the most common and produces the longest runs), on the standard of the master and on the number of copies taken. On average, around 100 to 250 copies should be possible from a good master.

Preparation is easy, although it can be a little tricky where it is desired to incorporate several colours on the one master, so necessitating changes of carbon. On the other hand, colour combination potential can be a plus, particularly for maps, charts and diagrams. Corrections are messy, requiring the removal of the carbon deposit from the master, either by scraping with a blade, painting over with a masking fluid or erasing with a special rubber, and then the substitution of a fresh piece of carbon paper if an alternative insertion is called for. Alternatively, masters can be prepared via a heat transfer copying process which has the advantage of producing a facsimile version of the original. Nonetheless, in strict business application terms spirit duplicating is infrequently found and where it is used it would be for internal purposes only. Typical users of the method tend to be schools and voluntary bodies. Machines can be manually or electrically operated and are available in different sizes to accommodate different widths of paper.

Stencil duplicating

Stencil duplicating has been around for a long time and works on the principle of ink passing through finely cut images on a very thin sheet of cellulose paper lightly coated with a special wax. This stencil is part of a special stencil set (different sets are available for different purposes and for different methods of preparation). The set will consist of the wax sheet, which is sometimes fronted with a protective film cover to protect the wax (particularly during preparation on an electric typewriter), a thin sheet of double-sided carbon paper and a stiff backing sheet. The carbon serves two purposes; it provides a copy on the backing sheet and also helps the typist see what is being typed given that the ink ribbon is always disengaged during stencil preparation to enable the metal keys to strike directly onto the wax to cut the letter images. Without the black showing through from the carbon behind the wax sheet, proofreading is very difficult. Preparation itself is straightforward, although an even pressure is required on the stencil for hand or manual typewriter preparation. Hand prepared stencils are drawn up using a special stylus pen.

Stencils can also be prepared by heat transfer or electronic means. The latter enables the preparation of a good facsimile copy and is useful where there is a lot of fine detail or diagrammatical work to produce onto the stencil. Electronic stencil cutters or 'scanners' (see Fig. 4.1) can also be used to reproduce drawings or half-tone photographs quite satisfactorily. An electronic eye scans across the original at high speed and a fine hair-like needle simultaneously cuts an identical image on a special stencil. In fact, used in conjunction with an ink duplicating machine, a scanner presents a feasible alternative to photocopying for the company which needs to produce a lot of copied material, particularly of a detailed nature, for internal use, although scanners are not inexpensive to buy.

Once again stencil duplicating machines may be hand or electrically driven and operation is relatively straightforward, although inexperienced operators can get into a mess when filling the drum container with ink or attaching/removing the stencil. Colour reproduction is possible, although it does necessitate changing drums. A more realistic

Fig. 4.1 Electronic stencil cutter
(By courtesy of Roneo Alcatel Ltd)

compromise is to run off material on coloured paper. Lengthier runs are possible with the stencil process as opposed to the spirit method, but once again the end product is more suited to internal use rather than for external circulation purposes.

Offset duplicating

Offset duplicating (see Fig. 4.2) provides by far the most professional finish. Also called lithography the process has gained popularity in recent years, particularly where organisations have established their own in-house print facility. The process, which originated in Bavaria in the latter part of the last century, operates on the principle that oil and water do not mix. When the blank areas of the plate become wet they do not pick up printing ink, while the graphic or printed matter has a greasy texture which rejects the water base but picks up the ink.

Once a plate has been prepared (see more on plate-making later) this 'master' is attached to a large roller (the master cylinder) on the machine. The plate is then inked up and the image is offset (hence the name) onto a second roller (the blanket cylinder) which, when it

Fig. 4.2 Offset duplicating machine
(By courtesy of Roneo Alcatel Ltd)

comes into contact with a third roller (the impression cylinder) feeds blank paper through and produces a copy. The process is a somewhat complex one and is dependent on the correct balance of the mix of ink and acid/water solution, which separates the non-image area on the plate. Operator skill in inking the rollers and adjusting the flow of fluid is of paramount importance, so training is essential.

Finished results are of very high quality and it is possible to set up very long print runs of several thousand copies. Offset duplicating requires careful setting up and machine preparation and consequently is best in circumstances where machines are in more or less constant use. Where machines lie idle they need to be stripped down frequently and well warmed up before they set about a new job. Machines can print in any colour, but, of course, this means changing the ink and cleaning the machine thoroughly beforehand. Some machines do have the capacity to produce multiple colour copies in a single pass through the machine but this is a specialised application and needs specialised equipment. Machines can be manual, semi-automatic or completely automated in operation. One of the main determinants of price will be the degree of automation. Table-top models are also available.

Other likely considerations when selecting offset equipment will include:

- the type of plates you are going to use, given that the purchase of special plate-making equipment adds cost;
- the maximum paper size to be printed;
- the operating speed;
- the accuracy with which the machine will feed paper through a second time (this is referred to as 'registration' and is important for dual colour work or where overprinting of any kind is required);
- the number of inking rollers (the more the machine has the better the likely results);
- the existence of a trained operator;
- special features eg automatic blanket cleaning;
- service and back-up support available from the supplier.

Typical applications of offset duplicating Offset duplicating is much more versatile than the other two systems described above and the end result is of much better quality, strongly resembling that prepared by a professional printer. Organisations employing offset systems use them for a wide variety of printing tasks, including, eg:

- all typewritten matter from which copies are required, eg reports, minutes, staff handbooks, telephone lists;
- diagrams and drawings;
- letterheads;
- blank forms;
- compliment slips;
- business cards;
- brochures;
- price lists;
- advertising material.

A recent new arrival

One new electronic machine to appear on the market is what is termed a Dri-Printer (see Fig. 4.3). This machine is something of a hybrid. It needs a special master which can be prepared using a word processor or electronic typewriter in that it can be cut using a daisy wheel (normal duplicating stencils cannot be prepared successfully in this way) and is therefore run off using typical duplicator technique, but it uses fast-setting, dri-print ink. This enables printing to be done

Fig. 4.3   A dri-printer
(By courtesy of Roneo Alcatel Ltd)

on copier bond paper, unlike traditional ink duplicating which needs a semi-absorbent paper.

The results are therefore of high quality, produced at speeds of between 50 and 150 copies per minute and yet less expensive than photocopies. Also the machine has a range of useful electronic features which make operation very easy.

Plate-making equipment

Offset duplicating presupposes the need to give some consideration to plate preparation and special plate-making equipment, in that the quality of the finished printed product will be to a large extent dependent on the type of plate used. Basically plates fall into four categories, viz paper, plastic, photographic and metal. There are many different ways of preparing these plates, but the following outlines will provide some idea of what is involved.

While paper plates can be prepared by hand or on the typewriter, by far the most common method of preparation is by photocopier. **Electrostatic plates** can be prepared quickly and cheaply on an ordinary electrostatic photocopier. In fact many plain paper copiers can also make offset plates. No special skill is required, only the careful feeding of the blank plate through the machine following the careful lining up of the original on the photocopier glass (as will be necessary with many ordinary photocopying jobs). While it is technically possible to store and re-use a paper plate, this is not recommended as a new plate will inevitably produce a better result.

Where an organisation wishes to print long runs and perhaps re-use special plates it is likely that metal plates will provide the answer. Whether the usage warrants the purchase of a plate-maker for the purpose will, however, depend on the extent of the requirement. It may well be more economical to have metal plates professionally prepared as and when required. There are several ways of making metal plates but the cheapest and simplest is by a process referred to as **chemical or diffusion transfer**. In comparison with electrostatic plate-making this is a complex, two-stage technique. The first stage necessitates making a negative of the original while the second is to process the negative by pressing it against a metal plate and passing it through a chemical solution. After a time lapse (not always easy to gauge) the negative and plate are peeled apart to produce the master. The exposure element in this process is critical and it may take several attempts to produce the desired result. This can prove time-consuming and costly but the end result is a plate which can be used, cleaned and re-used to print around 20,000 copies of high quality.

Where it is desired to make plates capable of a long run (say 40,000 copies) without producing a negative, **special photographic equipment** is needed to shoot the image directly onto a special type of plate. The end results will be superior, particularly on half-tone work, to the transfer process but the level of work done would have to justify the purchase of expensive equipment.

The ultimate technique employs what is termed **pre-sensitised plate making** but this is really only within the scope of the professionals as it requires photographing the material with a special type of camera and then special processing. An organisation wishing to use this type of plate would more than likely have its preparation contracted out to a supplier. Also, the cost of plate preparation by this method is much greater than the others described.

Fig. 4.4 Giant copier
(*By courtesy of Canon Business Machines Ltd*)

Copying equipment

The range of copying equipment currently on the market is extensive
and consequently considerable care needs to be taken to ensure that
users get what they need for the sort of money they wish to spend.
The types of copier available span from small, simple, desk-top
models for the small user (under 1,000 copies a month), through low,
mid and high volume copiers (ie those designed to accommodate over
30,000 copies a month) with all manner of special features and
capabilities, right through to giant copiers (see Fig. 4.4) which are
aimed at volumes in excess of 100,000 copies per month with the
capability to handle complex multi-page work. Price ranges too are
extensive and there is potential to buy, lease or rent. While most
copiers fall into the plain paper category there are still a few which
fall into the electrostatic category where they use specially coated

paper. The initial capital investment of such copiers is much smaller than for a plain paper copier, but the running costs are substantially greater, such is the cost of the special sensitised paper in comparison to plain bond paper. Therefore, these copiers are unlikely to be a good investment these days, unless for the very low volume user.

Selection criteria

Other than the volume of copying to be done, the following are worth considering when choosing a copier whether it is for outright purchase, leasing or rental:

- the speed with which copies are produced;
- maximum paper size taken;
- paper feed arrangement, eg sheet feed from one or two trays, or roll feed with a guillotine to cut paper according to preselected size;
- reduction and enlargement facilities;
- by pass facility to feed through single sheets, eg transparencies, letterheads, offset plates;
- ability to copy on both sides of the paper ('duplexing' is the technical term for this);
- potential to copy in colour (machines are available which make full colour copies of coloured originals, but they are very expensive);
- automatic document feed, ie where the copier will select and position the original on the glass, eject it on completion of copying and proceed to the next original;
- automatic selection, ie where the copier will automatically match the original to the appropriate paper size, taking into account any magnification or reduction ratio selected.
- job recovery potential, ie the ability to clear the paper paths after a jam during a complex multiple copy job and restart automatically without the need to reset the number required.

The need for certain of these features will depend on the type of copying work to be done by the machine and on whether or not it is the sole reprographics facility used. It will also be important to consider where any machine is located and the access arrangements which operate. Where no formal photocopying procedures are laid down, machines can be subject to serious misuse in companies. Such misuse can include any or all of the following:

- failure to operate the machine correctly, so adding to the likelihood of breakdown or malfunction and the consequent increase in maintenance costs;

- unnecessary copying, ie taking copies of material which is already available and easily accessible elsewhere;
- excessive copying, ie running off extra copies 'just in case' or providing individual copies of material which could easily be circulated amongst those directly concerned;
- uneconomic use of the machine, eg failure to reduce where feasible or to print on both sides of the paper.

Copy control and monitoring systems

Many organisations which operate a virtually 'open access' policy in terms of staff copying, do introduce certain control mechanisms whereby copies are charged to individuals or departments. These can operate in a variety of different ways including the following:

The maintenance of a log (This could be kept by one person who physically does all the copying or left to individual users to complete. As well as recording the identity of the copier, number of copies would be noted together with a description of what was being copied.)

The need to complete a requisition (This is common practice where a centralised reprographics service is provided.)

Authorisation forms (This could be a supplementary requirement of a requisition system but would necessitate securing the approval of a superior for all copying required or perhaps for copy requests exceeding a certain number.)

Key or card systems (These systems, as well as activating the equipment, record on a meter, the number of copies made. This may still necessitate completing a log, ie entering user name and the cumulative total recorded on the meter key on completion of copying.)

Code numbers (A more sophisticated variant is where members of staff are issued with a photocopying allocation and a personal user number which is programmed into the machine. Keying in the appropriate number accesses the machine's functions and the machine will automatically log the number of copies made and allocate to the appropriate user ID.)

Such systems have the following advantages:

- they enable an accurate record to be maintained of the number of copies used;
- they enable copying costs to be allocated on an individual or departmental basis;

- they help reduce waste;
- they help determine the type of equipment required and where it might best be located;
- certain systems reduce the need for supervision.

Renting, leasing or buying

Reprographics equipment represents an extremely competitive – some would say cut-throat – market and potential users need to be as well versed as possible on the facts and figures before entering into nego-tiation with a salesman. Selecting the best dealer can be problematic and will involve giving consideration to things like, service, discounts, number of years in business, willingness to trade in or part-exchange old machines, small print on leasing or rental agreements.

In terms of **outright purchase**, discounts will be important but so, too, will be the obsolescence factor. New models of machines are being introduced all the time, and when buying it is always difficult to decide when the time is right. Basically there is no best time and, as long as service and parts are guaranteed, it should not matter a great deal, provided adequate research has been undertaken to ensure that the machine has all the features required and that it is being secured at a competitive price with good back-up guarantees.

Many machines are available on a **leasing arrangement**, but here again care needs to be taken before signing on the dotted line. Some of the pitfalls to look out for are long-term commitment, high interest rates, inflexible finance arrangements compared, for example, to a bank loan or overdraft, and penalty clauses in the event of early settlement where it is perhaps decided to change machines prior to the expiry of the original lease. It is always important to study the small print. Another difficulty can arise where it is desired to discon-tinue a lease. Here the onus is on the lessee to give notice to the leasing company within a prespecified period, if he does not wish to renew the lease, otherwise the contract will be automatically renewed. This is common practice by leasing companies in the copier market, and care needs to be taken at the outset to establish when the contract ends and at what point notification needs to be given in respect of introducing a change or opting out altogether. An appropriate follow-up system needs to be set in motion. One answer would be to give written notification when signing the contract in the first instance. One strong plus on the leasing side, however, is the potential to buy the machine cheaply on the expiry of the lease or to renew the lease at a greatly reduced rate.

By contrast **rental** suggests a flexible, short-term option for an organisation which may wish to try out a machine prior to outright purchase or extended lease. However, terms tend to be for two or even three years, with very few companies operating on, say, a monthly basis to enable companies to ring the changes or cope with sudden fluctuations of work.

Where rental agreements tend to be the norm is in respect of giant copiers. These are extremely costly to purchase and maintain and the usual practice is for companies to enter into a rental agreement. Ultimately this will work out cheaper. Agreements usually cover approximately a two-year period and are costed out on the basis of monthly outgoings. As well as the actual machine rental the charge would encompass a charge for a minimum number of copies (a cost per copy would then be added to copies made over and above this), consumables (other than paper), service, replacement parts and any special staff training required. It is usual with such agreements for organisations to negotiate discounts where they may be renting several machines and undertaking a heavy volume of copying.

With the exception of the rental of giant copiers it is normally more economical to buy than to enter into either leasing or rental agreements.

Phototypesetting equipment

Phototypesetting equipment is gaining in popularity in that it provides a means by which text can be prepared (camera-ready) for publication and distribution. Phototypesetting has been one of the techniques which has revolutionised the newspaper industry. Modern equipment is little more complex than a word processor.

The difference between typed and phototypeset material

While few typewriters offer the facility of proportional spacing this is a standard feature of a phototypesetter. Right-hand margin justification and centring are also simple matters. A wide variety of type faces can be chosen and similarly variation is possible in terms of type size. These variables can be easily mixed and matched within a single piece of copy. Pages can be set up attractively and easily, according to house style or any other criteria. Formatting decisions can be made automatically with modern machines. In simple terms type is set by photographic means rather than by standard keyboard or printing conventions.

How does typesetting work?

Copy can be input into a system in two main ways, ie via a keyboard or through some peripheral device such as a word processor or optical character reader. When input is via a word processor the material does not need to be rekeyed. The original copy is simply transferred directly into the typsetter. There it is formatted according to the instructions fed into the machine. With optical character recognition (OCR) a device scans the typewritten copy converting it directly into codes which are understood by the phototypesetter and this again eliminates the need to rekey the copy.

Phototypesetting techniques, as well as producing attractive layouts, are capable of making considerable reductions in terms of the length of documents. It is estimated that savings in the region of 50 per cent can be achieved.

Intelligent copier/printers

An 'intelligent' or 'smart' copier/printer is something of a hybrid in that it combines the capabilities of a copier with those of a computer and phototypesetter, so enabling decisions to be made automatically about what to print. This marks another important step towards the totally integrated office system.

Whereas sophisticated photocopiers in general now have limited 'intelligence' in that they may have one or two microprocessors which control copying and paper handling processes, these capacities are extended in the intelligent copier/printer range to include the capture of digital data from computer, word processor or some form of communications line and the subsequent provision of a range of facilities for handling, processing and presenting tasks of all kinds. Consequently hard copy originals are no longer needed. Material of all types, ie text, graphics, even signatures, can be stored and repeated on demand thanks to laser technology. Large quantities of forms need no longer be stored, and precise details, placed perfectly in position on the forms, can be guaranteed.

The result, therefore, is the combination of a high quality fast copier with the flexibility of digital information processing. Such machines can serve not only as copiers *per se*, but as high quality, high speed printers for word processing and computing applications. They can also, via networking, serve as receiving and transmission terminals, which can automatically distribute information between workstations, even at remote locations.

Reprographics support equipment

Where a substantial amount of duplicating, printing and copying is carried out several other pieces of equipment will help to make the system complete.

Collating machines for arranging multiple page documents in order will be essential. While many of the larger copiers have this facility, duplicating machines do not and the time saved in high speed offset printing, for example, can soon be lost if the office staff have to resort to manual collation methods. Machines with different levels of auto-mation are available, but the procedure is similar, irrespective of the degree of automation. Vertical stations (the slots holding the separate bundles of paper) are loaded with the sheets to be collated and an arm with a rubber roller attachment moves back and forth ejecting a single sheet at a time from each station. With semi-automatic systems the operator will physically gather the sheets together in readiness for stapling or stacking papers prior to binding. Automatic collators are capable of handling greater volumes of paper and at much faster rates. Most machines can be programmed to skip certain stations or to detect double sheets and many have the capacity to add features such as stapling and folding attachments.

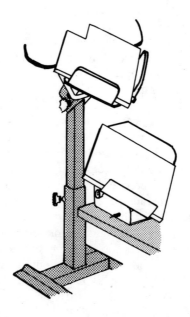

Fig. 4.5 Joggers

Joggers (see Fig. 4.5) are useful for accurately aligning sets of papers prior to stapling or binding. The electric machines vibrate gently 'jogging' the paper neatly together without damaging the edges of the pages.

Binding machines help to achieve a 'finished' product in respect of the effective preparation of multiple page documents and reports. A variety of different equipment is available but there are three most common types found in offices. One produces a spirally-bound document (see Fig. 4.6), following the punching of papers and threading of a binding spine of appropriate width. The one machine performs both tasks. A variation of the spiral binder is the 'flat comb' binder which produces a more permanent binding in that two plastic strips, one with spikes, the other with holes, are placed on either side of the papers to be bound (following the punching of suitably spaced holes), and once locked together are then heat-sealed. The third most common type uses the thermal 'perfect' binding technique whereby papers are bonded together by an adhesive seal extending along the spine of the cover. The finished product is like a modern paperback book finish.

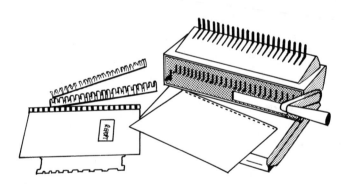

Fig. 4.6 Spiral binding machine

Lettering machines may also prove useful to give a document a more professional finish. It is often desirable to produce a larger, bolder print style on a title page and while this can be achieved using rub-on adhesive letters or via the enlargement facility on a copying machine, an easier technique is to prepare adhesive strips which can be attached to the page in a matter of seconds. Preparation is straightforward, the lettering machine operating on a dialling principle with a range of possible letter sizes and styles available.

Laminating machines provide yet another dimension in that they enable pages to be coated with a protective clear plastic seal. Not only does this make the cover more durable and easy to wipe clean, it can also enhance the image of the document or brochure by providing a glossy textured finish. The process used is a thermal one where the plain paper or card is bonded together with a specially glued sheet of the same size. Another popular application is to laminate on both sides and perhaps enclose a photograph, as, for example, with library or identity cards.

Setting up an in-house print room

Once an organisation starts to go in for reprographics equipment in a big way it is likely that consideration will be given to setting up a centralised printing facility. This can be beneficial in a number of ways not least of which is likely to be the reduction in outside printing costs. Such provision also serves to isolate a lot of noisy, specialised equipment in one area where it can be properly supervised and used to its full potential by specially trained staff. When considering the viability of such a reprographics centre the sort of issues which should be addressed will include the following:

- type of duplicating and copying work undertaken throughout the organisation;
- volume of work;
- turnround required;
- quality needed;
- extent of specialist applications, eg production of letterheads, brochures, etc;
- type of equipment needed;
- implications of outright purchase, leasing or rental;
- existing staff expertise to run the unit;
- essential training which would be required;
- procedures to be set up;
- location and facilities available;
- control and supervision aspects;
- cost considerations, eg setting up, running and maintenance;
- potential to extend and undertake additional printing tasks, possibly even for outside contracts;

- extent to which certain printing jobs would still need to be sent outside.

CHECKLIST

1 Duplicating techniques require the preparation of some form of master, stencil or plate.

2 Photocopies are facsimiles, ie exact copies, of originals.

3 The principal methods of duplicating are ink stencil and offset litho.

4 Photocopying is available from desk-top copier machines through to giant copiers with many special features.

5 Most large organisations introduce some system for monitoring, controlling and costing the amount of copying done.

6 Equipment may be rented, leased or purchased outright.

7 Phototypesetting equipment has revolutionised the printing industry by enabling the production of camera-ready copy for professional publication.

8 Intelligent copiers have programmable facilities built into their microprocessor circuitry and can be instructed to produce copies by remote control via communication links from computer or word processor.

9 A range of other equipment, eg collators, joggers and binders, contribute to the operation of a complete reprographics support system.

10 Many companies choose to set up their own in-house print facilities rather than place contracts with outside printers.

QUICK REVISION QUESTIONS

1 What is the distinction between photocopying and duplicating?
2 Name three ways in which a duplicating stencil can be prepared.
3 Describe one of them in detail.
4 Indicate four factors to be considered in selecting an offset duplicating machine.
5 Indicate three ways in which offset plates can be prepared.
6 What special features might be present in a modern photocopier?
7 Suggest two ways in which a company could monitor its photocopying.

8 Explain what you understand by the term 'phototypesetting'.
9 What are the advantages to be gained from a collating machine?
10 Suggest six points worthy of bearing in mind when considering setting up an in-house print room facility.

5 Office finance and documentation

All organisations have to be financed in some way in order that business may be conducted. For example, in the case of a manufacturing organisation, financial backing is needed to secure suitable premises, acquire any necessary plant, machinery and vehicles, as well as purchase raw materials, pay wages and meet overheads, until the finished product stage is reached and there is potential to distribute and make a profit. Similarly any service industry or professional business needs capital to establish itself and it is to the raising of capital that this section initially turns.

Other financial aspects which affect all types of business enterprise are the need to be insured, to pay wages and salaries and to comply with government regulations in respect of tax and social security.

All business transactions are supported by appropriate paperwork and there are a range of business documents designed specially to fulfil different purposes. Therefore, the section examines the usual documentation involved. At the end of the section a comprehensive glossary of terms associated with finance, insurance and import/export documentation is provided for easy reference.

At the end of this section you should be able to:

- list alternative sources of business finance;
- explain the principal business and financial services offered by commercial banks;
- recognise some of the services which would come into the category of 'electronic banking';
- explain the principles of insurance;
- identify the principal types of risk covered;
- outline a procedure for the payment of wages and salaries;
- understand the basic principles of social security;
- identify the documents in a business transaction;
- explain the functions of different business documents.

Types and sources of finance

Every type of business enterprise requires financial backing to get started, to operate and to expand. Just how much finance, of what type and for how long a period depends on the type of organisation, the nature of its business and the purpose for which the finance is required.

Finance is the lifeblood of any business and it is essential that it is available as and when required. This means that considerable forecasting needs to be carried out both in the short and long terms. Short-term planning helps establish initial capital requirements and has to be closely monitored and continually updated as needs change during the initial stages of a business's existence. Long-term financial forecasts are made in conjunction with a company's corporate planning process, ie where and how it wishes to develop, and has to be geared to the availability of finance.

Financial backing comes from a variety of different sources including other people's savings, banks, building societies, finance houses, insurance companies, unit and investment trust companies and from government grants and incentives. Just as private individuals need to examine the possibilities carefully so, too, do companies if they are to choose the most appropriate source or sources.

Commercial banks

Banking has been undergoing a process of evolution and the services offered today are wide ranging, very different from what they used to be and more sophisticated. In terms of the individual customer the principal services are outlined in Table 5.1 and it is to those used by companies, together with the more recent developments in banking technology, that this section now concentrates. In any event, all banks publish a wealth of detailed information on the services they provide and this is freely available and continuously updated. Also, the Banking Information Service, 10 Lombard Street, London EC3 produces useful materials and examples of cheques and other forms, which it is happy to supply to students.

Companies use commercial or joint stock banks, as they are sometimes called, to conduct their day-to-day business in very much the same way as private individuals. In other words the bank will process monies going in to and out of its current account, handle any direct debits or standing orders, pay its wages and salaries to its employees via the credit transfer system, offer night safe facilities, arrange banker's drafts and provide any of the other standard services which are available to all customers.

Table 5.1   Services of Commercial Banks

Current Account Services

cheque system
standing orders
direct debits
credit transfers
overdraft facilities
banker's draft facilities
personal loans
bank credit cards
*cash card service or ATMs
*debit cards
*EFTPOS
*home banking

Deposit Accounts

Budget Accounts

Savings Accounts

Miscellaneous other services

foreign currency and exchange dealings
services in the export field
economic information on overseas markets
discounting of Bills of Exchange
investment management services
intermediary in dealings with stockbrokers
income tax advice
insurance
executorship and trustee services
custodian of valuables
mortgage facilities

* These services are expanded on within the text

Additionally, in recent years, there has been increasing pressure on banks to secure business by granting loans, particularly of the short-term variety, and often to small businesses. The competition between banks to secure this business has been particularly fierce.

Banking and technology

Banks like every other aspect of business have been affected by developments in technology and systems and procedures have become increasingly automated with the resultant introduction of new and faster services for customers. This, in turn, has led to a reduction in the numbers of banking personnel. The following are a few of the more recent developments, and the explanations provided should help to dispel some of the mystique associated with the jargon.

Automated Teller Machine (ATM) Commonly referred to as 'cash round the clock' machines these self-service 'through the wall' machines are now well established. The customer simply inserts his personal plastic card in the slot in the machine, keys in his Personal Identification Number (PIN) which is a personal code, usually of four digits, and provided the machine can verify that the cardholder is the rightful user transactions can go ahead. Identification clearance is possible in that PINs are held in scrambled form on the magnetic stripe on the plastic card so that they can be verified when the system checks against a central register. While original terminals simply enabled customers to withdraw or deposit cash, more recent ones enable customers to produce their own statements, obtain individual, tailor-made quotations for loans and insurance and even purchase securities. The network of ATMs throughout the UK is extensive and still growing with the National Westminster Bank alone currently having the biggest network in the world. Future developments in this area will incorporate interactive video disks, intelligent printer and voice recognition and response.

Bankers' automated clearing services (BACS) This is the organisation set up by UK banks to handle and process automated payments between customers, eg direct debits and payrolls. Instructions can be sent to the BACS central computer by magnetic media or directly via the BACSTEL service, ie telecommunications link.

Clearing house automated payment system (CHAPS) This is the electronic inter-bank credit transfer system and unlike BACS has no central computer. The banks pass payment messages to each other via 'gateway' (ie links between networks) computers. The end-of-day settlement of high volume sterling payments is transacted via accounts held at the bank of England which is also linked to the system. CHAPS payments have the added advantages of being both instantaneous and guaranteed.

Cash management systems enable banks to call up information about balances and transactions on terminals located in their own offices. These terminals may be 'dumb' or personal computers (see also Section 8). Where they are the former the information accessed will be received in the format in which the bank chooses to send it and so may require to be reprocessed before it may be used locally.

However, where it is received on a personal computer it can easily be manipulated on screen.

Counter terminals are VDUs linked to the bank's central computer. They enable a cashier to call up information on customer accounts and enter counter transactions directly into the bank's accounting system. These terminals may also have card readers which can handle customer cards and so obtain instant authorisation for transactions, and some have passbook printers which enable customers' passbooks to be updated on the spot.

Debit cards are plastic cards which operate as cheque substitutes in that they are linked to current or savings accounts. They may be used to draw money from wall machines or to pay for goods. Retailers will seek authorisation for a transaction from the issue bank, just like they do currently with credit cards used to purchase goods over a certain value, but where they receive clearance the amount will be automatically debited to the account in the bank unlike with the credit card, where the user receives a monthly statement of account. There has been some reluctance on the part of retailers to handle debit cards in that they object to the charge which the banks make for the operation of the service and feel that they have been browbeaten into it without sufficient consultation.

Electronic funds transfer at the point of sale (EFTPOS) This refers to the electronic processing of a payment by a customer at a retail outlet. EFTPOS terminals can now be found in a variety of places, eg motorway service stations, garages and some retail stores. The payment may be by either credit card or debit card, but neither a cheque nor a credit card voucher is required to complete the transaction. What happens is that details of the transaction are entered into a terminal which also reads the data from the customer's card. Details of the EFTPOS transaction are then transmitted for electronic processing at the card issuer's computer either on magnetic tape, disk or cassette or by telecommunications link.

Home banking Another evolutionary facility is that of home banking. This enables personal bank customers to obtain information about their accounts or to initiate transactions from terminals in their own homes. A variety of different terminals is available and different countries seem to have opted for different ones. Some are linked to either public or private viewdata systems (see also Section 7 p 168) and so are used in conjunction with personal computers or adapted television

77

sets, while others use voice response systems accessible over telephone lines.

Off-line This refers to a system not linked directly to a central computer. Data is collected and dispatched by telecommunications link during cheap rate periods.

On-line This is one which directly connects a terminal, eg an ATM or EFTPOS, to a central computer so allowing two-way interactive communication.

Society for worldwide inter-bank financial telecommunications (SWIFT) This is a bank-owned organisation whose headquarters is in Brussels. It was set up to supply banks with a network for the fast, secure and inexpensive transmission of payments messages. SWIFT messages do not result in settlement being carried out as the messages contain instructions only.

Smart cards Also known as chipcard, carte à mémoire and integrated circuit card, the smart card is the French contribution to electronic banking. It is self-contained with a calculator-type keyboard and battery display. It does not require a terminal for its operation. A customer simply identifies himself by entering his PIN code on the card's keyboard then enters the amount of his purchase and the in-built microprocessor subtracts the amount of the purchase from the available balance. Transaction details are stored in the card, together with the new balance. The card computes and displays an authorisation number for each transaction.

A shop assistant can simply write down the authorisation number on a sales slip which is then imprinted with the numbers on the face of the card and the transaction is recorded in the same way as a credit card transaction except that the need to make a telephone call for authorisation is removed. The system is also receiving trials in Japan and the United States as well as several other European countries, but it is meeting with certain reluctance on the part of retailers who are not keen to invest in the terminals which are very expensive.

Super-smart cards These take the smart card a stage further in that they allow the user to access more than one account and choose his own PIN code.

Such developments are obviously altering the face of traditional banking methods and future years will bring even greater changes.

The merchant banks

The business transacted by merchant banks is different and separate from that conducted by the High Street chains of clearing banks described above.

They perform a range of functions which can broadly be divided as follows:

- they raise capital by arranging Stock Exchange quotations and new issues of shares and loan stocks;
- they advise on financial planning, mergers and takeovers;
- they provide advice for clients with large investment funds to manage, eg charities, companies, pensions, trusts and trade unions;
- they advise on the purchase, sale, development and leasing of property;
- they provide venture and development capital for small businesses;
- they finance home and overseas trade by accepting bills of exchange, buying and selling world currencies and advising on export financing.

Building societies

Building societies have long been recognised for their specialism in lending money to individuals for the purchase of their homes. Money is available from the investments placed in the societies by short-term savers who receive different rates of interest according to the type of share accounts they have.

However, after 100 years of restrictions building societies have, as a result of the Building Societies Act 1986, been free to diversify, since 1 January 1987. Since that date building societies and banks have been free to compete on equal ground for their customers. Therefore, building societies are now in a position to issue cheque books backed with guarantee cards, to provide personal equity and pension plans, special unit trusts, a broader range of insurance policies and a level of unsecured lending, as well as acting as estate agents.

There has, therefore, been a blurring around the edges of what were previously banking territories and what were building society ones to the extent that competition between banks and building societies has now become one of the central features of the financial system in the UK. This competitive environment has been growing since the early 1980s with the abolition of the building society cartel and the entry of banks and other institutions into the mortgage market. The abolition of the cartel made competition for mortgages much keener and had the effect of raising the mortgage interest rate relative to other interest rates.

So diversification of business interests came as an attractive proposition for building societies with much of the new business which came their way having considerable potential in terms of securing high profits, not to mention the advantages that are to be gained by spreading the risk over a range of financial activities rather than putting all their eggs in the mortgage basket.

The Stock Exchange

The London Stock Exchange has been transformed since 27 October 1986, the date of the so-called 'Big Bang' which literally revolutionised its operations and confirmed it as the world's leading electronic securities market, with quotations and trading information available at the touch of a button. However, its function remains basically unchanged, viz to put those who wish to sell in touch with those who wish to buy stocks or shares so that investments can change hands quickly, cheaply and fairly.

The 'Square Mile', as the City of London's financial quarter is termed, has been totally reshaped and reformed with the abolition of fixed commissions and the abandonment of the old split in functions between jobbers and brokers and the emergence of a new range of operators centring on the market-maker. Also since October 1986 trading has increased dramatically and there has been a drop in commission charges.

There has been a switch from dealing on the market floor, so often a feature of Stock Exchange photographs, to screen-based dealing behind the scenes. At the centre of the electronic market is the Stock Exchange Automated Quotations System (SEAQ). From individual SEAQ terminals market-makers transact business for the portfolios of stocks in which they are registered. Market-makers rely on the supply of financial information fed to them by services such as Reuters, Topic and Telerate.

This new mode of operations has been made possible by a revolution in information services. With technology, prices can be up to the minute at all times and global networking enables worldwide trading 24 hours a day. The replacement of video with digital switching systems (see also Section 7 on telecommunications generally) will enable a range of services to be delivered directly to individual desks with the potential to mix and match information on screen, presenting it all at one time rather than as separate pages. Digital systems are very much faster and the fact that they are compatible with computers means that there is no need for separate systems to handle and convert incoming information. It can be fed straight to a mini-computer which acts as a digital switch and so each individual user is in a position to access whatever information he needs at his own terminal.

Another likely development for the future is expert systems which are systems capable of giving the same advice as a human expert. In essence for financial applications this would mean software which held information typical of that contained in a textbook and which when combined with the power of a computer was capable of producing fast and accurate information which would enable sophisticated dealing opportunities to be undertaken.

Prior to Big Bang the Stock Exchange published no information at all in respect of individual deals and turnover in individual stocks. Protection for investors stemmed from the fact that brokers operated independently to secure the best price. However, with the end of single capacity dealing came the removal of such protection and screen-based information is now available to all brokers as well as anyone else who wishes to subscribe to the videotex service which delivers SEAQ information.

Types of share

There are two main types of share – ordinary and preference.

Ordinary (or equity) shares represent the highest risk of all in that ordinary shareholders have the last right to a share of the company's profits which are paid in the form of a dividend. Therefore, should a company get into financial difficulties and be liquidated, all creditors and other security holders would have a prior claim. However, offset against this is the fact that the liability of ordinary shareholders is limited to the extent of their capital investment so they can never be called on for more than the amount they agree to subscribe on their shares. Ordinary shareholders usually have voting rights which means that they are entitled to vote at an annual general meeting.

Preference shares, as the name suggests, have a prior right to a dividend before ordinary shares and are, therefore, a more attractive proposition for investors who prefer not to take a risk. Although they represent part of a company's share capital, preference shareholders do not normally carry voting rights. Shares are offered at a fixed rate of dividend, eg 5 per cent, but a dividend will only be paid when a company makes a profit. Consequently a company may withhold dividend payments when it considers that resources are insufficient to meet them but the most a 5 per cent preference share can expect to receive, even in an extremely good year, will be 5 per cent. Preference shares, however, are often cumulative which means that any dividend unpaid in one year is carried over to the next and paid out before ordinary shareholders are paid. Nonetheless in the event of liquidation preference shareholders are not entitled to dividend arrears and rank equally with other shareholders in terms of any money to come.

Debentures are not shares but loans to a company. They state the interest payable, the nature of the security (if there is any), the restrictive convenants and the timing of the scheduled repayment. They represent a very small degree of risk and interest is payable whether or not a company makes a profit. Debenture holders can, in fact, force a company into liquidation if interest is not paid and they have first claim if liquidation does take place. Debentures may be of different kinds, viz mortgage debentures secured on specified assets, eg property, floating-charge debentures on a company's total assets or convertible debentures, ie those giving their holders an option to convert to ordinary shares at a fixed price on a future fixed date.

'Going public'

One way in which a business can increase its financial resources is by floating a company or 'going public', ie issuing shares for purchase by the general public. It is unusual that a business would do this early in its existence and more likely that it will have existed in some other form, eg as a partnership or private limited company. There are several advantages in 'going public' including the following:

- access to the capital market through quotation of shares on the Stock Exchange;
- larger investors or institutions are more likely to be interested in public listed companies, so borrowing should become easier;
- shareholders have a ready market for their shares;
- a market price for shares is established;
- the possibility of buying out other companies becomes a reality in that shares may be offered in lieu of cash;
- there is a general increase in a company's financial standing.

Offset against these are certain disadvantages, including:

- the need to prepare special documentation;
- the costs of public flotation;
- the loss of privacy;
- the possibility of losing control to new shareholders;

- the risk of takeover due to the availability of shares on the stock market.

Registration

This represents that part in a company's formation process when it lodges documents with the Registrar of Companies in accordance with the Companies Acts. The documents are as follows.

Memorandum of association which sets out the purpose for which the company has been formed, its name, the location of its registered office, a declaration of limited liability, the names of its directors and the division of its share capital;

Articles of association which set out the regulations for the internal management of the company and cover matters such as appointment and powers of directors, issue, transfer and forfeiture of shares, rules governing meetings, payment of dividends, preparation of accounts for audit, alteration of capital structure and rights of different classes of shareholder.

On approval of these documents the company receives its Certificate of Incorporation.

Inviting the public to subscribe

This can be done by either issuing a **prospectus** which is an invitation to the public to apply directly to the directors for shares or by allotting shares to an issuing house which then resells the share to the public by advertising them in an **offer for sale**. Both represent advertisements drawn up to attract potential investors.

Relatively few companies, with the exception of really large, well-known ones, issue a prospectus as it is a very costly exercise. Smaller issues tend to be handled by an issuing house, eg a merchant bank, which receives the difference between what it bought the shares at and the issue price, plus, on occasions, a fee to cover administration costs.

Underwriting

All public issues are underwritten which means that underwriters, for a fee, agree to buy, at the issue price, any shares not taken up by the public.

Application and allotment

Prospective investors complete an application form requesting the number of shares they would like to buy. With the form they enclose a cheque either for the full amount or for the instalment payable on application. However, shares are often over-subscribed and so some form of rationing takes place, whereby investors will usually receive a proportion of the shares applied for. Allotment letters are then sent out detailing the share allocation and enclosing a cheque in respect of any overpayment.

Occasionally applicants may receive no shares at all in which case their cheques are returned together with a letter of regret.

Buying and selling existing shares

Where an individual or business wishes to buy shares which are already quoted on the Stock Exchange it will be necessary to secure the services of an investment expert of some kind, eg a broker, bank, building society or licensed dealer, and the procedure will be as follows:

- contact the investment expert who will contact SEAQ on his computer terminal (or arrange for a broker to do so) for up-to-the-minute share information;
- the broker will inform of the best price available;
- if agreement is made to purchase a verbal contract is made there and then and there is no backtracking;
- the broker will then complete the transaction with a market-maker;
- within a matter of days the purchaser will be sent a contract note telling him what he has bought, when and for how much, together with the date by which the transaction must be settled. The contract note will list the price of the shares, the transfer stamp duty (calculated at $\frac{1}{2}$ per cent), the broker's commission (how he makes his money), plus VAT on the commission.
- some weeks later the buyer receives his share certificate although it is possible for him to resell without it.

The procedure for selling shares is very similar. Once again the transaction will be handled by a broker acting on the seller's instructions. Therefore it is likely that the seller will have a minimum selling price in mind and, of course, he may only wish to sell a proportion of his holding, in which case he will eventually receive a new 'balance' certificate representing the shares he has retained.

Insurance

Any business enterprise runs certain risks and it is through insurance that risk is minimised. Insurance operates on the basis of 'pooling' risk, ie a central pool made up of the premiums from all the parties insured may be used to compensate those who have the misfortune to incur losses.

There are certain principles upon which all insurance agreements are founded and these are as follows.

Utmost good faith (uberrimae fidei) which means that insurance companies expect to be in full possession of all the facts relating to the risk which would influence the insurer in fixing a rate or even agreeing to insure at all.

Insurable interest In order to have insurable interest the person taking out the insurance must stand to lose something in the event of accident or damage or alternatively benefit from the fact that something is safeguarded in some way.

Indemnity This is the process whereby the insurer reimburses the insured to the extent of the losses but does not place the insured in a better position than formerly, ie the insured should not profit from the loss sustained – only be fully compensated. This is why it is important not to be underinsured. For example if a property and contents are insured only for £50,000 and the true value is £70,000, should the property be totally destroyed by fire the most the insured can expect to get back is £50,000, viz the extent for which his premiums covered him.

It should be noted that the principle of indemnity cannot be applied to life assurance, as clearly it is impossible to place a financial value on a life. The nearest that can be done is to estimate value in accordance with the type of life someone had. Therefore in the event of an accidental death or serious injury the insurance company would assess things like future potential earning capacity prior to the death or accident.

Subrogation Related to the principle of indemnity this comes into play when following insurance settlement to compensate for a loss sustained, eg fire destroying stock, there is found to be some value remaining in the remnants of damaged stock. In such a case the insurer would sell off the goods, hence you often see Fire Sales advertised, and retain the proceeds.

Contribution Also connected to indemnity this arises where an individual or company is insured with two or more companies. In such an instance insurance claims would be settled by the companies proportionately, according to the terms of the original policies.

Proximate cause This rule, also associated with indemnity, is concerned with the fact that insurance policies normally restrict claims to losses which are a direct result of an occurrence. Therefore compensation will only be paid out in terms of the immediate (or proximate) cause of the loss. For instance, if a property is insured against fire and a plane crashes into it, explodes and sets fire to the building, would the owner of the building have a claim against his fire insurance policy? Normally yes, but suppose the policy had an exclusion clause relating to fire caused by air traffic accidents in that the property was situated close to an airport runway. In this instance the plane crash was clearly the cause of the fire and so no claim could be made.

Types of risk

There are four main branches of insurance, viz fire, life, accident and marine, covering a wider range of risks including the following principal ones likely to affect businesses:

- **Public liability** which is concerned with the risks to third parties, ie persons other than employees, causing them injury or damage to their property consequent on things like defects in premises or negligence on the part of employees.
- **Employer's liability** which is an employer's statutory obligation under the Health and Safety at Work, etc Act 1974 (see also Appendix 1) to compensate employees for injury or loss sustained at work. Premiums are calculated according to the degree of hazard associated with the work and as a percentage of the annual wage bill.
- **Professional indemnity** covers firms such as solicitors or accountants against claims for damages resulting from professional negligence of some kind.
- **Products liability** covers manufacturers for claims against their products.
- **Goods in transit** covers all losses or damage to goods on the move either by air, road or rail. Separate policies are required for transport by haulage contractors and a firm's own vehicles.
- **Fidelity guarantees** are taken out against employees who handle money.
- **Forgery insurance** indemnifies a company against the consequences of their acting upon forged documents.
- **Bad debts insurance** helps reduce the effects incurred through bad debts.

- **Plate glass insurance** is taken out by shopkeepers in respect of their windows being cracked or broken.
- **Group life assurance** may be taken out in respect of groups of employees, particularly those offering a specialism of particular value to a company.
- **Hull insurance** which is an aspect of marine insurance relating to the actual ship in that it insures against damage to the vessel when it is at sea.
- **Cargo insurance** relates to the cargo itself and damage thereto.
- **Freight insurance** refers not to cargo itself but to the charge for carrying the cargo. In practice a shipowner often gets the freight in advance, although strictly speaking he is not entitled to it until the cargo is safely delivered, which means that in the event of trouble at sea the cargo could be lost so the shipowner insures against this eventuality.
- **Shipowner's liability** Akin to employer's liability and public liability, this aspect of marine insurance is what the shipowner takes out to meet possible claims from crew, passengers or other vessels including physical injury, damage resulting from collisions at sea and damage to berths when a ship is in dock.
- **Motor vehicle insurance.**
- **Fire insurance**, including consequential loss, eg inability to trade, or special perils, eg lightning damage.

Principal insurance documents

The main documents used in insurance are as follows:

- **claim forms** for completion by the insured in the event of a loss;
- **cover notes** issued by the insurer to certify that the proposer is covered for insurance purposes during a stipulated period until the insurer indicates that the proposal has been accepted or declined;
- **endorsements** which detail special conditions attached to a policy;
- **policies** which provide evidence of the contract of insurance;
- **proposal forms** which outline the personal details, and previous insurance history of the proposers.

Risk management

Large organisations may have their own insurance section or department one of whose duties will be to conduct periodic risk management exercises and submit reports and recommendations to management. The nature of risk management activities will include:

- identifying the activities of the organisation which are liable to risk;

- assessing areas of work which may be particularly vulnerable to criminal activity, eg computer fraud, industrial espionage, burglary, misappropriation of funds;
- valuing the organisation's buildings and equipment;
- performing a detailed analysis of computer installations;
- providing a full evaluation statement detailing areas of potential hazard in respect of employee safety, etc;
- suggesting areas which need improvement or further training;
- evaluating the extent of overall risk so that it may be budgeted for accordingly.

Risk management techniques are fairly sophisticated nowadays and well-conducted exercises can result in considerable savings in terms of insurance premiums as well as the introduction of suitable safe-guards and procedures for minimising accidents and loss. Additionally risk management should incorporate contingency planning so that, should an accident occur, immediate steps may be taken to reduce the adverse effects.

The future for insurance companies

Just as the banks and building societies have extended their areas of activity following deregulation so, too, have insurance companies in that they have the freedom to diversify should they choose to do so. Therefore it is possible that some of the larger companies may venture into mortgage finance, unsecured loans and deposit facilities to complement their normal range of insurance business.

The Financial Services Act 1986

Any section on finance would be incomplete without reference to the Financial Services Act 1986 which introduced new regulations affecting the savings and investment market. It regulated how investments are promoted, sold and managed and stipulated the type of advice which the different categories of investment company represented are entitled to pass onto clients. It stresses the importance of customers understanding the risks involved in particular investment transactions.

The Act established a new framework for investor protection by restricting the conduct of investment business to authorised or exempted persons. It introduces new rules for advertising and for the regulation of collective investment schemes (eg unit trusts) and contains new regulations relating to insurance companies, new provisions relating to the listing of securities and to the offering of unlisted securities and new regulations relating to insider dealing.

It also highlighted the need to establish new procedures, records and reporting mechanisms under the watchful eye of the Securities and Investments Board (SIB) which will act as the City's watchdog on investment matters with the right to take up cases on behalf of investors.

Wages and salaries

People working in organisations have to be paid, so another financial aspect for consideration is wages and salaries. This is something which affects all workers and whether or not they are directly involved in the preparation of wages and salaries it is important that they are aware of the basic facts in respect of employee remuneration and that they are able to check the accuracy of their own pay or salary slips.

Wages

Staff in receipt of a wage will normally be paid weekly and the amount is likely to be calculated either hourly on a flat (or basic) rate plus any overtime paid at a higher rate, or on piecework rates, ie those calculated on the basis of completing a given amount of work. Piecework is the method of pay predominant in industries such as engineering.

Hours are checked from employee clock records whereby employees register their arrivals and departures by 'clocking on and off' (see also Flexitime p 126). This traditionally meant a system where times in respect of starting and finishing were punched by the machine onto individual clock cards but most modern systems are computerised. Each employee has a personalised plastic key or card which, when inserted into the machine, records the time and feeds the information direct to a computer. A visual display enables employees to make their own time checks of hours worked.

Wages are calculated in accordance with number of hours worked taking into account overtime hours paid at different rates. Prior to any deductions the total hours worked provide the **gross pay**, but certain deductions both statutory and voluntary (see later) will reduce this figure to provide the **net pay**, ie that which the employee actually receives.

More and more employees are now having their wages paid direct into a bank, post office or building society account and this is encouraged by employers who are anxious to reduce the need to handle large sums of cash which are vulnerable to wage hoists and which need to have elaborate precautions taken for their safety whilst on the company's premises prior to the issue of wage packets.

The Wages Act 1960 made it legal to pay wages by cheque or credit transfer provided the employee agreed, and more recent wages legislation has totally done away with the nineteenth-century Truck Acts by which employees could insist on being paid in cash. However, where payment is made in cash additional procedures need to be set up to ensure the following:

- that wage packets are made up as quickly as possible in the interests of safety;
- that correct denominations of notes and coin are available;
- that suitable envelopes are used, viz the type which enable the contents to be checked prior to opening to prevent fraud;
- that appropriate checking mechanisms are incorporated to deal with any discrepancies;
- that each employee's packet contains a pay slip summarising how wages have been calculated and what deductions have been made;
- that arrangements are made to retain and store any uncollected wage packets.

Salaries

Salaries which are normally paid monthly are calculated as a proportion of the annual gross salary figure, less deductions, and usually paid directly into an employee's chosen account by the credit transfer system. All the employee will receive is a salary slip which will contain the following information:

- name;
- department and/or employee number;
- annual salary figure;
- tax code number;
- national insurance number;
- gross salary figure;
- any additions in respect of back pay, tax refund, overtime payment or additional expenses paid;
- statutory deductions in respect of income tax, superannuation or pension contribution and national insurance;
- any voluntary deductions, eg trade union subscriptions, contributions towards social, health or welfare funds or covenants undertaken.

The salary slip will often provide code numbers in respect of additions and deductions and these will usually be detailed in the form of a key on the reverse side of the slip for employee checking purposes.

Other means of remuneration

While wages and salaries represent the vast proportion of employee remuneration it is possible that other means may be used either instead of or to top up the basic wage or salary. These will include the following.

Commission This is usually added to a minimum flat rate and calculated as a percentage of, for example, sales.

Fees Certain professional occupations, eg medical consultants or legal practitioners charge a fee for their services, often charged according to a fee scale, in order to protect clients from being over-charged.

Incentive schemes Such schemes, eg profit sharing, are introduced to encourage increased employee interest and participation in the business of a company.

Bonus schemes These are often in the form of extra, or even double, money paid in recognition of extra effort, eg hard work during a peak period like Christmas or to ensure that an order is completed according to or ahead of schedule.

Expenses or allowances These are not strictly remuneration but are certainly things which would feature in the calculation of an individual's earning capacity. Rather they may be viewed as 'perks' of the job, eg the use of a company car, a clothes allowance, or travel and hospital expenses.

Statutory deductions

The main statutory deductions to come from wages and salaries are in respect of Income Tax and National Insurance.

All employees earning over a certain amount are liable to pay Income Tax on their earned income during a fiscal year, ie from 6 April in one year to 5 April in the next (in the UK). This tax is collected by employers via the PAYE (pay as you earn) system as applied to each employee's tax code.

An individual's tax code is calculated and allocated to him on the basis of information he has supplied to the Inland Revenue when he sent in his tax return and completed the tax claim form. Individuals may claim tax allowance against the following:

• personal allowance;

- married person's allowance;
- dependent relatives;
- certain expenses incurred in the nature of employment and not re-imbursed by the employer, eg trade union dues;
- certain types of interest paid.

The resultant code indicates the amount of money which may be earned before tax needs to be paid. All income over that amount is liable to tax within certain tax bands. Tax is paid at the standard rate up to a certain figure and thereafter is charged at higher rates. The code number is also issued to the employer in order that he knows how much tax free pay to allow. It is then taken in conjunction with tax tables issued by the Inland Revenue to calculate the amount of tax to be deducted.

It is important to note that allowances are liable to change and must always be claimed in accordance with the regulations applying at any given time. Likewise tax bands may move upwards or downwards and the rates which apply within the bandings may also alter following the Budget.

Notification of amended codes

Changes in circumstances may affect eligibility to allowances and consequently tax code numbers may require to be adjusted. Also, where errors may have occurred in the operation of the PAYE system, eg too little tax is deducted, the tax code number will be amended so that underpayment is made up gradually rather than taken all at once. Amendments to tax codes are notified to both tax payer and employer.

PAYE is a complex matter and full details are given in the Employer's Guide to PAYE issued by the Inland Revenue.

National Insurance

National Insurance helps finance a number of benefits including the following:

- sickness benefit;
- unemployment benefit;
- industrial disablement benefit;
- retirement pension;
- maternity benefit;
- child benefit;
- widow's benefit;
- death grant.

Contributions are related to earnings and are also collected under the PAYE procedure. All persons in employment are issued with a National Insurance number allocated by the DHSS (Department of Health and Social Security), on the commencement of the first job. This number remains the same throughout an individual's working life and must be given to an employer on request.

Contributions are payable by both employees and employers and are subject to lower and upper earnings limits which are reviewed annually. There are several classes of contribution dependent on whether contributors are employed or self-employed, but most people who work for an employer will fall into Class 1. The current National Insurance leaflet outlining all contribution rates together with those for Statutory Sick Pay is available from the Post Office. Another useful leaflet obtainable from the DHSS is the Employer's Guide to National Insurance Contributions.

Statutory sick pay (SSP)

Where an employee has a period of sickness covering four or more consecutive days, up to a limit of eight weeks in any tax year, an employer is responsible for paying SSP. For periods in excess of eight weeks, payment may be made from an employer's own sick pay scheme, the State scheme or some other benefit scheme.

An employer can get compensation from the DHSS broadly equivalent to his share of national insurance contributions paid on SSP. Currently the rate of compensation has been arrived at following DHSS consultation with employers organisations.

Business documents

Irrespective of apparent progress towards a paperless society businesses still process vast amounts of paperwork of one kind or another. Much of it takes the form of standard business documents related to a range of business procedures.

Elsewhere in this book, for example, reference is made to personnel documentation, to documents associated with meetings procedure, to financial returns, tax returns and other personalised formats prepared by organisations to complement their own systems and procedures. However, common to most companies involved in buying and selling activities are a range of documents linked to the various stages of a business transaction and it is to these that the section now turns.

Actual documentation and design will vary according to the nature of the business activity and the demands of individual systems but the main documents are likely to be the following.

Order

Orders may be placed verbally or in writing, but where a business orders a lot of goods, possibly through a central purchasing department, special order forms are likely to have been prepared to streamline the procedure. Also copy orders may be filed according to order number.

Invoice

This is the principal document in a business transaction and is made out when one person sells goods to another. Invoices may be used in a court of law as evidence of a contract of sale. The seller prepares the invoice, which may have as many as five different coloured copies for ease of recognition and which will contain the following information:

- names and addresses of both parties to the sale;
- VAT registration number of the seller;
- date of the sale;
- quantity of goods supplied;
- description of the goods;
- unit price;
- value added tax (VAT)
- details of any trade discount;
- terms of sale, ie discount which may be deducted and the credit period allowed;
- details regarding method of despatch.

What happens to the copies?

The top copy is sent to the customer as his contract of sale. He will process it through his Purchases Day Book (see Section 6 p 105), the second copy is retained by the seller as his copy of the contract of sale. He will process it through his Sales Day Book.

The third copy, usually referred to as the **advice note** may either be sent in advance of the despatch of the goods to announce their impending arrival or parcelled with the goods before they leave the seller's stores. An advice note is useful to the buyer in that it lets him know what goods are coming and whether there may, for example, be goods to follow separately and secondly it enables him to check the contents of the parcel immediately it is opened.

The fourth copy is an exact replica of the advice note but it is referred to as the **despatch note** in that it is sent to the seller's despatch department to help them monitor the progress of the order.

The fifth copy, often called the **delivery note** is issued with the goods to the delivery agent (perhaps a van driver) who will ultimately present it for signature when he hands the goods over to the buyer. The delivery note will then be returned to the despatch department for record purposes.

In addition to these five copies there may even be additional copies going, for example, to Head Office and the sales representative.

The preparation of multiple copy documents

Such documents normally take the form of continuous stationery packs, specially designed to a company's own specification in line with its systems and procedures. The documents will usually be of the NCR (No carbon required) variety for ease of handling and preparation. Not all copies will contain the full range of information in respect of prices and VAT. Advice, despatch and delivery notes, for example need only a description of the goods and the quantity. The exclusion of the pricing and VAT information is easily accommodated by a NCR system in that the special coating which produces the copies is simply eliminated from certain areas in the set of copies.

Debit note

A document very similar to an invoice in appearance, this is made out by a supplier when the purchaser has been undercharged on the invoice. For example, carriage may have been omitted or a typographical error may have been made against an item on the invoice, so necessitating an additional charge. In terms of bookkeeping a debit note is treated in the same way as an invoice.

Credit note

This operates in the reverse manner to a debit note, but is again issued by the supplier to the purchaser, this time to reduce the amount of an invoice. It may be issued, for example, where goods have been damaged in transit or where there has been an overcharge of some kind. To distinguish it from an invoice or debit note a credit note is printed in red. Credit notes normally have two copies, one which would go to the purchaser who has either returned goods or claimed for an overcharge the other being retained by the seller. The purchaser would enter the transaction in his Purchases Returns Day

Book while the seller would enter the transaction in his Sales Returns Day Book.

Statement

This represents the summary of transactions between seller and buyer and is usually issued on a monthly basis by the seller to inform the buyer of the amount which is currently owing in respect of goods supplied. The statement will not list all the details from the invoices, debit notes and credit notes but will simply provide appropriate reference numbers. It will also indicate any payments received during the course of the month. The final figure will represent the amount still owing.

GLOSSARY OF TERMS

Terms which have been explained in detail within the section are not necessarily included in this list.

actuary an expert in calculating insurance

annual wage audit a yearly review of all wage and salary levels (including perks) across an organisation to highlight differences and discrepancies and minimise possible future dispute

annuity retirement pension

APR annual percentage rate of charge

assurance a form of insurance to cover an *inevitable* eventuality, the timing of which is unknown, hence life assurance (to cover death)

bank rate the rate of interest at which a country's central bank is prepared to lend to other banks (in the UK the Bank of England sets bank rate)

bill of exchange a written order addressed by one individual (or company) to another requiring payment of a stated sum on demand at a specified time

bill of lading a document, in triplicate, of entitlement to goods being transported by ship; a copy is sent ahead of the shipment to give proof of title to the consignor, another copy is held by the exporter and the third is sent with the goods

blue chip share one regarded as a safe investment, ie in a well known and highly respected company

bonded warehouse a storage facility where goods are placed in the custody of Customs prior to re-export. This avoids the need to pay customs duty, VAT, etc

broker an agent (or middleman) acting as an intermediary between buyer and seller, eg an insurance broker or stock broker

cartel an agreement between several national monopolies or near monopolies to fix prices, market territories, etc to avoid competition

cash discount a reduction allowed to a customer to encourage prompt payment within a stipulated period.

cash flow   the flow of money required to finance an operation over a period of time

charge account   the type of account which provides credit in order that goods or services may be obtained prior to payment

clearing bank   one which is a member of the London Bankers' Clearing House. Cheques paid to these banks are cleared through this institution which calculates the discrepancies between banks and enables them to settle the net total of each day's business via one cheque drawn on the Bank of England. The process of bank clearing takes three working days

commission   payment (usually on a percentage basis) made for obtaining sales or orders

corporation tax   a flat rate of tax levied on all company profits

costing   the technique of identifying and allocating costs

cost, insurance and freight (cif)   where the seller pays all charges to the destination port

dividend   interest paid on shares

Dow Jones Index   the index of share prices on the Wall Street Stock Exchange in New York

ECU   European currency unit

EFTPOS   electronic funds transfer at the point of sale

EMS   European Monetary System

endowment assurance policy   one in which the sum assured is paid at the end of a fixed period if the insured is still alive

errors and omissions excepted (E & O E)   the idea is to print the letters on business documents, eg invoices, in an attempt to absolve the originator who issues the document from any errors contained in it but it is doubtful whether it would hold up in law

equity   the ordinary shares in a company or the value of its assets less its liabilities other than those to shareholders

Eurobonds   bonds which are negotiable within the member states of the EEC

European Investment Bank   established under the Treaty of Rome in 1957 it can make grants and loans in respect of schemes and projects which are of common interest to members of the EEC

excess   that portion of an insurance claim which has to be met by the insured

exchange control   a control introduced by one country over the ways in which it may exchange its currency for that of other countries

exchange rate   the rate at which a currency may be exchanged for other currencies

excise duty   a tax levied on the country of origin or manufacture on certain goods or services

export agent   a person or company acting in another country on behalf of an exporter

ex works   where the buyer is required to meet all expenses from the moment the goods leave the works, eg the buyer pays carriage

face value   nominal value as opposed to market value of a share

fidelity insurance   that taken out by an employer against the possibility of embezzlement by an employee

fiduciary issue   paper money unbacked by gold or silver

finance company   a firm in the business of lending money

Financial Times Industrial Ordinary Index   based on the average prices of 30 blue chip shares, it provides the indicator of the level of business in the UK stock market

first day premium   the difference between the issue price of a share and that quoted the next day

franchise   the licence to manufacture, market or distribute goods or services, often under a trade name

free on board (fob)   where the seller is responsible for all costs incurred, eg delivery charges and insurance, up to the point where the goods are on board ship

freight forwarder   (sometimes referred to as a shipping and forwarding agent) this is someone who provides a full service of transportation from the exporter's factory to the overseas buyer's premises, including determining the route, organising export documentation and arranging Customs clearance, warehousing and container services as necessary

gilt-edged securities   the term used for those stocks and shares – often Government securities – where there is little risk of loss in the investment

Giro   The postal cheque or money transfer system operated by postal authorities in many European countries

golden handshake   the colloquial term for the sum of money given to a senior executive on the termination of his contract – sometimes offered as an inducement to go!

golden hello   the term coined, particularly in the run up to Big Bang, to describe the large financial incentives offered to young executives to transfer from one finance company to another

gross income   that earned prior to any deductions

guarantee company   a UK company in which individuals have agreed to act as guarantors, ie they have undertaken to meet the debts, to a certain level, should the company go into liquidation

handover pay   the allowance made to shiftworkers in respect of their responsibilities to hand over to other workers on the following shift

hard currency   that which is not subject to dramatic fluctuations in the exchange rate

holding company   another name for a parent company or one which controls others due to the fact that it owns a majority of their voting share capital

home market   the market for a product within its country of manufacture so avoiding tariff barriers and customs duties

'hot' money   that attracted to a country because of favourable interest rates or that handled by currency speculators

IMF   International Monetary Fund

import duty   the tax or tariff imposed on a commodity when it is imported into a country

incomes policy   a government intervention in the free negotiation of rates of pay usually with the intention of minimising pay increases and keeping inflation down

index linked   adjusted in line with changing policies particularly in times of inflation

inflation   an economist's term to describe a situation in which there is a general increase of prices and a fall in the purchasing power of money

Inland Revenue   the UK government agency responsible for assessing and collecting income tax

insider dealing (or trading)   using inside knowledge of a company, its plans and financial state to personal advantage by using the information to make a profit before such information becomes public knowledge

insurance   covering against something which might happen

insurance underwriter   a member of a group involved with assessing and arranging insurance cover, eg Lloyds of London

investment   the placing of a sum of money on the expectation of receiving a return, eg in the form of a dividend, at a later date

invisible exports/imports   receipts/payments made for services of some kind, eg banking and insurance services or shipping and tourism, featuring in the current account of a country's balance of payments

letter of credit   a document issued by a bank which enables the holder to draw bills of exchange for a specified purpose. Used particularly by business personnel transacting large business deals in foreign countries

liquidated damages   damages estimated to have been incurred by a breach of contract

liquidation   legal proceedings causing a company to cease trading

merger   the joining together of two companies by agreement

minimum lending rate (MLR)   the rate at which the Bank of England is prepared to lend to UK banks

money broker   a financial institution specialising in dealing in the money market, ie buying and selling short-term securities and loans and in gold and foreign currencies

money supply   that amount of money circulating within the economy at any given time

monopoly   a situation where at least a third of a market is controlled by one company, so leading to exclusive trading privilege

Monopolies (and Mergers) Commission   a UK body appointed by the Department of Trade and Industry which may be called upon to investigate any apparent monopoly in the production or supply of goods and services, perhaps brought about following a merger

mortgage   a loan made by a financial organisation, eg a building society, to finance the purchase of property

nationalisation   State ownership of industry

Nikkei Dow Index   the index of share prices on the Tokyo Stock Exchange

non-contributory pension scheme   a scheme where only the employer contributes

open cover the insurance of goods for a general sum where precise volume is unknown

open market operations buying and selling of securities on the open market by a bank such as the Bank of England in order to regulate the money supply

overtime that time worked in excess of normal agreed working hours

paid up capital share capital on which all money due has been paid

par value nominal value of shares

pension a regular payment made to someone of retirement age

pensionable salary that part of earnings taken into account in calculating entitlement to pension

pensionable service those number of years of employment taken into account for calculating pension rights

perks fringe benefits

premium (1) the amount at which shares are sold above their issue price; (2) the rate paid for insurance cover

promissory note an IOU which incorporates a time clause

pure risk the insurance term for risk factors such as accident, fire, health and damage as distinct from the risk inherent in a speculative venture of some kind

quotation a detailed offer to carry out specific work for a given price

re-insurance the sharing of large scale risks between several insurers or brokers

Retail Price Index the official UK measure of changes in the value of money

rights issue a new issue of shares, on advantageous terms, to existing shareholders in proportion to their present holdings

scrip issue a bonus (free) issue or allotment of shares to existing shareholders, usually in proportion to their present holdings

share capital paid up capital

share index an index taken from a group of shares considered to be representative of the market

social security a government system whereby the disadvantaged may gain financial assistance

split shift where a work period or shift is divided into two or more periods within any one day. Common in the hotel and catering trades

statutory minimum wage the legal limit below which an employee cannot be paid

statutory pension scheme a compulsory scheme set up for certain workers, eg civil servants, teachers, servicemen

subsidiary company a company controlled by another company which holds more than 50 per cent of the issued capital

superannuation retirement pension

surety a person guaranteeing to undertake the liability for another's defaults

surrender value the cash value of an insurance policy

surtax additional tax above the standard rate

take-over bid where one company attempts to acquire another

tariff (1) customs duty; (2) a price list, eg in a hotel

taxable income   that income liable to tax, ie after deductions and allowances

tax avoidance   the reduction of a tax bill by legal means

tax evasion   the attempt to reduce a tax bill by illegal means, eg concealing information or inventing expenses

terminal value   the value of a sum of money after a given time, taking appreciation and interest into account

term shares   shares which cannot be sold for a specified period of time

trade discount   the allowance deducted by a manufacturer when selling goods to a wholesaler or between a wholesaler and another trader, eg a retailer

uncalled capital   that portion of a company's authorised capital which shareholders have not yet been called upon to subscribe

underwriter   someone guaranteeing to purchase unsold shares, eg a bank may agree to purchase unsold shares in a company, or insure a portion of a risk, eg an insurance company may agree to accept a proportion of a risk

unearned income   income derived from investments rather than employment

unit trusts   professionally managed portfolio of investments yielding an income but minimising any risk by spreading investment. Also the trust undertakes to buy back units from investors when requested

unsecured creditor   someone owed money but without any guarantee that it will be recovered

visible exports/imports   physical goods exported/imported and appearing as receipts/payments in the current account of a country's balance of payments

wage freeze   government ban on increases in wages usually to combat inflation

wholesaler   a middleman who buys goods from a manufacturer and resells to retailers, usually providing the facility of storing goods in a warehouse between transactions

winding up   the process of going into voluntary liquidation

without profits endowment assurance   a policy with a fixed sum assured as opposed to one 'with profits' which while guaranteeing more, requires the payment of a higher premium

yield   the return on an investment

CHECKLIST

1   All organisations need financial backing both in the short term and in the long term.

2   Finance comes from a variety of sources including private investors, institutions, banks, building societies, insurance companies and government.

3   Banks offer a wide range of services to their customers.

4   Commercial or joint stock banks concentrate on short-term finance and day-to-day business, whereas merchant banks are involved with company flotations, managing large investment

funds, providing venture capital and overseas business dealings.

5   Banking has recently undergone a transformation as a result of technological innovation with many of its systems becoming highly automated.

6   The 'cashless society' comes nearer to a reality with card systems and EFTPOS.

7   The Building Societies Act 1986 has enabled building societies to greatly diversify their financial operations.

8   The Stock Exchange underwent deregulation in October 1986 and since then its operations have changed dramatically.

9   The two main categories of share are ordinary and preference.

10 When a company 'goes public' a lot of complex procedures are involved.

11 The buying and selling of shares is conducted through a broker.

12 Business risks are minimised by insurance.

13 Insurance operates on certain basic principles which always apply.

14 Businesses may be affected by a range of risks, all of which may be covered by different types of insurance.

15 Large organisations often carry out what are known as risk management activities in the interests of organisational safety and security.

16 The Financial Services Act 1986 introduced new regulations in respect of the savings and investment market.

17 The calculation of wages and salaries is a complex procedure and much of it is now handled by computer.

18 To avoid the need to handle vast amounts of cash most wages and salaries are now paid directly to employees' chosen accounts via the credit transfer system.

19 In the payment of wages and salaries both voluntary and statutory deductions are made, the latter being in respect of income tax and national insurance via the PAYE system.

20 Business transactions produce a range of standard business documents.

QUICK REVISION QUESTIONS

1   Identify six principal sources from which finance might be raised.
2   List the principal services of a commercial bank.

3 Explain what you understand by 'electronic banking'.
4 Compare and contrast a debit card and a credit card.
5 What is an EFTPOS system?
6 Explain three of the main functions of a merchant bank.
7 Briefly explain what you understand by the term 'Big Bang'.
8 What is the difference between a share and a debenture?
9 What advantages does a company get from 'going public'?
10 What is contained in a company's Memorandum of Association?
11 What is the difference between application and allotment?
12 Outline a procedure for selling existing shares.
13 Apart from granting mortgages, what other areas of financial activity are now open to building societies?
14 What are the basic principles of insurance?
15 What are six categories of risk against which a shopkeeper would be likely to insure?
16 What are three special categories against which an exporter might insure?
17 Apart from basic wages and salaries what other methods of remuneration might be used?
18 Name five things which would be covered by National Insurance.
19 Explain what happens to three of the copies in a multiple invoice.
20 In what circumstances might a credit note be issued?

6 Office accounting and control systems

All financial matters are recorded and processed using standard accounting procedures and the co-ordination of all information collected enables accurate annual accounts to be produced. Business efficiency is also dependent on the types of control system a company sets up to monitor certain areas of activity and introduce financial savings as considered necessary.

Secretarial and office staff are often directly involved in the operation of many of the standard procedures and systems introduced and therefore need to be fully conversant with them. Also a general appreciation of company accounts and their interpretation is useful as it not only enhances awareness of how an organisation is progressing and where its strengths and weaknesses lie, but helps place office accounting procedures into perspective.

This section examines basic bookkeeping procedures used in offices and provides an introduction to the interpretation of financial accounts. It also highlights a few of the standard control systems commonly found in offices.

At the end of this section you should be able to:

- explain what is meant by a day book;
- define the principle of double entry;
- understand the purpose of a trial balance;
- maintain a simple cash book;
- define the imprest system;
- explain the procedure for issuing and recording petty cash transactions;
- appreciate the essential information required to prepare a basic set of final accounts;
- identify the items which constitute a set of final accounts;
- provide examples of assets and liabilities;
- distinguish between current and fixed assets and liabilities;
- explain the need for depreciation;
- explain what is meant by goodwill;

- identify the main financial statements prepared for the submission of company accounts and the preparation of an annual report;
- distinguish between different levels of profit;
- appreciate the order of presentation for a company's balance sheet;
- understand what is meant by budgetary control;
- list items to be found in a typical office expenditure budget;
- describe how a stock control system could be set up;
- devise a procedure for issuing stock;
- define flexitime and explain the operation of a typical system;
- identify the advantages and disadvantages of flexitime.

Bookkeeping procedures

The day-to-day financial activities of a business are recorded in the first instance in 'day books' or 'books of original entry'. As these terms suggest they are simply books used to record transactions or list business documents received in chronological order. They consist of Cash Book, Petty Cash Book, Purchases Book, Sales Book, Purchases Returns Book, Sales Returns Book and Journal. With the exception of the Journal the contents of the others are self-explanatory and the Cash and Petty Cash Books will be discussed in more detail later. In short, the Journal contains details of any transactions which cannot be entered into one of the other day books. An example of such an entry would be the purchase, on credit, of a typewriter for use in the general office. This would not be entered in the Purchases Book as it has not been bought with the intention of reselling, but as an asset for general business use.

Double entry bookkeeping

Where only day books are kept this is referred to as the single entry (or incomplete) method of bookkeeping. It is only when the entries in the day books are transferred to the Ledger, which is the main book of account, that double entry takes place. This means that for each entry in a day book both a debit entry and a credit entry will be made in two separate Ledger accounts. For example, where goods for resale are purchased on credit from J Smith the transaction is originally entered in the Purchases Book on receipt of the invoice. In double entry bookkeeping this entry would be transferred subsequently to the Ledger; a debit entry made in the Purchases Account and a credit entry made in the account of J Smith as illustrated in Fig. 6.1.

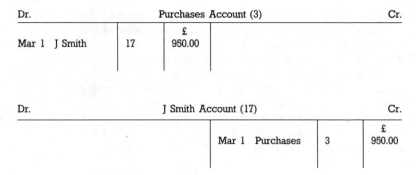

Fig. 6.1 Specimen Ledger entries

Consequently the fact that J Smith Account now has a figure on the credit side provides an instant indication that the business has a creditor in J Smith to the sum of £950. In practice separate ledgers would be drawn up to hold different types of account, eg all the creditors' accounts would be kept in one ledger (the Creditors or 'Bought' Ledger) and all the debtors' accounts would be kept in another ledger (the Debtors Ledger or 'Sales' Ledger).

Trial balance

In order to prove that double entries have been consistently made a bookkeeper may at any point draw up a trial balance to check the accuracy of the books by adding up all the debit entries and all the credit entries. Technically this is done by first working out a balance for each individual account by totalling each side and adding the difference to the lesser side to make the account balance. Therefore, where debit entries amount to more than credit ones there is a debit balance in the account and vice versa. It is the actual balances of all accounts which are listed in a trial balance and if there is not an equal total of debit and credit balances an error or omission has been made somewhere in the bookkeeping.

Cash Book

Although the Cash Book is a book of original entry it also serves as a record for all cash and bank transactions and any entry made may serve as one half of the double entry, the other half requiring to be made in an appropriate ledger account. The exception to this rule is where cash is transferred to or from the bank, in which case both

Dr. CASH BOOK **Cr.**

Date	Details	Fo	Dis All	Cash	Bank	Date	Details	Fo	Dis Rec	Cash	Bank

Fig. 6.2 Cash Book ruling
Note: 'Fo' represents Folio which is a column used to cross-reference entries to elsewhere in the accounts.

'Dis All' represents Discount Allowed by the business to its debtors. Therefore when a bill is settled by a debtor money is received in cash or in the bank but the full debt included a sum which has been allowed as discount, and this, too, must be accounted for.

'Dis Rec' represents Discount Received by the business from its creditors.

entries are made in the Cash Book – one on either side. This is known as a 'contra entry'.

Basically then, a Cash Book is a comprehensive record of cash and bank receipts and payments – the receipts being entered on the debit side, the payments on the credit. It is kept separate from other ledger accounts simply because many entries require to be made and it is important to be able to establish a business's cash position at any time.

A Cash Book is generally drawn up on a columnar basis with separate columns for cash and bank entries. Additionally it is customary to record any discounts allowed or received in the Cash Book as illustrated in Fig. 6.2.

Mechanised or computerised bookkeeping systems

Although the principles will still apply, many of the techniques already explained are likely to be mechanised in some way, if not computerised, certainly in larger offices. Such systems enable the simultaneous preparation of entries to day book and ledger as well as producing necessary documents such as statements of account to send to debtors. Also in many modern systems, eg the preparation of bank statements, it is usual to produce a running or continuous balance after every transaction.

Petty Cash Book

Another book of original entry which many secretaries will find they are required to maintain is the Petty Cash Book.

Even in an age when we are fast approaching the so-called cashless society, small amounts of actual money are indispensable to the running of any business. Not everyone is prepared to be paid by cheque or credit card, nor is it always appropriate or convenient. Consequently most offices will operate some type of petty cash system to cope with such contingencies. The sorts of expenditure typically associated with petty cash are as follows:

- small travelling expenses, eg taxi and bus fares;
- window and general cleaning expenses;
- small items of stationery which are not normally stocked;
- occasional postages;
- supplies for the office coffee breaks;
- flowers for reception.

Occasionally, although much less frequently, an office may be in receipt of small sums of money, eg cash left for personal telephone calls made.

In any event some sort of formal accounting mechanism needs to exist to record these minor transactions. In larger organisations in particular, many such systems will operate, and taken collectively they can represent a surprising amount of money on an annual basis. In bookkeeping terms the maintenance of petty cash is relatively straightforward, although it still follows the general principle of double entry.

The imprest system

The most usual method of operating petty cash is by what is known as the 'imprest' system. This is simply a system whereby the sum of money allocated for petty cash purposes is determined, eg £50 a month, and topped up at the end of the period to get back to the £50 in readiness for the next month's expenses. Therefore, if during the accounting period of the Petty Cash Book £35 has been paid out on various expenses, there should be £15 left in the cash box, so to restore the imprest the Cashier would reimburse the person in charge with £35.

What does a Petty Cash Book look like?

A typical Petty Cash Book, duly balanced, is given as Fig. 6.3. Note the analysis columns on the right-hand side. The purpose of these is to provide a detailed account of exactly where each item of expenditure goes and columns are headed up to suit particular needs. The totals of these columns provide a useful cross-check for the overall total column and are ultimately transferred to the appropriate accounts in the Ledger.

In practice it is unlikely that anyone will rigorously complete petty cash entries as and when they occur. This is where the voucher system helps. Whenever payments are made to members of staff or others these payments are supported by an authorised and dated voucher in respect of the sum involved. When the money is paid out the recipient will also sign for it on the voucher. Vouchers are kept with the cash box and are serial numbered for reference purposes. Alternatively the Petty Cashier may accept dated receipts instead of vouchers, where, for example, a member of staff has already paid out personal money for goods or services. It is through vouchers and receipts that accurate account can be kept of where and when the money goes out and for what purpose. From this information the person in charge of petty cash can, at a convenient time, make up the book. The total of the vouchers and receipts, together with the money still remaining in the cash box should always represent the imprest.

Dr. PETTY CASH BOOK **Cr.**

Receipts				Payments										
Date	Details	Fo	£	Date	Details	V. No	Fo	Total	Trav. Exps.	Post-ages	Clean-ing	Misc	Ledger	VAT
1/3	Bank	CB	50.00	2/3	Stamps	1		3.90		3.90				
9/3	Tel. call		1.50		Coffee	2		2.35				2.35		
				5/3	Flowers	4		5.00				5.00		
				6/3	Bus fare	3		1.75	1.75					
				7/3	Windows	5		3.50			3.50			
				10/3	Parcel	6		2.68		2.68				
				13/3	Parking	Rec		3.50	3.50					
				15/3	Sundries	7		1.42				1.42		
					J Jones		L2	8.00					8.00	
				18/3	Taxi	8		3.40	3.40					
					Repair	9		8.92				8.50		0.42
				26/3	Stamps	10		2.60		2.60				
			51.50					47.02	8.65	9.18	3.50	17.27	8.00	0.42
			4.48	31/3	Balance		c/f	4.48						
			47.02					51.50						
1/4	Balance	b/f												
	Bank	CB												

Fig. 6.3 Specimen Petty Cash Book

Presenting final accounts

While general office accounting procedures are likely to involve activities like keeping straightforward records of transactions and the monitoring and checking of ledger accounts together perhaps with the maintenance of Cash Books or Petty Cash Books, it is the ultimate drawing together of all the information, following the preparation of a trial balance, which constitutes a set of final accounts. In simple terms, ie for a small business, this is represented by the Trading and Profit and Loss Account and Balance Sheet.

The trading account

This is a summary of the actual trading position in an accounting period, usually twelve months. It details the stock, purchases and sales figures for the period and provides the gross profit on trading, ie the difference between total sales and the cost price of the goods sold.

The cost price of goods sold is determined by adding all purchases of goods (*plus* any expenses such as carriage, *less* any goods returned) to any existing stock figure, so arriving at the total goods available for sale. From this figure any remaining stock (ie that calculated at stock taking at the close of the financial period) is deducted to arrive at the actual price of the goods sold.

The profit and loss account

The gross profit calculated and shown in the trading account is carried down to the profit and loss account. Added to this figure are any other profits made from other investments, while offset against it are all items of expenditure incurred in the process of operating the business, eg rent, rates, lighting, heating, wages, salaries, travelling expenses, telephone charges, stationery and advertising costs, repairs and any other costs which had to be met, before the true or net profit could be determined.

The balance sheet

Finally a balance sheet can be prepared and it provides a summary of all the balances of accounts still remaining in the trial balance after the preparation of the trading and profit and loss accounts. Those remaining accounts represent the assets and liabilities of the business and will principally be made up of cash and bank balances, debtors, creditors, premises, fixtures and fittings, any loans to the business and the capital invested by the owner (or owners in the case of a part-

111

BALANCE SHEET OF D BOYD
as at 31 December 19 . .

Fixed assets
Shop premises	10,000	
Fixtures and fittings		
(less depreciation)	2,000	
		12,000

Current assets
Stock	2,600	
Debtors	380	
Cash in bank	1,205	
Cash in hand	115	
	4,300	

Less current liabilities
Creditors	1,300	
Working capital		3,000
		15,000

Represented by
Capital:
Balance at 1 January	10,000	
Add net profit	4,500	
	14,500	
Less drawings	3,500	
		11,000

Long-term liability:
Loan from J Miller		4,000
		15,000

Fig. 6.4   An example of the balance sheet of a sole trader

nership) together with any drawings made against the business and the profit or loss incurred during the year.

Traditionally balance sheets were displayed horizontally with assets listed on the right-hand side and liabilities shown on the left. However, it is more common now to arrange items vertically with one group on the top of the other as indicated in Fig. 6.4.

Assets and liabilities

Assets represent items of value to the business and are usually divided into current assets, ie those which can be turned quickly into money, viz cash in hand, cash at bank, debtors and stock, and fixed assets, ie those representing a long-term investment and to be used by the business, viz premises, furniture, fittings and equipment and motor vehicles.

Liabilities, on the other hand represent the financial obligations of the business and are represented as current and long-term liabilities. Current liabilities would include a bank overdraft, if a business had one, together with any creditors to whom the business owed money, while long-term liabilities would include any business loans acquired from other people as well as the amount due to the owner, ie the capital invested.

In terms of the order in which items are listed it is usual to list them in descending order of liquidity, ie arranged according to how quickly they may be turned into cash (in the case of the assets) or settled (in the case of the liabilities).

The interpretation of company accounts

Handling day-to-day accounting procedures and even preparing a set of final accounts for a small business is one thing, but understanding the complexities of the accounts of public companies, submitted with an annual report, is something else.

Annual reports and accounts provide the principal means by which companies can communicate information about their financial affairs to those who may be interested, eg shareholders, employees, competitors, the Inland Revenue. The form of the Directors' Report and published accounts is set by the Companies Act of 1985, in conjunction with all previous Companies Acts which dealt with this subject. The documents are sent to each shareholder, debenture holder and other interested party and are also filed with the Registrar of Companies in a prescribed format. The fact that they are 'filed' with the Registrar means that they are available for public inspection on the payment of a search fee (see also Section 15 p. 376).

Changes in requirements

In recent years there has been an enormous growth in the amount of information required of statutory accounts as a result of pressure from the Government and the general public, as well as the consequence of joining the EEC. This pressure for more information is understandable in that not only does the Government feel that the public has a right to certain information, particularly when confidence is shaken by take-overs, mergers and even cases of blatant fraud, but the publication of information can also have a beneficial effect for industry and commerce generally. In times of inflation and rising prices companies need to exercise stringent economies if they are to remain competitive. Consequently the availability of comparative results can provide such an impetus while the opportunity to view trading figures may help to stimulate the export trade.

In short people want to know how companies are managed and whether or not they are financially sound so the series of Companies Acts in the 1980s has set increasingly stringent demands for the disclosure of information, while accounting standards have been continually tightened following the setting up of the Accounting Standards Committee (ASC) which prepared standard guidelines for the preparation and presentation of final accounts.

Three main financial statements are prepared, viz the Profit and Loss Account, the Balance Sheet and the Source and Application of Funds and these are briefly explained below.

Profit and Loss Account

The Profit and Loss Account measures a company's operating performance over its financial year. This may be neither the calendar year, ie January to December nor the tax year, ie April to April, but rather the period during which business is best conducted according to the demands of the particular enterprise. Therefore a company's financial year may, for example end on 30 June each year.

The Profit and Loss Account shows the revenue (or income) for the year and offset against this is the cost of goods sold together with all expenses incurred. As well as detailing revenue from actual trading it will show income acquired in other ways, eg interest on investments and dividends from associated companies. Therefore the ultimate profit or loss will have taken into account both trading profit and other income.

Deducted from this total income or profit figure are all interest payments on borrowed capital (eg overdrafts, mortgages, debentures). It is the profit at this point, ie before taxation, but after interest payments, which is the best indicator of a company's performance and of the efficiency of its management. Tax is calculated on any profit made *after* interest has been deducted. Therefore, the more interest a company pays out the less it has to pay in tax.

Any other items which may appear on a Profit and Loss Account are usually referred to as 'extraordinary' items of either income or expenditure in that they are unusual in the company's normal operations and, therefore, must be shown quite separately. An example of an extraordinary item of expenditure in a company's accounts might arise where a company pays out a lot in redundancies which would, of course, affect that financial year only. Another example, this time affecting a company's income, would be where a company has sold off or 'disposed of' (to use accountancy terms) some of its properties and made a profit on the book value (ie the valuation as it appeared in the Balance Sheet).

It is only when all these additions and/or subtractions have been made that the net profit or loss for the year is reached, ie the amount available for distribution to shareholders.

A word of caution about 'profit'

When examining a set of company accounts and asked to comment on the profit be sure that you are clear which profit is being referred to as it could be any one of the following:

- **gross profit** ie the total sales less the cost price of goods sold;
- **trading profit** ie the profit on sales having taken into account the cost price of the goods sold, together with all expenses thereon;
- **total profit** ie the trading profit plus any other profit from investments, etc;
- **net profit before tax** ie the total profit less any interest payable;
- **profit on ordinary activities** ie net profit after tax;
- **profit available for distribution to shareholders** ie the net profit plus or minus any extraordinary items.

Therefore it is essential to have a precise definition of which level of profit is being referred to.

When the bottom line of profit is reached there are essentially two things which can be done with it. It may either be paid out in full to shareholders or some of it may be held in reserve (eg where there has been a particularly good year). Strictly such a split would be shown in what is termed a Profit and Loss Appropriation Account which is just a continuation of the ordinary Profit and Loss Account.

Notes on accounts

Whatever format a set of final accounts takes there will always be a set of explanatory notes accompanying them. They provide a detailed and often complex interpretation of the principal figures and will also outline how the money has been distributed in terms of dividend payments. For example, two dividends may be paid during a financial year – an interim dividend half way through the year and a final dividend after the AGM. It will be up to a company to determine the proportion of profits to dividends and it may be all, something or even nothing. A company may also, where it may have had a poor year, elect to pay a dividend out of its reserves where it has kept a surplus aside in earlier years. Remember that the order in which dividends are paid out will depend on the nature of the stock held (see Section 5).

The balance sheet

This is the statement indicating what a company owns (assets) and what it owes (liabilities). It comprises three major classes of item: assets, liabilities and equity capital.

Assets The simplest assets to explain are those which are fixed and tangible, like premises and fixtures in Fig. 6.4, although even those assets present problems in accounting terms as the values do not remain constant. They will either appreciate, eg land and buildings, or depreciate, eg equipment, fixtures and vehicles. Such factors need to be taken into account when reading a balance sheet as the assets are likely to appear at their acquisition value with perhaps a proportion written off each year by way of an allowance against depreciation (the fixtures and fittings sum in Fig. 6.4 was a net figure after allowing for depreciation, but the shop premises figure was likely to be the sum for which the property was acquired).

Another asset which is sometimes seen in a balance sheet, particularly in the first year or so, following the acquisition of a company, is goodwill. Goodwill is an intangible asset and is the fictitious sum of money which may be paid for the future potential profits of a company, based on its past reputation and clientele. In most instances it will be written off as quickly as possible but initially it may feature as an asset as the company has had to pay for it. Other examples of intangible assets would be patents or trade marks.

Finally there are current assets, ie those which are most quickly converted into cash, viz cash itself, money in the bank, debts owing to the company, its stock of finished goods, together with any prepaid expenses, eg rent or rates paid in advance.

Stock valuation Auditors pay particular attention to the way in which stock is valued and insist that it is shown in the accounts as the lower value between cost price and net realisable value, otherwise a high stock figure will produce an unrealistically high profit figure when calculating the cost price of goods sold.

Liabilities Liabilities represent the obligations on the part of a company to pay, in the foreseeable future, for goods or services already received. Legally a company must distinguish between short-term creditors, ie current liabilities and those to which payment is due after more than a year, ie long-term liabilities. Typical examples of current liabilities are short-term loans, creditors, tax dividends due to be paid, overdrafts and deposits from customers (ie where customers have prepaid certain monies, eg the deposit for a holiday or for accommodation prior to receiving any benefit from it). Long-term liabilities, on the other hand, would be represented by debentures, mortgages and secured loans, for example.

Equity capital Finally a balance sheet shows how the capital is made up, ie the type and allocation of shares and any share premium raised through offering shares above their nominal value (eg supposing 10 million shares with a nominal value of £1 per share are sold at £1.25 per share, the share capital will be shown at £10,000,000 but there will be an additional entry against a separate share premium account showing £2,500,000, which represents the 25p share premium per share), together with any reserves, ie any profits retained from previous years.

Balance sheet formats

As was indicated earlier the traditional British method of presenting a balance sheet, viz horizontally, has been replaced by the vertical method, and the Companies Act 1981 actually details two alternative formats in its section on the presentation of company accounts. The intention behind this schedule in the Act was to bring every company within the European Economic Community (EEC) into line in terms of presentation.

An example of the vertical format in accordance with one of the alternatives specified in the schedule is given as Fig. 6.5.

Source and Application of Funds Statement

This statement, while not required by law is produced as standard accounting practice and provides an indication of how and why a company's financial situation has changed during a year. It shows where the financial resources (funds) have come from and explains how they have been used. In short a statement of source and application of funds should, when considered in conjunction with the other financial statements, help answer the following key questions:

- Where have the profits gone?
- Is the company making enough to continue to pay out dividends?
- Where did the company get money from during the financial year?
- How healthy is the company – is it solvent, ie has it sufficient liquid assets to meet its short-term obligations?

	Notes	This year £'000	£'000	Last year £'000	£'000
BALANCE SHEET OF A-TYPICA PLC as at the end of the most recent financial year					
FIXED ASSETS					
Intangible assets	7	6		7	
Tangible assets	8	91		79	
Investments	9	13	110	10	96
CURRENT ASSETS					
Stocks	10	49		36	
Debtors	11	42		43	
Cash at bank and in hand	12	5		7	
		96		86	
CREDITORS: amounts falling due within one year	13	60		44	
NET CURRENT ASSETS		36	36	42	42
TOTAL ASSETS LESS CURRENT LIABILITIES			146		138
CREDITORS: amounts falling due after more than one year					
Debenture loans	5	25		30	
Bank loans	5	4	29	5	35
PROVISION FOR LIABILITIES AND CHARGES:					
Pensions and other obligations	6	11		9	
Deferred taxation		5	16	3	12
SHAREHOLDERS' FUNDS			101		89
Being: **CAPITAL AND RESERVES**					
Called-up Share Capital			50		50
Share Premium Account			20		20
Revaluation Reserve			5		4
Profit and Loss Account			26		15
			101		89

Fig. 6.5   An example of a company balance sheet format

In order to answer these questions it is necessary to consider:

a how money has come into a company in the course of a year, ie sources or inflows, and

b how money has gone out of a company in the course of a year, ie applications, uses or outflows.

The main sources of funds are as follows:

- profit on ordinary activities (before tax and interest);
- depreciation (this needs to be added back to the profit figure as it is merely an accounting adjustment in recognition of the falling value of fixed assets and so is bound to distort the actual money flowing in);
- proceeds from the sale of fixed assets, eg an item of equipment no longer needed, or surplus land and buildings;
- by calling in monies owed by debtors during the previous financial year and minimising the amount of sales on credit during this financial year;
- by taking longer to settle with creditors;
- by raising loans;
- by taking on a bank overdraft.

Conversely the main ways in which funds are used are as follows:

- paying out dividends;
- paying tax;
- paying interest on loans and overdrafts;
- buying new fixed assets;
- stockpiling goods;
- extending the credit period allowed to debtors;
- paying off creditors faster.

The difficulties which non-experts have in deciphering a Flow of Funds Statement (another name for this statement) arise from the fact that many of the figures which appear cannot be directly traced from the Profit and Loss Account and Balance Sheet. For example a figure shown for taxation will not be the same as that shown in the Profit and Loss Account. However, what such a statement does show to the layperson is the difference between the funds available (ie the sources) and the funds required (ie the application) to carry on the business of the company and this will of necessity result in either an increase or decrease in net liquid funds.

Budgetary control

When people speak of control systems one that always seems to spring readily to mention is budgetary control. Budgets of all kinds are prepared with the intention of helping to make an organisation run more efficiently and so be more profitable. Budgeting is a management

119

tool which is essential to short-term planning. Budgets can be drawn up for any period of time and they can cover virtually any area of operational activity within an organisation. For example there may be budgets affecting production, sales, R & D and administration. What is important is that they are co-ordinated by senior management within the framework of the organisation's overall budget.

Advantages and disadvantages

There are many advantages to be gained from budgets, including the following:

- they enable an organisation's aims and objectives to be translated into financial terms;
- they act as yardsticks by which to measure efficiency;
- they highlight key actions which need to be taken;
- they provide an overview of an organisation's activities and this can assist top management in decision making;
- they provide an indication of areas which need corrective action;
- they can provide positive motivation for staff;
- where they are the responsibility of individual departments (budget centres) they endorse the principle of delegation.

In terms of disadvantages budgetary control systems may be thought to present problems in that:

- they impose yet another routine which needs to be performed;
- they may be thought to be merely another way of bringing about cost reductions;
- they can be time-consuming and costly in terms of administration and staff effort required to prepare them;
- they may be so complex that they are misunderstood by those whose responsibility it is to prepare them.

Budgetary control in the office

Budgetary control systems play their part in the control of all offices and it will be the Office Manager or Administrator who is responsible for preparing the budget(s) for an office. The sorts of expenditure which need to be budgeted for includes the following:

- staff salaries;
- equipment;
- consumables, ie stationery and other office supplies;
- running costs, eg heating and lighting;

- rent, rates and insurance;
- telephone charges;
- printing and postage.

Budgets are prepared by forecasting likely expenditure which will be incurred during the ensuing budget period. Some of this will be relatively straightforward to predict, based on past records. For instance, salaries can be calculated fairly accurately with the help of the salaries section and taking into account pay increases in the pipeline together with any anticipated additions to the staff. Likewise it will be possible to calculate rent and rates, being a proportion of the overall charge made to the company, possibly based according to floor space occupied.

Where difficulties are likely to arise is when a department is undergoing considerable innovation and change, eg the introduction of office automation or departmental restructuring of some kind and where the knock-on effects cannot be fully appreciated. Similarly unanticipated changes in the volume of business either up or down will affect the outgoings of an office. Costs of all kinds need to be closely monitored and areas of concern reported. Any significant variations need to be investigated as they may seriously affect the budget allocation.

Costs incurred fall into different categories according to whether they are influenced principally by time factors or volumes of work undertaken but basically they will be either fixed, eg rent and rates or variable, eg telephone charges and postages. Therefore, in the knowledge that some costs are bound to fluctuate a budget needs to be flexible.

Capital and revenue expenditure

An office manager needs to distinguish between capital and revenue expenditure as he may have separate budget headings between which he may not be permitted to switch expenditure, and where a capital item such as a new piece of equipment eg a microcomputer, photo copier, etc. is required he may have to obtain management support and approval before he can go ahead and place an order if the cost exceeds the amount of his allocation in respect of capital expenditure.

In terms of revenue expenditure, there will tend to be more flexibility, although it is unlikely that a manager will find that he is able to save on consumables, eg stationery, and use the money for capital items. Once a budget has been worked out by a departmental head, submitted to management and approved, perhaps following minor modifications, it is the responsibility of that head of department to manage expenditure within that budget. Variations will be noted and actual expenditure will be compared with that forecast. Such feedback will be used as a basis for calculating the next year's budget.

Stationery and stock control

Another control system familiar to those who work in offices is that set up to monitor the supply and issue of office stationery and supplies. Offices get through large amounts of stationery and supplies in the course of a year and provision has to be made within departmental budgets for such items of revenue expenditure.

Needs will vary between departments and the ways in which materials are ordered, stored and issued will vary according to the size of the organisation. Small businesses, for example, may buy on a fairly *ad hoc* basis according to requirements, relying largely on the availability of supplies from local stationers or office equipment suppliers. Much of their ordering may even be done from a catalogue, over the telephone. Small users will be unlikely to have the time to 'shop around' to get the best deal. Besides they are likely to buy in such small quantities as to be unentitled to special discounts. Large organisations, on the other hand, will get through a lot of supplies in the course of a year and are able to benefit from bulk purchase discounts, special offers and contract supply terms.

Within large organisations all supplies may be ordered via a Central Purchasing Department. This means that literally all supplies, irrespective of the type of goods, will be ordered centrally using standard procedures. The idea is to enable management to exercise tighter control over buying, by rationalising supply sources, while securing the benefits of specialist purchasing staff who are skilled in securing the best terms and who know the markets and the suppliers.

Although actual orders may be placed by the purchasing department, it will be the responsibility of individual departments and sections to determine their particular requirements within the parameters of their respective budget allocations. They will then advise the purchasing department of their needs by means of a requisition, sometimes suggesting preferred or alternative suppliers.

Establishing requirements

At least once a year departments will be requested to estimate their requirements for the current year in terms of stationery and other supplies. Within a small section this may simply be done by the section head on a fairly rule-of-thumb basis, but where there may be a large department comprising a range of secretarial and clerical staff with varied duties and responsibilities, requirements may be more difficult to assess and the procedure may be to request staff to fill in a pro forma of some kind listing their estimated individual requirements over a certain period. The pro forma may comprise a specific list against which staff stipulate their requirements or have an open format where staff are free to request whatever they feel they need, or a combination of the two.

Following the submission of appropriately authorised departmental requisitions the Central Purchasing Department will collate all requests, and proceed to order from suitable suppliers. When the goods are received they are checked off against the different requisitions and distributed to the individual departments for ultimate issue.

This will frequently mean that some form of interim storage and control will be required on a departmental basis, with the need to set up appropriate procedures for recording stock and issuing supplies.

Storage facilities

Depending on the volume of materials to be stored departments will need to set aside either lockable cupboards, or perhaps even a locked storeroom for this purpose. Storage facilities need to be kept locked as many of the items held are easily carried and open access will frequently result in indiscriminate usage and even pilfering.

Where a special room is used it is important that it is dry, well ventilated and adequately lit and that it is fitted out properly with shelves and the necessary steps to reach the supplies. Heavy items should be stored on or near floor level, while less frequently requested items can be stored on higher shelves. All shelves should be appropriately labelled and a note of all stock received should be recorded in an appropriate system.

Stock control systems

Various systems exist but one common method is to prepare a stock card for each item of stock held. These cards may be stored in any suitable indexing arrangement, but a good way is to insert the cards within a visible edge system (see Fig. 6.6) either the flat drawer variety, or in book form. This technique has the advantage that stock items can be easily and quickly located and yet the cards are held

123

Fig. 6.6 Visible edge card index system

securely in place and the information contained on the cards is kept relatively confidential. Also signals (eg coloured plastic tags) can easily be inserted into the plastic strip which secures the visible edge, so flagging the need to re-order. A typical card layout is shown above.

This procedure greatly facilitates annual stock taking as the final column on the card represents a running balance. What is in effect being maintained is a **perpetual inventory** of all stock held.

Why the need for stock records?

Throughout an entire organisation stationery and consumables will account for a substantial amount of money over a year, particularly where a lot of photocopying is done and paper consumption is high. Such expenditure will feature in the company's annual accounts as will stock held (see earlier in this section) and it is essential that accurate records are maintained. Also, records help to highlight areas of waste and heavy usage. Tighter controls may be introduced and it may be possible to secure better terms or consider alternative suppliers.

Maximum and minimum stock levels

When handling large quantities of stock it is essential to establish

Item _____ Unit of isssue _____						
Description _____ Ref No _____						
Supplier _____ Maximum held _____						
Shelf location _____ Minimum held _____						
Date Received	Requisition Number	Quantity Received	Date Issued	Quantity Issued	To Whom	Bal
DESCRIPTION OF STOCK ITEM HELD						Ref No

Fig. 6.7 Stock record card

maximum and minimum holding levels. Maximum will be determined by space availability for storage, by shelf life considerations and by the amount of capital which it is realistic to tie up in holding the stock. Minimum levels will be determined by the speed with which supplies can be replenished.

FIFO

Most stationery and consumables are stored and issued using the FIFO (First In First Out) principle. This is particularly important where goods have a limited shelf life or where deterioration of some kind is likely, the significance for the actual storage of goods being that when new stocks are delivered it is important that old stock is brought to the front of the shelves with new stock placed behind.

Issue procedures

Where stationery and office supplies are kept under lock and key some form of issue procedure needs to be established and a member of staff has to be given authority to operate the system and so be responsible for its smooth operation. Usually supplies will only be issued at set times, otherwise the member of staff with this responsibility will find that he/she is called upon to issue supplies at all times, so disrupting other work. A typical procedure will operate as follows:

• all staff are issued with a list of stock carried;

- the person requiring an item of stock will complete a stationery requisition (usually prepared in duplicate);
- this is signed by someone in authority;
- requests are usually made in predetermined units of issue, eg reams of paper, packets of envelopes, boxes of paper clips, individual pens, etc;
- the stationery clerk retains one copy of the requisition, the member of staff keeps the other;
- all staff are notified of issue procedures and times;
- record cards are updated after each issue of stock.

Flexitime systems

Flexible working hours are yet another type of control. Flexitime has operated in offices for many years now and, as the name suggests, it provides for the operation of flexible working hours. Within certain predetermined limits, staff may choose when they start and finish the working day to fit in with their personal circumstances and preferences and are allowed certain flexibility in terms of lunch-time arrangements.

Coretime and flexitime

Most systems operate on what are defined as coretime and flexitime hours. **Coretime** represents the time during which all staff must be in the office, usually between 1000 hours and 1200 hours in the morning and 1400 hours and 1600 hours in the afternoon, although variations will be possible. **Flexitime**, represents the bands of time at the beginning, middle and end of the day when staff may choose whether they will be present or not, with the proviso, of course, that sufficient flexitime hours are worked to bring the number of working hours up to contract total within a week or month. Additionally most organisations will indicate the earliest a person can start work in the morning, the minimum time which must be taken as a lunch break (usually half an hour) and the latest time at which a person may remain in the office in the evening. These requirements exist to ensure that the demands of an office's work can always be met.

Advantages and disadvantages

In addition to the control which such systems provide for staff to organise their own working days, there is the advantage of avoiding rush hour traffic; the potential to accommodate personal arrangements, eg shopping, hairdressing appointments, extended luncheon engagements; and also the ability to accumulate time which can be set off against half days or even full days out of work (although here again, there are usually limits to the number of hours anyone can have credited to them over and above contracted hours during a particular accounting period).

From the point of view of management the introduction does mean additional work in terms of the calculation of contracted working hours over each period, as well as the need to install special time-recording machines, for which each member of staff will have a personal key. Also the extension of the working day does add to overheads, eg lighting and heating and perhaps canteen facilities. However, on the plus side flexitime does tend to be viewed favourably by staff, which is good for morale, and to eliminate any problems which might have been encountered in terms of bad timekeeping.

CHECKLIST

1 Day books form the basis of double entry bookkeeping which requires a debit entry and a credit entry to be made in two separate ledger accounts.

2 A trial balance is a testing mechanism to prove the accuracy of the double entry system prior to the preparation of final accounts.

3 All cash or bank transactions are recorded in the Cash Book which is usually drawn up on a columnar basis with separate columns for cash and bank as well as columns for recording discounts allowed and received.

4 With the introduction of sophisticated software many systems are now handled by computer.

5 Petty cash is needed to cover small items of expenditure incurred in the day-to-day running of an office and the usual method of keeping a Petty Cash Book is on the imprest system.

6 A set of final accounts comprises Trading, Profit and Loss Account and Balance Sheet.

7 Assets represent items of value to a business whereas liabilities represent its debts or financial obligations.

8 It is usual to distinguish assets as being either current, ie those which can be quickly converted into cash or fixed, ie those having long-term value and liabilities as either current, ie those which should be met within a year or long term, ie those which will stand for a period greater than a year.

9 Companies are all required by law to file their annual accounts with the Registrar of Companies and certain standards of presentation are expected.

10 The three main financial statements which are prepared are the Profit and Loss Account, the Balance Sheet and the Source and Application of Funds.

11 A Profit and Loss Account shows the income for the year together with the expenditure incurred and the consequent profit or loss.

12 It is possible to interpret profit in many different ways dependent upon which stage in the operation it is calculated, eg before or after tax.

13 A Source and Application of Funds Statement shows where a company's resources have come from and how they have been used.

14 Budgetary control systems are short-term forecasting and planning activities which may be centred on any area of an organisation's activities in line with the overall budget.

15 An Office Manager is responsible for budgetary control in the office and needs to distinguish between capital and revenue expenditure in drawing up his budget.

16 Stationery and stock control systems enable a company accurately to monitor materials used and replenish as necessary possibly via a Central Purchasing Department.

17 Supplies will only be issued on presentation of a properly authorised requisition.

18 A system of stock issue, checking and recording will be set up, usually on a departmental basis.

19 The operation of flexible working hours in offices enables staff to control their contracted working hours within certain preset limitations.

20 Flexitime has advantages for both staff and management.

QUICK REVISION QUESTIONS

1 What day books are likely to be kept by a small business?
2 What do you understand by the term 'double entry bookeeping'?
3 How and why is a trial balance prepared?
4 What is meant by a 'contra entry' in the Cash Book?
5 Explain what you understand by the imprest system of operating petty cash.

6 What do you understand by the voucher system in connection with petty cash?

7 What is the purpose of a Profit and Loss Account and what would be some typical entries?

8 What is the difference between current and fixed assets?

9 Why is it necessary to show depreciation in a set of final accounts?

10 In what circumstances might a payment be made in respect of goodwill?

11 Name three different levels of profit which can be calculated in financial accounting.

12 What method is now recommended for presenting a balance sheet?

13 When would a company's balance sheet show an entry under 'Share Premium Account'?

14 What is an alternative name for a Source and Application of Funds statement and what does one contain?

15 Name four items which would need to be considered in an office's budgetary control exercise.

16 What are three advantages of budgetary control?

17 What three principal factors influence maximum stock levels?

18 What are the essential features of a stock issuing procedure?

19 What is meant by 'coretime' when operating a system of flexible working hours?

20 What are the main advantages of flexitime?

7 Office communication systems

The office is the hub of an organisation's communication network whether the facilities are the most basic or the most up-to-date imaginable. Communication is both internal within the organisation itself and external, including worldwide contacts. Communication is concerned with transmitting and receiving information in all forms.

Information is central to all aspects of an organisation's activities. It is vital in terms of planning, controlling, problem-solving, decision-making, motivating, negotiating, interviewing, buying, selling or any other managerial pursuit. Without reliable, up-to-date information organisations simply cannot function effectively and it is the way information is communicated and the systems which are used that are vital.

Managers spend more time communicating with others than they do on any other activity and good communication is an essential key to management effectiveness. This section identifies the different media available and examines the principal communications systems available to offices today.

At the end of this section you should be able to:

- identify the different communication media available;
- explain the criteria which influence choice of media;
- identify barriers to effective communication;
- suggest how effective communication is achieved;
- identify different types of written communication;
- outline a procedure for dealing with incoming mail;
- explain a procedure for the internal circulation of mail;
- have an awareness of the operation of an outgoing mail system within an office;
- identify the principal Post Office mail services;
- identify different kinds of meetings;
- explain the functions of different committees;
- outline the role of the chairman;
- identify the key factors in effective meeting participation;
- describe standard telephone and switchboard equipment;

- outline recent advances in telephone systems and services;
- appreciate the uses of telephone answering machines;
- explain what is meant by 'call logging';
- compare and contrast telex and teletex;
- appreciate the complexities of datacoms;
- explain the workings of an electronic mailbox;
- understand the operation of a local area network;
- understand the operation of a database;
- outline the advantages of facsimile transmission;
- explain how videoconferencing operates;
- outline the services of couriers.

Media selection

A wide range of communication media is now available and office personnel need to be familiar with the possibilities which exist. Basically it will be a question of determining whether something needs to be conveyed in print, whether direct face-to-face contact is preferable, or whether transmission via electronic means might be more appropriate.

Initial consideration will be concerned with the type of communication and whether it is internal or external. Literally every action taken by personnel working in offices will involve communication of some kind. It may be providing information, seeking information, giving advice, solving problems, undertaking some form of public relations activity or simply transacting day-to-day business.

Selecting the appropriate medium is important as it will influence both impact and outcome as well as being a consideration in terms of efficiency, economy and expediency. An initial guideline will be to ask the question '**Who** wants to ask **what** of **whom**?' As well as reducing communication to basic human terms this helps highlight other issues which will best be solved by posing certain questions. The following are examples:

- **The time scale involved**. How urgent is the communication and which method would produce the quickest result?
- **The distance factor**. Is the communication internal, external, local regional, national or international?
- **The cost factor**. What are the available options and how significant a consideration is cost?
- **The human element**. How significant a factor is consideration for the other party's feelings, expectations and impressions on receipt?

- **The credibility factor.** Will the communication be taken seriously if delivered in a particular format? For example a verbal reprimand may need to be supported by a written warning or a telephone call may not carry the weight of a request on letterheaded paper.

Barriers to effective communication

Even where selection criteria have been carefully considered communication will fall down when somewhere along the line of communication there is a barrier between the transmitter and the receiver. In the case of telephone calls, for example, this may be a line engaged or a technical fault, while with a letter it may be a postal strike or an inadequately addressed envelope which causes the problem, not to mention ambiguity in the actual letter content.

In verbal communication there are obvious physical factors which can contribute to problems, eg difficulties in hearing or interruptions from extraneous noise. However, it is important for any communicator to be aware of other barriers which can seriously hamper effective communication and these can include the following.

Language problems This refers to difficulties in interpreting what is being said or written either because it is in a foreign language or delivered in an unfamiliar accent or because the language used is very technical or too specialist in nature and so beyond the comprehension of the receiver.

Non-verbal cues (often referred to as 'body language') This is where the transmitter of the communication accompanies or substitutes remarks with physical gestures like shrugged shoulders or raised eyebrows. Attitudes are also conveyed by the way people stand or sit, where they stand in relation to others, how much eye contact they maintain and how they look and dress (see also p 342).

Differing perceptions There is a strong likelihood that different people will interpret the same thing in different ways. Study Fig. 7.1 as an example. What do you see when you look at it first? Differences of interpretation arise as a result of differing previous experiences, influenced, among other things, by age, sex, nationality, culture, education and personality.

Prejudgement There is a tendency in many people to prejudge issues by adopting the attitude that they have read, seen or heard something before. Consequently they do not give the matter their best attention and make judgements based on previous knowledge and experience.

Fig. 7.1 Young girl–old woman

Filtering out This is somewhat similar but usually happens where people are resistant to change and will only hear what they want to hear, twisting new information to fit what they believe already.·

Labelling or stereotyping This happens where someone has a precon-ceived notion about someone, eg, 'He never has anything worthwhile to say' or 'She's just a dumb blond'. Consequently he has made up his mind about what the person is about to communicate before the speaker has even opened his mouth.

'Two and two make five' or (mental closure) This happens where the receiver fills in the gaps – something we can all do naturally with printed matter, eg accepting incomplete words, but which may have severe repercussions in verbal communication as it can be difficult to back-track to reality.

Superior–subordinate relationships Barriers can exist where one party will tell the other what he thinks the other wants or expects to hear rather than what is really the case.

From these few examples it can be seen that effective communication is not without its problems and that communicators need to be aware of likely pitfalls when preparing to transmit information whether in written form or orally.

Written communication

Written communication takes many forms but can be comfortably divided as indicated in Table 7.1.

Whatever the form of written communication certain basic questions need to be addressed before any material is prepared. These are as follows:

- What is the purpose of the communication?
- To whom is the communication addressed?

Table 7.1   Types of written communication

Internal to the organisation	External to clients/customers	External to the wider environment
memoranda*	letters*	reports*
reports*	invitations	notices
notices	circulars	returns
agendas	price lists	official forms
minutes	publicity leaflets	press releases
contracts	estimates	advertisements
handbooks	quotations	information booklets
manuals	orders	articles
questionnaires	invoices	application forms
job descriptions	debit notes	job details
job specifications	credit notes	promotional literature
interview assessment sheets	statements	
house journals	export documents	

Note: The three asterisked items are elaborated on pp 288–294.

- From whom is the communication coming?
- What is the purpose of the communication?
- What is the status of the recipient?
- What tone should be adopted?
- What sort of reply, if any, is required?
- How confidential is the information?
- What style/layout should be used?
- Is the communication complete in itself or does it need enclosures?
- How brief or how detailed should the communication be?
- What sort of impact or impression needs to be conveyed?
- What would be the likely implications of an error or misunderstanding?
- How complex is the information/detail which needs to be explained?

Irrespective of the trend towards less paper with the upsurge of electronic mail and data communications, written correspondence still features strongly in most offices. It is central to office operations and integral to the vast majority of systems and procedures which rely on the preparation, processing, dissemination and collation of paperwork of some kind or another. Consequently sound procedures for handling what can loosely be referred to as mail are essential.

Mail handling systems

Most large organisations have established procedures for handling mail. These will operate at the incoming and outgoing stages as well as throughout the working day and will be run from a centralised mail room through which all mail, both internal and external, passes. The larger the organisation the more complex and automated the procedures.

Incoming mail

Efficient procedures for processing and distributing incoming mail are essential to the effective operation of any organisation. The morning post, for many office personnel, will be the catalyst which sets the wheels in motion for the day's work. Precise procedures will vary according to the specific requirements of individual organisations but are likely to operate along the following lines:

- mail arrives in the mail room having been delivered by the Post Office, collected by messenger or picked up from a locked postbag/box service;

- any Registered or Recorded Delivery mail is signed for and recorded in an appropriate log-book;
- any special precautions introduced as a result of letter bomb scares would be taken (mail is also put through routine scrutiny by the Post Office);
- a preliminary sort is undertaken, eg basic letter mail is separated from printed paper and packages;
- Private, Personal or Confidential mail is placed to one side, unopened, even where it is company practice to open all mail;
- other mail is opened, probably using a letter opening machine if the volume of mail is sufficient (in some organisations mail which is specifically addressed to an individual or department will be sorted and sent unopened);
- where mail is opened all contents are removed;
- enclosures are checked and any omissions logged;
- enclosures are attached, where necessary, to main item, eg letter, using a semi-permanent staple;
- remittances (eg cheques) are recorded in a special Remittances Book which is checked and signed by someone in authority;
- all correspondence is date stamped or stamped with any other official stamp;
- where necessary additional copies of items of correspondence are made for circulation purposes (alternatively circulation/routing slips are attached);
- mail is sorted into appropriate departments/sections or individuals (usually using baskets or pigeon holes) ready for collection or distribution;
- envelopes are often retained for a few days in case of queries, although where considered of special importance or significance they would be attached to the correspondence earlier in the procedure.

In order to ensure that mail is sorted and available for collection or distribution as early as possible mail room staff normally operate special hours. This means an early start, particularly given the operation of flexible working hours for many office staff generally.

Internal circulation

In many organisations the volume of written communication which circulates internally can be significant. This will take the form of memoranda, notices of meetings, agendas, minutes, reports, newsletters, magazines circulated amongst staff, copies of correspondence received by other members of staff (passed on for information), files for return to Central Filing Department and so on. It is usual that several collections of mail may take place during a day in addition to those made when distributing mail in the morning and collecting mail for the final post in the evening. Just how many collections there will be will depend on the size and physical spread of the organisation and the number of mail room staff.

Messengers may visit individual offices or they may simply call at certain pick-up points in which case office staff need to become familiar with the approximate pick-up/distribution routines. A typical method will be one set of incoming pigeon holes and another set of outgoing ones. The latter may well be subdivided according to, for example, Internal, Local mail, Outside the area, International and Special. Mail room messengers may use special trolleys where the volume of mail is heavy.

Outgoing mail

The efficiency of outgoing mail procedures depends largely on the awareness of office staff of the methods used together with the time-scales to which they must operate. Everyone needs to know what the deadline is for the last collection by mail room staff and what alternative arrangements exist where this collection is missed. Secretaries must try to have all correspondence checked, signed and prepared in good time. Any special instructions should be clearly given and where an authorisation (eg for the use of First Class mail), is needed this too should be secured in good time. Mail may be collected from individual offices or alternatively pick-up points may be placed at convenient places throughout the building(s). The mail room should always be notified in advance when a large mail shot is to be expected.

Postal services

Staff within organisations need to be aware of the services offered by the Post Office in terms of written communication. Full details of all such services are contained in the *Post Office Guide* as well as in a series of useful leaflets.

Basically the services provided can be categorised as indicated in Table 7.2, but you are advised to refer to your local Post Office Headquarters for fully up-to-date information and details of any special services provided locally.

Table 7.2   Post Office Postal Services

Inland		*Overseas*	
Letter post:	Advice of delivery	**Letters:**	Europe – ALLUP
	Airway letters		(no air mail label
	Bulk rebate		required)
	postings		Outside Europe:
	(2nd class only)		Surface mail
	Business Reply		Air mail
	Service		Aerogrammes
	Cash on Delivery		Express:
	(COD)		normal service
	Certificate of		plus additional
	Posting		fee
	Discount services		Small Packet
	(for 5000+ letters)		service
	Freepost (2nd class	**Parcels:**	Various additional
	only)		services, eg
	Recorded Delivery		Certificates of
	Registered Post		Posting
Parcel post:	Cash on Delivery		Customs
	(COD)		Declarations
	Compensation Fee		International
	Parcel		FDD (Franc
	Contract services		de Droits)
	Postage forward		Prepayment of
Miscellaneous:	Ad mail		customs
	Consequential loss		charges to the
	insurance		addressee
	Datapost – same		Cash on Delivery
	day and		(COD)
	overnight	**Printed papers:**	Reduced rates for
	services		bulk postings of
	Electronic post		books,
	Franked mail		newspapers,
	Free collection		circulars, etc
	service		Surface mail
	(for 1000+		Accelerated surface
	letters and		post
	100+ parcels)		Air mail
	Intelpost	**Miscellaneous:**	Intelpost
	Late posting		International
	facilities		Datapost
	Poste Restante		International Reply
	Printed Postage		coupons
	Impressions (PPI)		Registered packets
	Redirected mail		Swiftair
	Selectapost		
	Unaddressed		
	household		
	delivery		

Meetings

Meetings take up a major proportion of time in most organisations and their degree of effectiveness in achieving their objectives is conditioned to a great extent by the following:

- standard of organisation;
- level of preparation;
- quality of paperwork provided;
- competence of the chairman;
- efficiency of the secretary;
- level of participation by those present;
- awareness of participants of their respective roles;
- terms of reference;
- frequency with which they take place.

Types of meetings

Many different types of meetings take place within organisations. These range from the very informal 'encounter' on the corridor and the exchange of information which may follow, to the more structured but still informal progress-type meetings which may take place in the manager's office with a few of his subordinates every Monday morning, through to the more formal committee meetings, board meetings and statutory meetings like an AGM.

The degree of formality of meetings will be determined by the following:

- the rules and regulations governing procedure;
- the structure of proceedings;
- the existence of formal paperwork, eg agenda, minutes;
- the presence of a chairman;
- the venue;
- the number attending;
- the frequency of the meetings.

Committees

Many organisations rely on a variety of formal committees as a means of channelling communications within their complex structure. Committees will range through the following.

Executive committee represented in most companies by the Board of Directors;

Standing committees, permanently established to meet on a regular basis to discuss and deal with specific matters, eg finance (standing committees are to be found particularly within the committee structure of local councils, eg the Housing Committee, the Education Committee, the Social Services Committee);

Subcommittees, established by any parent committee with the requisite power to relieve the parent committee of some of its routine work in a specific area. Members of subcommittees are appointed because of their interest and expertise and are required to report back to the parent committee. A good example in a local council committee structure would be the Further Education Subcommittee of the main Education Committee.

Advisory committees would normally be set up to advise the Executive Committee on some matter of importance or issue of interest, eg the introduction of office automation within an organisation. The remit of such a committee would be to gather information, carry out investigations, collate the findings and report back to the Executive Committee with recommendations.

Ad hoc committees are set up with one purpose in mind. This may be a fact-finding mission, a preliminary investigation into the feasibility of a scheme or proposal or a problem solving activity of some kind. Such a committee would be disbanded as soon as it had fulfilled its function.

Joint committees are set up to pool the expertise of two or more other committees. These will often be joint consultative committees, where the desire is to enhance the level of communication between management and the workforce, for example, so improving industrial relations.

Committees serve a particularly useful purpose where the representation is sufficiently diverse to enable a wide range of expertise to be called upon in order to advise and contribute to reaching a conclusion on a complex problem, the decision of which may have far-reaching implications.

Purposes of meetings

Meetings are called to serve a variety of different purposes which include:

* providing information to a group of people together and so saving time;

- providing a forum for putting forward ideas or proposals;
- solving problems;
- exchanging opinions;
- reporting back;
- co-ordinating activities;
- reaching joint decisions;
- dispelling rumour;
- creative thinking;
- pooling talents and resources;
- benefiting from the introduction of a breadth of knowledge and experience;
- fact finding;
- fulfilling a statutory obligation;
- teambuilding;
- developing staff via committee representation;
- encouraging maximum participation and involvement;
- speeding up a process by acting as a catalyst.

Procedural matters

The procedure followed by a meeting will depend on the type of meeting and the rules and regulations governing its conduct. Basically it will be a matter of the chairman guiding the meeting through the agenda, supported by the secretary to whom he will refer for rulings on procedural matters, eg rules in respect of seconding and voting, who is entitled to vote, any specific results necessary to carry or defeat a motion, etc. (Such information will be set out in the rules, viz the Articles of Association of a company, the Constitution of a society, the Standing Orders or By-laws of a local council.) The effectiveness and success of any meeting or committee will, therefore, depend to a large extent on the way in which it is chaired.

The role and duties of a chairman

A chairman's duties are really threefold, viz his conduct outside the meeting, the way in which he handles meeting procedure and the way in which he controls the committee members. Many individuals who chair meetings will find that it is a regular aspect of their work, but by the same token they would be likely to agree that no two meetings are the same and that different knowledge, skills and expertise will be called upon to cope with each one, depending on the purpose of the meeting, the composition of its membership, the regularity with which it meets and the extent of formality.

Briefly the duties and responsibilities of a chairman before, during and after a meeting are as follows:

- agreeing a draft agenda;
- liaising with the secretary in respect of the physical arrangements;
- planning the way he wishes discussion to proceed;
- delegating any administrative work needed in advance;
- being businesslike and starting promptly;
- making any necessary introductions and/or announcements;
- ensuring that there is a quorum;
- taking apologies for absence;
- going through the previous minutes and signing them if accepted as an accurate record;
- dealing with matters arising out of these minutes;
- guiding the meeting through the agenda items;
- initiating discussion and sustaining a co-operative atmosphere;
- pacing the discussion which takes place and being mindful of time;
- controlling discussion but encouraging everyone to have his say;
- ensuring that members keep to the point and that the discussion is within the remit of the group;
- taking chairman's action if/when necessary;
- clarifying points as required in consultation with the secretary;
- sustaining objectivity and impartiality;
- limiting discussion where deemed necessary because of irrelevance or time constraints;
- summarising discussion;
- putting matters to the vote;
- declaring results;
- closing or adjourning the meeting;
- liaising wth the secretary to agree draft minutes;
- taking any necessary follow-up action agreed;
- monitoring progress and events between meetings.

Effective participation at meetings

The composition of a committee may arise out of the rules and regulations and members may be there for a variety of reasons, eg the position they hold in the organisation, as a representative of a group of individuals, or a particular interest group or faction, either by nomination, selection or as a volunteer, because of particular expertise possessed or as an observer.

While much of the responsibility for effective meetings can be put down to the chairman, the way in which those present contribute is also significant. Meaningful results can only be achieved when participation is positive and there is plenty of informed discussion.

People will be more likely to be in a position to make a useful contribution when:

- they have studied the agenda and supplementary paperwork and done the necessary homework;
- they have canvassed the opinion of others as appropriate;
- they are prepared to put forward their views in a logical and constructive way;
- they are willing to listen to opposing views;
- they are prepared to support others;
- they are prepared to disagree if/when appropriate;
- they are sufficiently conversant with meetings procedure;
- they are prepared to become involved and take follow-up action if requested to do so;
- they are prepared to report back to colleagues.

The paperwork connected with meetings

Since the preparation of much of the paperwork associated with committee attendance is the responsibility of the secretary, full discussion of this is given in Section 14, together with a glossary of meeting terminology.

Telephone systems

Advances in the telephone have been considerable since the days of Alexander Graham Bell and the range of sophisticated facilities via modern systems is extensive, greatly enhancing the commmunication potential which exists in this somewhat taken-for-granted medium. Long gone are the days when telephones were a novelty and a status symbol, used for emergencies rather than as a popular means of communicating. Gone too are the days when choice was limited to British Telecom.

In the UK now there is not only the option of selecting telephone equipment (available for purchase in the local High Street), from a range of manufacturers but the possibility of subscribing to an alternative independent public telephone service called Mercury, which already covers large areas of the country, serving a large proportion of the business community, as well as offering some international services. But more of Mercury later.

Types of system

While there are a range of telephone instruments with various facilities, the sort of decisions that businesses have to make are in terms of overall system selected, as well as whether to buy outright or go for rental. Choice will largely depend on the size of the organisation and the number of lines and extensions required, as well as cost considerations.

PABX systems

Traditionally companies have tended to select a PABX 'private automatic branch exchange' with one, or where it is a large system, several switchboard operators who answer all incoming calls and route them accordingly. Extension users will be able to dial their own outside calls, unless the system operates a barring device (see below). Modern PABX systems (see Fig. 7.2) are controlled by microprocessors which means that they no longer have a confusing array of plugs and cords, but rely on the operation of buttons, keys or touch-sensitive panels. When extensions are in use this is indicated by a light. Such systems also have in-built self-diagnostic panels which display any faults occurring in the system. In addition they offer a wide range of special features to both operator and extension user (see below) as well as sophisticated call-logging facilities (see page 155).

PABX systems dominate the switchboard market particularly where companies need a lot of extensions, although there are smaller mini systems designed for very small offices. It should be noted also that the term PMBX, 'private manual branch exchange' whereby both incoming and outgoing calls are handled by the operator (found in smaller organisations) has virtually disappeared and the equipment is no longer supplied. Therefore the term PBX 'private branch exchange' has become synonymous with the automatic system.

Key systems

An alternative to the PABX is a key system. Here any extension user may answer incoming external calls. This type of system is more popular within smaller offices and no switchboard operator is required. Incoming calls may be answered on any of the extensions and calls can be transferred to other extensions as required. This means that each extension user has a special type of telephone handset with special keys for each of the extensions. Lamp displays indicate whether or not the extensions are engaged. Communication can also be made simply between extensions. These systems have a very good

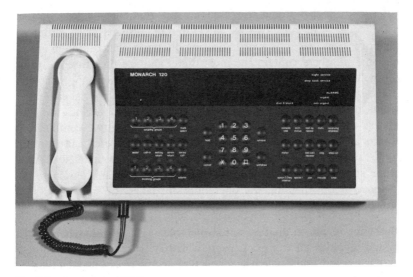

Fig. 7.2 A modern PABX
(*By courtesy of British Telecom*)

range of sophisticated features. It is worth noting that some key systems may in fact be something of a hybrid in that they may be linked to a PBX and so not all extension users will answer incoming external calls.

Internal systems

In large organisations separate internal systems may also exist to enable communication between extension users and so relieve the pressure and congestion on the PABX. Much of the frustration experienced by external incoming callers finding lines engaged can thus be avoided. These internal systems are also microprocessor-controlled and so it is possible to programme special features, eg to transfer calls to other extensions.

Special systems features

A wide range of features is available in modern systems and the main ones are detailed below. Sometimes the same feature is referred to by a different name, according to different suppliers, so alternatives are given in brackets.

Abbreviated dialling (memory dialling) refers to the facility to program the system or even an individual telephone instrument to automatically dial frequently used outside numbers by keying in a brief code – usually two keys. Different systems have different memory sizes, so it is worth bearing in mind that although international numbers contain the most digits and are therefore the most difficult to recall not every system can cope with them. (Where such usage is regularly required it may pay to invest in a special callmaker which operates with the insertion of a programmed plastic card into a desk-top unit, or via a keypad where each button combination selects a preselected number or by magnetic tape which can store up to 400 telephone numbers and dials the numbers automatically.) Also, while such features save dialling a lengthy number and eliminate the chances of mis-dialling, the operation still takes the same time as it still has to go through at the speed of the analogue system.

Call back (camp-on dialling or camp-on busy) is a feature whereby the system enables an extension user, who has tried to contact another extension and found it engaged, to replace his receiver and be called back automatically when the engaged extension becomes free. By lifting his receiver the call will ring out to the other extension. This feature is very useful where certain lines are frequently busy as it saves redialling over and over again.

Call barring is a facility which enables both PABX and key systems to restrict the placing of certain categories of call, eg long distance or international calls, from certain extensions. Such calls may only be placed via the switchboard operator.

Call-diversion enables the extension user to programme his telephone and so divert his calls to another extension. This is a useful facility where someone may have to attend a meeting or leave his office and yet is expecting an important call which he does not wish to leave unanswered.

Call parking enables an extension user to place an outside caller on another extension without the extension actually answering the call, eg where he may perhaps take a call at someone else's workstation but need access to material at his own he may 'park' the call at his extension before he actually sets off to return to his own workstation.

Call queueing comes into operation where all extensions are engaged. This means that a queue of incoming calls is lined up and each will be automatically routed in sequence as soon as lines become free. (Note that this will often be what is happening where you may call a number which you expect to be permanently manned, eg British Rail Passenger Timetable Enquiries, and yet cannot get through. Therefore replacing the receiver and dialling again will not help – it will simply put you to the end of the queue!)

Call re-routing (call transfer) enables the extension user to programme his telephone so that when it is not answered after a given number of rings the call will automatically reroute to another designated extension.

Call waiting tone (engaged interrupt) is where an audio or visual signal is given to the extension user while he is talking on the telephone to someone to indicate that another incoming caller is trying to get through. This facility can help minimise the frustration experienced by many incoming external callers who meet with engaged lines, as well as helping to cut short lengthy calls.

Conference calls enables calls to be set up between two or three extensions and one outside caller. (Note: where you wish to set up a conference call with several outsiders based at different locations this can be arranged via BT.)

Direct dialling in is a PABX feature which enables outside callers to access a specific extension by by-passing the switchboard. This necessitates the caller knowing the special number required.

Extension group hunting is a PABX feature whereby when handling incoming calls the system can search or 'hunt' around a number of designated extensions till it finds a free one. This is useful in a section which deals with general enquiries which may be dealt with by any of several people.

Last number recall (repeat last number, redial last number) enables the extension user to automatically redial the last number called. This is useful where a number is frequently busy. (Note: this does not include a number on the memory dialling programme.)

Messaging (message waiting light) is a feature of key systems and is used to indicate (usually by means of a flashing light) that another extension has been trying to make contact.

Music on hold is where background music is played to 'entertain' the caller while he is waiting to be connected. While the choice of music may not be to the caller's taste, at least he knows he is still connected and hopefully receiving attention!

Override (priority interruption) is where designated extensions may break into calls between other extensions. This is a useful feature where urgent matters need attention. It should be noted that the interrupter is prevented from listening in on the conversation as an audible warning sound alerts those engaged in conversation.

Paging is possible via different facilities dependent on whether the system is a PABX or a key system. With the former, paging is not built-in but a separate tannoy system can be accessed from certain extensions. As far as the latter is concerned any extension user can make an announcement which will come through the loudspeaker of any telephone not in use. It is, however, possible to bar paging where an extension user does not wish to be disturbed.

Waiting return is a PABX feature whereby incoming calls are automatically sent back to the switchboard if the extension to which the call was originally routed does not answer within a specified time.

Telephone equipment

There is a variety of associated equipment on the market to complement these systems and assist in the operation of the special features. The following provides a summary of the main items.

Individual telephone instruments

The selection available caters for all purses and tastes. The type of handset will, of course, be largely dependent on the overall system and where, for example a PABX is in operation an ordinary push button extension will be the norm, although even here there is a good choice of styles available. Basically the handset selected will need to match the needs and preferences of the user. Now that individual approved instruments (ie those carrying the green sticker) may be plugged into any telephone socket the choice is considerable with the option to change instruments at will.

Loudspeaking telephones

A busy executive may find a loudspeaking telephone very useful. This would enable him to have his hands free to shuffle papers, make notes or even move away from the telephone while also proving useful where he wished someone else in the room to listen or take part in a conversation. The majority of loudspeaking units operate on what is termed 'switched duplex' which means that speech can only come in one direction at a time. Therefore the caller and the receiver must speak in turn.

Fig. 7.3   A cordless telephone

Cordless telephones

Another possibility is the cordless telephone (see Fig. 7.3) which as the term suggests operates without a direct cable link. A base unit powered via a transformer from mains electricity announces the calls as well as automatically recharging the handset which is battery powered and may be used within a certain radius of the base unit. Such sets are designed to be used as extensions off a main exchange line and are somewhat of a gimmick. They do possess certain programmable features like personal paging, automatic redialling and an inbuilt security code to prevent unauthorised access by other cordless telephone users.

Cellular telephones

Cellular telephones are mobile phones which may be used in a car or anywhere else while on the move. Two rival networks operate in the UK – Cellnet, which is a joint venture between BT and Securicor, and Vodafone which is owned by Racal. Neither company sells systems and equipment direct, both working through distributors who handle the operation on behalf of the networks.

Basically a cellular phone enables the user to place calls to other cellular users or to any other ordinary telephones regardless of whether they are in this country or abroad. What is not possible, however, is for a cellular user to receive phonecalls on a cellular phone unless in an area in which cellular phones are operational. Currently, there are certain areas of the UK which are still not within either cellular network, eg the whole of Wales (at the time of writing), although by 1990 it is estimated that 90 per cent of the UK population area will be covered.

The concept of mobile telephones is not in itself new, as radio car phones have been around for a long time. What makes cellular phones

Fig. 7.4 A cellular car phone
(*By courtesy of British Telecom*)

so different is the speed with which technology enables the connections to be made following direct dialling, together with the vastly superior quality of the lines. Also there are no availability problems.

In terms of actual equipment all cellular phones need to be approved by the British Approvals Board for Telecommunications (BABT) just like any other telephone equipment. A substantial range of equipment is available, most of which will operate on either network. An example of a cellular car phone is given as Fig 7.4.

The services which are available on either network are as follows:

- call barring;
- call forwarding;   All explained under the earlier
- call transfer;   section on telephone systems
- call waiting;   (pp 146 and 147)
- conference calls;
- directory enquiries (each network has its own free service),
- itemised billing;
- operator service.

Types of cellular phone

There are three types of cellular phone. **Mobiles** are for use only in cars. **Portables** are battery-operated and as the name suggests may be used anywhere, although the batteries frequently need recharging. **Transportables** are larger, heavier units, also battery-operated, and are capable of use as carphones as well.

Like standard telephones cellular phones have a range of sophisticated features dependent upon model and price range. One feature, particularly worthy of mention is 'hands free' speech, which comes with most mobiles as either a standard feature or optional extra. From a safety point of view alone this is a very worthwhile feature because it is difficult to steer, change gear and talk on the phone all at the same time! In fact, there is every likelihood that such a feature will become a legal requirement such is the lobby by road safety experts. Already, where this feature is not present, the Highway Code recommends that drivers pull over before making a call on a carphone.

Enabling carphone users to have their hands free while using the phone is relatively straightforward. A small built-in microphone can be fixed to the sun visor or to some other position on the dashboard where the driver's voice may be easily picked up. However, providing the means by which a driver can have his hands totally free, ie eliminating the need to dial a call (even if this only means using an abbreviated dialling facility), is more complex. The answer rests in some form of voice-activated dialling and experiments with this provision are already being carried out on several systems. The idea is that the user can announce something along the lines of 'Call the office' and the system will recognise the instruction and automatically dial the call. However, like most voice recognition systems it sounds simpler than it really is.

Telephone answering machines

The range of equipment now on the market for outright purchase or rental is extensive and machines have certainly grown in popularity. Basically there are three types of machine: (1) those which answer only, (2) those which answer and record, and (3) those which form a combined telephone and answering machine.

Some machines now have additional useful features which include the following.

Remote control which enables the user to contact his own machine and listen to any messages left. Remote control is activated either by a 'bleeper' which sends a message to the machine when the gadget is held to the telephone receiver, or by voice. The latter removes the need to carry a bleeper gadget but does necessitate the caller's making somewhat strange noises over the telephone as the system reacts to a sequence of speech pattern rather than a specific command. Some systems have special security codings to avoid unauthorised access to messages. Another advantage of remote control exists where the system enables the prerecorded message to be altered from a distance. This can be particularly useful where, for example, an instruction or contact number needs to be changed.

Recording of telephone conversations This is a useful feature available on certain machines.

Call screening/monitoring This permits the user to listen to messages as they are being left and to interject if he decides to take the call personally.

Radio paging

BT's radio paging rental service which currently handles 80 per cent of the paging market in the UK enables subscribers to contact people while on the move. The service covers virtually the whole of the UK population and where wide-area paging is required remains an organisation's only real paging option despite being more expensive and having less special features than many of its competitors.

How does paging work?

Basically there are three types of wide-area system, viz tone, display and voice.

Tone-only pagers merely 'bleep' and subscribers then need to dial the relevant number from a normal telephone. At that point the call is switched automatically to a transmitter network operated by the supplier and is subsequently relayed to the user via radio wave. Modern, more sophisticated tone-only pagers can emit a range of different tones, each signifying a variation in the message, eg one tone may mean 'call the office' while two tones may mean 'call home', but there can be problems in distinguishing the signals.

Display systems (see Fig. 7.5) incorporate a small light-emitting diode (LED) which can display brief messages, some purely numeric, eg a telephone number, while others are alphanumeric and capable of providing limited written information, eg confirmation data such as 'appointment fixed for Tuesday'. Many also have a memory facility to store a message or number, although capacities of systems vary considerably. However, it is possible to find a system which will store up to 400 characters broken into as many as 10 separate messages where required.

Voice systems only operate on UHF frequency and are less useful over a wide area. Besides, given that they only operate one way (the

Fig. 7.5 A radio pager with a LED display
(*By courtesy of British Telecom*)

receiver still needs to use a telephone) they have been largely superseded by cellular telephones.

Incidentally, it is also possible to have a silent pager so that the signal does not cause a disturbance, eg by going off during a meeting. These work with either flashing lights (not very convenient in a pocket or briefcase!) or by producing a shock wave via a small vibrating device attached to the user!

British Telecom services

Despite the sophistication of modern telephone equipment BT still provides a range of special call services which are listed as follows:

- advice of duration and charge (ADC) calls;
- alarm calls;
- conference calls (see p 147);
- credit card calls;
- fixed time calls;
- freefone calls;
- personal calls, including international ones;
- subscriber controlled transfer;
- temporary transfer of calls;
- transferred charge calls.

Full details of all these services are available from BT, together with a free leaflet of charges, by dialling 100 and asking for Freefone 2500.

Telemessages

A 24-hour telemessage service has replaced the former inland telegram service. By dialling 100 and asking for the Telemessage Service your message can be dictated and transmitted via telemessage computer to Royal Mail Sorting Offices for postal delivery on the next working day. In order to ensure such delivery it is essential to telephone the message through before 2200 hours Monday to Saturday and before 1900 hours on Sundays and Bank Holidays

International telemessage is available, but only to the USA, while special occasion cards are available for UK only.

An alternative means of transmission is available to Telex subscribers who may send a telemessage by dialling the special code listed in the *Telex Directory* and it is also possible to send messages via PSS (Packet Switching Service), via electronic mail (see p 164) or via an organisation's own computer.

Charges are calculated on the basis of message wordage, ie a basic charge for the first 50 words, with a reduced charge for the next 50 or part of 50 up to a maximum of 350 words. Therefore it is advisable to be concise. Charges are included with the normal telephone or telex accounts.

International telegrams

It is important to note that the term 'telegram' still remains in the international context and International telegrams are available world-wide. These too may be submitted by telephone or telex for trans-mission from main Telemessage offices to the Telegram Retransmission Centre which has a computerised system designed to forward messages over international routes.

There is a standard charge for this service plus a rate per word (plus VAT). Messages to Europe, North America and North Africa are costed at one rate, while those to the rest of the world are costed at a higher rate.

Call logging

Call logging is the term used to explain the monitoring and analysis of all traffic on a telephone system. Every call is recorded by computer in terms of duration, time of day, number dialled and the extension from which the call has been placed. Such systems not only enable management to keep a record of expenditure and where necessary put bars on certain extensions to prevent unauthorised use, but they also provide data which can help assess the suitability of equipment for an organisation's needs and determine any better distribution of extensions or perhaps the need for additional external lines. Also they provide a useful check against any query over a telephone bill.

A call logging facility need not be viewed by staff as a 'Big brother is watching you' type of exercise as data will not necessarily be printed out continuously simply to keep an eye on staff! Rather the facility exists to run the program as and when required with a view to improving the efficiency and effectiveness of the system as well as highlighting any problems or abusive practices. It is also important to appreciate that call logging itself cannot solve problems it can only provide the necessary information for management to use.

Digitisation and System X

The UK telephone system is being digitised which means that tele-phone calls will soon use digital rather than the current analogue lines. This will ultimately ensure a faster, higher quality service for subscribers. The changeover system is referred to as 'System X' and when it is complete, new optical fibre cables will replace the existing system throughout the country. Optical fibres are very thin strands of glass, as fine as a human hair, and are capable of carrying far more simultaneous conversations than existing copper cables, so system efficiency will be greatly improved, with better quality and faster dialling.

A word about Mercury Communications

As mentioned earlier the UK now has an alternative independent network in the shape of Mercury Communications Ltd, established in 1982. While most of Mercury's customers still centre in areas where business is most thriving, viz SE England, Mercury, which uses digital technology, has laid fibre-optic cables alongside British Rail's InterCity network, so basically these will be the areas ultimately covered by the service. Access to international communications is also available and is achieved via Mercury satellite communication centres, eg transatlantic calls are handled from Mercury's satellite station at London Docklands.

Mercury offers two different services to its customers; 2100 is aimed at larger businesses while 2200 is aimed at the smaller end of the market, including the private consumer. The former connects its customers directly to the Mercury network, while the latter accesses Mercury indirectly via BT lines. This system makes the BT connection through a device rented from Mercury and referred to as a 'smart box'. The device recognises outgoing trunk calls placed by the 2200 system and reroutes them initially to BT lines which forward the call to the nearest point on the Mercury network. Eventually it is anticipated that the need for a 'smart box' will disappear with the arrival of an individual telephone instrument which connects directly to a BT exchange line.

This is not the place to go into the technicalities of the operation, but suffice it to say that the service is providing competition for long-established BT and it does work out less expensive at the present time. The main disadvantage, if indeed there is one, would seem to be a question mark over Mercury's ability to respond to and cope with sudden increase in demand and, of course, back-up support is still something of an unknown quantity, given that it is early days in terms of establishing a competitive telephone network. Also, given that the service does not operate nationwide, most subscribers would also need to retain BT lines and pay the rental charges for both systems.

Telex and teletex

Telex

The telex service, short for 'Telegraphic Exchange', as it has its basis in the original telegraph network, has been around for a long time. It has about $1\frac{1}{2}$ million users worldwide and is the oldest form of electronic mail. In a nutshell, telex enables any two subscribers to transmit written communication via telegraph lines, but leaving a printout and, of course, the service will operate whether or not the other machine is manned, provided it is switched on and fitted with paper to receive the message.

Since the liberalisation brought about by BT's loss of monopoly in the supply of equipment, telex has undergone a series of improvements bringing it into better line with the electronic age. The arrival of the electronic telex machine has seen a tremendous improvement from preparation via paper tape, the big bonus being the edit facility which is unavailable with paper tape so necessitating a retype in the event of a mistake in the message. Also with an electronic system the preparation of outgoing material is not interrupted by the arrival of an incoming message as was the case with the older systems when the two processes could not operate simultaneously, and the new machines are much quieter.

Basically electronic telex machines are like word processors attached direct to telex lines and are likely to have the following types of special features.

Abbreviated dialling similar to that available on modern telephone systems with memory facility, although with systems run on floppy disks, a very large directory of abbreviated coded addresses is possible.

Automatic retry where if a number is engaged the system will automatically redial the number several times more at regular intervals to gain contact. This can be a very good time saver in a busy office.

Batching where the system will automatically search through its memory for any other communications bound for the same destination and send them all one after the other so avoiding the need to redial on several occasions.

Conversational connection enables users to continue 'conversation' once the initial connection is made, ie messages may be sent to and from terminals without the need to redial.

Delayed transmission enables the sender to program the machine to transmit the message at a later time, although given that there is no cheap rate time on telex the facility does not save money as such but does help a company to prioritise and dispatch messages according to urgency.

Multiple address is telex's equivalent to word processing's mail merge facility (see p 188) whereby the machine will automatically repeat the same message to a series of addresses.

Queueing enables messages to be lined up in the order in which they have been keyed in for ultimate dispatch in that same sequence, although there is normally a system of prioritising whereby the queue can be jumped to transmit an urgent message.

Received in background means that incoming messages will be stored in the system's memory if received while a message is being prepared for transmission. There will normally be some form of signal, eg a screen message or a flashing indicator light to alert the operator that a message has been received.

Telex equipment

While it is possible to buy a dedicated telex machine (see Fig. 7.6) it is likely to be more economical to opt for a microcomputer with an adaptation which enables it to double as a telex terminal or to upgrade a memory typewriter by adding what is known as a telex box which incorporates the essential telex software. Either of these latter alternatives to a dedicated system are worthy of consideration where the volume of use of telex is relatively low. Where it is very low indeed it may be even better to consider employing the services of an electronic mail or telex bureau. These bureaux operate on a subscription basis and will send and receive any telex messages by communicating with their clients either via computer or over the telephone for dictation and relay purposes.

Telex via message switching

High volume users of telex, on the other hand, will find that a single line is insufficient for their needs and so they need the back-up of a dedicated system that operates along the lines of a PABX in that it supports several lines and terminals and can automatically route messages by switching them around and searching for free lines.

These systems will incorporate all the features of single terminals mentioned above but will also have added facilities similar to many

Fig. 7.6   A dedicated telex machine, the new Leopard telex terminal
from British Telecom.
(Photograph by courtesy of Manners, Borkett & Partners Limited, Crowthorne)

found on modern PABX systems and be designed to generally
improve the efficiency of the system. Passwords may be introduced
to prevent unauthorised access to messages held and there may be a
facility to log the cost of messages sent, together with a device to spot
errors or 'illegal' characters which cannot be sent down line, eg any
lower case characters as telex only operates in upper case.

Teletex

Despite recent improvements in the telex provision it is somewhat
ironic that it has been during this time that telex has been threatened
by the arrival of teletex (not to be confused with teletext which refers
to specially adapted television sets designed to handle the BBC's
Ceefax and the IBA's Oracle viewdata information services).

Also from BT the teletex service is based on a set of internationally
agreed standards set up by CCITT (the International Consultative
Committee for Telephones and Telegraphy based in Geneva) to ensure
the compatibility of intercommunicating equipment and designed to

transmit and receive electronic mail via the Public Switched Telephone Network (PSTN) or via Packet Switchstream (PSS), BT's packet switched network. The main differences between this new service and telex are as follows:

- teletex is a memory to memory system;
- final print quality is influenced by the type of printer used, which may be dot matrix, daisy wheel, ink jet or any other;
- there is a capability of producing text of letter-quality featuring a wide range of characters (remember that telex uses only upper case characters);
- faster transmission speed of teletex means that an A4 letter can be sent in about 10 seconds whereas telex transmits at around 70 wpm;
- as an integral part of the telephone network, transmission is via normal telephone lines, whereas telex necessitates the rental of its own separate lines which are also more expensive than ordinary telephone lines;
- calls made via teletex at off-peak times will cost less and, using the 'store and forward' facility, messages may be prepared at any time and stored by the terminal for automatic transmission after 6 pm;
- ease of operation, particularly compared to the older type of non-electronic telex machine, hence little operator training is required;
- more supervisory safeguard features are built into teletex, eg a log has to be kept to record what happens to every call, ie whether it has been successfully transmitted, whether it is still in a queue or whether it has been aborted.

Another important thing to note is that while telex has legal status in that its documents are accepted as legal evidence the position in respect of teletex is as yet unclear.

Links with telex

Thanks to an interconnecting facility known as Interstream 3 teletex and telex subscribers can communicate, but only at the lower telex speeds, on the PSTN or PSS or on the telex networks. While this facility greatly enhances the user base available to teletex subscribers (currently teletex has relatively few subscribers in comparison with the enormous user base enjoyed by telex), it does, of course, slow down the speed of communication and substantially increases the cost in that teletex users need to access the telex system via what is termed a 'gateway'. This means that it will be necessary to contact the gateway (which is currently based in London) first of all via a standard phonecall, then there is a fee for using the gateway, plus the actual charge for sending a telex message from London. However, at least the interconnection does exist should teletex subscribers need to use it.

Nonetheless, despite the seemingly attractive options offered by teletex and accepting that equipment costs are fairly expensive, it has yet to take off in the manner originally anticipated and its future is far from clear.

Datacoms

Computer communications or datacoms is a growth area and such are the advances in microcomputer technology, together with the reduction in hardware and software prices, that it is no longer the sole province of large-scale computer users. Intercommunicating computers and word processors are a reality. Communication can take place between microcomputers over a local area network (see page 165), but it is also possible for remote terminals to communicate with a large host computer, eg to access information from a database (see page 167). An example of the components to be found in a typical datacoms link between a personal computer and a mainframe computer situated somewhere else is given as Fig 7.7.

While it may look relatively straightforward in diagrammatical form there are complexities, largely as a result of equipment incompatibility and these need to be ironed out for successful communication to take place.

A few of the technicalities involved

The crux of computer communications is digitisation which is the operation of an 8-bit binary code to represent the information transmitted. When data encoded in this way is transferred between computers the speed and sequence of receipt need to be the same as that of transmission.

Not only that but to ensure compatibility the same datacoms codes need to be used and there is also the question of protocols, which in simple terms refers to agreed sets of rules which enable different devices to recognise one another. 'Rules' cover such things as ensuring that data is only transmitted when the receiving terminal is ready to receive, ie the incorporation of some form of answer-back code or some form of error detection/correction facility to minimise corruption of information. Here again many different protocols exist and it is only recently that attempts have been made to standardise. Hence the need to introduce protocol converters to enable incompatible

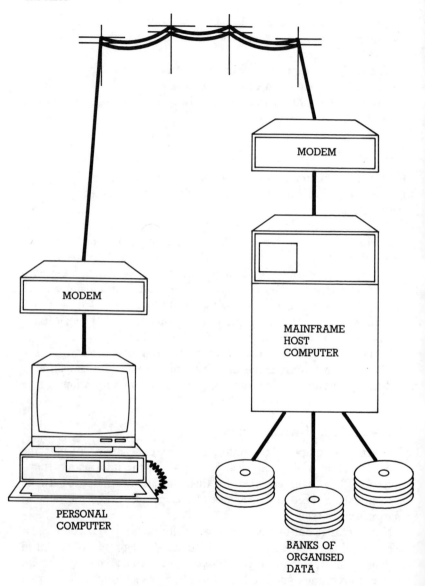

Fig. 7.7   The components in a datacom network

computers to communicate. All in all this is a complex area for the non-specialist and awareness of the problems will suffice.

Modems and acoustic couplers

Two pieces of hardware associated with datacoms which are likely to be familiar are modems and acoustic couplers. Given that most computer communication takes place via ordinary telephone lines modems (taken from *mod*ulator and *dem*odulator) are needed to connect a computer to the telephone system at the transmission end and to reconnect the telephone lines back to the computer at the receiving end. These modems are necessary in that computer and telephone lines cannot currently be linked directly because computers use digital binary signals while telephone lines are analogue. A modem is simply a small electronic box which forms a bridging link between digital and analogue and vice versa. Built-in modems are now commonly found within modern micros.

An acoustic coupler is an alternative linking device which is popular because it is very portable. For example, a businessman using a portable computer would need one to link to any telephone to transmit data back to his base. It operates by connecting the coupler to the communications port at the rear of the computer and then placing the telephone handset in a cradle device which forms the link (see Fig. 7.8).

What about the telephone lines?

Once the telephone line stage of transmission is reached complexities still exist in that there are a variety of different networks which may

Fig. 7.8 An acoustic coupler

be used for transmission purposes. The standard network is PSTN and it is accessed by simply dialling the connection as in a normal call and has corresponding line charges. While this facility may be adequate for relatively low volume datacoms usage it will be likely that organisations who use the facility a lot will lease a private line.

A higher level service with greater error free transmission is PSS. This system offers a faster more efficient service for large volume users. The term 'packet' switching arises out of the fact that messages are broken down into 'blocks' or 'packets' for transmission.

With the progress towards full digitisation BT also offer several private digital transmission systems under the collective name of X-stream, after System X digitised exchanges. Referred to as Kilo-stream, Megastream and Satstream they provide very fast, sophisti-cated data and voice transmission services, the latter being a national/international provision operating via a customer's personal satellite dish.

Electronic mail

The term 'electronic mail' is used to describe a range of electronic data transmission services but is most often applied either to the services supplied by electronic mail bureaux such as Telecom Gold or to describe an organisation's internal mailbox system operated via its own computer.

In terms of electronic mail bureaux, they are based on large central computers whose storage is then allocated as 'mailboxes' or 'electronic pigeon holes' to all subscribers who may then interchange messages. Basically the idea of electronic mail bureaux is to provide a general messaging facility as well as the means of transmitting and receiving telexes without the need for separate telex equipment. Take Telecom Gold as an example.

Established by BT in 1981 Telecom Gold operates from a large computer centre based in London. Subscribers may access the system via standard telephone lines connected to a variety of different types of terminal, eg microprocessors, or word processors. The mailbox is strictly private, is available 24 hours a day and may be accessed simply by keying in a private password. This enables the user to operate his own electronic office from his workstation.

He can transmit and receive messages, he can set up a record-keeping system, he can manage his own diary and appointments, contact any telex subscriber, receive telex messages, page his mailbox when out of the office and even keep in touch when travelling abroad.

He can also make use of a wide range of business data and services and have up-to-date travel information at his disposal. In fact he has the basis of office automation, including electronic publishing, literally at the end of a telephone or at the tip of his fingers.

A word about 'nodes'

It is worth noting that, while most large computers are based in London, users from other parts of the country will not end up paying large phone bills to access their mail. Nodes are remote access points scattered throughout the country and linked on leased lines to the central computer. Therefore users outside London will contact their nearest node which acts as a relay station and sends messages from their mailboxes direct to their workstations on a private network at no extra cost.

Intra-company systems

At the more local or organisational level, electronic mail is 'addressed' to the mailboxes of individual company personnel. These boxes are areas of the computer allocated to specific users. Messages, addressed in code, are received by the computer and held in memory storage until the recipient chooses to access them at his terminal by using his password. At this point he may choose simply to view the list of mail held in his mailbox by scanning through it, he may choose to read some of it, print some out, transfer it to his own storage, on another disk, forward it on to another user or, having read it, delete it altogether. It is this sort of use of electronic mail which gets us closer to the concept of a paperless office.

Local area networks (LANs)

While the telephone network is the means of connecting external electronic mailboxes, internally it is likely to be done by using a local area network or LAN. A LAN is simply a means of linking together, via coaxial or fibre-optic cable, a number of electronic devices over a restricted geographical area for communication purposes. The introduction of LANs has considerably enhanced the potential for decentralising electronic facilities as well as reducing resistance to the introduction of new technology in that many of the mysteries, so often attached to computers, have been minimised.

All types of electronic device may be interfaced to the LAN, eg microcomputers, word processors, management workstations, OCR, printers and auxiliary storage (see Section 8 for a more detailed

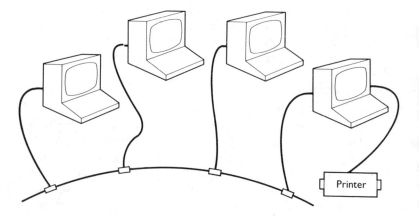

Fig. 7.9   A bus network

account). There are three main type of networking arrangement – bus, ring and star. The **bus network** (see Fig. 7.9) is where all devices are connected to and share a single cable, information travelling in either direction. One major advantage is the ability to attach devices at any point on the network without affecting other users. The same applies to the need to remove devices from the network. The **ring network** (see Fig. 7.10) is where all the devices in the network are connected

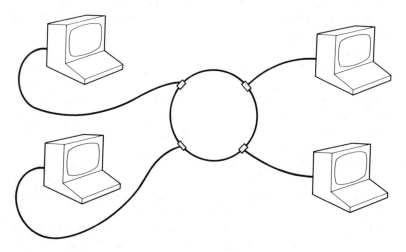

Fig. 7.10   A ring network

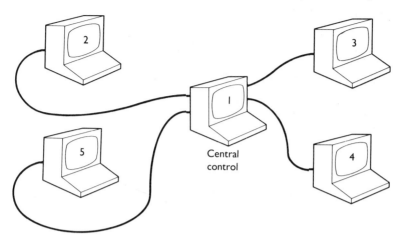

Fig. 7.11   A star network

by a single communication cable which runs in a circle. Messages are sent from one device to another around the ring. This type of network has a disadvantage in that failure of a single device renders the entire network inoperable. Finally the **star network** (see Fig. 7.11) is where each device is connected via a central control unit which receives and routes all messages from the various devices or terminals. The major drawback with this system is where the central control unit breaks down and the entire system is affected as a result.

Via such techniques communication is much faster than over telephone lines because all data is in digital form and transferred in 'blocks' or 'packets' of information throughout the network. Data is only picked up by another terminal on the line when the system recognises the 'address' on the 'packet' and delivers it to the appropriate terminal. Note that where a greater geographical distance is required than can be serviced by a LAN a wide area network (WAN) may be set up via a telecommunications supplier.

Databases

Information is an important resource to any organisation and the potential to store, manipulate, update and retrieve it via the sophisticated file handling systems of a computer is considerable in that the space needed is virtually negligible given developments in technology. Such is the state of the art that it is possible to store data equivalent

167

in volume to all the entries in a large telephone directory on the head of a pin!

A database might, therefore, well be described as an electronic encyclopaedia of well organised business information held on computer. The vital thing in such a database is its standard of organisation. Like any other extensive filing system the more records that are collected the longer it takes to find a particular one. Therefore the logic of storage in terms of file organisation affects the ease with which it may be retrieved, just as in the case of any manual system. Also the more 'views' the database can provide of the same data (rather like cross-referencing in a manual system) the easier it will be for multiple users to locate the information they require, regardless of the fact that they will be requesting and viewing the data from a range of different perspectives.

While databases may be set up at individual or departmental levels using database management systems (DBMS) software in conjunction with a personal computer (see also Section 8, p 199), there are many large scale facilities available which enable subscriber organisations to access and make use of information stored on central computers. Such high volume usage enables a system to operate more cheaply in that large numbers of organisations are able to interrogate certain areas of the database, displaying the information on their own terminal screens.

Open and closed systems

Often referred to as viewdata systems, information held on computers may be 'open' in that it is made available to all subscribers (eg Teletext data). Alternatively, access may be restricted to what are defined as 'closed user groups'. This will largely be a matter for information providers to decide and where providers do supply restricted access information many organisations install private viewdata systems to link into particular networks. For example, information supplied by holiday companies and tour operators will tend to be restricted to travel agents, while information on cars may be available only to dealers who will be able to interrogate the database and discover the precise availability of cars in respect of models, engine capacities, colours, special features and locations. Similarly estate agents make use of this type of provision in respect of the availability of property.

Another advantage of such a system is that providers of information are able to update information very quickly. This not only ensures the provision of a more efficient service, it also produces substantial savings in terms of reducing printing costs by continually reproducing catalogues and information sheets. Basically, however, the idea behind viewdata is to make large quantities of data available cheaply to as many users as possible.

Prestel

The most common UK public viewdata system is still BT's Prestel which holds an array of useful everyday information, including airline and train times, financial information, news updates, sports and entertainment guides which can be accessed on an adapted television screen over telephone lines, via a microcomputer interfaced to a modem and carrying appropriate software, or via a dedicated Prestel desk top machine.

Prestel can also be used in an interactive capacity, ie a subscriber may order goods, book holidays and in some instances pay bills via the system. Several other facilities like links to telex and the option of using an electronic mailbox are also possible, although additional support equipment is needed. Charges are based on equipment rental and telephone charges plus any special charge levied by an information provider.

Specialist databases

There are a growing number of large databases, both nationally and internationally (see also Section 15, p 377). Many hold specific types of information, eg Dun and Bradstreet operate 'Who Owns Whom' while Butterworth Telepublishing has a legal database designed for solicitors. The Stock Exchange has its own viewdata system for access to up-to-date stock prices with updates as changes take place and the database at the House of Commons Library – the Parliamentary On-Line System (POLIS) – is geared to use by MPs. This latter facility will obviously save hours of researchers' time in ploughing through back copies of *Hansard* and all manner of other publications. Material held on the database dates from 1979 and can be accessed by the simple entry of key words which will vary according to the nature of the enquiry, the knowledge of the enquirer and the capacity of the system.

Cost and other factors

Costs are still high for the operation of most systems and, of course, charges will depend on when and for how long time was spent on-line. Sometimes it will be sufficient to glance at information but on other occasions it may be necessary to study it more carefully, in which case it will make sense to print out or ask for an on-line print-out to be sent. Alternatively it may be possible to store certain information on disk.

Another important consideration will always be the ease with which a database can be accessed and then the simplicity of moving through the system to locate the desired information. Some systems are infinitely more simple to use than others.

Databases in more general use

It is interesting to note that some public libraries now hold their catalogues on a database, possibly linked to the Town Hall's main computer. This library data can be accessed by the public, often out of library opening hours (rather in the manner of a bank's cashpoint). Such a service will not only state what books are held on a certain topic or whether a specific title is in the catalogue, but how many copies there are and whether they are in or out of stock. Sometimes other local information may also be accessed from such a database, eg local events and local theatre programmes for the season.

Facsimile transmission

Facsimile machines, telecopiers or, as they are most commonly referred to, 'fax' machines, are certainly a growth area in office telecommunications. In fact there are more fax users worldwide (because of the large number of users in Japan) than there are of telex. More and more suppliers are entering the market and machines now have many additional features.

What exactly is fax and how does it work?

Faster than telex, fax is a system whereby it is possible to transmit an exact copy (a facsimile) of a document, drawing, graph, or any other material which can normally be photocopied, over telephone lines to be received by another fax machine somewhere else. That somewhere may be in a neighbouring office, one hundred miles away or on the other side of the world. Distance is no object; it only costs more in that charges accrue according to the destination and the time it takes to send the message.

There is a lot of similarity with photocopiers in terms of the type of reproduction, but the similarity ends there as the techniques differ substantially. When a document is fed into the transmitting fax machine it is scanned and the information which is encoded into a

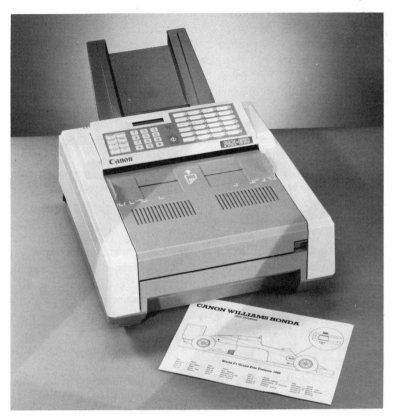

Fig. 7.12 Facsimile machine
(*By courtesy of Canon Business Machines Ltd*)

series of electrical pulses is then sent down the normal telephone lines. At the other end the image is reconstructed by a printer to produce the original image (see Fig. 7.12). Somewhere in between, of course, the encoded images are converted from digital to analogue and back to digital via built-in fax modems. This is necessary in that while images are encoded digitally, telephone lines still cannot handle digital traffic (remember that currently they operate in analogue although digitisation is in progress).

Compatibility factors

One big bonus of fax over many other items of communicating equipment is that the two communicating machines need not be of the same make. This arises in that fax machines conform to 'Groups' or industry standards as established by CCITT. There are currently four groups although the vast proportion of machines now fall into Group 3 whose standards were ratified in 1980. The main difference between groups is one of transmission speed. Group 3 machines are capable of transmitting a page of A4 in between 20 and 30 seconds while the older Group 2 and Group 1 machines are much slower and the recent Group 4 machines which have been designed to operate with digital telephone lines (and as such are really restricted currently as far as general use is concerned to Japan) will be able to produce A4 sheets in as little as 3 seconds.

It is technically possible to transmit between machines in different groups although transmission speed is determined by the lower group and cost is correspondingly greater.

Speed factors

While it is possible to estimate the speed with which a document can be transmitted it is important to realise that speed is dependent on the modem which transmits data in bits per second (bps) and while some modems connected to new Group 3 machines may be capable of transmitting as fast as 9600 bps, they can only do this if the modem at the other end is capable of operating at the same speed. Otherwise the transmitting machine will need to 'step down' to the slower speed of the receiving machine.

Also speed is affected by the quality of the telephone line which may not always be good enough to handle high speed transmissions. Machines which operate at 9600 bps all have automatic step-down modems to ensure transmission compatibility.

Dialling features

The dialling feature of a system is a major determinant of performance and cost effectiveness. Some systems have auto-dialling features which as the name suggests incorporate some automatic element, eg an automatic redial where a line is busy or an abbreviated dialling facility, or a delayed dial whereby it is possible to program the system to transmit the document later at a predetermined time which will save money by using cheap-rate lines – particularly for international calls. Some systems also incorporate a group codes facility which enables automatic dialling of all the numbers held in a particular code group.

Reduction and enlargement features

Most machines, and certainly those at the cheaper end of the market can only handle A4 materials, but some of the newer machines offer reduction facility while others will transmit B4 documents size for size. Where reduction facility is useful for things like architects' or engineers' drawings, as well as computer print-out, an enlargement facility will be useful where a lot of small-sized and perhaps poor quality material needs to be faxed.

Printing methods

Although thermal printing is still the dominant technique, using heat-sensitive paper, plain paper is beginning to catch on and will undoubtedly be increasingly used in future. The great disadvantage of thermal paper is its poor, flimsy quality. It is also expensive, although it is worth remembering that where fax documents are to be handled a lot they can be photocopied first of all! Another likely printing technique to enter the fax market will be laser printing, particularly for Group 4 systems.

Output quality .

The images produced via a fax machine are never quite up to the standard of those produced by a photocopier although they are improving. The sharpness of the end product is determined by what is termed 'resolution' which is the intensity of 'lines' that contribute to the final image (like the lines which make up a television picture or a graphics display on a VDU monitor). In essence the higher the resolution, the sharper the image. Some machines do possess a facility to improve the result by switching to what is known as 'fine mode' and there are even some machines which offer 'extra-fine mode', but only machines of the same make can communicate at these resolutions. While a higher resolution improves the quality it also puts up the cost as transmission takes longer.

Another aspect which contributes to quality is the ability of the scanner to distinguish between black and white. While this will be easy and obvious with straight line texts, documents which contain half tones, ie shades of grey, can be problematic and require that the machine be set accordingly. Electronic stencil cutters (see Section 4 p 56) require the same care in setting.

Detecting and correcting errors

Regardless of how sophisticated the fax machine's features, it will still be the quality of the telephone line at the time of transmission which affects the ultimate copy most significantly. Line interference can distort the image or lose part of it altogether making messages difficult if not impossible to read.

Machines do have an automatic cut-off when a certain level of image corruption is reached (about 15%) but it is the other errors which are actually transmitted that need to be detected. Machines do provide some indication often in the form of a print-out detailing transmitted pages with problems. The difficulty rests in assessing the extent of the problem. While the safe bet will always be to retransmit any faulty page, this can be time-consuming and expensive and perhaps not always necessary. The alternative, however, is to risk the possibility of delay or error caused by illegibility, coupled with the need to rely on the receiver to alert the transmitter of any difficulty.

A better option is to correct the error before it reaches the receiver – the maxim being that prevention is better than cure. However, this facility is still in its infancy and is largely restricted to use between proprietary brands, although it is a distinct possibility that CCITT will establish an error standard.

Memory features

As well as the memory facility associated with auto-dialling features, many machines have memory which can store complete documents. Memory can be introduced in two main ways – as RAM (Random Access Memory) and as hard disks (see Section 8 for a more in-depth explanation of these facilities). One of the benefits of memory in a fax system is the capacity it provides to 'store and forward' or 'broadcast'. Broadcasting can be done a document at a time or as a multiple document 'fax shot' (as opposed to mail shot). The latter 'batching' of documents for transmission can be time-saving where many organisations have to receive copies of the same document. Where the text is in the system's memory the entire process can be programmed to take place automatically at cheap rate time.

The future of fax

New and improved features are coming onto the market all the time and there are certainly likely to be more plain-paper machines, as well as more laser fax. There have also been an increasing number of neat portable machines introduced. Group 4 systems will be on the increase with the introduction of digital telephone systems and the consequent increase in transmission speeds. Also more fax and computer link-ups are likely whereby messages compiled of a mixture of graphics and text will be prepared on a computer and then sent via fax networking to another fax subscriber who will be able to view it on his VDU without printing out a hard copy first.

Videoconferencing

Any section on office communication would be incomplete without reference to videoconferencing, particularly given the number of meetings that take place in business every day. Irrespective of how good any written or verbal communication might be there is often nothing to compete with face-to-face exchanges, and yet attending meetings can be so time-consuming, not only in terms of actual meeting time but in respect of the time taken up travelling.

With the technology already discussed it is, of course, perfectly feasible to conduct a conference over the telephone and substantiate conversation by accessing stored or transmitted data and sending facsimile copies. Nonetheless there will still be occasions when it is preferable actually to see the other parties, hence the need for video- or teleconferencing, as it is sometimes called.

Confravision, introduced by BT quite some time ago, started the ball rolling as far as this sort of provision was concerned by enabling groups of people situated at different locations to be linked up in sound and vision. While this provision dispenses with the need to travel long distances there is still the need to go to one of the regional Confravision studios. Public videoconferencing rooms are currently located in London, where there are two, Birmingham, Manchester, Bristol, Belfast, Aberdeen, Glasgow, Ipswich and Douglas (Isle of Man). The rooms can generally accommodate six people and display facilities enable documents and diagrams to be shown to the distant location. Videoconferencing calls can be made both within the UK and internationally.

Now with the developments in BT's digitisation programme full colour signals can be achieved via Videostream. This service (see Fig 7.13) enables customers to be connected by high speed digital links and so hold conferences between their own meeting or conference rooms. The equipment also has the facility to send documents and other graphic material. No special studio accommodation, with all the attendant lighting and acoustic facilities, is required and a range of camera and monitoring equipment is available for purchase or rental.

The advantages of videoconferencing

Such attractive conferencing facilities have the following advantages:

- they enable business to be conducted live;
- any features introduced at an ordinary meeting may easily be incorporated, eg the display of graphics;

175

Fig. 7.13   BT's Videostream service in operation
(*By courtesy of British Telecom*)

- participants can both see and hear one another;
- a permanent recording may be made;
- travel time and costs are vastly reduced, in fact in some instances they will totally disappear;
- contributors should be less tired and therefore more effective;
- maximum contributions can be secured from any one with anything valid to say, eg a colleague with a limited, but perhaps specialist contribution to make can be contacted to go to the conference room and put over his view via Videostream where it would be unlikely that he would be released from his duties to travel to a distant meeting. (More likely in such an instance someone else would be briefed to represent him and, of course, this may prove inadequate where additional specialist information is required or where a decision needs to be reached and the representative is insufficiently briefed);
- access is readily available to any files, data or opinion which may be needed urgently or unexpectedly;

- the effects of travel problems or adverse weather conditions are avoided;
- information will be more easily kept confidential within organisations' own premises than where they are holding a meeting in a hotel or other outside premises.

The disadvantages

Disadvantages would seem to be relatively few other than the obvious ones of equipment malfunction or signal failure of some kind. Other possible difficulties might include the following:

- a chairman may find it more difficult to keep order by remote control and would certainly need to adopt different strategies (consider the difficulties which television interviewers can experience when operating in this sort of medium);
- there is no opportunity for members to get together in the same way informally prior to a videoconference (any premeeting contact would have to be made over the telephone);
- some executives may resent the removal of an opportunity to get away from the office for a while – on expenses – although evidence would seem to suggest that many executives begrudge the time they spend travelling;
- some members may find it difficult to act naturally in front of a camera, certainly at first, and this may affect the natural swing of a meeting.

Charges

All videoconferencing charges are calculated according to the length of transmission which must be a minimum of 30 minutes. Where companies make regular use of the service they will qualify for a lower rate of tariff.

International videoconferencing is also available with links to Canada and the USA as well as certain European countries. Where users use Confravision and travel to a studio to make the link-up they will have studio fees as well as transmission charges, but those with their own equipment operating from their own premises will only pay the international rate for the service.

Special Event Videoconferencing

A highly flexible application of videoconferencing is what BT term Special Event Videoconferencing. The idea is to apply the concept to events such as product launches, press conferences, annual general meetings and opening ceremonies in order that these occasions may reach a range of different locations which have previously been precluded.

Requirements may take the form of live videos of national events or the relaying of proceedigs to a number of locations both nationally and internationally. The service also enables speakers who may normally be unobtainable to be brought together. Bespoke packages of video and audio facilities can be provided by BT, together with links between literally any two venues via transmitting stations and satellite.

Courier services

In addition to the forms of communication which have already been described the following courier services should be borne in mind as ways of communicating office data quickly and safely, particularly given the criticism that is frequently levelled at the Post Office in terms of lack of speed and general inefficiency in delivering mail.

Special messenger services

At the local and regional levels special messenger services exist to deliver documents and small packages from one location to another at high speed. In the London area many of these services operate using powerful motor-cycles and provide a very useful supplement to other methods of transmitting data.

National courier services

At a national level courier services guarantee delivery within the country the next day or even within the same day. A large number of these services exist including the Post Office's own Datapost service, which does enjoy a very favourable reputation, and other well known names such as Securicor, Red Star (a British Rail service) and Roadline (part of National Freight). Charges differ dramatically among the services as do arrangements for pick-up or deposit but the major determinants are distance and weight.

Overseas document delivery services

These offer desk-to-desk document deliveries using air courier services. Here again a range of operators and price options are available to cover anything from next day to third day delivery, dependent on where in the world the package is destined. Once again the Post

Office's International Datapost is possibly the service which springs readily to most people's minds but a range of alternative private operators is also available such as Express Air Ltd, Transworld Couriers, World Courier (UK) Ltd.

It is also worth mentioning the alternative option of using one of the international fax services rather than a courier. Certainly for shorter documents this medium is worth considering. The Post Office variants of this service are known as Intelpost or Test-Fax, which is an electronic mail alternative enabling appropriately adapted microcomputers to access the Intelpost network direct.

CHECKLIST

1   Good communications are essential to the effective and efficient operation of all aspects of any organisation.

2   More time is spent communicating than in any other form of business activity.

3   A range of factors affect the selection of a communication medium.

4   There are always barriers to overcome in communicating successfully with others.

5   Communication can basically be broken up into written, verbal, oral/aural and machine/technology assisted.

6   An organisation's mail handling procedures are vital to its communication system.

7   The Post Office provides a useful range of support services in respect of processing urgent and valuable mail, both within the country and overseas.

8   Meetings form an important element of any organisation's communication network.

9   Meetings can be called for a variety of purposes and in some instances may be regular features on a committee's calendar of events.

10 Procedural matters relating to meetings are formally documented in Articles of Association, Constitutions, or By-laws.

11 The chairman performs an important role at any meeting.

12 Meetings have more likelihood of being effective when there is a high level of participation.

13 Telephone systems have undergone vast improvements in recent

years and are now extremely sophisticated, offering a variety of equipment with many useful features and options.

14 Still greater improvements in telecommunications are scheduled in line with the digitisation of the network.

15 Telex is the oldest form of electronic mail and still serves about $1\frac{1}{2}$ million users throughout the world.

16 Intercommunicating computers are a reality and datacoms is very much a growth area.

17 Modern electronic mail systems tend to refer to an organisation's mailboxes which are operated over a LAN and enable users to convey messages directly to one another, on screen, via computer; but it can also refer to a range of other data transmission services supplied by electronic mail bureaux such as Telecom Gold.

18 A database refers to a large store of logically arranged business information centrally held on computer, either locally within an organisation, regionally, nationally or even internationally.

19 Fax refers to the transmission, over telephone lines, of any material which can normally be photocopied, for receipt by another fax machine situated elsewhere, irrespective of distance.

20 Videoconferencing provides the means by which persons situated at distant locations may be linked by sound and vision, so enabling a meeting or conference to be conducted without the need for time-consuming and expensive long-distance travel.

QUICK REVISION QUESTIONS

1 Indicate three factors which would be considered in advising a valued client of a delay in a production schedule which will affect the delivery date agreed for his order.

2 Describe three barriers which a speaker might encounter in attempting to communicate effectively with a large, unfamiliar audience.

3 Devise a step-by-step procedure for distributing mail within a medium-sized organisation of six departments located within a four-storey modern office block.

4 What Post Office services might a secretary request to ensure the safe delivery of valuable items of mail?

5 Indicate three aspects which determine the degree of formality of a meeting.

6 Outline the functions of a Standing Committee.

7 List six possible reasons for holding a meeting.

8 Describe the qualities you would expect to find present in an effective chairman.

9 Assume that you have been selected to represent your department on an important committee.
   a What steps would you take to ensure you were adequately prepared?
   b What would you aim to do when attending meetings?

10 Briefly describe six features you would expect to find on a modern PABX system.

11 What is the difference between a 'mobile' and a 'portable' cellular phone?

12 What is meant by 'call logging'?

13 Explain the following features of a modern telex machine:
   a abbreviated dialling;
   b delayed transmission; and
   c received in background.

14 What are the major differences between telex and teletex?

15 What device enables a portable computer to be linked to an ordinary telephone and communicate with another computer?

16 Explain the following terms and abbreviations:
   a node;   *e* Satstream;
   b star network;   *f* BABT;
   c modem;   *g* PSS;
   d System X;   *h* PSTN.

17 What is the difference between an open and a closed user system of viewdata?

18 Suggest three aspects of fax which a new subscriber might consider prior to selecting a system.

19 What are the main advantages and disadvantages of videoconferencing?

20 In what circumstances might a company call on the services of a courier?

8 Office equipment

Modern offices are well blessed with time- and labour-saving equipment designed to take the drudgery out of routine tasks as well as improving office productivity. Many such items of equipment have already been discussed but this section sets out to consider those others most directly associated with secretarial work, viz typewriters, word processors, computers, dictation/transcription machines, calculators and mailing machines.

At the end of this section you should be able to:

- describe different types of typewriter;
- suggest criteria for selecting a typewriter;
- explain the concept of word processing;
- describe different word processing configurations;
- identify the main features of word processing equipment;
- discuss the impact of word processing on the office;
- explain the components of a computer system;
- distinguish between mainframe, mini- and microcomputers;
- list different functions which can be performed on a computer;
- identify different input/output devices;
- identify types of auxiliary storage;
- consider different software application packages;
- explain different types of dictation/transcription equipment;
- describe the features of calculating machines;
- compare and contrast different calculating machines;
- list the types of modern mailing equipment which are available.

Typewriters

As indicated in Section 1 of this Unit the first typewriters were successfully marketed in the 1870s but typewriters have come a long way since then and there are a great many models to choose from. Unlike the days of manual machines when they all did pretty much the same thing, modern electronic machines now boast a list of features which can be difficult to unscramble when selecting a typewriter.

Apart from the introduction of electric, followed by electronic machines, the single most significant change in typing and typewriters was brought about by the introduction of single element machines. Here the carriage remains stationary, unlike with standard typebar machines where it is the movement of the carriage which enables the keys to print onto the paper. The single element (originally most commonly a 'golf ball' head, but now more likely a daisy wheel – both elements so called in keeping with their appearance), revolves and moves backwards and forwards along a bar inside the machine to produce the print.

This single element brought great flexibility in terms of type size and print style. The golf balls or daisy wheels can be changed very easily – even within the same line of a document – so enabling the introduction of different sizes and styles of print. The pitch, ie the character spacing, (usually pica or elite) and perhaps even pro- portional spacing) can be altered at the flick of a switch. This was a great move forward as traditional typebar machines offered no possi- bility of such changes.

Another significant feature was the introduction of correcting features whereby the machine, at the depression of the appropriate key, back-spaces to the error. Dependent upon the sophistication of the machine the typist can then either strike the wrong key again at which point a lift-off correcting ribbon is activated to literally 'lift' the error from the page (it should be noted that the error is removed, not covered up) or where the machine has a memory, the depression of the correction key will perform the entire function automatically. For the first time typists could produce perfect copies without the need to erase or paint over errors.

The QWERTY keyboard

Year by year new machines are introduced, all of which have new features. The one thing which has remained standard, however, is the traditional QWERTY arrangement of the keys, irrespective of any additional keys which may have been added to perform special functions.

Experiments have, however, taken place in terms of the size and shape of keys, their distance apart and the slope of the keyboard (modern machines tend to be much flatter) in attempts to maximise user comfort and such tests continue. These are aspects which should be borne in mind when selecting a machine and it is advisable that the user should have the opportunity to try the machine out.

Other aspects which have affected typewriters are size and weight. While larger heavy duty models would still be recommended for situations where the machines are getting a lot of use, lighter compact ones will usually be adequate where the workload is less and perhaps backed up by other machines or word processing facilities.

It would be wrong to suggest that manual typewriters are totally a thing of the past, although there are decidedly fewer around. They do, however, have the advantage of operating anywhere and not being affected by power cuts or electrical faults. Even the most sophisticated office may still keep a manual machine for emergencies.

Electronic typewriters (see Fig. 8.1)

Given that most recent advances in typewriters have been in the electronic models these will be described here. Basically an electronic typewriter is a cross between an electric typewriter and a word processor. While still retaining the general appearance of an electric machine the microprocessor component gives the machines some of the advanced features and capabilities associated with word

Fig. 8.1 Electronic typewriter
(*By courtesy of Canon Business Machines Ltd*)

processing. All electronic machines have a memory of some kind ranging from correction-only memory, which is the capacity of the machine to recall previous characters typed and with a single key stroke make lift-off corrections (as described above), to the sort of memory capacity which enables the storage of phrases and short paragraphs frequently recurring in letters so that they can be recalled and typed automatically, to the most sophisticated memory machines which allow not only the storage of text but incorporate editing potential as well. The latter variety vary tremendously in their capabilities dependent on the power of the machine.

Memory typewriters

It is at this level that typewriters and word processors converge. Technically any machine with more than 2K of permanent memory can be classed as a word processor, although it can be difficult to draw a dividing line in pure technical terms. Memory typewriters do not, of course, have the benefit of full or half screens like word processors (unless they are upgraded – see below). However, many do have single line displays showing about 30 characters. This is extremely helpful in undertaking editing work, but one thing that it is important to consider is that the more sophisticated memory typewriters with the greater capacities can work out to be fairly expensive, and unless the nature of the work warrants such a large memory a less expensive model would possibly suffice. There again, where the full capacity of the memory is being utilised this raises the question of whether or not the machine should be properly upgraded or even exchanged for a word processor.

In general the experts would recommend that potential typewriter buyers who would like the advantages of a memory feature select the sort of machine which has a memory of approximately 8000 characters and which can also be edited. Such machines can cost somewhere in the region of £500–£700. Users who need more memory capacity would in most instances be well advised to consider word processing.

Features of electronic typewriters

Apart from correction facility, pitch variation and memory features electronic typewriters benefit from a variety of other features which greatly enhance presentation and improve the typist's productivity. The following are some of the more common features which are likely to be present in modern electronic machines:

- availability of different lengths of carriage;

- single line display (this provides the ability to type 'on line' so enabling corrections to be made before printing the text on paper. Also where the machine has a memory – which is usual on line display machines – the typist can scan the contents of the memory 'on line', making any essential alterations before committing the text to paper;
- automatic centring at the touch of a key;
- decimal tabulation whereby figures can be lined up automatically on the decimal point;
- automatic underscore where it is possible to select to underline characters automatically as they are being typed;
- half spacing which is useful in proofreading where a letter may have been omitted or where a word may be replaced by a slightly longer one;
- justified right-hand margin, which enables the right-hand margin to be straight like the left. When used in conjunction with, for example, a proportionally spaced wheel the end result can be extremely effective;
- emboldening, where words may be emphasised when the wheel strikes the ribbon twice for each letter;
- automatic paper insertion, whereby paper is fed into the machine at a predetermined point ready for typing, so enabling each line to commence at the same point on a multi-page document;
- repeater keys which enable continuous repetition of the same character merely by continuing to depress the key;
- automatic carriage return which enables the typist to continue typing even when the print wheel has moved to the next line. The extra characters are retained in a buffer memory and automatically added to the words on the next line;
- stop code feature whereby it is possible to halt the automatic printing of a paragraph called up from the memory so that additional words, phrases or sentences may be inserted and when the insert is complete the machine will start up again when prompted by the typist and complete the portion of stored text;
- automatic column calculation is available on some of the more sophisticated models. Here the machine will determine automatically the position of the tab stops when it is given the largest word or phrase in each column.

Electronic typewriters have been one of the early 1980s success stories accounting for a sizeable proportion (estimated at 33 per cent in 1983) of expenditure on text-producing equipment and they have the flexibility to be upgraded to the status of a word processor.

Typewriter upgrades

Many electronic typewriters can be upgraded to word processors by adding disk drives and a VDU via interfacing. The typewriter then serves as both keyboard and printer in the word processor system but can still function ordinarily to produce short memos and envelopes. The technique represents word processing at its most basic, although upgrading is likely to work out more expensive than buying a micro-computer with the appropriate WP software, and price is the main drawback of any upgrade system.

The major benefits of upgrading electronic typewriters are to be had from those with the smallest memory capacity. Upgrades are available on two levels, viz those with disks and those without. The diskless variety provides a screen and an internal memory of varying capacity depending on the model of the machine. Text is displayed on the screen as it is typed and can be stored in the internal memory for future use – even once the machine has been switched off. Where the upgrade has disk drives, additional material may be stored permanently on floppy disk as in a conventional WP system, and this option has a greater repertoire than the diskless one, particularly in the availability of the mail merge function. A realistic variation on the upgrade theme is to consider interfacing the existing typewriter with a microcomputer which has an inexpensive, draft quality, dot matrix printer. This would enable work to be prepared on the microcomputer but printed out when required using the high quality daisy wheel printer.

Most electronic typewriters operate with daisy wheel print heads which are available in a variety of type styles. However, a more recent arrival on the market is the thermal printing process, exemplified in IBM's 'Thermotronic' typewriter. This is a form of non-impact printing as the print is achieved by the machine 'drawing' the letters by shooting beams of heat at a special thermal ribbon which then deposits the projected characters onto the paper. The advantages are that the method is high speed, virtually silent, the end result of a high quality and there is potential to incorporate a wide variety of print styles and sizes. Nonetheless, being non-impact it is impossible to make carbon copies and the original is very easily erased. Also it is currently very costly both in terms of the machine itself and the ribbon supplies.

Word processors

The term 'word processing' was first coined by IBM in the mid 1960s to represent the linking to a typewriter of a computer processor. Initially there were only limited storage capacities and editing facilities, but the microelectronics revolution has brought with it sophisticated technology which now enables much greater storage, together with a wide range of software features.

The functions of word processors

The main functions of word processing are concerned with the storage, retrieval and subsequent editing of text. In simple terms this means that text, once created, can be kept indefinitely, redisplayed, added to, updated, corrected or totally revised and printed at will. To facilitate these functions word processors are able to incorporate massive deletions and/or insertions, major movements or substitutions of text, pagination and repagination, column changes, global searches and replacements and the inclusion of headers and footers.

The features which are built into the software to achieve these ends are more than pure text editing features. They have wide scope, including the potential to merge lists of names and addresses with standard letters and produce personalised documents, maintain and update a database of information, sort and re-arrange data held, build unique documents from recorded blocks of text and standard paragraphs, held in the processor's memory and capable of recall at a keystroke. The following is a list of typical more advanced features found on WP software:

Mailmerge The merging of two sets of distinct information to form one discrete personalised document. Some systems offer a selective system which would print only selected information while others would print, for example, the names and addresses of an entire file. (Note that some systems require a separate software package to perform this list processing activity.)

Database Once again this application may necessitate separate software, although it will tend to be more sophisticated than integrated databases. Basically it is a sort of computerised card index with a range of file and sort capabilities, akin to data processing *per se*. Information can be stored in a variety of categories or fields and called to the screen in any form required.

Spelling check This is a built in dictionary of varying size which will highlight any error in a word included in its dictionary. Smaller dictionaries, eg 20,000 words, have their limitations but it may be possible to add frequently used technical words and/or names to the dictionary.

'Help' facility This is a useful feature during the learning stages, but may not always be sufficiently detailed to solve a problem without reference to the manual.

Disk directories While all packages have some sort of index facility some are more sophisticated than others in that they automatically arrange in alphabetical order, provide details of number of pages, date of creation and number of subsequent edits, together with the date of the last edit.

'What you see is what you get' (WYSIWYG) Not all VDUs provide on screen the final version as it will appear when printed out, eg with emboldening, underscoring, right-hand margin justification, although it will usually be possible to check all this by a 'View Mode' of some kind which will indicate, via symbols exactly where new lines are taken and so on.

Initially many of the more sophisticated special WP features (ie those indicated below) could only be found on dedicated systems but gradually micro packages have begun to keep pace by including many of them in their programs. The following are typical examples:

- **concurrent printing** ie the ability to print out one document while working on the screen on another;
- **line drawing** – both vertical and horizontal;
- **scientific or mathematical symbols** – once the prerogative of dedicated systems these are now available on several micro packages;
- **wide document work** – possible via horizontal scrolling;
- **'windowing'** ie the ability to split the screen and view more than one document at a time. This is particularly useful where integrated packages are used, eg WP with database, financial modelling or graphics;
- **foreign languages** – like scientific symbols this was once only possible on dedicateds but micros have now bridged the gap.

In the last ten years the word processor market has grown substantially. Original predictions of word processor sales were fast outstripped and sales volumes increased almost seven-fold between 1981 and 1983, and have continued to increase even more since. One thing which has changed of late, however, is the movement away from dedicated systems towards the more versatile microcomputer systems which operate on greatly improved word processing software packages.

Dedicated word processors

As the name suggests these are systems 'dedicated' to and designed specifically for word processing. Previously when software packages were far from user-friendly there was much to be said for selecting a dedicated system and where a company or individual has virtually no requirement other than to manipulate text there may still be a strong case for opting for a dedicated system, particularly if funds are available. Certainly dedicated systems are very easy to use and some offer the luxury of a full A4 screen (see Fig. 8.2) which is not available on a micro. All dedicateds have special word processing keyboards with a range of special function keys which are clearly labelled to represent the action which can be achieved by depressing the particular key, eg 'MOVE', 'COPY', 'DELETE'. This is a decided advantage over the usual micro keyboard which has general function keys which are usually labelled numerically so necessitating familiarity with the system manual. Also the positioning of the keys on micros is often less well thought out than that on dedicateds.

Fig. 8.2 **A dedicated word processor with A4 screen**
(*By courtesy of Sony UK*)

Dedicated systems are more costly and the potential to perform tasks other than word processing may be restricted in that such systems will usually run only on the manufacturer's own proprietary word processing software, although more recently there has been a move towards enabling dedicated word processing users to run other manufacturers' micro software applications, eg spreadsheets, payroll, maths packages, via the system. While such options exist it should be recognised that they tend to be fairly expensive and limited. Therefore, where flexibility is called for it is probably a better bet to invest in an inexpensive microcomputer which has the power to operate a wide range of inexpensive software rather than use a dedicated word processor, leaving the word processor free for the purpose intended.

Microcomputers

Most microcomputers are capable of running word processing software of some kind. The questions to be answered are 'which kind?' and 'which will run on which?' In terms of the particular package, eg Wordstar, Wordcraft, Word Perfect Jr, it will be a matter of individual needs and preferences, otherwise it will be a matter of hardware compatibility, ie the software needs to be compatible with the operating system of the micro. In practice the latter is not as simple as it sounds.

This dilemma has been largely alleviated by the introduction of what are termed 'IBM-compatible' machines which means that the micro uses the same type of disk and has the same keyboard configuration as the IBM PC and can therefore run any program designed for the IBM PC. So it will be a question of determining whether to make a selection in hardware or software terms and to check the compatibility factors very carefully.

Word processing configurations

Having looked briefly at the various ways of achieving the benefits of word processing, the next step which most organisations need to consider is the type of configuration which is best suited to their needs. The basic configuration is stand alone. This comprises a totally self-contained system of keyboard, VDU, processor (CPU) and printer which is designed for use by one person at a time and the term may be used with dedicated or non-dedicated systems. It is perfectly possible to extend the stand alone system into a cluster formation with several screens sharing the same printing facility. This can be further extended having the potential to call on central hard disk storage as well as individual floppy disk storage. The configuration is then frequently referred to as a Shared Resource system.

Alternatively, where work stations comprise only a VDU and keyboard, depending on their power from a centrally located mainframe or minicomputer and, most likely, remotely situated printing facilities (often of determinable quality, eg draft or letter quality), this sort of configuration is termed Shared Logic. This configuration has one decided disadvantage, viz where the computer has any malfunction all terminals are out of action. This can largely be eliminated by opting for a compromise in substituting 'dumb' terminals (ie those with no intelligence of their own) with 'intelligent' or 'smart' terminals with their own central processing capacity achieved via floppy disk drives.

As word processing advances and the trend is increasingly towards convergence, ie the merging of word and data processing together with other technologies such as telex, voice recognition and photo-typesetting, there is a strong case for selecting the most versatile and flexible configuration which can bring to one workstation as many capabilities as possible.

Visual display units (VDUs)

When choosing a word processing system, although software will be crucial in terms of enabling the user to perform the functions he needs, it will also be important to give some thought to the VDU. This can vary in size, colour and clarity and ideally the word processing operator should be given the opportunity to sit at the screen and try it out before a final decision is made. Also, given the concern about the relationship between VDUs and health, their importance cannot be over-emphasised. In terms of pure ergonomic aspects the features which need to be considered will include the following:

- size, colour and display capability of the screen;
- tilt of the screen and contrast control;
- scrolling capacity – both vertical and horizontal;
- highlighting and reverse video capabilities;
- glare and screen flicker;
- accessibility of switches, ie ON/OFF switch, contrast control;
- status information provided on screen;
- clarity of characters in terms of ascenders and descenders and number of characters per line.

A word about VDUs and health

While there has been a certain amount of adverse publicity in respect of VDUs in connection with pregnancy, epilepsy, radiation, eyestrain, facial dermatitis, tenosynovitis (ie repeated strain of the tendons in the wrists), posture problems and stress, much of the research has been inconclusive. There is, however, a wealth of information and research findings available.

Nonetheless, in broad terms most of the problems associated with the use of VDUs can be substantially alleviated by the following:

- the provision of adequate working conditions with ergonomically designed workstations;
- suitable lighting;
- flicker-free screens;
- regular medical testing and monitoring;
- sufficient office cleaning to reduce static electricity;
- the introduction of adequate rest periods for operators;
- research into job design and the introduction of technology to the workplace.

Printers

Two main types of printer are used in conjunction with word processors – impact and non-impact – although it is also possible to produce direct input from word processors to phototypesetters. With impact printers, as the name suggests, direct contact is made with the paper, while non-impact printing forms images by placing ink on the paper without direct contact being made.

Impact printers

These are the most common type, using either serial (ie producing a letter at a time and operating at speeds of between ten and several hundred characters per second (chps) or line printing techniques (ie capable of producing a line at a time at speeds of up to 3000 lines per minute). Where it is desired to produce high quality printing the daisy wheel (or thimble) will usually be the answer. Daisy wheels and thimbles are available in a range of type styles and pitches. They can also incorporate special characters like foreign accents and scientific symbols. Such printers use the same technology as the electronic typewriter, the only difference being that instructions are sent from the central processing unit (CPU) as opposed to the keyboard.

Where speed rather than quality is the principal criterion for selection, the alternative is a dot matrix printer where characters are formed by a series of tiny dots. This technique is also capable of printing graphics, something virtually impossible with a daisy wheel. While the quality of print from a dot matrix printer is not up to the standard of a daisy wheel, great improvements have taken place, and when printing speed is reduced it is possible to achieve 'near letter quality' (NLQ) printing.

Non-impact printers

The principal alternatives to impact printers are ink jet, laser and thermal. Ink jet printers use a high speed stream of tiny electro-statically charged droplets of ink aimed at the paper or other surface (they are capable of printing on metal, glass or plastic). The end product is of very high quality, particularly where graphics are being printed, although the quality reduces as the speed increases and it is only possible to produce one copy at a time.

Although laser printers continue to be expensive, prices have fallen since their introduction and are likely to continue to fall still further. Laser printing is based on the photocopying principle where the computer directs laser beams which draw the image onto the copier drum which in turn reproduces the paper image as per the normal photocopying process. Where laser printers come into their own is in an application such as desk-top publishing (see page 201) where it is required to mix varied images of different type styles and sizes as well as graphics work, all in the one page.

Thermal printers (see also page 187) produce copy not via individual characters on a print wheel but via a machine programmed to 'draw' the characters on a heat sensitive or thermal ribbon which then deposits the characters onto the paper (no special paper is required). The advantages of this technique are that as well as being of good quality, fast and very quiet, the machine has a range of type styles and is capable of printing out in expanded or condensed forms. However, running costs are high, carbon copies cannot be made and top copies are easily erased.

Printer selection criteria

Irrespective of which type of printer is being considered certain basic selection criteria need to be borne in mind. These will largely include the following:

- independent operation from the VDU and keyboard so that concurrent editing work may be performed along with the printing;
- user-definable printing priority where the printer is shared;

- the capability of halting the printing at any point;
- the ability to cater for or introduce a range of type styles;
- special paper handling arrangements, eg sheet feed, continuous stationery;
- speed factors;
- costs – both initial and running;
- noise and the ability to fit an acoustic hood.

Computers

Computers have been around in offices for a long time, although they now come in various types, shapes and sizes. Irrespective of their size all systems operate on the same basic principles as illustrated in Fig. 8.3 below.

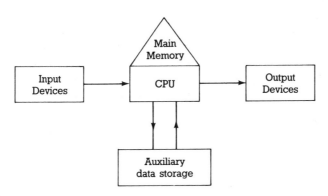

Fig. 8.3 A computer system model

What, then, is a computer? It is 'an electronic device operating under the control of instructions stored in its own memory unit, which can accept and store data, perform arithmetic and logical operations on that data without human intervention, and produce output from the processing' (Shelley G and Cashman T, *Computer Fundamentals for an Information Age*, Anaheim Publishing Co. Inc., 1984). From this definition it can be seen that computers are capable of performing certain specific operations. These operations are not complex in themselves but it is the speed and reliability with which the computer can perform them which renders it such a powerful tool in the business environment.

Components of a computer

The processing of data by computer is performed by four specific units (see Fig. 8.3), which together form the computer's hardware, viz

1 Input units, eg keyboards, light pens, graphics tablets, OCR, voice recognition.
2 The processor unit comprising two distinct parts, viz the main (or internal) memory consisting of RAM and ROM (see below) and the central processing unit (CPU).
3 Output units, eg printers, or VDUs or speech synthesisers.
4 Auxiliary storage (or external memory), eg hard disks or floppy disk drives.

RAM and ROM

Random Access Memory (RAM) refers to the computer's short-term working area and is measured in kilobytes or K. RAM may be over-written indefinitely with new data and programs and so by way of comparison is akin to an audio cassette which can be recorded over or wiped clean and recorded on again. The only difference in operation from an audio cassette is that RAM can be accessed by the computer at any point in its memory whereas a cassette would have to be run through in sequence to find a specific place. The thing to remember about RAM is that when the machine is switched off everything is lost unless it has been committed to disk storage first of all.

Read Only Memory (ROM), on the other hand, is by comparison like an LP record which can only be played back and which is inscribed for all time. ROM, therefore is supplied by the computer manufacturer and is used to store internal memory information which will be required constantly to enable the system to function.

Software

Despite the size and tangibility of the hardware components the system would be incapable of functioning without the software or computer program. Software itself comes in two types – system software and application packages. The former refers to the operating system which is the set of programs stored in the computer's internal memory which control the computer's operations. Alternatively they may be specially written by computer programmers to solve specific problems. The latter are written in one of the common programming languages, eg BASIC (Beginners All-purpose Symbolic Instruction

Code), COBOL (Common Business Oriented Language) or FORTRAN (*Formula Translation*).

Once the programs are written the program languages need to be converted by translator programs called compilers into machine (binary) language in order that they may be understood and interpreted by the computer.

Frequently the computer user will have little or no knowledge of programming as such and it will be immaterial to him whether the program is 'off the shelf' or custom designed as long as it is capable of producing the desired results. Where programs are bought from software suppliers they are generally referred to as software or application packages (see page 198).

Types and sizes of computer

The following are examples of typical modern computers and configurations.

Mainframe computers Prior to the development of the microprocessor all computers were mainframe. They were huge, highly sensitive machines which needed to be located in controlled environments around which an air of mystery and awe seemed to permeate. Such computers were very much at the centre of an organisation's activities, not least in that they represented a substantial investment. This in turn demanded that optimum use be made of the computing facilities provided, so round-the-clock workloads were scheduled in order that there should be no idle time. This meant the production of special schedules and adherence to new deadlines imposed by the machine.

Despite the emergence of mini- and micro-computers many organisations had developed their data processing capabilities around large-scale highly powerful and very expensive mainframe computers. A lot of money and expertise was invested into these systems and the view is frequently taken that it makes good sense to exploit their potential by using them as corporate databases and support for office automation.

Minicomputers The term minicomputer was coined to distinguish smaller computers introduced by Digital Equipment Corporation (DEC) from the larger, more expensive mainframes. Initially (in the mid 1960s) they not only differed in size, cost and power but in terms of their less extensive range of input/output devices and lack of software. However, they have come a long way since then and now have a wide range of applications including many in the business field. In fact they now play a major role in the computing world by either, in a stand alone capacity, accomplishing specific tasks previously tackled manually, or by supplementing larger computer installations, perhaps by operating at departmental level for, say, accounting functions, but networked at organisation level to the mainframe facility.

The future for minicomputers Although many minicomputer firms still survive, the market has declined in recent years, since the arrival of up-market, more powerful micros, some of which can now out-class the minicomputers. Also micros are less expensive and often have just as much expansion potential in terms of additional disk storage and extra terminals. Possibly one of the main reasons why minicomputers will still retain their position in the computer market for some years to come is that a lot of high quality, specialist software has been written specially for them and software support is good. However, the position is changing as micros become better and more powerful all the time.

Microcomputers The first complete microcomputer made its market appearance in 1977 thanks to the silicon chip as a means of computer storage. Advancement has been such that many micros or Personal Computers (PCs) are sufficiently powerful to enable them to function as small business computer systems. A typical configuration is shown as Fig. 8.4. As well as being the smallest these systems are the least expensive. They can be programmed in two ways. Firstly and most commonly it can be done via ROM memory chips which contain the instructions essential to direct the operation. Alternatively the system may be programmed by the user using a language such as Basic. A wide range of software applications packages are now available for microcomputers but it is important to check compatibility. Dependent upon the operating system the choice of programs may be restricted.

Typical uses of personal computers All levels of personnel within a variety of departments in an organisation may find use for a PC. The following are six common uses, apart from word processing, to which a PC could be put, provided it has the appropriate application packages:

- database and file management;
- spreadsheet;
- graphics;
- electronic mail;
- desk-top publishing;
- integrated applications.

Fig. 8.4   A microcomputer configuration
(*By courtesy of Canon Business Machines Ltd*)

Database and file management

A useful feature of any computer is its ability to store large volumes
of information and to retrieve it speedily at a later date. File handling
software used with a PC enables the user to swiftly locate the desired
file, display it on screen, update it, add to it, delete it, print it, sort
it or list it with other files held on disk. For example, where it is
desired to locate a particular customer's file it would be a matter of
inserting the appropriate name and instructing the computer to
search.

Alternatively, where it may be desired to circulate certain information to all clients in a particular area or within a particular age
group or credit rating, feeding in the appropriate variables will enable
the computer to search the database and produce the information. To
undertake such a task manually would be extremely time-consuming
by comparison. This type of software is capable of largely replacing
the conventional filing system in an office. DBMS (Data Base
Management System) enables a PC to function in much the same way
as a mainframe computer, as regards its ability to access and manipulate data.

199

Spreadsheet

This type of program enables the user to reach decisions on financial matters, budgets and other plans and forecasts. The user simply enters the figures which he has as the basis of his calculations, together with the formula to be used in reaching the projection and the software does the rest. As the name indicates the package enables the user to emulate a grid – wider and deeper than the VDU in order that horizontal and vertical scrolling may be done with the figure projections entered automatically.

One particularly useful feature of good spreadsheet software is the ability it provides to pose a 'What if . . .?' question. Here the software will reach projections based on assumptions fed in by the user. For example the user could request the software to project profits based on a 5 per cent increase in sales and a percentage decrease in costs or a change in the rate of VAT and then ask the system to recalculate on the basis of different percentages. An example of a spreadsheet package as it would appear on a screen is given as Fig. 8.5. Electronic spreadsheets are an invaluable tool for management decision support.

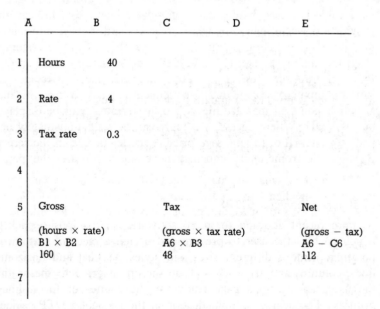

	A	B	C	D	E
1	Hours	40			
2	Rate	4			
3	Tax rate	0.3			
4					
5	Gross		Tax		Net
6	(hours × rate)		(gross × tax rate)		(gross − tax)
	B1 × B2		A6 × B3		A6 − C6
	160		48		112
7					

Fig. 8.5 An example of a spreadsheet

Graphics

This type of software enables PCs to produce charts on screen by transferring numerical values into some appropriate form of chart or graph for easier analysis and more eye-catching presentation, often in a variety of colours. Here again the software does all the work and something which might previously have taken hours to draw up is produced in a matter of seconds. Where it is desired to print out the results seen on the screen this can be achieved using a dot matrix printer or where better results are required using a graphics plotter (see page 207).

At the top end of graphics are packages connected with computer-aided design (CAD) used by engineers, architects and the like to test out their design ideas. This area of software development is improving all the time in terms of both its scope and quality. Computer graphics can greatly improve management communications and considerably enhance presentations to colleagues and clients.

Electronic mail

Where personal computers are networked within a department or company there is great potential for personnel to communicate with one another. A networked system where terminals are linked together via a cable is referred to as data communications. Not only can this provide a powerful means by which to access and transfer information held on another PC but it can also provide the basis for a system of electronic mail (see page 164). With the appropriate software users of PCs can transmit messages to other network users. Messages are stored in auxiliary storage until the recipient is ready to 'read' his mail at which point all mail 'addressed' to his terminal will be displayed on his VDU. Where necessary a reply can be sent immediately or a hard copy taken of the message prior to its deletion from the screen. By using electronic mail companies move one step nearer the 'paperless office'.

Desk-top publishing (DTP)

A more recent addition to micro software is a composite package which enables the user to prepare and design a piece of text incorporating print of different sizes and styles, vertical and horizontal lines, columns and art work – all on the one page. This means that the user can set up a page ready for the printer or for in-house printing. The degree of sophistication of the particular DTP package will determine the range of options available but different packages containing libraries of images can be stored for future use. Such a facility enables a company to produce much of its own illustrated literature and is useful in the preparation of house magazines, advertising materials, brochures and pamphlets.

This type of software allows users to exercise whatever creative talents they may possess in terms of devising an eye-catching layout. It is somewhat akin to an artist being faced with a blank canvas. The DTP user starts off with a blank screen and is able to combine text, graphics, rules and boxes, headlines and captions all to form a finished page. It is helpful to employ additional input devices other than the keyboard. For example, a mouse (see page 205) will be useful for selecting menu options and sizing pages, while a light pen or graphics pad (see page 207) will prove useful for drawing images on the screen.

It is, however, advisable to have a clear idea of what is required first of all and to draft initial ideas with pencil and paper. Once the page has been designed on the screen (an example is provided in Fig. 8.6) it may be either printed out using, ideally, a laser printer, which will be of sufficiently good quality to be accepted as 'camera-ready artwork' or saved on disk and typeset direct at a later date.

Fig. 8.6 VDU screen with DTP software
(*By courtesy of Apricot Computers plc*)

DTP is growing in popularity and an increasing range of packages of varying quality, cost and ease of use are available. As with any other software it is important that potential users have a good idea of their own needs and that they have the package demonstrated before reaching a decision to purchase.

Integrated software

Frequently it would be useful to be able to combine data or functions intrinsic to particular software packages. For example, it could be useful to be able to move from word processing directly into spreadsheet or graphics. This is now technically possible via the use of integrated packages. Therefore where a sales manager wishes to incorporate a spreadsheet or a bar chart into a report this can be done using the WP function of the software.

An added bonus of this sort of application is the use of windows. This enables portions of the VDU to be divided up to display a range of aspects all at the same time – the technological equivalent to various sheets of paper spread out on a desk.

Input devices

Data can be entered into and accessed from computers in a variety of ways dependent upon the type of data entered, the computer configuration, the options open to the user, preference, speed, convenience and cost factors. Hardware devices for data entry fall into two broad categories – terminals and other devices specifically designed for data entry.

Terminals

Terminals consist of a keyboard and VDU linked to the computer but they have varying capabilities. For example, at their most basic they have very limited functions and as such are often referred to as **'dumb' terminals**. This means that they can virtually be used only to transmit data to the computer although they are likely to be capable of receiving limited messages from the computer. With developments in microprocessing **'smart' terminals** were introduced and these possess added capabilities such as text editing. Smart terminals are now commonly used for data entry applications and are frequently tailor-made for the tasks they undertake. The next step up is **'intelligent' terminals** which have much more sophisticated capabilities which enable the user to 'program' various tasks, eg mathematical checks on data entries made. Intelligent terminals frequently have the additional processing power of their own disk drives and so PCs are often used in this capacity as part of an overall computing configuration within an organisation.

In terms of the actual VDUs and keyboards the same selection criteria will apply as did for word processors in the previous section. Two other types of terminal can also be used to input data, viz keyboard/printer terminals and integrated workstations. The former is the old teleprinter which transmits data via a keyboard to a central computer. With the increase in VDUs these have become much less common although portable versions have proved popular with, for example, sales representatives, who can easily transmit orders directly to a distant computer at the end of the day, by simply linking a portable teleprinter to a telephone via an acoustic coupler.

Integrated workstations, on the other hand, are becoming something of an executive necessity. The idea is simply to provide the facility whereby it is possible to enter data into a computer, retrieve it as required, communicate with others either verbally or in writing and all from a single unit of equipment (see Fig. 8.7). Such executive workstations are high in the list of priorities for automated offices as

Fig. 8.7 Executive workstation

they are capable of providing all the essential communications functions in one compact unit.

Other personal 'preferred' devices

A range of alternative input devices exists but these are additions to rather than substitutes for the keyboard. The **'mouse'**, virtually designed by Xerox, is something of an alternative to the 'joystick' which is associated largely with early computer games where it helped pinpoint something on the screen by moving the cursor around. A mouse is used in a similar way and was designed largely to counteract alleged resistance to the use of keyboards (particularly by male executives). It is a small light-weight, box-like device attached to the system. By moving it about on the desk top (it has several small wheels underneath to facilitate movement), the user can control the cursor on the screen. Then by pointing the arrow at the desired selection item and pressing a button on the mouse the selection is automatically activated. While being easy to use, a mouse does necessitate a clear desk and one hand has to be taken off the keyboard to use it.

Alternatives to the mouse are the **'light pen'** or **'touch sensitive screens'** which react when contact is made with the desired item on the screen. While natural, easy and fast to use, ergonomically (see page 234) this is less comfortable for the user who needs to stretch towards the screen to make the necessary contact and they can lack precision.

MCR, OCR and bar codes

Magnetic character recognition (MCR) has been around for some time and is used by banks to process the large volume of cheques in a quicker and more accurate way. Special numbers are printed in magnetic ink across the bottom of the cheques, viz cheque number, the bank's sorting code number and the drawer's account number and the data can then be encoded and read by machine at very high speed.

Optical character recognition (OCR) devices are becoming increasingly popular as a means of scanning typed, printed or in some instances, handprinted data, by laser or photo-electronic device and comparing the readings with characters stored in the device's memory. Such machines are capable of amazingly high speeds.

Bar codes provide another means by which information can be fed directly into computer. Many items sold in shops and supermarkets now have a bar code and where point of sale (POS) terminals are in operation the assistant passes the code mark over an optical reader. The data, represented by the lines on the bar code, are transmitted directly to a minicomputer which retrieves the price and description and automatically displays it on the terminal display and prints out a cash receipt for the customer. An alternative means of reading bar codes is to pass the tip of an optical penlike device over the bar code (as in computerised libraries) whereby the data from the code is read and automatically stored in computer.

Graphics input devices

In addition to light pens which can be used successfully to draw lines on a screen, **digitisers** can convert analogue signals picked up from points, lines and curves on sketches, drawings or photographs into digital impulses for transmission to computer. Digitisers are principally used by engineers and medical specialists.

Graphics tablets (see Fig. 8.8) work in a way similar to digitisers. They enable shapes to be traced with a pen and transmitted directly into the computer, but additionally they contain unique sets of commands which enable the user to implement complex movements on the drawing he is working on, eg altering the angle so that it can be viewed differently, so saving an immense amount of time. Graphics tablets are used extensively in computer aided design (CAD).

Voice recognition

The idea of being able to 'speak' directly to the computer and enter data is an exciting prospect but 'matching' problems still inevitably exist and systems which do operate voice recognition still have a fairly restricted and precise vocabulary. Technology still has a long way to go to perfect this method and bring it into common use.

Output devices

Given that the primary purpose of a computer is to produce useful information, the form in which that information is presented is significant. The type of output device needed will be dependent on the type of computer and the functions it performs. Basically it will boil down to a choice of printers and displayed output on VDUs, with the additional possibilities of plotters, COM and voice output.

Since printers have already been discussed in the section on word processors it is not intended to consider them further here. In terms

Fig. 8.8   A graphics tablet

of screen output this is important in that with any interactive computing system responses are displayed on VDUs and so quality and user comfort are important considerations. Display monitors come in many sizes and qualities and are capable of monochrome (black and white) or colour display. In addition to the ability to display standard text many monitors can now display graphs and charts with some having the capability of displaying very high resolution graphics in a full range of colours. With the development of portable computers flat panel displays have been one essential and these are frequently supplied in the form of liquid crystal displays (LCD) similar to those used in calculators.

Plotters

These devices have come into their own with the increased capability of computers to produce graphics and their price has dropped

207

considerably. Several types are available. Pen plotters which will be of either the flat bed or drum variety plot the drawing or diagram by pen, or a series of pens, where multi-colour work is being created. Drum plotters are used frequently to create large two-dimensional drawings. Alternatively there are electrostatic plotters which work something on the lines of an electronic stencil cutter in that a drum rotates and creates an electrostatic charge on the paper on which the drawing is made via a row of special styli (pens) spread across the width of the paper. The paper then passes through a developer and the drawing appears. This method is very much faster than pen plotters and the output is of a high quality.

Computer output microfilm (COM)

This technique (see also page 44) records computer output as tiny images on microfilm or microfiche. Data comes directly from computer where an on-line facility exists or from magnetic tape where the facility is off-line. Data is then read into a recorder, displayed internally on a VDU from which it is photographed onto film. The big advantages of this technique are the high speeds with which data can be produced, compared with standard printing techniques, and retrieved from film, coupled with the reduced costs both in terms of production and storage.

Voice output

Voice output can be achieved by a machine encoding spoken words in a digital pattern, storing on disk and then retrieving and reinstating the digital data into voice sound (as with the speaking clock) or by voice synthesis. The latter is a more promising development but is infinitely more complex. It operates on the basis of words stored in a computer's memory being analysed by a special program which then generates phonemes for the letter combinations. Phonemes are then combined to form sounds. The special software is able to determine pitch and loudness by applying special rules of intonation and stress so that the speech sounds real.

Auxiliary storage

The final element of Fig. 8.3 yet to be considered is that of auxiliary storage or back-up and here again this will be determined by the particular computing configuration in use. For a large computer, back-up will be in the form of magnetic tape or disk. Where magnetic tape is used it is stored in tape libraries where there may be literally thousands of reels of tape carefully categorised and stored ready for processing as required. However, tape is not so readily used nowadays as retrieval has to be sequential, whereas the type of access required is frequently random in nature. Nonetheless, tape can provide useful back-up in terms of holding duplicate data.

Magnetic disks, however, provide the most widespread form of additional storage for large scale computers. Disks can be of the removable (exchangeable) or fixed variety. The former can be removed from the disk drives and stored in special packs or transferred for use with other compatible systems while the latter are totally sealed in an enclosure and permanently mounted so that they cannot be removed from the disk drive. Although these fixed disks cannot be removed they do have extremely large capacities (eg a large disk drive can store 2.5 billion characters) and yet access time is very fast.

Disks, of course, are also the most popular medium for smaller systems including PCs, although some microcomputers do use audio cassette tapes for storing programs. Smaller disks frequently referred to as flexible, floppy or diskettes, come in a range of sizes, although the most common is still the $5\frac{1}{4}$-inch floppy disk. These disks are enclosed in a protective vinyl jacket lined with friction free material to protect the disk and enable it to turn easily. Storage capacity is determined by three factors, viz whether the diskettes are single- or double-sided, by recording density and by the number of tracks per inch. Consequently double-sided, double-density, double-track diskettes are capable of the most storage.

A more recent popular development has been the microdisk or microfloppy. This is a $3\frac{1}{4}$-inch diskette built into a strengthened rigid protective plastic casing with a cover which slides back to expose the disk when it is inserted in the disk drive. This type of disk is extremely resilient and has a storage capacity in keeping with the larger floppies.

Where a small system user has a need to provide extensive auxiliary storage hard disks are used. Some hard disk storage units contain removable disks while others are permanently mounted as in the larger systems described above. One type of fixed disk drive, referred to as a Winchester disk, is frequently used with smaller computers. These were originally developed in the early 1970s by IBM where the idea was to hermetically seal, ie encase the metal disks, the read/write heads and the control mechanisms within a case with air continuously filtered and circulating to prevent contamination. Originally the disks were 14 inches in diameter but for PC use they are now available in $5\frac{1}{4}$- and $3\frac{1}{2}$-inch sizes.

Optical disks

Where large storage back-up is needed, optical disks represent a more recent form of very high density storage. Currently they are very costly, although prices will undoubtedly drop. In appearance they are similar to laser disks used in video or audio systems, being plastic disks on to which digital information is burned by a laser beam, so enabling it to be read by a light source. Currently their best use is in terms of archival storage (as an alternative to microfilm) as once the data is entered on disk the disks cannot be overwritten. However, once erasable disks become readily available the potential of optical disks to store vast quantities of data will become a reality.

Computer selection criteria

As with any other office equipment careful consideration needs to be given to selecting computers, whether they be full-blown mainframe systems or small micros. Few purchasing decisions will be as crucial and it will be important to avoid making mistakes. In short the question which needs to be posed is 'What can a computer do for you?' If this question is put to a company the type of response suppliers are likely to provide are as follows:

- improve your ability to produce up-to-date information at high speed;
- increase your overall efficiency;
- enable you to make better use of your resources;
- enhance your management decision-making capability;
- allow you to introduce checks and controls;
- increase your profitability;
- help you keep pace with your competitors.

However, what the company then needs to take into account are the following:

- the type of system and its options;
- the configuration;
- compatibility and integration potential with other systems;
- the present capacity and potential for enhancement;
- the cost – present and subsequent;
- the ease of installation;
- the ease of operation;
- space factors and environmental considerations;
- back-up from the supplier;
- training;

- maintenance;
- supplies.

Similar criteria will apply to the small user in terms of selecting a PC and it will be important to analyse requirements thoroughly before attempting to make a decision on the wide range of microcomputer systems which are available. Special considerations in respect of PCs will include:

- the main purpose for which the system will be used;
- the type of operating system;
- the size of the memory;
- the availability and range of software packages;
- the clarity of the VDU;
- the quality of the printer;
- the 'feel' of the keyboard;
- the quality of any operator manual provided;
- the number of disk drives;
- the type of auxiliary storage;
- the potential to interface with peripherals such as OCR, plotter, phototypesetter.

Computing is and always has been a dynamic area of activity and consequently it will always be difficult to make a decision on what to have. However, the best that companies or individuals can hope to do is to call on whatever expertise is available having done a thorough analysis of requirements in the first instance. That way it should at least be possible to pinpoint precise requirements and avoid the danger of being dazzled by science and coaxed into accepting a system which has more features than necessary or which is outmoded or about to be replaced by something better.

Dictation/transcription equipment

Audio typing is a long-established alternative to the use of shorthand for taking down dictation and thereafter transcribing it at the typewriter or word processor. Its major appeal is that it is a direct technique whereby material can be dictated directly into the machine for playback and transcription sometime later by the typist who can listen to the material and simultaneously type what is heard.

Types of equipment

As with much other office equipment a wide range of systems is available, although the market leaders are undoubtedly Philips, Grundig and Dictaphone. In selecting equipment it is important to consider the following points:

- who will use it;
- how many people will use it;
- where it will be used;
- whether audio equipment already exists – compatibility factor;
- the type of cassette to be used;
- the uses to which the equipment will be put;
- whether an installation is to be free-standing or whether there is a case for a centralised provision;
- how simple is it to use;
- how expensive is it to buy, install and maintain;
- what sort of back-up and service support is available from the supplier.

Basically where equipment is being selected for non-centralised use it will be a matter of deciding whether to opt for portable (hand-held) or desk-top machines. Portables cost less and are convenient in that

Fig. 8.9 Pocket memo
(*By courtesy of Philips Business Systems*)

they can be carried about easily, hence the term 'pocket memo' often applied to such machines (see Fig. 8.9). However, desk-top varieties tend to be more sturdy and reliable but are, of course, more expensive. Additionally desk-top models do have more features and many dictators prefer to speak into a hand-held microphone rather than directly into the recorder itself.

Desk-top models

These may be a fully-fledged dictation/transcription unit (see Fig. 8.10) with all the special features such as loudspeaking facility, telephone interface socket by which the machine can be connected to a telephone in order to record important telephone conversations, eg calls from abroad, calls containing a lot of vital statistical information or calls which other staff may like to hear at a later date. (*Note*: This does not transform the dictating machine into a telephone answering machine. It simply enables a recording to be made.)

Playback can be through the loudspeaker or through the microphone, although such models may, of course, also be used by the

Fig. 8.10   Dictation transcription unit
(*By courtesy of Philips Business Systems*)

Fig. 8.11   Transcription unit
(By courtesy of Philips Business Systems)

secretary who would attach a foot control and headset for typing back the recorded dictation.

Alternatively desk-top machines may simply be transcription units with playback facilities for use by the typist (see Fig. 8.11). Here again such units will have all the features which facilitate audio typing such as fast forward and fast rewind buttons, voice, pitch and speed control level buttons, which can be very helpful to the audio typist in transcribing badly dictated tapes, as well as the facility to playback through the loudspeaker or via earphones controlled by a foot pedal.

Types of recording media

While it is technically possible to use a non-magnetic or inscribed technique whereby permanent recordings are made by cutting grooves into a plastic belt or disk, magnetic media are more usual in that material can be erased both during dictation and after transcription so enabling the disks, tapes or cassettes to be altered and re-used.

Fig. 8.12 Mini-cassettes
(*By courtesy of Philips Business Systems*)

Mini-cassettes (see Fig. 8.12), ie those capable of recording 15 minutes dictation on each side are still the most popular media although the introduction of the micro-cassette which allows 30 or even 60 minutes of dictation a side is increasing in popularity. However, many systems bought for use with minis will not operate with the micro-cassettes, hence the continued use of minis. Also a minus in terms of the micro-cassette is that it is increasingly used with domestic equipment and this could lead to pilfering of the cassettes!

Some systems operate on standard cassettes and this can provide flexibility where dictators may wish to use their personal cassette recorders to do work for the office. While it is possible to use any length of tape, ie C60, C90 or C120, C60s are more advisable in that the constant starting, stopping and rewinding associated with audio dictation methods is not recommended for the thinner C120 tapes.

Additionally certain manufacturers have their own special brand of cassette compatible only with their system. These often have the advantage of incorporating special indexing features, but the disadvantage is that it becomes very costly to even consider changing a system while it is impossible to interchange tapes with any different system used elsewhere.

Indexing methods

One problem of audio dictation can be in relation to locating a desired point on the recording. Most machines do have a scale on the front of the dictation/transcription units and the typist will be able to gauge starting and finishing points fairly accurately where the dictator has marked the points on a paper index slip which is inserted in front of the scale. These marks can be made either manually by the dictator or electronically by the machine when a button is pressed. Likewise it is possible to provide an indication of the order in which material should be transcribed or indicate by a different mark an omission or special instruction.

Some of the more sophisticated machines are able to locate these bleeps automatically, ie the typist runs the tape through on fast forward until there is a bleep, at which point the tape will stop automatically. Even more advanced are those which have automatic visual indexing via flashing lights or other signals but, of course, the facility is reflected in the increased cost.

While such features can greatly assist the typist in helping her prioritise a heavy workload and in enabling her to judge more accurately the paper size required it must be said that they are frequently under-utilised or even disregarded entirely by many busy executives.

One useful feature present on a lot of machines is a 3-digit tape counter, similar to that found on audio or video cassette recorders. Some even have light-emitting diode (LED) or liquid crystal display (LCD) and these greatly facilitate locating points on the tape.

Centralised dictation installations

Whereas individual units may prove satisfactory in smaller organisations, larger outlets may wish to offer the facility to the maximum number of staff in the hope of sharing typists' workloads more equitably and generally saving on staff and equipment. Centralised dictation will, therefore, frequently be a feature of a typing pool, secretarial services unit or secretariat within a large organisation.

Three principal types of installation are found and they may be either automatically controlled or monitored by a supervisor.

One is referred to as the **tandem** system in that two units, one for dictation and one for transcription, are stacked on the typist's desk so enabling a recording to be made on one machine while the typist plays back and transcribes from the other. Contact is made via the PABX (telephone system) or via an independently wired network and any queries which either party may have regarding the dictation/transcription can be made over the telephone. Typists tend to favour this over other centralised methods as it is a bit more personal.

Another is called a **multi-bank** system and here a 'bank' of machines is installed in the typing centre and wired to the offices of users. Once again access to the equipment will be via the PABX or an independent link. The difference is that users of this system are simply routed to a free machine and it will be the supervisor's duty to distribute the work once the dictation is completed and deal with any queries which may arise. This system is much more impersonal and places greater responsibilities on the supervisor who must distribute the work fairly, monitor progress and liaise with the dictators.

The **continuous or endless loop technique** which is a variation of the tandem system refers to a centralised system which receives dictation on one long tape (holding up to 6 hours dictation) accessed by either the PABX or a private line. The tape is enclosed in special cases and may be used over and over again. The distinction between this system and the previous one is that not only can dictation and transcription modes operate simultaneously but the typist can in fact begin to transcribe within seconds of the dictation commencing. The major disadvantage of this technique is that material will generally be transcribed in the order in which it has been dictated. However, with some systems a VDU is linked to all units in order to keep track of the dictated material and even distribute work according to typist efficiency levels. It also enables loops to be scanned to locate certain dictation passages which require priority treatment.

A word about computerised systems

Computer technology has greatly enhanced the potential of centralised audio facilities in that not only has it meant that a supervisor's task is made easier by the existence of special features which continually monitor the work but from an organisation's point of view it becomes possible to greatly improve turnround of work. Systems automatically route jobs to certain workstations, eg those with the best turnover record, and generally improve control. Also they log all tasks so that they can be costed automatically to the relevant department or individual.

Many systems even have the facility whereby a dictator who is working late in the office may access the system and dictate work for transcription first thing the next day. Remote home links are another growth area in audio dictation.

Audio linked to word processing

Given that voice input is still something for the future many organisations view audio dictation as the natural intermediate step, and so where secretarial services are largely provided by a word processing centre it is more than likely that word processing operators may use audio as a medium for preparing text from authors situated in any department within the organisation. With networked computing systems it will be possible for authors to 'OK' word processed material 'posted' to them by electronic mail for checking before hard copies are printed out.

Pros and cons of audio

The advantages of audio systems and dictating equipment can be summarised as follows:

- dictation can be recorded any time and anywhere at the convenience of the dictator;
- the audio typist can be occupied with other work while dictation is taking place;
- non-urgent material may be transcribed at a convenient time, whereas when shorthand is used both dictator and secretary need to be present at the dictation and it is preferable to transcribe shorthand notes as quickly as possible;
- any audio typist can transcribe dictated material but it is unlikely that secretaries can easily read one another's shorthand notes;
- where executives share a secretary only one can dictate shorthand to her at a time, but where audio is used all executives may dictate at the same time;
- secretaries can listen to audio recordings as often as is necessary or can ask someone else to listen to part of the tape which is causing problems rather than rely on deciphering shorthand notes;
- it is also claimed that typing accuracy is improved with audio as typists are less likely to misinterpret what they hear over the transcription unit than they are to misread or alter an outline which they had difficulty with due to the speed of the original shorthand dictation;
- it is possible to accurately measure the volume of work undertaken by audio typists and so improve overall efficiency and increase productivity;
- where a centralised system is in operation staff savings may be possible;
- it is possible to send cassettes through the post when an executive

is away from the office on business, so avoiding a backlog of work on his return.

In terms of disadvantages of audio the main one is simply that some people do not like using machines. This will apply to both dictators and typists. Also there can be a novelty factor in using dictating equipment and this can wear off causing users to revert back to shorthand or even longhand notes. Other possible disadvantages could include the following:

- the cost of equipment, accessories and possible installation charges;
- breakdowns, including power failure and the inconvenience of slow repairs coupled with heavy maintenance charges;
- the impersonal atmosphere and reduced morale that can result in offices which use audio exclusively, particularly via a centralised system;
- the need to train dictators and typists in the use of systems and equipment.

Dictating machine bonuses

As well as providing a useful means for recording material for subsequent transcription at a later date, dictating equipment can prove useful in a variety of other ways. For example, desk-top machines, can provide a useful means of leaving messages, particularly where the boss and secretary do not come into contact on a regular basis. In such situations it could easily become part of the routine for either or both parties to check their respective machines each morning or evening in the same way as one would check an answering machine or an electronic mailbox.

Such a technique, as well as personalising the contact between secretary and boss can enable much more detailed information to be included than would be possible with handwritten notes.

Dictating machines can also be useful in rehearsing speeches, or for 'brainstorming' initial ideas prior to the final preparation of a report. Hand held machines can also prove extremely useful as a form of pocket aide-memoire where they can easily be used to make notes or observations, eg when an architect or surveyor may be visiting a building site and making a progress report. Hospital doctors also find them useful when making their ward rounds. Similarly they can be useful during an activity like stocktaking or checking through catalogues or shelves of books when it is convenient to have a hand free and yet not have the need to make physical notes.

Calculating equipment

While major calculations within organisations will be performed by computer and using electronic accounting machines there is a need for routine calculating and checking to be carried out. The calculator revolution has made the electronic calculator an essential support tool for anyone who needs to count!

Calculators come in all shapes and sizes, in all price ranges and with varying degrees of sophistication and memory. Therefore, it is important to analyse requirements carefully in order to ensure that any calculator selected is capable of doing what is required.

Generally speaking all calculators can add, subtract, multiply, divide and work out percentages in a fraction of a second but many have additional capabilities including inbuilt memory. While pocket calculators will provide totals on a liquid crystal display (LCD) some larger desk-top varieties are available which print results on a tally roll. This can be particularly useful for checking figures, and in offices this is a useful feature where entries may be constantly interrupted by, for example, the telephone. Here the existence of a printout will often reduce the likelihood of error.

When selecting a calculator it is worth while examining the actual keyboard in that like any other keyboards some possess features which make them easier and more comfortable to use. For example, in addition to the ten 0–9 keys some have double or triple cipher keys which save depressing the 0 repeatedly to get hundreds and thousands. This feature will be useful where a lot of high figures are used. Another useful feature is a raised spot on the centre (5) key to aid touch operation. (Similar spots are found on the F and J keys of some word processor keyboards.) The keyboard may also provide a function key by which it will be possible to select the number of decimal places required in a particular calculation. The positioning of this facility together with that of the delete key are also significant considerations.

Pocket calculators are battery operated and it is important to remember to switch them off when not in use, although most now have an automatic cut-off facility built in by which the calculator switches itself off after a given period of inactivity. Desk-top varieties, too, are usually battery driven for convenience although most have the facility to be converted to mains operation.

When batteries are running low the brightness of the display becomes impaired and there may be intermittent flickering. More sophisticated models will incorporate a red warning light to indicate that the battery is nearing the end of its life.

Whatever type of calculator is being used it is important to study the instruction book carefully and carry through some of the practice exercises which are usually included prior to attempting to use the calculator.

Mailing equipment

It is in terms of outgoing mail in particular that procedures can be highly mechanised or automated. As far as incoming mail is concerned the main item of equipment that might be used within a large organisation is likely to be an **automatic letter opening machine**. With these machines letters are stacked up and fed swiftly through, the machine slicing a thin strip of paper off the top of each envelope. It is important to place all envelopes the right way up so that the top of the letter is guillotined. Also given the way in which these machines work it is important that mail is folded carefully and that large enough envelopes are used, otherwise the contents could be damaged, with even complete lines of type lost in the opening process! The only other items of equipment likely to be used during the incoming mail handling stage are stapling machines, date stamps, sorting trays and delivery trolleys, with, of course, photocopying machines serving an important function in making essential copies and shredding machines being used to shred used envelopes for recycling or packaging purposes.

In terms of outgoing mail the principal items of machinery and equipment are as follows:

- letter scales;
- parcel scales;
- collating machines (see p. 68);
- joggers (see p. 69);
- folding machines;
- addressing machines;
- sealing machines;
- inserting machines;
- parcel tying machines;
- franking machines.

Of these there are two particularly worthy of further elaboration.

Addressing machines
Addressing machines are useful where an organisation frequently sends correspondence to the same address. They are used a lot by mail

order companies, clubs and societies. Various techniques exist for the preparation of the addresses on the envelopes, letters, cards, invoices, payslips and so on. The more traditional types follow one of the standard duplicating processes, ie spirit masters, stencil plates and foil or metal plates. The latter operates from embossed plates rather than the photographically prepared type, although like stencil plates they produce print by coming into contact with the paper through an inked ribbon. Preparation of address masters, stencils or plates is fairly simple. Spirit masters, stencil and foil plates can be prepared directly using a typewriter, while the metal plates are embossed using a simply operated embossing machine.

Spirit masters are only suitable for short-term use but ink stencils and plates last for a long time. The problem with the latter types is that they become very inked up and difficult to read. Sorting therefore presents a problem, although one useful device which can be applied to stencil plates is to use colour coded mounts. That way it is possible to isolate specific criteria for sorting purposes or to skip printing certain plates as they pass through the addressing machine. Possibly one of the principal reasons for experiencing difficulty in removing one's name from mailing lists could be the difficulty of isolating plates. It is a dirty and time-consuming task and probably simpler and cheaper in the long run to simply run all the plates through the system regardless.

Modern addressing techniques

Three more usual techniques used now to produce addresses involve the use of photocopiers, word processors or computerised equipment. With the former it is a simple matter to produce printed addresses on a plain sheet of paper, appropriately spaced out and then have them photocopied onto special peel-off self-adhesive labels which are made up on A4 size sheets. Where a word processor is used names and addresses are stored on disk and can be summoned up as needed for envelopes or incorporated into standard letters as part of a mail merge sequence. As far as computerised systems are concerned again several variations exist from which addresses stored on computer can be selected according to certain criteria and automatically printed out on, for example, continuous stationery address labels. The big advantage of any form of computer storage is the ability to update and to retrieve in a variety of different ways, according to particular needs. The significant variables are keyed into the computer which will perform an automatic sort and print out only the addresses required.

Franking machines

Franking machines produce a postage stamp design of an appropriate denomination, together with a date and cancellation mark – all printed in red ink – instead of having to rely on adhesive postage stamps. There is also the option of incorporating a company logo or advertising slogan with the frank. This slogan may be switched on or off as required. Machines can be bought or rented from several different suppliers, who must secure official authority from the Post Office which also has a regulation that machines must be inspected at least three times a year.

Franking machines have the following decided advantages:

- they dispense with the need to keep vast quantities of stamps of different denominations;
- they may be set for any denomination within the value range of the particular machine;
- machines are relatively easy to operate and fast to use;
- expenditure on postage is automatically recorded so control is better;
- departmental costing for postage can be more easily managed;
- electronic machines can be interfaced to other mail room equipment, particularly postage scales. This means that the machine will automatically register the weight and adjust the meter reading, printing out the correct postage;
- some machines incorporate other special features, eg automatic feeders whereby letters can be stacked and fed automatically; automatic sealing where envelopes are moistened as they pass through the meter and sealed automatically; automatic date change which avoids what can sometimes be something of a tricky operation to perform and one which can easily be overlooked, although many machines now have a built-in warning signal which emits when a date is left unchanged;
- they are hygienic to use;
- they incorporate free advertising or a return address which can save money;

The disadvantages are as follows:

- where no postage book is kept, private mail can easily be passed through the system;
- errors can be made, eg junior staff may frank letters with the wrong amounts or the wrong dates;
- machines can be quite expensive;

- breakdowns are very inconvenient;
- there is still the need in most cases to visit the Post Office to have the meter refilled;
- franked mail cannot be placed in a post box, but must be properly bundled according to Post Office regulations and handed in over a Post Office counter (alternatively arrangements can be made for large volumes of mail to be collected by the Post Office);
- franking machine control cards need to be completed and submitted weekly to the Post Office;
- machines must be inspected at least three times a year;
- maintenance contracts can prove costly;
- it is still likely that organisations or departments will maintain a supply of stamps so that mail may be stamped and posted after the franking machine meter has been read for the day and the machine locked to prevent unauthorised use.

How does the system work?

Machines operate on a meter system with two meter registers to read each day. An ascending register records the number of units of postage used, while a descending one logs the number of units still in hand. Therefore, when units are purchased from the Post Office the descending meter registers the total units in credit.

Meters can be refilled in several ways, dependent upon the type of machine. Some machines, particularly of the older type have to be taken in their entirety to the Post Office to have the purchase of additional units recorded on the meter. Others have detachable meters (this is the most common method) and while saving the need to take the whole machine, which can prove to be quite heavy, there is still a need to join the Post Office queue. Yet another alternative is what is known as the 'value card'. These cards can be bought in different value denominations from the Post Office but are only available for certain manufacturers' systems. When inserted in the machine the meter is automatically credited with the appropriate amount.

The most promising method is the 'remote setting' technique where everything is done at a distance. A cheque is sent to the Post Office, the amount required is registered on computer and when the machine needs to be reset the user contacts the computer which reads out a coded number via voice synthesis. This number is then keyed into a numeric keypad attached to the meter and the new reading is entered into the meter.

One final possibility is a personal visit by a Post Office representative but this is extremely costly for the Post Office to operate and is at the discretion of local postmasters. There will usually be some sort of handling charge for the service.

CHECKLIST

1 Office work is supported by a vast range of office equipment.

2 Modern typewriters possess many special features and it is important to carry out a thorough analysis of requirements before making any new investment.

3 It is possible to upgrade typewriters to word processors by adding screens and disk drives.

4 Word processors may be dedicated or non-dedicated.

5 Word processing systems may be stand alone or part of a shared system of some kind.

6 Word processor screens come in different sizes and there are a variety of possible colour combinations for the background and printing.

7 Printers are basically impact or non-impact.

8 Computers may be mainframe, mini or micro.

9 Hardware refers to the tangible physical equipment of a computer system, eg the circuits, disk drives, printers and VDUs.

10 Software is the generic name for the computer's operating program and is also frequently used to refer to application packages supplied by software houses.

11 Extensive software packages are available for micros or personal computers (PCs).

12 Compatibility factors are a major consideration, ie the application software must be compatible with the system software.

13 A range of input and output devices exists and selection will be largely determined by the types of application undertaken and the finance available.

14 An important aspect of any computer system is that of auxiliary storage or back-up facilities.

15 In selecting computing equipment organisations need to address many issues and satisfy the essential criteria they have identified.

16 Audio techniques for dictation and transcription are widely used and a varied range of systems and equipment is available.

17 All office personnel should be conversant with the operation of basic calculating equipment.

18 There is relatively little equipment associated with the processing of incoming mail but outgoing mail can be a highly automated activity.

19 Addressing machines *per se*, tend to have been largely superseded by advanced photocopying techniques or the application of computers and word processors.

20 Franking machines are used by most companies which need to process large volumes of mail.

QUICK REVISION QUESTIONS

1 Suggest eight typical features likely to be found on a modern electronic typewriter.
2 Distinguish between dedicated and non-dedicated word processors.
3 In what circumstances might a company opt for a dedicated system?
4 What do you understand by the term 'typewriter upgrade'?
5 What is the difference between shared logic and shared resource when describing WP configurations?
6 Name two types of non-impact printer.
7 Explain the difference between RAM and ROM.
8 Briefly explain the functions of two application packages commonly used on PCs.
9 When is a computer terminal referred to as 'dumb'?
10 Suggest two alternatives to a keyboard for inputting data to a computer.
11 What do the following abbreviations or acronyms stand for: CAD; COM; WYSIWYG; BASIC; OCR; LCD?
12 Name two alternative sources of output from a computer, other than a VDU.
13 Which offers higher density storage – a Winchester disk or an optical disk?
14 When selecting computer equipment indicate 10 things that you would consider.
15 What facilities would you expect to find included in an executive workstation?
16 What are the advantages of audio over shorthand?
17 Imagine that you have been asked to investigate the possible introduction of audio systems into your offices. What options are available in terms of systems and equipment and what advice would you give?

18 Without referring to a calculator can you provide a diagram giving the arrangement of the numbers and any other function keys? (Check your diagram for accuracy against a calculator!)
19 Suggest three items of equipment you would expect to find in an average mailing section.
20 What are the main advantages of franking machines?

9 Office environment

It is all very well to have a range of up-to-date equipment but it is equally important that working conditions are of a comparable standard. It is not so very long ago that office conditions were, on the whole, very poor indeed, with virtually no legislation to govern the environment. Yet it is unreasonable to expect a high level of office productivity unless conditions are good. Given that such a high proportion of workers now occupy office-based jobs, increasing attention has been given in recent years to office accommodation and facilities. Not only is it important to view offices in structural and economic terms but also in terms of the people who work there and the jobs they do.

At the end of this section you should be able to:

- compare and contrast different types of office layout;
- list the advantages and disadvantages of open plan offices;
- suggest what constitutes a good working environment;
- suggest criteria for the selection of desks and chairs;
- explain what is meant by systems furniture;
- consider different types of heating and lighting systems;
- appreciate the importance of adequate ventilation;
- identify factors which contribute to noise in an office;
- draw up a safety checklist for an office;
- identify possible security problems in an office;
- suggest ways in which security might be improved.

Office layout and design

A variety of different layouts will be found in offices today but they are still likely to fall into two broad categories, ie closed or cellular offices or some type of open plan. The former are based on the concept of staff occupying separate, sometimes even individual, offices and the work being transacted 'behind closed doors'. Offices may be

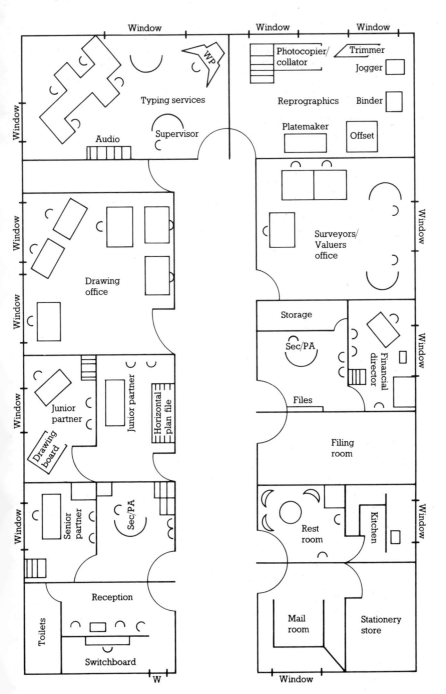

Fig. 9.1 A corridor office layout

229

entered from either a centrally located corridor (see Fig. 9.1) or from one running along one side of a building. Such arrangements have the following advantages:

- more privacy;
- persons occupying status positions are easily identifiable (eg names on doors, larger, better furnished rooms);
- improved security (individual offices may be locked);
- fewer distractions;
- the possibility exists to control one's own immediate environment in terms of heat, light and ventilation;
- isolation of noisy equipment;
- the ability to personalise one's surroundings.

However such layouts also have disadvantages, most of which would be seen from the point of view of management and which will include the following:

- difficulties of finding/making sufficient single rooms available for all those who need or request them;
- sharing may be unpopular;
- communication is less direct;
- supervision is more difficult;
- valuable space is taken up by corridors, walls, doors and radiators;
- the expense of providing individual items of equipment.

Open plan offices

The original concept of 'open plan' was simply to organise large numbers of workers in one large office rather than in shared or individual rooms. Early examples of open plan show very formal classroom-like rows of clerical workers and/or typists – sometimes very large numbers of them – working in the same huge office. Such arrangements were thought to have the following advantages:

- saving of space;
- better control and supervision;
- improved workflow;
- better organisation of repetitive tasks (the assembly line treatment);
- ease of adding an extra desk;
- more direct communication;
- more potential to share expensive equipment;
- easier cover in the event of absence.

However, they were extremely impersonal and, although they were inexpensive for management to set up, they were unpopular with staff who resented the lack of privacy and the over-close supervision as well as the difficulties of catering for individual preferences, and it was felt that the spread of infectious diseases was virtually unchecked.

Bürolandschaft

In the late 1950s studies were conducted by German consultants into maximising the use of office space while taking into consideration the needs of individual workers. They introduced the term 'Bürolandschaft' or 'office landscape' and applied it to the arrangement of groups of office workers involved in related activities occupying a vast area of office floor. These large schemes, sometimes referred to as 'panoramic office planning' could accommodate literally hundreds of people on a large-scale open plan layout.

Although large numbers were located on the same open floor, with their work areas set out in a random-looking arrangement, each work-station was carefully designed and positioned and it was considered important that every worker should be able to see daylight irrespective of where he was situated on the open floor.

Adapted open plan designs

Such huge open plans were not entirely successful and are now viewed as the dinosaurs of office layouts by architects and planners. However, ideas have not turned full circle back to closed offices but rather tended to adapt the 'Bürolandschaft' idea, resulting in smaller-scale open layouts which are both functional and attractive (see Fig. 9.2).

The emphasis of these new adapted layouts is on the sharing of facilities and accommodation. Much of this can be put down to the growth in office technology. While actual work space becomes smaller the support space (ie that taken up by sophisticated equipment) is growing. With the equipment comes the need for increased wiring and the added noise and general disruption that any item of equipment produces. All these facts make it unrealistic to operate in traditional open plan offices which were, after all, designed to achieve increased productivity in routine activities. Hence modern offices seek to strike an effective balance between the wide open spaces of the early German-style open offices and the cramped Dickensian conditions of many older-style corridor offices. The result is the provision of a working environment designed to support activities performed by a range of different office staff and tailor-made to suit their individual needs and requirements.

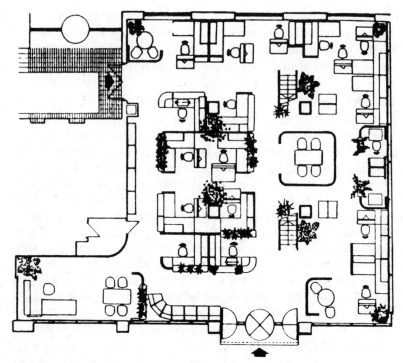

Fig. 9.2 A modern award-winning open plan office occupied by Building
Design Partnership in Sheffield

Such modern designs are a product of a systematic examination of
the space requirements of each worker in terms of the job he does,
the equipment and facilities he uses and the contact he has with
others. From this kind of information it is possible to work out
individual requirements for space and communications and then
translate these to an overall plan of the available area.

These design principles may be applied to floor areas of varying
shapes and sizes accommodating staff involved in a wide range of
activities. Irrespective of the scale of the project the points which a
designer would consider are:

- communication networks;
- types of heating, lighting and ventilation;
- provision of essential services, eg wiring, telephones;
- maximising the use of acoustic materials;
- positioning of desks (workstations) to avoid constant eye to eye
  confrontation;

- design of workstations;
- access to work areas;
- extent of privacy required;
- location of machinery and shared equipment;
- servicing of facilities and equipment;
- location of meeting areas;
- reception areas for visitors;
- inclusion of rest and refreshment facilities;
- siting of storage facilities;
- location of toilets;
- allocation of 'free' space;
- inclusion of planters and other natural foliage.

Consequently the end result of such a design is a 'total concept' – something carefully thought out and planned from start to finish. It is not haphazard. It is designed in an attempt to make office work as efficient and effective as possible but with the interests of people in mind. Office staff will, therefore, benefit from such layouts in a variety of ways. Their need for privacy will be respected by the introduction of sufficient acoustic screening and foliage, and at the same time any feelings of isolation and non-involvement will be prevented. Workers whose job contents are closely related can get together more easily without moving from the comfort and convenience of their own work areas. The provision of amenities such as rest areas and refreshment facilities also dispenses with rigid tea and coffee breaks and studies suggest that this actually increases productivity rather than exploitation of the new freedom and the consequent wasting of time which might be envisaged. Environmental conditions generally will tend to be superior with special attention given to the provision of adequate and suitable lighting, heating and ventilation coupled with high quality furnishings and decor throughout.

This type of office environment also has advantages from the point of view of management, which will benefit as follows:

- maximum flexibility is ensured in that individuals, sections or departments may be easily moved around;
- layout is adaptable to changes in emphasis either within the organisation structure or in the orientation of the business enterprise;
- 'team spirit' is more easily achieved;
- working relationships tend to be improved as a result of the greater accessibility of colleagues;
- staff benefit from the installation of expensive equipment which could not be justified unless shared;

- status consciousness is less prevalent within the staff as everyone shares similar accommodation and facilities;
- discipline and general standards of behaviour tend to improve in that there is pressure to conform with those around;
- furniture and fittings are of superior quality in that there is frequently a tendency to standardise at a high level;
- the sort of reception area which is essential to this type of design, viz one which is conducive to receiving guests in an area of comfort and style, creates a very favourable first impression.

Office decor and furniture

The attention that is given to office layout necessitates consideration being given to decor and furniture as well. This is only reasonable when we consider that office workers spend half their waking lives at work. Design specialists and furniture manufacturers and suppliers have grown in number and there is a wide variety to choose from.

Just as colour schemes and fashions change within the home so, too, in offices, but basically it will be a matter of selecting things which are pleasant on the eye, comfortable and yet practical and business-like. In terms of colour most offices tend to opt for muted shades which are acceptable to most people and which are likely to cause the minimum of visual distraction or disturbance. The aim is to achieve a pleasant blend of paintwork, fabrics, floor coverings and furniture which reflects the image of the company.

Carpets are an important feature of most modern offices in that they help absorb sound, prevent heat loss and generally add to comfort. Colours, designs and textures will be selected with care both to blend with the overall scheme and be sufficiently hardwearing and easily cleaned.

Furniture

The type of furniture selected depends to a large extent on the type of layout together with the nature of the work undertaken and the finance available. Other important considerations are ergonomic and anthropometric ones.

Ergonomics, according to *The Concise Oxford Dictionary* is the 'study of efficiency of persons in their working environment' while **anthropometry** is concerned with 'measurement of the human body'.

Therefore, careful studies are performed to see that all office furniture is designed to ensure the comfort and efficiency of the user.

Chairs, for example, should be the correct height for the type of work being done. They should be fully adjustable, provide adequate back and/or arm support, have sufficient depth of cushioning, be capable of swivelling and/or tilting as required and possibly have fitted castors for ease of movement. A comfortable chair is of vital importance to a sedentary worker and although many modern office chairs are costly the investment will be more than justified. An example of an ergonomically designed chair for a clerical workstation is given as Fig. 9.3.

Desks are also important and need to be considered in terms of the following:

- shape and height;
- type of work;
- size of the worktop and amount of overlap;
- knee clearance;
- drawer space and whether locking is necessary;
- whether single or double pedestal and if single whether right- or left-hand fitted drawers;
- the finish, eg wood, veneer, metal, plastic;
- freestanding or panel-hung, ie part of a workstation;

Fig. 9.3 An ergonomically designed chair at a clerical workstation
(*By courtesy of Project Office Furniture plc*)

Fig. 9.4 'C' frame furniture
(*By courtesy of Project Office Furniture plc*)

- with a 'C-frame' (see Fig. 9.4) rather than the traditional four vertical legs, ie a cantilever construction, usually associated with systems desking and designed both to look smart and to make it easy to move in and out of the desk area;
- whether it has a secondary worktop at right angles to the main desk surface – referred to in the trade as 'pedestal return';
- weight and mobility;
- continuity of supply, ie the knowledge that the design selected will be available for some time to come.

Systems furniture

Initial attempts at the Bürolandschaft concept utilised freestanding desks and standard fittings plus perhaps the introduction of portable screens and plants to create a more pleasant atmosphere. However, it soon became clear that, if better use were to be made of available space to produce a more efficient environment, then special furniture was needed and so came the birth of systems furniture as we know it today (see Fig. 9.5).

Fig. 9.5 Systems furniture
(*By courtesy of Project Office Furniture plc*)

As the term suggests systems furniture is more than matching desks, chairs and storage units. It is a total concept of specially designed and co-ordinated furniture components which when assembled together make the best use of valuable floorspace while ensuring maximum flexibility. In open plan offices in particular a lot of space above desk height can be wasted. Although office rates are calculated on the basis of square feet or metres, total space is measured according to cubic proportions, and it makes strong economic sense to attempt to utilise some of the space above desk height.

Systems furniture enables individual workstations to be created, tailor-made to the user. For example the workstation may be built up of a selection of screens, work surfaces and storage compartments geared to the particular user and his work. Shelving can be attached to the screen to accommodate books and files, work surfaces can be of different heights, eg lowered wells to accommodate electronic keyboards, and a selection of mobile storage units of different widths and internal fittings can be designed to slide neatly under the work surfaces. An example of a secretary's workstation set up with systems furniture is given as Fig. 9.6.

Workstations may then be linked together in a variety of ways so

Fig. 9.6 A secretarial workstation designed with systems furniture
(*By courtesy of Project Office Furniture plc*)

ensuring great adaptability and versatility. All sorts of configurations are possible using systems furniture and many useful optional accessories are available in a wide range of co-ordinated colours and materials.

Wire management

While systems furniture really came into its own with open planning there was also a need to handle the proliferation of cables and wires associated with sophisticated office equipment. Sometimes referred to as 'cable management' this refers to the facility to accommodate all such wires and cables, viz telephone wires, computer cabling etc, within special channels designed as part of systems furniture. Not only is loose cabling of any kind unsightly but it also represents a particular safety hazard in a busy office. Therefore wire management enables all the cables and wires to travel unobtrusively through the furniture (see Fig. 9.7) in that all sockets are countersunk and out of sight with access via traps in the channelling all of which forms an integral part of the workstation.

Computer aided design (CAD)

It is perhaps interesting to note that office design, layouts and associated planning problems have been greatly alleviated by the application of computer aided design (CAD) techniques. These enable

238

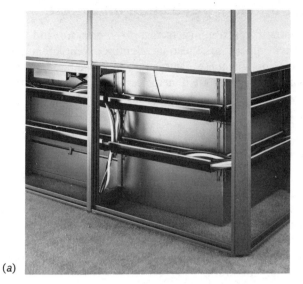

(a)

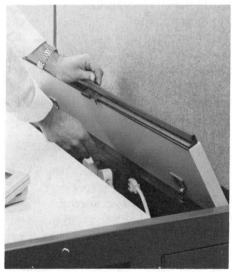

(b)

Fig. 9.7 Wire management
(By courtesy of Project Office Furniture plc)

designs to be drawn, specifications and schedules to be updated and problems and new situations to be responded to quickly and economically using a computer.

Heating, lighting, ventilation and noise

Other important contributory factors to a pleasant and productive working environment are heating, lighting, ventilation and noise reduction. Although these factors are not visible indicators like furniture and decor, they are nonetheless significant in that they affect the quality and comfort of the working environment as well as the morale of the staff.

Heating

According to the Offices, Shops and Railway Premises Act, 1963, offices should have reached a temperature of 16 °C within the first hour of work to be considered reasonable. Like of lot of legislation the word 'reasonable' is not easy to define, but most office workers would tend to agree that 16 °C is still rather low and that a more comfortable temperature would be nearer 21.1 °C given that much of office work is of a sedentary nature.

From the point of view of management, trying to provide heating that is acceptable to all members of staff is no easy task. Individual preferences inevitably vary, and in terms of the degree of control which can be exercised over many systems this can often be very difficult throughout a large building where some parts may seem too hot while others are relatively cool. Variations will occur dependent upon the siting of offices in respect of sunlight and prevailing winds, and of course many modern buildings have a lot of glass which can render offices like greenhouses in summer and iceboxes in winter.

Basically heating options will be by gas, oil or electricity but consideration will need to be given to:

- size and type of building;
- whether there is sole or shared occupancy;
- the need for a back-up facility;
- how flexible and responsive the system is in terms of controlling the temperature;
- safety features;
- installation, running and maintenance costs;
- availability of supplies and back-up support;
- potential to update or upgrade the system;
- the space taken up by boilers, pipes and radiators;
- the appearance of the system;
- the cleanliness of the system;
- its overall suitability to the needs of the office.

Lighting

Lighting too has its problems, although in legislative terms the guide-lines laid down are even less specific, viz that it should be 'suitable and sufficient' and many organisations may wish to seek expert advice in terms of their lighting.

While natural light is always to be recommended, most modern offices rely on supplementary lighting to some extent. The type of supplementary light required will depend on:

- the type, size and style of building;
- the level of natural light available;
- the nature of the work undertaken;
- the age of the workforce;
- the use of equipment, including VDUs;
- the degree of reflection or shadow present;
- the colour and texture of wall coverings and furniture;
- the existence of curtains or blinds;
- the level of maintenance and cleaning available.

Ventilation and humidity

Adequate ventilation is also important and this can be ensured by anything from opening windows, using extractor fans and air cleaning equipment to installing full-scale air conditioning. The last of these alternatives will often be preferred in city centres, particularly, where noise, dirt and pollution from outside make it impractical to rely on opening windows. Six air changes per hour are recommended to ensure maximum comfort and high productivity, while helping to reduce the spread of disease.

As well as poor ventilation the dryness of the atmosphere can produce problems. Many offices provide humidifiers which expel moist air and help counteract the drying factors brought about by central heating. Humidifiers also help reduce static electricity generated by certain synthetic materials found in offices, eg many types of carpet.

Noise

A final environmental consideration worthy of mention is noise. Society is bombarded by noise more than ever before from all directions and sources. In offices noise, which is measured in decibels, will come both from outside and within the building. Noise reduction and control are, therefore, important issues which need to be addressed if good working conditions are to be achieved. Some of the more obvious things which will have a bearing on noise will be:

- the location of the building;
- the general nature of a company's business, eg the amount of people coming in from outside;
- the layout of departments;
- the size and glazing of windows;
- the number of doors and whether they are fitted with non-slam hinges;
- the types of acoustic materials and the level of soundproofing employed;
- the siting of noisy equipment;
- the number of telephones.

White noise

One interesting thing which some organisations have experimented with is what is termed 'white noise'. This is background noise channelled through ducts above ceiling level, and designed to mask general conversation and noise from machines. You may also have noticed the use of background music in lifts and sometimes over the telephone while you are waiting to be connected.

Facilities management

This is the term used to describe that area of management activity specially concerned with the total provision of all facilities within a building – heating, lighting, ventilation, communications, furnishings, fittings and equipment. It is the Facilities Management Group of the Institute of Administrative Management (IAM) which organises the bi-annual competition for the 'Office of the Year Award'.

Safety in the office

All organisations have a statutory obligation under the Health and Safety at Work, etc Act, 1974 (see Appendix 1) to produce a health and safety document for publication or issue to employees. Such a document sets out the company rules, regulations and procedures in respect of safety practices within the working environment and will be likely to include:

- some sort of general statement of intent on behalf of the organisation acknowledging its desire to promote the interests of health and safety and operate within the spirit of the Act;

- an acknowledgement of the responsibility of the company as a legal entity in respect of safety matters, but emphasising the need for company-wide involvement and recognition by all employees of their personal duties and responsibilities with regard to health and safety;
- a reporting mechanism for accidents or injuries;
- the location of the first aid box and accident book;
- a statement of procedures in respect of the provision of safety training;
- a code of safe working practices, broken into different areas of work, including the office;
- where and from whom advice on safety matters can be sought;
- details of the roles and duties of official safety representatives;
- the name of the executive responsible for ensuring that the policy is fulfilled.

The Health and Safety at Work, etc Act can be enforced by local environmental health officers who are at liberty to visit and inspect office premises at any time.

Office safety factors

Offices like any other work areas, have their own types of hazard and special attention should be given to the following:

- the building, its layout and facilities;
- entrances, corridors, lifts and staircases;
- doors, including the need to keep firedoors closed;
- the opening and closing of windows;
- the provision of adequate lighting;
- ensuring unobstructed gangways;
- qualified installation, maintenance and servicing of electrical appliances;
- proper training in safety procedures and in the use of equipment;
- the provision of stepladders and trolleys;
- the display of warning notices on faulty equipment or other potential hazards;
- the arrangement of furniture to facilitate workflow but minimise the likelihood of collisions;
- the elimination of trailing wires of any kind;
- correct storage procedures for flammable liquids and other dangerous materials;
- proper guards on all equipment;
- training for staff in the use of fire extinguishers;

- regular equipment checks, including fire extinguishers;
- the elimination of horseplay and practical joking in the office;
- total familiarity of staff with the fire alarm evacuation procedure.

Security

Security within offices has become increasingly important in recent years for two principal reasons. Not only have break-ins become more prevalent with thieves recognising the value of technological equipment, but the potential to be gained from acquiring information and using it elsewhere cannot be ignored. The former is largely a question of ensuring the physical security of property but the latter – the security of information – is a more complex matter, covering such things as breaches of company security and industrial espionage which might involve anything from the theft of a company's designs, its R & D plant, its client lists or even its wage rates.

Security is a total concept and something which needs to be reflected throughout an organisation from the design stage. It is a particularly vital design feature in new buildings where there is multiple occupancy as it can be relatively easy for anyone to walk in from the street and literally disappear either up the stairs or into the lifts. A large proportion of office crime and theft is of the 'walk-in variety' rather than specific planned break-ins. In existing buildings security measures need to be introduced to minimise problems and staff need to be aware of the procedures in operation.

Periodically organisations will review their security arrangements and undertake what is termed 'risk management' (see also p 87) which is an exercise designed to identify, evaluate and judge potential areas of risk. In short it explores the costs of alternative means of protecting an organisation from chance losses. Such an exercise will be likely to examine ways in which security risks could be avoided or reduced and the types of thing which are likely to be considered are:

- access potential and car parking arrangements;
- the roles of the gatehouse, commissionnaire and reception staff;
- the use of security personnel and agencies;
- alarm systems;
- guard dogs;
- closed-circuit television (CCTV);
- the vetting of staff;
- the issue and control of keys, particularly master copies;
- alternatives to keys, eg the use of code numbers;
- the introduction of identity cards and visitor's badges;

- restricted access areas;
- restricted handling of confidential information;
- frequent audits of computer systems and users;
- the introduction and frequent changing of computer passwords.

At the more attitudinal and procedural levels individual office staff need to be encouraged to be more security conscious and generally more vigilant as well as introducing personal security safeguards which will minimise unintended 'leaks' of information. The types of thing individual staff can do include:

- being alert;
- being prepared to challenge strangers;
- being tidy;
- locking away all confidential papers;
- destroying, preferably by shredding, all confidential documents that are no longer needed;
- taking extra care when photocopying, not to leave originals in the flat bed of the photocopier;
- introducing coding systems as appropriate, eg when indexing files and disks;
- noting the serial numbers of all machines and equipment and marking with indelible ink or a special marker that can only be read under ultra-violet light;
- escorting visitors to the premises at all times;
- taking extra care when telephoning;
- avoiding idle gossip;
- marking confidential papers accordingly;
- using appropriate messenger services as required.

CHECKLIST

1 The conditions in which office work is carried out have received increasing attention in recent years.

2 Layouts fall into two main general categories, viz closed or open plan.

3 Open plan arrangements tend to offer certain advantages, particularly from a management perspective, in terms of economies, improved workflow and communication and better control, but careful design principles need to be applied.

4 Office decor and furniture are growth areas and a wide range of schemes and designs is available.

5   Increased attention is given to ergonomic considerations in the selection of office furniture.

6   The use of systems furniture increased with the tendency towards open plan.

7   The increased reliance on electrical and electronic equipment brought with it an array of cables and wires into offices and furniture specialists introduced what they term 'wire management' to accommodate this.

8   As well as furniture and fittings, offices need to give attention to heating, lighting, ventilation and noise.

9   The main piece of legislation in respect of health and safety in offices is the Health and Safety at Work, etc Act, 1974.

10 Security has become an increasing problem for offices, both in terms of the physical security of tangible items from theft, break-ins and vandalism and from the point of view of the security and confidentiality afforded to information, which is a valuable commodity.

QUICK REVISION QUESTIONS

1   What are the advantages of individual offices opening onto a corridor?
2   What do you understand by the term 'Bürolandschaft'?
3   List six factors which need to be taken into consideration when designing an open plan layout.
4   What are the advantages of open plan?
5   What factors would you consider when selecting a chair?
6   According to the Offices, Shops and Railway Premises Act, 1963 what temperature should be reached in offices after 1 hour?
7   What do you understand by the term 'white noise'?
8   Assume that you are going to give a talk on Office Safety during an Induction Programme for new office staff. Draft a list of the points you would include.
9   Where do you consider the main security risks are likely to be in a large company?
10 As a secretary, what could you do to minimise risk and maintain confidentiality in your immediate working environment?

10 Office personnel

Any organisation is only as good as its staff who represent the most valuable resource it has. Therefore all personnel matters are of the utmost importance if there is to be a reliable, efficient and productive workforce. Office staff form a substantial proportion of any workforce and it is to their recruitment, selection, training, development and appraisal that this section now turns.

At the end of this section you should be able to:

- identify the principal categories of office personnel;
- describe their duties and responsibilities;
- appreciate the significance of sound recruitment and selection procedures;
- draw up job descriptions;
- prepare suitable advertisements for insertion in the press;
- design and complete a job application form;
- prepare your own curriculum vitae;
- describe typical interview procedures;
- appreciate the preparations an interviewee needs to make;
- outline the procedure for making an appointment;
- identify the legislation which needs to be observed;
- identify different types of training;
- devise a simple training programme;
- appreciate the purpose of appraisal;
- suggest possible appraisal techniques which might be used to assess office workers.

Categories of office personnel

The job titles and grading systems applied to office personnel in different organisations will vary but they will tend to fall into the categories identified in Table 10.1 which also briefly outlines the

Table 10.1 Typology of office personnel

Job title	*Duties and responsibilities*	*Qualities, qualifications and experience necessary*
Office Manager or Senior Administrative Officer	Be responsible for the overall direction of the office; Direct and control the work of the office; Supervise office staff; Organise the office to maximise efficiency; Devise systems and procedures; Select office equipment; Delegate duties among staff; Identify training needs; Communicate management policy; Handle staff problems; Motivate and encourage staff; Offer advice to junior personnel; Ensure a healthy, safe and pleasant working environment.	Good general education; Administrative Management training – a professional qualification in Admin. Management would be a bonus, eg MIAM; A good communicator; Leadership skills; A team builder; Experience appropriate to the job.
Personal Assistant (PA) or Executive Secretary	Full secretarial support for executive at director level; Supervision of junior staff; Deputising for superior. (See Unit 2 for full details)	Good general education; High level of secretarial and communication skills; Organisational ability; LCCI, or RSA Diploma for Executive Secretaries or Personal Assistants or a degree plus perhaps a post-graduate qualification.
Senior Secretary/PA	Full range of secretarial support for one (or more) executives at top management level ie Head of Department or Principal Officer	Good education; Excellent secretarial and communication skills; Sound secretarial qualifications of an advanced level.
Secretary	Full range of secretarial support for middle management	as above but secretarial qualifications at Intermediate level, eg LCCI, PSC.

Table 10.1 (*cont'd*)

Job title	Duties and responsibilities	Qualities, qualifications and experience necessary
Junior Secretary	Secretarial support for supervisory level staff, possibly operating as a team or group secretary	Good education and good all-round secretarial and English language skills; possibly a college/school leaver.
Shorthand-Typist	Taking shorthand dictation and transcribing onto a typewriter. Often a member of the Secretarial Services Division or Support Unit providing services for any staff without access to a secretary.	Good general educaton; Sound English skills; Good shorthand and typing, preferably with a Shorthand-typist's certificate; Flexible attitude; High standards; Minimum need for supervision.
Audio-Typist	Preparation of material from audio dictation, again possibly based in a centralised unit. General office duties.	As for Shorthand-typist but substituting audio for shorthand; The ability to operate more by 'remote control'.
Copy Typist	Preparation of typewritten material from draft longhand notes. General office duties.	Fast, accurate typing; The ability to decipher poor handwriting; Good layout and presentation skills; High level of concentration; Preparedness to undertake routine, repetitive work.
Secretarial Services Supervisor	Scheduling and co-ordination of work undertaken by the unit or department. Prioritising work submitted. Responsible for allocating work, setting standards, advising on preparation, monitoring progress, evaluating and checking results.	A proven background in secretarial work, displaying competence in all essential skills. Excellent communication and people skills. Good organisational ability. Sound judgement. Ability to inspire

Table 10.1 (*cont'd*)

Job title	Duties and responsibilities	Qualities, qualifications and experience necessary
	Liaising with staff requesting the service. Selection of staff. Identifying strengths and weaknesses. Providing training or arranging for it.	confidence in others and to cope under pressure. High degree of professionalism. Attention to detail. Some supervisory training.
Word Processing Supervisor	Similar to those of a Secretarial Services Supervisor but with the emphasis on word processing. Possibly a slightly greater need for an awareness of the working environment, eg ergonomic factors, health considerations when working with VDUs. The maintenance of an up-to-date knowledge of the office equipment market in terms of new technology in order to advise on the change and purchase of new systems.	As per the Secretarial Services Supervisor but additionally someone who enjoys working with office technology and is aware of the need to provide value for money by ensuring a high level of productivity in return for the high level of investment in capital equipment.
Word Processor Operator	The preparation of text from longhand, shorthand or audio. Text editing functions. Data storage and retrieval. General housekeeping associated with word processing.	In addition to a good general education and office communication skills, knowledge and experience of word processing, possibly with a formal qualification in WP. High level of concentration. Prepared to work alone with minimum supervision. Spatial awareness for layout. Logical thinking. Good proofreading. Flexibility to learn new

Table 10.1 (*cont'd*)

Job title	*Duties and responsibilities*	*Qualities, qualifications and experience necessary*
		systems or change from one to another. A feel for machines.
Clerks	A range of administrative duties, according to grade and specific job description, eg completion of returns, general record keeping and file maintenance, processing of all standard paperwork. Perhaps some supervisory and training responsibilities in respect of juniors.	Good general education. Competence in English language. Competence with figures. Familiarity with standard office systems and procedures. Systematic and meticulous.
Office Junior	General office duties as instructed by superiors.	Good basic education. Interest in office work.
Receptionist	Greet and receive all visitors. Act as the 'link' person – the first contact with the outside world. Employ screening procedures as necessary. Liaise with security personnel. Entertain guests when required. Receive hand-delivered letters, packets and parcels. Maintain a visitors book. Issue identity badges. Liaise with office staff re the escort of visitors.	Good general education. Excellent communication skills. Pleasant, welcoming and warm personality. Good appearance. Accomplished in 'small talk'. Good memory for names and faces. Well organised. Perhaps a qualification in Reception Duties.
Telephonist	Receipt and routing of incoming calls. Placing calls at request of staff. Monitoring and logging calls as required. Training relief operators.	Clear, pleasant voice. Plenty of patience and tact. Helpful and organised. Good memory, unflappable and quick thinking. Good with technological equipment. Post Office training a bonus.

duties and responsibilities and the qualities, qualifications and experience sought.

Recruitment and selection

These are the areas most readily associated with the Personnel Department of any organisation in that they are directly concerned with the identification of vacancies and of filling them with appropriate staff. During times of high unemployment there will be fewer vacancies but conversely there will frequently be more applicants for all available positions and so, while actual recruitment is relatively low profile, the selection element will require a lot of careful attention in order to secure the right candidates for jobs.

Vacancies may arise for various reasons, including any of the following:

* retirement;
* promotion;
* resignation;
* dismissal;
* increased workload;
* creation of a new post.

How a vacancy is advertised will be largely dependent upon company policy, eg some organisations will always advertise internally in the first instance (this is thought to be good for staff morale), whereas others are legally bound to advertise outside, possibly even nationally. Other possibilities will include:

* going through existing files of unsolicited applications;
* putting the position in the hands of a Job Centre or an employment bureau;
* direct contact with local educational establishments;
* contact with professional bodies;
* advertising in specialist journals;
* using local radio;
* by word of mouth or personal contact.

Advertising vacancies

Where a job is to be advertised it is essential that a suitable advertisement is prepared. A selection of typical secretarial advertisements is given in Section 11 p. 283. Basically a good advertisement should make reference to the following:

- job title;
- details of the job;
- necessary qualifications;
- essential requirements of the person sought (skills, experience and abilities);
- nature of the organisation's business;
- location;
- grade and/or salary details;
- how prospective candidates should apply;
- closing date for applications (where applicable).

Different styles are used for different purposes and by companies which wish to project different images, but all advertisements should aim to attract attention, stimulate interest and ensure quick responses from suitable applicants. It is also important that the framing of any advertisement should take into account the law in respect of racial and sex discrimination.

Job details

Advertisements will frequently be prepared from job descriptions and specifications. The former provides details of title, grade, location (if relevant), purpose, main duties and responsibilities, specific duties, position within the organisation's structure, ie to whom responsible and for whom responsible (if relevant), working environment, training opportunities and conditions of employment. The latter identifies particular knowledge, skills and attitudes which are required to perform the job effectively. Detailed job specifications analyse each associated task separately in respect of knowledge required. They may also state minimum qualifications and levels of skill sought as well as providing an indication of previous experience which would be considered desirable. An example of a job description is given as Fig. 10.1.

Application forms and CVs

Many organisations adopt a standard application form which will be sent to all applicants together with job details while others will ask candidates to send a copy of their curriculum vitae or CV, often together with a letter in support of their application.

Either way it is important that the information is completed fully, neatly and accurately, taking special care to comply with any specific requests, eg to complete the form in black ink or using a typewriter (this is so that the form may be photocopied and circulated to

JOB DESCRIPTION	
Title	Secretary
Department	Personnel (12 staff)
Location	Head Office – Central London
Responsible to	Senior Personnel Officer
Responsible for	Office Junior and YTS trainee
Job Summary	Full secretarial support for Senior Personnel Officer
Essential Education	Good general education to 'A' level; Secretarial Studies to at least Intermediate level, eg LCCI PSC
Hours of Work	37-hour week (Flexitime in operation)
Scale	3
Salary	scp's 17–2 + ILWA

Main duties and responsibilities

1 To undertake secretarial and administrative duties as requested by the Senior Personnel Officer.
2 To liaise effectively, by telephone, with staff from regional offices and deal with personnel queries from the public.
3 To set up and maintain necessary filing and record systems.
4 To undertake secretarial and administrative duties for the internal and external advertising of vacancies.
5 To organise and document selection interview panels.
6 To prepare and distribute agreed agendas for Job Evaluation Panels and undertake any necessary follow up.
7 To supervise the Office Junior and YTS trainee.
8 To train other staff in the operation of the word processor.

Fig. 10.1 Specimen job description

members of an interview panel) or to reply in your own handwriting. A typical application form is provided as Fig. 10.2.

Where you are relying on a CV this does provide a good opportunity to demonstrate your typing and presentation skills. You should endeavour to keep CVs brief, supplying only essential information. The sections included in Fig. 10.2 provide good guidelines for what to include. Some organisations go as far as to suggest that one side of A4 is the optimum length of a CV, and indeed where you can adequately display the necessary detail on one sheet this is to be recommended. However, if you have a lot of information to include two sides of A4 is perfectly acceptable.

APPLICATION FOR EMPLOYMENT		

Vacancy ....

SURNAME (block letters)	FORENAMES
	Mr/Ms

ADDRESS

Tel no

Age last birthday	Date of birth	Nationality Place of birth	If registered under Disabled Persons (Employment) Act YES/NO

EDUCATION Schools attended	From	To	Examinations passed (state subject, board, level and grade attained)
Colleges, university attended			Qualifications attained
Training courses attended			

Membership of professional or other similar associations

Hobbies/sports/other interests

(a)

Fig. 10.2   Specimen application form

255

DETAILS OF PREVIOUS EMPLOYMENT (Please commence by stating your present employment first. Use an additional sheet if required)

Name and address of employer	From	To	Brief description of duties

Earliest date at which you could take up this appointment	Present salary
	£ per annum

Names and addresses of *two* persons to whom reference may be made in relation to your experience and suitability for this post

ADDITIONAL INFORMATION in support of your application. You may continue on a separate sheet if necessary

Signature	Date

(*b*)

Fig. 10.2   Specimen application form (cont'd)

Accompanying letters

Where you have completed a formal application there will usually be a space for additional information or details you wish to add in support of your application, and it is essential that you use this space for that purpose rather than ramble on in a covering letter. However, where you have been asked to submit a CV you will need to sell yourself, in the hope of securing an interview, in your covering letter or in additional information sheets. Here also, it is preferable to be cogent but concise. Remember that your application may be one of hundreds.

It should be sufficient to write three main paragraphs in a letter – one an introductory one indicating how you learnt about the vacancy and signifying your intention to apply, a paragraph (or perhaps two) outlining why you think you are suitable for the post and what contribution you feel you could make to the company if appointed (you can often refer the reader to your CV within the body of your letter to substantiate what you say here), and a final paragraph indicating when you could be available for interview if shortlisted. It is unnecessary to add anything else and you should certainly not close with an ungrammatical statement such as 'Hoping to hear from you.'

Shortlisting

Good advertisements should bring plenty of applications and once all are received by an organisation they are thoroughly scrutinised and a shortlist is drawn up of the most likely candidates, ie those who best fit the job details and who have submitted the best applications and/or CVs. These candidates are then invited for interview.

Incidentally it is preferable at this stage to notify unsuccessful candidates who have not been selected for interview, rather than wait until the end of the entire interview and selection process. However, with the large numbers of applicants now applying for many jobs it is quite usual for applicants to hear nothing further unless they are called for interview.

References

Sometimes references are taken up at this point in the proceedings, while on other occasions an appointment may be made conditional upon the receipt of satisfactory references. Either way, the idea behind requesting references is to provide an extra dimension on the candidate. Referees are sent job details and are sometimes asked to answer very specific questions in relation to the candidate's abilities, personality, integrity, health record and general suitability for the job.

References are usually supplied 'in confidence', but with the changes in data protection legislation some organisations will permit staff to have access to certain data in personal files (this would certainly be the case with data held on computer), and it is important to seek clarification on such matters if there is any cause for doubt that a reference will be treated as 'confidential'.

Testimonials

A testimonial is a general statement, testifying to the character, integrity and professional competence of an individual. It is often supplied when someone leaves a position, and is usually made out 'To whom it may concern'.

The interview process

Interviewing is a two-way process designed to fill in the gaps between the application or CV and the job description. The prospective employer attempts to determine the suitability of the candidate for the job and the interviewee has the opportunity of learning more about the vacancy, deciding whether it really appeals and, if so, selling himself or herself to the company as the right person for the job.

Interviews are never easy situations for either party in that they are somewhat artificial social encounters with a lot hinging on a relatively short space of time. Nonetheless, both parties can take certain steps to ensure that they secure the maximum from an interview.

Company preparations

Once a shortlist has been drawn up candidates will be informed of the date, time and venue for the interview, together with any other arrangements that have been included, eg preliminary talks, tours of the organisation, tests to be undertaken. It is important that candidates are sent comprehensive details of the way in which the day, or sometimes more than one day, is to be organised, so that they are in no doubt as to the format. Included with the information will be details of how to get to the venue (often a location map is provided), as well as the name and extension number of a person to contact should there be any problems.

Sometimes all candidates will be interviewed on the same day and there may even be a preliminary group interview when all candidates are seen together. Alternatively candidates may be called for interview over a period of days and so may never come into contact with one another. Either way, the company needs to make sure that its arrangements are adequate.

Reception needs to be made aware of the candidates expected, so that they may be welcomed and directed to the appropriate area of the building for the interview. Staff involved in the interview process need to be made aware of the times scheduled and of their particular roles, eg what sort of questions they will ask, what sort of information they need to have available in response to questions from candidates, what materials are needed for any tests to be carried out. Additionally there will be arrangements to make in respect of the waiting area and any refreshments which are to be served.

The interview room itself needs to be organised. This is important in that the wrong environment will not help the candidate to relax and it may be difficult to get the best out of an interview where, for example, there are a lot of interruptions or where the room is uncomfortable in terms of the seating arrangements or in that it is too cold or too warm, with perhaps too much strong sunlight shining into the eyes of the participants.

Panel interviews

One other feature worth mentioning is the panel interview. This is much more common these days, particularly where the successful candidate will be required to work as part of a team and where it is considered important to judge an interviewee's performance in responding to a range of questions presented by a variety of different people. The resultant cross-section of opinion can be useful in reaching a balanced decision.

Panel members will have received photocopies of all candidates' application forms and/or CVs in advance of the interview and having studied them will be in a position to suggest questions which they would like to raise during the actual interview. Members of a panel interview will usually have a briefing meeting before the interviews take place in order to determine the order of events, the role each panel member will adopt and the questions which each will put.

All interviews need to be well structured, but in the case of a panel interview close attention to structure will be even more vital, otherwise a candidate may feel totally confused by being bombarded by questions from all directions. The person chairing the interview panel is responsible for ensuring that after the necessary preliminaries have been dealt with the interview proceeds along logical, predetermined and agreed lines.

Legal aspects

It is also the responsibility of the person carrying out or chairing a selection interview to ensure that no questions are posed which contravene any relevant employment legislation. The main pieces of legislation in this respect are the Equal Pay Act 1970, the Sex Discrimination Act 1975 and the Race Relations Act 1976.

During interviews it may also be that other aspects of employment legislation are encountered and so it is important that the interviewer or a member of the panel (often a representative from the personnel department) is able to refer as necessary to the relevant Employment or Trade Union Acts. Since the early 1970s there have been numerous pieces of legislation, some of which amended or consolidated information set down earlier, so it is important that accurate interpretations are placed on any legal aspects raised at interview.

Candidate preparations

While it will be virtually impossible to predetermine the format and conduct of any interview, candidates can take certain steps to ensure that they are as well prepared as possible and that they are best able to do themselves justice.

Preparations will include things like being sure about where and when the interview is to take place and that sufficient time (taking account of possible unexpected delays) is allowed to arrive at the destination with time to spare. A trial run never goes wrong here. Attention should also be given to general appearance, bearing in mind the importance of first impressions.

Also there is usually a certain amount of advance research which can be undertaken in an attempt to find out a bit more about the organisation before the interview. Sometimes company literature will have been included with the job details and if so time should be spent reading it through. Where no information is included it is worth undertaking a little personal research, by asking around, reading up about the company – in the library perhaps – or trying to obtain copies of company newsletters or information sheets. One note of caution, however – research should not result in the interviewer feeling that he is being lectured by the interviewee on the successes and achievements of his own company! All this does is prove that the interviewee has done his homework and has a retentive memory for facts. As with most things it will be a matter of striking an effective balance by showing a level of awareness and interest, without going 'over the top'.

Questions

In general the best advice to candidates on how to respond to questions is to listen carefully and to take time in replying. Straight monosyllabic 'Yes/No' replies may be what is required to certain direct questions, but usually it will be necessary to expand a little.

Interviewers can put questions in a variety of different ways, all aimed at bringing the interviewee out and enabling him/her to demonstrate knowledge, express opinion, exercise judgement and demonstrate assertiveness, tact, aggression, discretion (or any other quality sought in a candidate). It is useful to watch television interviews to assess how successful the participants are in achieving their objectives.

One difficult thing in any interview can be when the interviewee is given the opportunity to ask questions. As was mentioned earlier, interviewing is a two-way process and it is only reasonable to expect that an interviewee may have questions. However, even given that most people attending interviews will have given thought to possible questions they can ask if given the opportunity, when the time comes they frequently experience difficulty in thinking of anything. Whether there are any questions and of what type they are will depend to a large extent on how the interview has been conducted and on how forthcoming the interviewer has been in providing information as the interview progressed. Where a candidate does have a question (or questions) the opportunity should certainly not be passed over.

Assessment forms

Where a large number of candidates are interviewed some kind of interview assessment form may be used to provide a profile of each candidate. Such a device can help remind panel members of particular attributes or qualities identified or lacking in individual candidates, as well as helping to ensure that all aspects have been sufficiently probed during the interviews. All interviews are bound to be largely subjective, but the use of an assessment form can be helpful in providing structure to the proceedings. Also where used in panel interviews they can help in reaching a group decision.

Assessments can be made on either numerical or alphabetical gradings and would be likely to cover a range of job-related aspects including the following:

- educational background;
- qualifications;
- training;

- relevant experience;
- communication skills;
- other essential skills (these would be listed according to the requirements of the job);
- appearance;
- self-confidence;
- personality;
- facial expression;
- courtesy and manners;
- attitudes;
- interest in the position;
- awareness of the company and its objectives;
- general knowledge;
- preparedness to undertake training;
- reaction to specific aspects, eg unsocial hours, overtime;
- present salary level (if appropriate).

The appointment

Once all the interviews have been conducted the interviewer or interview panel will be in a position to decide whether or not an appointment can be made. It should not simply be a question of selecting the best person on the day, unless that person fits the selection criteria for the position.

Where a decision is reached, at the end of a series of formal interviews, and it is decided to make someone the offer of a position, the procedure will be to make the offer verbally, explaining any conditions, eg subject to a satisfactory medical report. Alternatively, where interviews may have been taking place over a number of days, or even weeks, the procedure will be to make the offer in writing or perhaps over the telephone, and, on receiving the candidate's formal acceptance of the offer the unsuccessful candidates will be notified. Such a delay may be advisable where, for example, more than one of those interviewed was suitable, so that any rejection of the offer on the part of the first choice, would mean that the second choice could still be approached.

Whatever the procedure the successful candidate should always receive a written letter of confirmation and this is usually accompanied by a document outlining the terms and conditions of employment (or even an actual written Contract of Employment).

Employment legislation under the Employment Protection (Consolidation) Act 1978 requires that full-time employees should receive, within 13 weeks of starting work, details of the major items of the contract. Technically a contract is made when an offer of employment is made and accepted and it is not necessary for the contract to be in writing to be legally binding. A verbal contract is sufficient. However, where a contract is provided in writing any misunderstandings or difficulties arising later will be more easily dealt with.

Where a full written contract is provided it will be likely to include:

- job title;
- outline duties;
- commencement date;
- rate of pay;
- hours of work;
- holiday arrangements;
- sickness allowances and notification requirements;
- periods of notice, either side;
- grievance procedures;
- disciplinary procedures;
- union membership arrangements;
- rules appertaining to the work;
- arrangements for terminating employment;
- any special rights or conditions;
- any rights to vary the contract.

The contract will be in duplicate and the applicant will be asked to sign and return one copy, retaining the other for personal reference.

Training and staff development

Personnel work and responsibilities towards staff do not begin and end with the appointment. Thereafter all manner of other employee-related matters need to be given due consideration and one particular aspect is the training and development they receive once they are in the job.

The induction process

The first element of training is usually an induction programme, ie an exercise devised by the organisation to help new employees to settle down quickly and feel a part of the organisation. Such programmes, as well as being good for the morale of new recruits, provide a company with an opportunity to welcome new employees and generally create a good and lasting initial impression.

Induction courses come in all shapes and sizes, ranging from a half-day familiarisation session to a full-blown programme of events which may extend over several weeks. The format will largely be dependent on the scale and nature of the organisation and on the number of new recruits taken on at any given time. Programmes may be organised on a company-wide basis (even, in some instances, involving new staff from different branches throughout the country), departmentally or possibly a combination of the two. In any event the types of things covered will be likely to include:

- company background information;
- organisational structure;
- company development plans;
- health and safety information;
- salary arrangements;
- employee profit-sharing schemes;
- pension scheme information;
- disturbance allowance provision;
- sickness notification requirements and procedures;
- procedure for requesting leave of absence;
- holiday arrangements;
- company rules and regulations;
- company systems and procedures;
- a summary of centralised services;
- education and training facilities and provision;
- travel and subsistence allowances and how to claim them;
- appraisal schemes;
- promotion procedures;
- transfers;
- grievance procedures;
- disciplinary procedures;
- union matters;
- medical services and first-aid facilities;
- social and sports facilities;
- restaurant and canteen facilities;
- employee welfare arrangements.

Such information may be imparted in a variety of ways including talks, films, company tours and social events but, certainly within larger organisations, it will be likely that staff will be issued with a loose-leaf Staff Handbook. This will provide full details of all the aspects covered during the induction programme, together with any other useful information, eg specimen forms to be completed in respect of special requests.

There is a lot to learn when starting any new job and it would be unrealistic to expect new employees to absorb it all at once, so a manual will provide useful back-up. Also it enables management to update information with ease as well as incorporating any new information as it becomes available.

Another aspect of induction will be the introduction of new staff to their immediate superiors with the opportunity to have at least a brief chat and so remove any initial feelings of isolation and general unease which may exist.

Job specific training

Induction is really a process rather than specific training and dependent on the nature of an appointment a new employee may experience other more specific training during the early days of a new job. This may range from training of a relatively informal nature whereby a new employee is apprised of departmental systems and procedures probably by 'sitting next to Nellie', ie learning from an existing member of staff, to training in the operation of a piece of equipment, perhaps by attending a course put on by the manufacturer or supplier, eg a word processing training course.

Reasons for training and staff development

Organisations need to undertake or arrange training for a variety of reasons, not least of which is the need to ensure the provision of efficient staff, who are able to work in ways that will improve productivity and enable a company to operate effectively in an increasingly competitive market.

The provision of training and staff development is good for staff motivation and morale. Staff will experience increased job satisfaction where they are able to work to their full potential and experience the knowledge and gratification which comes from a job well done. Additionally, particularly in times of high unemployment, when there may be relatively few prospects of being promoted or having the opportunity to apply for new positions, staff will welcome development programmes which at least provide hope for the future and endorse an organisation's concern and interest in the personal and professional development of its workforce.

Training and staff development need to be part of an organisation's manpower plan. They should not be undertaken as an *ad hoc* response to a sudden crisis or shortfall, but as part of a rational plan where training and development needs have been clearly identified and programmes selected or devised to meet these needs.

Kinds of training and staff development

Many different categories of training and staff development exist, from those conducted in-house in response to a particular need, eg operator training for new equipment or safety training following a run of poor accident statistics, to full-time secondments or short specialist courses for managers.

A wide range of programmes is available to cater for all levels of achievement and previous experience – from school/college leavers in their first jobs to members of the Board of Directors. Programmes are put on by in-house units, by educational establishments, by freelance training providers, by manufacturers and suppliers and by large external training specialists such as Industrial Society (IS), British

Table 10.2   Short Courses and Workshops for Office Staff

Course title	Provider	Duration (days)
Effective Letter Writing	GBS	2
Quicker Reading	GBS	2
Basic Report Writing	GBS	2
Recruitment and Selection	GBS	4
Coping with Stress	GBS	2
The New Secretary	GBS	4
The Personal Assistant	GBS	5
Receptionist/telephonist	GBS	2
Producing a House Journal	GBS	2
Appraisal Interviewing and Coaching	BIM	1
Performance Appraisal	BIM	2
Body Language for Managers	BIM	2
Leading Effective Meetings	BIM	2
Introduction to the Personal Computer	BIM	1
The Techniques of Time Management	BIM	2
Getting the best from your staff	BIM	2
Team Building	BIM	2
Time Management for Secretaries	BIM	1
The Executive Secretary (Part 1)	BIM	2
The Executive Secretary (Part 2)	BIM	2
The New Supervisor	BIM	2
Employment Law – An Update	BIM	1
Delegation	IS	1
The Experienced Secretary	IS	2
Helping Your Manager	IS	2
The Secretary's Role	IS	2
The Senior Secretary as an Administrator	IS	3
Senior Secretary in Management Today	IS	3
The Team Secretary	IS	2

Institute of Management (BIM) and Guardian Business Services (GBS).

Courses which are offered on-site, locally, regionally, nationally and even internationally are of varying duration and may or may not carry an award at the end. Providers are often happy to design programmes to meet specific requirements in respect of content and timescale and there are courses for literally anything imaginable, from the very general to the very specific. A selection of the types of short courses and workshops which are offered by the major providers and are especially applicable to office staff is given as Table 10.2.

Whatever the format used it needs to be selected with great care and attention to detail in order to ensure that it is the most appropriate type to meet the objectives identified.

On or off the job?

One thing that will need to be determined is whether the training or staff development can best be achieved within the company or outside. Several factors will be instrumental in reaching a decision. The types of thing likely to be considered by any organisation will be as follows:

- the sort of training needed;
- the time which can be made available;
- the respective advantages and disadvantages of being 'on the spot' or 'away from it all';
- the ultimate aims and objectives to be satisfied by the training;
- the availability of suitable courses both within the organisation and outside;
- the content and structure of programmes;
- the training methods used;
- the accommodation and facilities;
- the experience and suitability of the trainers;
- how the course is assessed and evaluated;
- the standards of performance expected of the training;
- the need for a programme to be company-specific;
- the advantages of interaction with others from outside the company;
- the level of motivation of employees;
- the cost implications, ie the fee for the course, the need to replace a course member while he/she is attending the course, the loss of production incurred if the trainee is not replaced, the time it will take to recoup the loss once the trainee returns.

There are advantages and disadvantages with both techniques and it is a question of weighing up the pros and cons and judging each programme on its own merits.

Performance appraisal

Appraisal is a systematic exercise designed to assess an employee's performance in his/her job. At its most informal it may consist of a 'chat' with the boss to see 'how you are getting along', while at the other end of the spectrum it may mean the completion of various assessment forms and appraisal interviews, perhaps even at half-yearly intervals.

Staff are appraised for a variety of reasons, including the following:

- to collect data which may be used to improve a company's overall operation;
- to identify training and staff development needs;
- to assess the present and future potential of staff;
- to identify staff deserving of promotion;
- to motivate staff to improve their personal performance;
- to provide an opportunity for staff to discuss their career aspirations;
- to provide a forum at which staff may be offered guidance, advice and constructive criticism regarding their future development;
- to provide an opportunity to offer praise and commendation;
- to provide an opportunity to point up weaknesses or shortcomings in work and attitude;
- to provide staff with an opportunity to raise issues of concern to them;
- to provide a basis for the consideration of future pay awards;
- to check on the effectiveness of recruitment, selection, training and promotion procedures on the part of the personnel department.

The three main elements of appraisal

The first element of appraisal is **performance review** which, as the name suggests, analyses what an employee has done and what he is doing in his job, with a view to helping him improve his personal performance and, by extension, enhance the effectiveness of the organisation. Such reviews should help identify strengths and weaknesses, enable discussion to take place between employer and employee and allow for counselling for the future.

Secondly there is **potential review** which is designed specifically to identify where an employee's career should be heading and within what sort of timescale. This is a very speculative and subjective area of appraisal and is never easy to determine. Some companies choose to involve someone who is unfamiliar with the employee undergoing the appraisal in an attempt to secure greater objectivity.

The third element is that of **reward review** where certain companies link increments and bonuses to performance. Technically rewards may be given or withheld according to performance during an assessment period, but such a process can obviously have severe implications for staff motivation and morale, and the presence of monetary reward may serve to cloud other relevant issues. Therefore, it is more appropriate if any pay reward review is arranged to take place at a separate time from other aspects of appraisal.

Appraisal techniques

Various techniques are available in terms of carrying out staff appraisal but the following are the most common in respect of assessing the performance of office staff.

Overall assessment where the superior prepares a written statement about the employee. He will often be given a checklist to work to and will be required to comment on points such as reliability, enthusiasm, acceptability as a working colleague and appearance. This is a simple technique and at least forces superiors to sit down and gather their thoughts, but it is bound to be largely subjective and will also be influenced by the superior's skill at expressing his thoughts in writing.

Guideline assessment requires the superior to consider more specific questions, the theory being that answers should be more precise. However, in practice comments are often relatively unhelpful in that the guidelines are too vague.

Grading takes the guideline technique still further by providing a framework of reference from which the person carrying out the appraisal is required to select the statement which most closely describes the individual being assessed. The range of statements might include descriptive words such as outstanding, good, satisfactory and poor, but the problem rests in determining how good is 'good' and what would constitute 'outstanding'.

Merit rating is similar to grading but relies on numerical allocations rather than descriptive words and has the advantage in that results are at least quantifiable. While this can be helpful in determining pay scales and identifying training needs, it still falls a long way short of being objective and will do little to boost morale or improve motivation. Also many appraisers are reluctant to operate the range of possible ratings tending to stick to the middle band.

While all these techniques operate on a one-way basis it is common in many companies for employees to be asked to evaluate their own performance by completing a questionnaire which will form the basis of a counselling session with their superior.

It is also common practice in some companies to give employees the opportunity to exchange their versions with those prepared by superiors and then engage in frank problem-solving discussion. This ensures that everything is brought out into the open. The technique provides both sides with the opportunity to defend or justify their actions, answer criticisms and mutually arrive at a plan of action for the future.

Appraisal interviews

Irrespective of what technique is adopted in terms of preparing and/or submitting written reports, the activity is likely to have more credibility, certainly in the eyes of employees, where there is also an interview. Although the whole idea of appraisal may be decidedly unpopular with employees in that it is frequently viewed as a threat, or a farce in that much of what takes place is viewed as 'going through the motions', from a more positive standpoint it can, where conducted skillfully, produce meaningful results for both employer and employees.

To achieve such results appraisal needs a sense of purpose and well structured appraisal interviews need to be an integral part of the whole exercise. Otherwise appraisal may be viewed as a waste of time.

All employees need to be fully conversant with the operation of the scheme and with their roles in it. Suitable pro formas need to be prepared (see Fig. 10.3). Interviews need to be carefully scheduled and well structured as well as being held in a suitable environment which will help encourage maximum interaction between interviewer and interviewee. Any decisions reached, preferably as a result of joint agreement, need to be carefully recorded and communicated to the interviewee at a later date as part of a positive action plan for the future.

Successful appraisal interviews will lead to improvements all round in respect of steps taken to rectify problems, to introduce changes,

---

PERFORMANCE APPRAISAL FORM

Name _____

Department _____

Job Title _____

Date joined company _____

Date of present appointment (if different) _____

Period covered by this review _____

A) Overall performance during review period

☐ ☐ ☐ ☐ ☐ ☐ ☐

Exc.   V Good   Good   Satis.   Fair   Poor   V Poor

Tick box as appropriate

B) Strengths and weaknesses

Comment according to how performance is affected in the areas stated. Add other areas as considered appropriate.

	Comments	Action agreed
a) Knowledge of overall job		
b) Knowledge of essential systems and procedures		
c) Communications skills		
d) Machine familiarity		
e) Attention to detail		
f) Member of a team		
g) Level of co-operation		
h) Punctuality		
i) Reliability		
j) Initiative		
k)		
l)		
m)		
n)		

(a)

Fig. 10.3 Specimen staff appraisal form

C) Potential

□	□	□	□	□	□
Overdue Promotion	Ready for Promotion	Has Promotion Potential	Not ready for Promotion	Has no Promotion Potential	Unable to Comment

Tick box as appropriate

D) Training Needs Identified

List any identified together with any specific required

E) Career Aspirations of Interviewee

Indicate any discussed which might be accommodated by the company, suggesting any recommended action

F) Other Comments

G) Objectives for next appraisal

Summarise main objectives agreed

Prepared by _____   Countersigned by _____

Signature of   Signature of
Interviewer _____   Interviewee _____

Date _____   Date _____

(*b*)

Fig. 10.3   Specimen staff appraisal form (contd)

to arrange necessary training and to monitor future progress. In fact, there needs to be a continuous monitoring and evaluation process to ensure that implementation is effective.

CHECKLIST

1 A large number of people are employed in office work and each category of worker has his own duties and responsibilities.

2 The recruitment and selection of appropriate staff is the responsibility of the Personnel Department.

3 Following the identification of a vacancy job details are prepared, the position is advertised and interested parties are invited to apply.

4 The application forms or curricula vitae provided by applicants are studied carefully and a shortlist for interview is drawn up.

5 Both candidates and those conducting the interviews need to be well prepared.

6 Interviews, which may be conducted by a panel, need to observe the law in terms of discriminatory practices and questioning employed.

7 Following his appointment the new employee is entitled by law to receive details of his contract and this is usually supplied in writing, certainly for most office workers.

8 New employees are often put through what is termed an induction process when they join a new company, to help them settle in and familiarise them with company policies and procedures.

9 In the course of anyone's career in office work they are likely to undertake some form of training or staff development.

10 Appraisal techniques of some kind are applied within most organisations to measure performance and gauge future potential.

QUICK REVISION QUESTIONS

1 What distinctions would you make between a secretary and a shorthand-typist?

2 Suggest three special qualities which an interview panel might look for in someone applying for a position as a Secretarial Services Supervisor.

3 List the requirements of a good advertisement for a vacancy.

4 What is the difference between a job description and a job specification?

5 List the things anyone shortlisted for interview may do by way of preparation.
6 Name three pieces of legislation which may require to be adhered to or interpreted during an interview.
7 List five things which should be included in a contract of employment.
8 Outline the things you would expect to be covered during an induction programme.
9 What factors need to be considered in deciding whether staff training should be undertaken on company premises or elsewhere?
10 Briefly explain two appraisal techniques which might be used to assess office workers.

UNIT 2
The Secretary

Just as people have their own idea of an office so, too, do they have their own perception of a secretary. The word 'secretary' means all things to all people and certainly many of those who work in offices choose to shelter beneath the secretarial umbrella. In some people's minds a secretary will simply be someone who works in an office, answering the telephone and doing the typing. At the other end of the spectrum a secretary may be seen as someone holding a very responsible position within an organisation, who provides a full range of management support which calls upon a variety of skills and abilities that would certainly not be prerequisites of office staff generally.

Also, there is no precise model of a secretary. Roles differ considerably in that there are certain factors which undoubtedly influence where the emphasis lies and hence the type and range of skills which will be required. The following are some of the things which are likely to influence the role:

- the size and structure of the organisation;
- its geographical location;
- whether it is in the public or private sector;
- the nature of its activities, eg manufacturing or service;
- the position of the boss within the organisation's hierarchy;
- the boss's external involvements and commitments;
- how much the boss is absent from the office;
- how much is delegated to the secretary;
- whether the secretary has her own span of control, ie subordinates to whom she may issue work;
- whether the secretary works exclusively for one person or for a number of individuals;
- where the secretary's office or work area is in relation to that of her boss(es);
- the amount of technology which is present in the work place.

Additionally there will be the inevitable personality factors present in both secretary and boss(es), as well as their styles of working and their overall expectations of their own jobs and of one another.

A brief glance through this list should indicate the complexities of being a secretary and how difficult it can be to be precise in terms of indicating what secretaries actually do. Different jobs require different skills, abilities and attitudes.

This unit examines the range of support skills which are likely to feature in most secretarial roles while considering the qualities and attitudes that are desirable and in keeping with those engaged in secretarial work. It also highlights specific areas such as diary and time management, meetings, conference and travel arrangements – all of which require a special blend of organisational flair and administrative ability. Nonetheless such aspects frequently represent an increasing amount of many secretaries' work at a time when employers are becoming more demanding and calling upon a mixture of old and new skills.

Traditional secretarial roles are gradually changing and secretaries, given the support of information technology, are able to exercise more of their administrative and support functions, which, after all, is what secretarial work is all about. Many find that their careers are now encompassing a wide range of the more administrative-type tasks, that their work is becoming more interesting and challenging with their roles extending into management.

A Secretary's life – what it's really like

Helen Weinhardt is a secretary with the National Computing Centre in Manchester. The Centre was created over twenty years ago by the government of the day, primarily to promote the use of Information Technology throughout the UK. Originally funded by the Government, the Centre is now self-supporting – a company limited by guarantee. Unlike a normal limited company, there are no shareholders to compensate, therefore the profits from the sale of products and services help to pay for what is known as the 'National Role', in other words NCC pays 50 per cent of all research and development and the Government pays the other 50 per cent.

I work as a 'shared' secretary to two of the senior managers at the Centre, Dr Matthew Dixon, who is manager of Knowledge Management Systems (KMS) and Mrs Frieda Darling who heads the Consultancy Division. KMS covers three departments, Expert Systems, IT in Training and Data Protection and Security with a staff of 19, while the Consultancy Division has a staff of 13 and deals with all NCC's consultancy assignments. Working for two people and two separate areas of work obviously creates some complications but for the most part things run fairly smoothly.

I cannot really describe a 'typical' day as every day is different, but I can highlight some aspects of my job which occur on a regular basis. Most days begin with the post which I open, followed by a run through of the diaries to co-ordinate the movements of the day. The diary also serves as a reminder for deadlines, etc. Aspects of the job which happen on a regular basis are those normal for any secretary, viz typing (word processing), shorthand, filing, fielding callers, making arrangements for meetings, travel, accommodation, etc. All my typing is done on a Tandon PC using the Wordperfect word processing package. Although I do some typing it is not on a grand scale – the Centre has a typing pool where all major typing is carried out. Shorthand I use less frequently, but I do take dictation on occasion and use my shorthand for taking long and complicated telephone messages.

A large percentage of my time is spent using the phone. All calls to both managers come through me and it is my job to take messages in the case of absence and, where possible, pursue queries, ensuring that requests of whatever nature are responded to as quickly as possible. I also take calls for consultants in their absence and usually keep a written record of all external calls and messages.

Organisation plays a major role at every level of my job, whether it is a case of organising the day's workload or making the arrangements for a major meeting. Working for two people (and often more!) it is important to prioritise. Normally when I am asked to do something and I already have a backlog of work, I ask for a time limit. This allows me time to organise the rest of my work and make provision for any shortage of time or a potential clash of priorities.

Organising meetings is another regular occurrence and it is normally my job to make all the necessary arrangements. I book the room, refreshments and any equipment needed. I also deal with the paperwork such as organising dates and sending the appropriate material to the attendees. Before every meeting, I make a point of checking the arrangements so as to avoid any problems. It is also my job to receive all external visitors as well as those attending meetings.

Other tasks which occur regularly are using the fax machine, following up requests made by managers to their staff and noting the weekly movements of staff so that communications remain good within each division. I also deal with all administrative procedures concerning the division such as ensuring timesheets are given in on time, expenses are signed and recorded and orders processed.

I enjoy my job – it is varied and often unpredictable but this certainly makes it interesting and it provides a challenge.

Mandy Robinson is Secretary to the Executive Director of the Educational Health Care Division of Gardner Merchant (a division of Trusthouse Forte plc) and is based in Manchester.

One of the best aspects of my job is that even though some parts of my day are spent on routine tasks I rarely have a typical routine day. Being involved with the sales and operational side of the contract catering business, I always have to be prepared for the unexpected. A letter or a telephone call can cause plans to be altered at the last minute and lead to other areas of activity such as preparing reports, sales proposals, or rearranging hectic travel schedules for my boss.

It helps to be 'un-flappable' and to be prepared to use your own initiative. My boss spends a large percentage of his time out of the office, so if problems arise, I have to be able to deal with them, or at least find someone who can. On his return, there is usually a lot of correspondence to deal with, which I have to prioritise, so that his time is not wasted in sorting through what is and is not important. Occasionally I may have been able to take action myself and respond to queries and requests in the absence of my boss, otherwise I will summarise the contents of letters as we go through them. My shorthand skills are required here, as my boss dictates a reply there and then. Occasionally he dictates letters over the telephone for me to type and send off in his absence.

I like to have an organised working environment, though occasionally it is anything but organised. I always make lists of tasks to be completed and tick them off when I have dealt with them – a basic yet crucial exercise.

Managing time is vital. I keep not only my boss's diary, but also those of three other people, who can also call on me for any secretarial work they want doing. Everyone believes his own particular work is the most important and I have to be quite firm in deciding what must take priority. I soon discovered I would never please everyone all the time and how important it was to learn to delegate work to other colleagues or subordinates in the team.

Good telephone skills are essential. I speak to clients and senior members of the company regularly and take messages when I am not able to deal with queries or requests for information myself. Shorthand is very useful here and I always transfer messages to a message book so that I never forget to pass on the information given.

A good working relationship is vital with those around me, not only my boss and people in the office, but also those with whom I am in regular contact by telephone. It is great to be accepted as one of the 'team'.

Libby Sturrock is Personal Assistant to the Sales and Marketing Director of Glasdon Ltd in Blackpool.

Typically I arrive at 8.55 am and re-sort correspondence into priority order, so that all important documents are dealt with first. From 9 till 10 am has been designated 'Happy Hour' and is allocated to routine correspondence, dictation, signing documents for approval and planning requirements for future meetings. For me this time is often enlightening, as Roger may explain the background of certain memoranda and I can learn from the action he instigates. It's also vital in maintaining ordered administration and in ensuring regular communication between principal and secretary, hence an effective working relationship.

Ideally it should provide an hour of uninterrupted work, but in practice Roger is telephoned with news of significant developments and a stray member of staff may enter to request a 'quick word'. Roger is the Sales and Marketing Director with extensive responsibilities for promoting and planning the sales of the company's wide range of waste management, environmental and safety products. Despite his hectic schedule, he likes to remain accessible to all his staff.

While Roger prepares for his first meeting, I open the first post in my neighbouring office, aiming to redistribute mail to appropriate staff and so reduce Roger's post to a minimum. 'I wouldn't mind a coffee, Libby', ventures Roger through the adjoining window. A junior provides the refreshment, while I begin typing up my dictated notes.

Between frequent phone messages and calls from colleagues popping in with information and news, I also type an offer of employment letter on behalf of a Sales Manager and open the corresponding new Personnel file.

Roger now has an internal planning meeting with our Production Director, followed by a discussion on new product development in Design.

Meanwhile I need to change a couple of meetings to accommodate a visitor next week, so liaise with secretary colleagues and advise the schedule co-ordinator, the 'schedule' being a useful company diary of management movements.

The second post arrives and is sorted before lunch; I'm able to respond directly to one personnel enquiry regarding clerical vacancies, while the rest is for Roger's attention.

Roger has requested competitor information for the following day and I ask our Librarian to source this for me, before going to lunch.

Suddenly at 1.30 pm we hear that our caterer has crashed on the way to Glasdon and the lunch for some important visitors is spread over a Blackpool road. With only half an hour to cobble together a presentable buffet, it's all secretarial hands on deck and a potential crisis becomes a relatively enjoyable challenge.

Back to the telephone I call an agency to source suitable venues for the Christmas Sales Conference, and as Secretary of the Social Group chase up some staff for payment of theatre tickets.

As I also have responsibility for the recruitment, training and welfare of three Junior staff based in the Post Room, I try to assist their promotional prospects by securing weekly afternoon placements in suitable departments. Having liaised first with their Supervisor, I contact the appropriate Department Heads who agree to train and assess the Juniors for a period.

Roger has been delayed for his afternoon meeting and I pass on apologies before dealing with the last internal post. The next half hour is spent showing our corporate video to the newest Junior as part of his induction programme, then I must catch up with Roger to ensure that his outgoing letters are signed ready for franking and collection.

For the nth time I check over my message pad and tidy up any loose ends before locking the cabinets around 5 pm.

Maybe tommorrow I'll catch up on that filing!

Janet Schofield is Secretary/PA to the Export Director of Shubette of London Ltd.

The world of fashion is exciting, glamorous and demanding. My company is one of Britain's leading manufacturers of ladies' garments and children's wear and I provide full secretarial and administrative support to the Export Department and am responsible to the Managing Director and Company Secretary.

Work begins formally at 9 am and the first task is to sort the post. This has to be grouped and distributed according to department, along with any telexes and facsimiles (it is my responsibility to keep centrally-filed copies of these documents). Amongst the post for our department are customer orders from all over Europe, which must be processed daily and export sales figures based on these orders are collated weekly.

Shorthand dictation is normally taken in the morning and often becomes drawn out due to telephone interruptions. Important telexes are sent immediately in French, German or English. At 11 am each day I collect any cheques to be signed by the Managing Director.

Throughout the day I have to take and pass on messages to the Export Director. Whenever he is abroad (approximately 8 weeks in the year), I assume full responsibility for the running of the office and must keep him informed daily of major events. As a prelude to his travels, I have to make flight arrangements, book hotels and confirm appointments.

Extensive administrative work is involved in making stand applications and ordering equipment for the European Fashion Exhibitions. On occasions, when the Export Director is unavailable, I may be asked to attend a meeting with the British Overseas Trade Board (BOTB) or the British Knitting and Clothing Export Council (BKCEC) regarding exhibition organisation.

Following the completion of the season's range, time is spent welcoming buyers from abroad, and being hostess to our agents. The busiest time of the year is immediately after the exhibitions when the orders come flooding in, and any problems with deliveries may occur.

After lunch (taken between 1 and 2), I usually spend time typing up any letters, reports, or memos still outstanding from the morning. I may also have to translate documents from French or German into English and make telephone calls abroad chasing customers for payment of outstanding invoices or placing fabric orders where prompt delivery is most important.

It is essential that I prioritise my work from day to day and divide my time in accordance with the hierarchical set-up of the company. The Managing Director's work must be done first and foremost! Each day also has its mundane aspects like making coffee, filing, watering the plants and making constant checks on the levels of stationery. However, when work is slack, the Export Director is eager to teach me more about export documentation and the methods of payment, all of which I find most interesting.

11 Technical skills

An examination of the skills associated with secretarial work is essential as such skills provide the foundation on which the job itself will take shape and flourish. Even the range of technical skills – the mechanics of the job – has grown since the early days of secretarial work. No longer is competence in shorthand and typewriting sufficient, although, of course, it is still expected. Employers now seek as standard the additional skills of word processing, business communication (including top class telephone technique) and, increasingly, a level of competence with figures.

It is towards these 'tools of the trade' that this section now turns before going on to examine the wider range of additional skills, qualities and attitudes that are required in the performance of the secretarial role.

At the end of this section you should be able to:

- indicate the traditional technical skills required by secretaries;
- identify additional skills which are likely to be called for;
- indicate points to bear in mind when taking dictation;
- identify the features of good audio dictation technique;
- compare and contrast the relative merits of shorthand and audio;
- explain the role which a secretary plays in relation to the preparation of written communication;
- identify the essentials of a good business letter;
- appreciate the importance of good layout and presentation in all written communication;
- appreciate the importance of good telephone technique;
- advise a junior member of staff on telephone usage;
- identify instances where a secretary's numerate skills would be called for.

Traditional skills

Irrespective of how fast office work is changing due to office tech-

COLLEGE LEAVER

Take this opportunity to consolidate your recently acquired secretarial skills including shorthand, audio and word processing whilst providing all-round secretarial support to two executive/ managers in a small national company. Benefits include free lunch, BUPA and car parking facilities. Telephone to discuss this and other opportunities.

EXECUTIVE SECRETARY/ OFFICE ADMINISTRATOR

We are an American Computer Graphics Company the world leader in our field and growing fast. We are looking for an Executive Secretary/Office Administrator to provide first-class secretarial support to the Group Managing Director, with some support for the Company Secretary and North European Sales Manager.

You will be a key member of a small, highly professional team. You will need to be outgoing, self-motivated and capable of working under considerable pressure. You will take responsibility for:-

- the smooth running of the European Headquarters in Kensington
- organising and attending conferences and meetings
- extensive travel arrangements
- frequent contact with U.S. head office, European subsidiaries and distributors.

110 wpm+ shorthand, 65 wpm typing.

Please apply in confidence with your CV to:-

PERSON FRIDAY (Audio)

Insurance Company is currently seeking an organised person who is able to work under pressure and enjoys a busy and varied work load. Although work has a high admin. content you will require audio skills, a knowledge of Wang, WP, and rusty shorthand (50 wpm). A refresher course is available for Wang. Ref: 2243.

A true PA/executive assistant is required by this major US company. You will provide full administrative back-up to the staff administrator and handle PR matters as well as doing research. A career-minded and ambitious secretary can expect to progress to an admin/managerial position. An 'A' level education and 90/50 skills with WP experience is required.

Design/Advertising

Reception

Articulate and stylish receptionist/secretary with bags of initiative to work for rapidly expanding West End company handling design and advertising for blue-chip clients. Varied reception duties handling a busy switchboard, telex and WP — typing 45wpm essential, meeting and greeting clients, organising couriers and composing your own correspondence.

COLLEGE LEAVER SEC LEADING MERCHANT BANKERS £ EXCELLENT + Bonus + M.S.

This leading firm of Merchant bankers have requested that we recruit a college leaver secretary educated to "A" level standard with good shorthand and typing qualifications, applications are invited from college leavers who may not leave until June. Our Clients are prepared to wait for self confident candidates with flexibility and the desire to be part of one of the most prestigious City Bankers. Superb working conditions and excellent salary structure, full training will be given in all aspects of the position within their Corporate Finance area.

Fig. 11.1 Advertisements for secretarial positions

nology, the skills traditionally associated with secretarial work remain, viz shorthand and typewriting. Additionally many advertisements now specify a knowledge of word processing which is increasingly included as a standard skill which any secretary will be expected to possess. A glance at any page of newspaper advertisements will indicate that these skills are still demanded for a large proportion of secretarial positions. Figure 11.1 represents a typical selection.

Qualifications

The examining boards, notably the London Chamber of Commerce and Industry (LCCI), Pitman Examinations Institute (PEI) and the Royal Society of Arts (RSA) have long been setting examinations at all levels to test competence and ability in these traditional skill areas. Many employers will particularly specify certain standards and will recognise certificates and diplomas from these bodies as evidence of success.

Where a school or college leaver uses one of the many secretarial employment bureaux to secure initial employment, whether of a permanent or temporary nature, they too will attach importance to the technical skills which the prospective employee has, and will invariably require a range of tests to be taken to assess these skills and provide details for their own records.

The importance of English

One skill that should not be overlooked is that of English language. Unfortunately it is still common to hear employers lament the standards of grammar, punctuation and spelling that come out of their offices, passing remarks like 'If only someone could invent a typewriter that could spell!'.

Without these skills the other areas, regardless of how good the speeds might be, are rendered virtually useless. For example, where a secretary is using a lot of shorthand it will be absolutely vital that she can punctuate her notes. Similarly, where a secretary is working from audio her ability to transcribe with ease what she is hearing will depend on the extent of her vocabulary. Likewise typing from illegible handwriting will be infinitely easier where the secretary has a good command of the language and is confident in her spelling.

Many secretaries are also given the task of preparing their own correspondence, either from brief notes or from a simple 'Say "no" to that' approach. Composition skills are called for here, while different skills such as précis or minute taking are required in other situations.

Taking dictation

Certainly one of the more traditional skills associated with secretarial work is taking dictation. Dictation can be given direct to the secretary who will make notes in shorthand or it may be provided on some sort of recording medium (see p 211), in which case it will be listening and comprehension skills rather than memory and deciphering skills which will be to the forefront. Either way the secretary's command of language is of paramount importance.

Shorthand dictation

Despite rumours to the contrary many employers still favour the personal approach of dictating to a secretary. Also for many employers shorthand is still considered a prerequisite skill of a first-class secretary. Irrespective of what shorthand system is used (there are several different ones) it will be important to take account of the following:

- *Be organised* – always have your notebook and pencil or pen ready. Many bosses even dictate over the intercom! An elastic band around used pages helps you to find the first blank page very quickly.
- *Rule up pages in advance* to accommodate notes, alterations and reminders.
- *Date all pages* – it can be helpful in locating something later.
- *Concentrate when taking dictation* – try not to let your mind wander even though you are capable of making notes automatically while your thoughts are elsewhere (a skill most shorthand writers acquire)! Unless your notes are perfect, transcription will be likely to prove difficult as you will have little or no recall of content.
- *Ask the dictator to repeat something or to slow down.* Where you have failed to hear, or lost the drift, or where the dictator is going too fast, admit your shortcomings quickly. There is little point letting someone continue when you know you will not be able to read back your notes.
- *Ask for clarification* on any point you are not quite sure of at the end of that piece of dictation, while it is still fresh in the dictator's mind, rather than at the end of the complete session.
- *Read through your notes* as soon as the dictation is finished.
- *Prioritise* in terms of the order in which you transcribe. Sometimes it will not be in strict order of dictation.
- *Draw a line through transcribed notes* as you complete a page.
- *Prepare a draft in double line spacing* where you may have been

unable to seek clarification and yet have only omitted a few words. Ask your boss to check it and fill in the blanks. He will probably take the opportunity to made other changes as well! Where you are using a memory typewriter or word processor making the changes will be very easy.

- *Type back your notes at the earliest opportunity*. Try not to leave things overnight, or worse still over a weekend. The longer you leave them the more difficult transcription tends to become.
- *Always check your typing* before removing the paper from the type- writer or proofread from the screen before printing out.

Audio dictation

Many executives now choose to use audio dictation methods and this requires a different type of transcription ability. The ease with which transcription is undertaken will always depend to a great extent on the quality of the dictation. While equipment itself has improved immensely, mumblers unfortunately still exist and consequently the secretary may experience problems.

Hints for good dictation

One of the problems of audio can, therefore, be the poor quality of the dictation. There is little point in a company investing in expensive equipment if staff do not know how to make the best use of it. Most secretaries will experience difficult recordings at some time in their careers where it may be virtually impossible to decipher what the dictator is saying.

Making a good recording is not as easy as it may at first appear and like any other skill it requires practice. It may not only be the boss who needs to practise, secretaries themselves may find that it is useful to record certain work on tape and delegate the typing to a junior member of staff. The following list of points provide useful guidelines for anyone who is preparing an audio tape or cassette for transcription:

- Where the same person may not always be the one to transcribe the tape, begin by introducing yourself – your name, position, department and extension number.
- Provide a clear indication of what it is that will follow, eg a memo, a letter, a report or whatever, indicating where possible its length. Even 'This is a short letter' will prove helpful to the typist.
- Indicate whether the copy is a draft or in its final form.
- State the number of copies required.

- Specify any special instructions, eg 'confidential', line spacing or special layout required.
- Indicate how the document is to be referenced or indexed, particularly where it may be typed on a word processor and stored on disk, in which case it will also be useful to indicate the retention period, if any.
- Speak clearly and at a steady pace, holding the microphone or recorder near the mouth.
- Avoid shuffling papers or moving around too much.
- Distinguish via tone and voice inflection between instructions to the typist and actual text to be typed.
- Switch off the machine when pausing for thought or when interrupted.
- Be conscious of background noise and the machine's capacity to pick it up and so adversely affect the quality of the recording. Therefore be aware of open doors and windows and extraneous noise such as traffic, music or even loud ticking clocks!
- Dictate essential punctuation, eg full stops and new paragraphs or something unusual which is required, but don't overdo it. Too many instructions can prove to be obtrusive.
- Spell unusual words or names.
- Have necessary papers to which you need to refer close to hand.
- Clearly indicate the end of a particular piece of dictation.
- Indicate any special complimentary close you wish to use.
- Indicate where the typist can find any enclosures referred to in the text or say that you have them ready.

The pros and cons of audio systems were discussed in Unit 1, Section 8.

The case for shorthand

The great debate still continues as to whether audio is better than shorthand and at the end of the day it will be very much a matter of preference, and ideally it will be useful for a secretary to have both skills at her boss's disposal. There are occasions when it is still preferable and more convenient to make shorthand notes, eg when attending meetings or taking down the gist of a telephone call. Equally there will be times when the use of audio will make better sense and offer greater flexibility.

A word about machine shorthand

Stenotyping is the correct name for machine shorthand. It is based on a phonetic system whereby the operator types phonetic syllables, striking the keys with both hands simultaneously very much in the manner in which chords are struck on a piano. The machine is light-weight and portable and can be operated on the lap (an alternative to a shorthand notebook). Each time the keys are struck syllables or words are printed out, almost noiselessly, on a continuous roll of paper. Just like shorthand notes the roll of paper needs to be tran-scribed, but this may be done by anyone with an understanding of the theory of stenotyping.

Stenotyping systems are available in different languages and any stenotypist can take dictation in any foreign language in which she is proficient. The advantages of this technique arise where verbatim notes need to be taken continuously and where there is a need for immediate transcription. The stenotypist can take the notes using the machine and the printed roll can be passed to another typist for tran-scription, so enabling continuous reporting in, for example, courts of law, at conferences and during parliamentary debates.

Written communication skills

Given that secretaries' roles are gradually evolving largely as a result of the introduction of office support technology and the consequent removal or reduction of many of the labour-intensive tasks formerly associated with secretarial work, a greater emphasis will be placed on the cultivation or acquisition of other skills. One of these is undoubt-edly the ability to handle a wide range of written communication, not purely from the point of being able to transcribe someone else's thoughts but as an originator.

Where a secretary works closely with her manager or as part of an office team her knowledge of the work undertaken will become exten-sive and there is no reason why she should not feel competent to compose routine replies in the form of business letters, send out inter-office memoranda and compile or draft reports. Likewise, the nature of her job may be such that it requires the completion of returns, the drafting of newspaper advertisements or press releases and the taking of minutes (see Section 14).

Business letters

Thousands of business letters are written and read every day. Some will be well written and well received but others will fall into the opposite category. Basically business letters are written to inform or to make arrangements and organise something. Where they are well prepared and presented they can achieve a great deal for a comparatively low outlay.

Where a secretary prepares a lot of correspondence personally it is important that she takes time to perfect her technique and is watchful of her spelling, grammar and punctuation. Many useful books are available to help in the art of letter writing and it will be well worth her while to find one which meets her needs and to keep it by her for reference. However, the following are a few points to bear in mind when composing business letters:

- plan first of all;
- always quote any reference and insert your own;
- date all letters;
- be sure to use the correct name of the addressee;
- insert an attention line where appropriate;
- use the appropriate opening salutation (where you do not know the person you are writing to, begin 'Dear Sir' or 'Dear Madam' and end 'Yours faithfully' but where the letter is on a more personal level begin 'Dear Mr . . .' or 'Dear Mrs (Miss or Ms) . . .' and end 'Yours sincerely');
- where appropriate include a subject heading;
- be brief, clear, pleasant and courteous;
- avoid using clichés within the body of the letter;
- decide on suitable paragraph breaks, giving a separate paragraph for each point;
- be logical in your presentation;
- number your points if the letter is long and complex;
- try to finish on a positive note which will, where necessary encourage a quick response;
- avoid adopting redundant or outmoded closing remarks;
- use an appropriate complimentary close;
- adopt your organisation's conventions in terms of designatory close, eg some organisations include the company name in all correspondence followed by the name and designation of the signatory (in some instances only certain officials will have the authority to sign);
- remember to check spelling, grammar and punctuation before presenting the letter for signature (in fact before removing it from the machine!);
- remember to include any enclosures referred to;
- prepare an envelope of a suitable size and mark it with any special instructions for the mailing department.

Finding the right words

Sometimes it can be difficult to find the right words and to adopt the appropriate tone. This will come with practice and experience but you should avoid using phrases like the following:

- We acknowledge receipt of your letter . . .;
- We are in receipt of your esteemed favour . . .;
- We have to hand your communication of the 16th instant (or ultimo);
- A copy is enclosed for your convenience . . .;
- Enclosed please find . . .;
- Allow me to say how . . .;
- We beg to remain your obedient servants;
- Hoping to hear from you. (This is grammatically incorrect as 'hoping' is not a full verb.)

Such phrases are hackneyed, inappropriate and often redundant, adding nothing to the letter. It is better to adopt straightforward language like the following:

- Thank you for your letter of 19 March;
- I am enclosing . . .;
- We are happy to . . .;
- We hope to hear from you . . . .

Similarly your choice of individual words and phrases is important if you are to establish the right tone and convey the sentiment you wish to express. Do not sound over-familiar, indifferent, aloof or hostile and avoid ambiguity and long-windedness. Always try to keep your writing crisp and concise, avoiding lengthy phrases when one word could be substituted. For example, substitute 'now' for 'at this moment in time' and 'because' or 'as' for 'due to the fact that'. Even small things like the points just mentioned will improve your style and produce a much more acceptable letter.

Layout and presentation

Organisations all have their own house styles for all their communications and it is essential that you adopt the preferred format where there is one. Layouts will frequently be dependent on the design of the letterhead and the inclusion of any logo. Sometimes the information included in the printed letterhead can take up as much as 25 per cent of the page and there may even be additional information printed in the bottom margin, so it will be essential to gauge the avail-

LETTER HEADING AND LOGO

Your Ref:
Our Ref:

Today's date

Any special classification, eg CONFIDENTIAL

Recipient's name
and address

                      either a specified individual or the company name in
_____ general

_____

An attention line if recipient not named above

Salutation

SUBJECT HEADING

_____

_____

_____

_____

_____

_____

Complimentary close
NAME OF THE COMPANY OR ORGANISATION?

         Space for Signature

Name of Writer
Official Designation

Enc

Letter copy(ies) reference

Fig. 11.2 Component parts of a letter in fully blocked style

able space accurately, setting margins and commencing continuation pages at suitable points.

Where there is room for some variation it is important to opt for a style which is clear, attractive and consistent. Most business offices now tend to favour a fully blocked layout and an example of this is given in Fig. 11.2 which provides details of the component parts of a letter.

Memoranda

The memorandum or memo represents the most common form of inter-office written communication. It serves a variety of purposes from conveying information, to seeking clarification, to making suggestions, to indicating progress, to confirming arrangements, to outlining decisions reached, to amplifying existing information – in fact to virtually any type of internal message. Most organisations have their own preprinted forms for this purpose, often in both A4 and A5 formats. These can have different designs but are likely to include the following component parts:

- company's/organisation's name;
- memorandum heading;
- to and from;
- date and sometimes reference;
- subject heading (sometimes included).

Memos will serve as a channel of communication throughout an organisation and will operate in all directions and between all levels of staff. The style, content, tone and degree of formality will vary dependent on the status of originator and receiver. The most important function of a memo is the provision of a written record.

Some organisations even adopt multiple copy memo packs which may be colour coded for filing purposes. Others have forms designed which incorporate a reply section on the same form which is useful in terms of record keeping as well as saving time and taking up less storage space. Memos may be circulated within an organisation as separate sheets of paper or they may be enclosed in an internal envelope where increased security or confidentiality is necessary.

Memos should always be dated and carry the initials of the sender (it is not usual to sign them).

Reports

Reports vary considerably in style, content length and format, dependent upon the purpose for which they are intended and upon the audience they are aimed at. They range from those set out on an A4 memo sheet to formal documents of several hundreds of pages.

Short, informal reports can be conveniently broken down into three main component parts, viz the introduction, the findings or body of information and the conclusions, together with any recommendations, where appropriate. Where a more formal report is called for it will be usual to divide it up as follows:

1 Heading or title page
2 Terms of reference
3 Procedure adopted (modus operandi)
4 Findings
5 Conclusions
6 Recommendations
7 Appendices.

Where a report is even more formal and possibly much lengthier it will be usual to insert a Contents page and a Synopsis after the title page but before the terms of reference, and, where supporting documentation has been used and consulted, it is usual to finish with a Bibliography.

Style and presentation

The key to effective report writing lies in the style and presentation used to convey the message. The style should be clear, factual and objective, demonstrating an informed and balanced view. It is an accepted convention in report writing – particularly those of a more formal nature – that impersonal constructions should be used, ie the writer would use 'It was evident' rather than 'I noticed'.

In terms of presentation, typewriting texts will supply useful guidelines and examples, as will many books on communications. The principal things to bear in mind are logical sequence, good links between different sections and clear indexing.

This can be ensured by giving sufficient thought to the use of spacing, both in terms of line spacing and indentation and to utilising different styles of type, together with features such as emboldening (where the facility exists) as well as making good use of letters and numerals to sub-divide sections.

A special word about indexing

As is the case when preparing minutes (see Section 14) careful indexing can greatly facilitate the reader while being particularly helpful when one reader wishes to communicate with others and draw their attention to a particular section of the minutes or report. Providing a numerical reference will help greatly in this respect.

Another benefit is that the use of numbers can help the reader of a report to recognise the importance of a particular section or paragraph. The use of single numbers, eg 1, 2 and 3 may be used to denote main sections while a numeral followed by a full stop and another number, eg 1.1, 1.2, 1.3, will highlight subsections. A further subdivision to a particular paragraph may be represented by the addition of yet another full stop and number, viz 1.2.1, 1.2.2 and so on. This technique is adopted by most government departments and is also commonly used by organisations which operate on a committee structure where formal minutes are prepared.

An alternative method is to use large Roman numerals, ie I, II, III to denote main sections, adopting arabic numerals, ie 1, 2, 3 for the subsections and small arabic letters, ie a, b, c (on their own or within brackets thus: (a)) to denote paragraphs. The ultimate possibility would be to enumerate points within the paragraphs by small Roman numerals, ie i, ii, iii (on their own or within brackets). Therefore the hierarchy of a formal report would be as indicated in Fig. 11.3.

```
I First Main Heading
1. Section Heading
   (a) First Sub Heading
        i) First point within sub heading
       ii) Second point within sub heading
   (b) Second Sub Heading
2. Section Heading
II Second Main Heading
```

Fig. 11.3   Hierarchical arrangement for a formal report

Telephone skills

The telephone is a major feature in all modern offices and the proportion of the average secretary's time spent using the telephone is estimated to be somewhere in the region of 10 per cent. Given that the telephone plays such a major part, it is essential that the secretary masters the mechanics of its efficient and effective use. Without the support of good telephone communications the business world would virtually grind to a halt. However, telephones can be both a curse and a blessing for a secretary. Many frustrating hours can be spent trying to make contact or returning calls, and the interruption of other activities can in some situations be almost constant.

Receiving calls

Secretaries need to be very positive in their attitude to the telephone and have an excellent telephone manner and technique. Prompt answering is important together with a pleasant greeting announcing your name or position or indicating the department. In most large companies the call will have come from the switchboard which will have given the organisation's name and routed the call. It will be usual to ask about the nature of the call and whether you can help. Dependent on the response you will then be in a position to judge whether to handle the query yourself, reroute it elsewhere if appropriate, take a message or perhaps put the call through to your boss.

Screening calls

Many secretaries as well as acting as physical gatekeeper to their boss operate a stringent telephone screening service. In some jobs it will be vital to be on your guard against bogus 'personal callers'. Often they may turn out to be representatives or press people so it is important to tread carefully. Do not hesitate to 'interrogate' a little if in doubt but try to develop an instinct for such calls as an over-inquisitorial approach can place you in an unfavourable light with genuine personal callers who will resent such treatment.

The 'Hold' facility

Sometimes it will be necessary to ask the caller to 'hold' while you check with your manager whether he wishes to speak with the caller. Where you do use this feature be sure that you neither leave the caller 'holding' for too long nor inadvertently cut him off.

Taking a message

Always be ready to take a message when answering the telephone and be sure that you get full details of name, title, company, telephone and (where appropriate) extension number of the caller. Listen carefully to what the caller has to say and be sure to ask for confirmation of any details you have taken down before you ring off. Where you do take a message be sure that you record the date and time together with all the relevant details and add your own name and extension number, if you have one.

Some organisations use specially designed telephone message pads for this purpose and one of the advantages of this is that the design is immediately recognisable for what it is and is consequently less likely to be overlooked or lost among a lot of other papers on a desk. One other vital ingredient will be clear handwriting. Better still, if the message is a complex one, type it.

Keeping your cool

Sometimes the telephone seems to bring out the worst in people and they can be short-tempered, rude and abrupt, showing little or no patience and consideration. This achieves nothing and it is vital that you always remain calm and co-operative regardless of the behaviour of the caller.

Placing calls

Most secretaries will place the majority of their boss's calls as it is extremely wasteful of executive time to dial telephone numbers and then find that something like 70 per cent of the calls do not produce results for one reason or another.

Sometimes a secretary will have a string of calls to make and where the first recipient of a call is not available it will make best sense to try again at the end of the list of calls rather than ask for a return call when you know that the phone is likely to be busy.

When placing calls either personally or on behalf of your boss the following points can help ensure efficiency and save time:

- find the numbers yourself – do not ask the switchboard operator, unless you are really stuck as this should not strictly be part of her job;
- have the numbers of the calls listed ready;
- know your contact wherever possible;
- where you know an extension number use it (if you do not have one make a note, where appropriate, for future reference);
- have clear notes made on the content of each call in order to avoid, waffle, omission or repetition;
- have any relevant papers to hand in case you need to refer to them during the conversation;
- when you are connected, announce clearly who you are and the purpose of your call;
- be prepared to leave a message – even with an answering machine;
- observe standard telephone conventions, eg if you are cut off during a call which you initiated it should be you who rings back –

otherwise both parties can be dialling at once and finding the lines engaged;

- when placing calls for your boss be sure that he is ready to receive them and that he is suitably briefed.

Transferring calls

Even the most efficient switchboards will sometimes route calls wrongly or it may be, as is the case in many large organisations, that extension numbers are frequently changed as a result of staff or accommodation transfers. In such instances it is helpful to the caller if you can transfer them direct rather than reroute them back to the switchboard.

Most systems have a transfer facility and by pressing this button and dialling the appropriate extension the call is held until you either locate the required extension in which case your replacing your receiver will automatically reroute the call to the new extension or you depress the transfer button again to return you to the caller. Where this is likely to be a feature of your organisation it is useful to make a special note of the new extension to which the previous occupant of your telephone has transferred, otherwise you will have to spend time consulting the internal directory which may not be up-to-date!

Equipment familiarity

One final point worthy of comment in terms of telephone technique is mastery of the equipment. Modern telephone systems are extremely sophisticated and possess a range of very useful features (see Unit 1, Section 7), but the benefits to be gained are seriously eroded where staff are not fully conversant with such features.

Numeracy skills

No longer is it acceptable for a secretary to profess ignorance or fear of working with figures. Where an advertisement states that someone who is 'comfortable with figures' or 'likes working with numbers' is preferred, this is unlikely to mean that the position would only be suitable for someone with a degree in mathematics! What it probably means is that the secretary will be expected to undertake certain tasks which require her to work with figures, checking totals, calculating expenses, keeping simple accounts, working out VAT, discounts and percentages and completing standard financial returns.

While it is likely that some people will feel happier in this area of work than others, every aspiring secretary should at least feel confident and competent in respect of basic numerical work. Also it is important to be able to keep track of personal finances, salary and tax. Besides, with the advances in calculators (see also Section 8, p 220) so much of the actual calculation is now done for you by the machine. All that is really called for is the patience to study the instruction booklet and to perform some practice exercises.

Never pass over the opportunity to learn to use any of the financial and statistical software packages that are currently available for micro-computers. Their operation is surprisingly straightforward even for those with little or no previous knowledge of mathematics at this level of manual application.

CHECKLIST

1 As technology advances the role of the secretary evolves but there is still an expectation that secretaries will possess certain 'tools of the trade'.

2 The standard technical skills are still those of typewriting and shorthand, although a knowledge of word processing is now frequently included.

3 The importance of English to a secretary cannot be over-emphasised.

4 Despite the increase in the use of audio dictation systems there is still a sound case for the use of shorthand.

5 All secretaries need to feel confident in the preparation of business correspondence.

6 Presentation and layout are important in all types of written communication.

7 Minutes and reports are greatly improved and more easy to follow when careful indexing is included to help highlight the importance of different sections and make the location of particular sections much quicker.

8 Another essential skill for any secretary is the efficient and effective use of the telephone.

9 Telephone systems tend to be fairly sophisticated and equipment mastery is an important aspect of any good telephone technique.

10 It is usual for employers to expect a level of numeracy from secretarial staff and advertisements for some positions actually make specific reference to such a requirement.

QUICK REVISION QUESTIONS

1 Suggest four useful tips for anyone taking shorthand dictation.
2 Assume that your company is changing over to a centralised audio dictation system and that you have been asked to provide guidelines for staff on good dictation technique. Draft the points you would wish to stress.
3 Briefly explain what is meant by stenotyping.
4 List the component parts of any business letter in the order in which they would appear when typed on letterheaded paper.
5 Provide suggested alternatives for the following phrases taken from business letters:
   a We acknowledge receipt of your communication of the 15th inst.
   b Enclosed please find . . .
   c Hoping to be favoured with an early reply.
6 When might a memorandum be used?
7 What are the main sections into which a report can normally be divided?
8 Design a simple telephone message form.
9 Suggest three important points which a secretary should remember when placing a telephone call.
10 Give three examples of occasions where a secretary's numeracy skills may be called upon.

12 Organisational skills

As well as a good range of what have been termed 'technical skills', secretaries need good organisational skills. Such skills will help ensure the smooth running of an office, section or department and help all parties make the best use of their time. The type of organisation which is called for will vary according to the type of company, the size of office section or department, the nature of the work and the personalities of those involved.

Some situations will demand a lot of forward planning to accommodate everything which needs to be done or fitted in to a very tight schedule. Imagine what it would be like to be secretary to a major international orchestra conductor who has concert tours arranged months and possibly years in advance! Another situation might involve a lot of routine tasks, eg the completion of monthly returns, the operation of cycles of committees, scheduled deadlines and annual events, which would make it necessary and possible to anticipate events and estimate the time involved so that other activities could be organised around them. Yet another might be difficult if not impossible to predict in that the situation is dynamic with the picture constantly changing so that successful organisation will rely on ability to handle arrangements at short notice, respond to changes of plan and cater for the unexpected.

In any event it will fall to the secretary to co-ordinate the essential elements of the schedules of those individuals for whom she provides support. This will involve, keeping diaries and appointments schedules, handling travel arrangements and generally trying to manage everyone's time to best effect.

At the end of this section you should be able to:

- list the essentials of maintaining office diaries;
- indicate typical 'thieves of time';
- suggest measures to ensure the more effective management of time;
- identify problems which can arise when working for more than one person;
- suggest strategies to overcome time-sharing problems;

- identify the principal features of making effective travel arrangements;
- prepare itineraries;
- compare and contrast travel arrangements necessary for different parts of the world;
- give advice on booking travel and hotel accommodation;
- suggest a selection of useful travel reference sources which a secretary might consult.

Keeping diaries

The diary is the focal point and linchpin when it comes to organising an office. It is both the reference for the day's activities and the basis for all forward planning. Therefore sound diary management is an essential element of any secretary's role. Wherever possible it is preferable to have only one desk diary, as great confusion can arise where the secretary has one diary and the manager another. Obviously any executive will carry a personal pocket diary into which he will doubtless enter appointments agreed while he is out of the office and it will be difficult enough to incorporate that information without having two desk diaries as well!

The maintenance of several diaries is not only time-consuming but there is always the risk of making errors when transferring information and a need to constantly confer, update and cross-reference. Also where you may have omitted to transfer information there is the danger that double bookings or missed appointments will result. Therefore it is more efficient to keep one official desk diary into which all appointments are entered.

Ideally all appointments should be made through you. Even where your manager is out of the office and finds that he is asked by another executive to agree a further appointment, he should suggest to the other party that secretaries liaise. This can save a lot of confusion and often avoids the need to cancel or reschedule appointments later.

Filling in the diary

Many different diary formats are available and it is important to select one that is in keeping with the amount and type of entries that need to be made. When an executive has a very busy schedule it will be essential to have enough space to enter all the necessary details. Some executives may prefer to have daily details transferred to a card or have the actual diary page photocopied for ease of reference, particularly where they may have a series of appointments away from the office.

In terms of filling in actual detail the following are useful guidelines:

- write neatly and clearly;
- print all names;
- include telephone numbers where possible;
- make initial appointments in pencil and confirm in ink;
- transfer pre-arranged appointments and fixed information, eg AGM dates, set meeting dates, subscriptions due, birthdays and anniversaries from the old diary into the new as soon as you have it;
- don't overload the diary – cross-reference to a file or follow-up system where necessary;
- provide all essential detail, eg precise meeting places and exact appointment times;
- allow for thinking and/or travelling time;
- give thought to the overall programme for the day and week;
- remember the need to consolidate after a holiday or a lengthy period of absence from the office;
- try to allow some time for yourself so that you can liaise as necessary with your boss.

The secretary's own diary

Some secretaries may also keep their own office diaries and this will be a decision based on individual preference in terms of the type of aide-mémoire required. It will be useful to note down all the advance preparations required to ensure the smooth running of the boss's schedule. For example, the preparation of essential paperwork may need to be started several days before a particular meeting or appointment, and restaurant bookings may need to be made and confirmed or flight tickets collected and taxis booked in advance. In such instances the secretary's diary will function as a back-up and checklist against which the progress of arrangements may be monitored.

Additionally where the secretary herself may find that she has personal responsibilities in terms of committee representation or instances when she is required to deputise for her boss, these would always be noted in her diary. Likewise it will be useful to include certain events and appointments external to the organisation as it will be useful to assess their implications in respect of time, travel and workload. Most secretaries will find that their jobs are rarely strictly 9 to 5 and that some form of (what will often be negotiated with her boss) flexitime will operate. In any event it will be useful to know in advance what personal arrangements need to be accommodated into the working routine.

Electronic diaries

Technology enables organisations to operate an electronic diary management service via computer. This means that all executives' diary details are keyed into the system by secretaries and can be recalled to the VDU for updating and co-ordination purposes.

The system will respond to any variable required, eg dates, times, names, types of meetings or venues. Therefore where one secretary is trying to arrange a meeting of her manager with another three executives she can either check the diaries of the other executives involved by accessing them and displaying them on her VDU (the window technique of display is particularly useful here – see p. 203) or she can get the computer to do all the necessary checking and comparing for her and come up with a selection of possible dates and times. When a time is selected a message can then be sent to the other parties via electronic mail, asking that they confirm or state an alternative.

Some electronic workstations have reminder systems built into the software whereby appointments will be signalled automatically on screen or there will be a warning signal to remind the secretary to check the diary or appointment schedule held in the system.

While such systems can save a tremendous amount of time they are dependent on the quality of information fed into the diary management system by the secretaries. Continuous monitoring and updating is essential – just as with a manual book version – if the system is to work effectively.

Managing time

Time is something none of us ever has enough of and consequently the way in which we manage our time is important if we want to be effective in achieving the things we set out to do. In a secretary's day a lot of her decisions in terms of how she manages her time will involve her in prioritising and this ability to prioritise is something on which bosses set high store.

Sometimes it will be a physical impossibility to get through everything that is in an in-tray in the course of a day, given the many other interventions which typically occur. What is important is that the essential things are completed. Things will invariably fall into four principal categories, viz:

1 Things that *must be done*.
2 Things that *should be done*.

3   Things that *could be postponed*.
4   Things that *can be delegated*.

Therefore it will be a matter of checking through the workload and assessing priorities. Categorising according to the four types mentioned above should help you make the right decisions. This does become easier the more familiar the secretary is with her boss's work and with the operation of the organisation as a whole, so it is important to learn as much as you can as quickly as you can.

Know yourself

How effectively you manage your time will have a lot to do with you as a person. Be honest with yourself when you answer the following questions and you will have a better idea of the sort of work habits you have.

- Do you have a tidy desk?
- Do you rely on your memory?
- Do you make lists?
- Do you stick to your list?
- Do you lose your list?
- Is your list invariably too long?
- Do you make your list in order of priority?
- Do you tend to do the things you enjoy best, first?
- Do you always arrive at work on time?
- Do you frequently arrive early?
- Do you stick to tried and tested techniques?
- Do you experiment with new ways of doing things?
- Do you find yourself grumbling and complaining?
- Do you ever turn to another job before you finish the one you started?
- Do you procrastinate?
- Are you optimistic or pessimistic?
- Do you think of yourself as a perfectionist?
- Do you worry a lot?
- Do you tend to get flustered?
- Do you have a preferred time of the day, eg are you better in the morning or are you a slow starter who gets into her stride as the day progresses?
- Do you find it difficult to delegate?
- Do you find it difficult to say 'No'?
- Do you ever feel pressurised or under stress in your work?

Most of these questions can be posed whether you are a practising secretary or whether you are still studying. There are no right and wrong answers, but where you are honest with yourself you will have a fairly good idea of what your working habits are like and where there may be room for improvement.

Some things may be obvious and relatively straightforward to remedy. For example, if you are guilty of having an untidy desk the solution is obvious if not necessarily easy to adhere to. Also it will be relatively easy to try to be more punctual or to experiment with making lists and establishing priorities.

It is the personality factors which are more complex to deal with and it will mean persevering and trying to rid oneself of bad habits or insecure reactions to the pressures and demands of others. However, self awareness is the first step, and the realisation that certain habits or traits are responsible for much of the time we waste can at least point us in the right direction for making some adjustments which will help increase our efficiency and make us more effective.

Typical thieves of a secretary's time

One thing that will enable a secretary to manage her time more effectively is her ability to pinpoint typical things which will eat into time in the course of the day's work or make it difficult to establish an efficient routine.

The following are some likely culprits:

- failing to listen carefully to instructions first time round and having to ask again later;
- not setting any time aside to liaise with the boss;
- unnecessary interruptions;
- lack of planning;
- setting unrealistic targets;
- trying to tackle far too many things at once and ending up with nothing completely finished;
- doing things that could easily be delegated to someone else purely out of habit or just because you like doing them;
- lacking confidence to do the task straight off, ie making drafts of routine things;
- not getting straight before tackling a task, eg starting a job in the certain knowledge that you should make a phone call first or not taking a few minutes to tidy your desk before settling to a task;

- not having essential reference materials to hand, eg dictionaries, timetables, telephone directories;
- trying to short-circuit something, eg failing to consult an instruction manual when using an unfamiliar piece of equipment or attempting a new function on a familiar machine;
- reading slowly;
- careless proofreading;
- making unnecessary checks;
- looking for things which haven't been put back in their rightful place;
- retracing one's steps, eg going backwards and forwards to the files or photocopier;
- ploughing through mountains of unfiled material;
- hoarding, eg failing to discard unwanted papers, and then being constrained for space;
- frittering time away on personal activities, eg office gossip, personal phone calls, reading newspapers;
- indecision;
- lack of assertiveness;
- untidiness.

Managing your boss's time

Part of a secretary's job will also be to help her boss manage his time most effectively. So not only does she need to know herself and her own working habits but she needs to know her boss as well. This will include recognising his preferences in terms of things such as when he likes to deal with his paperwork and whether he likes to conduct business in a social atmosphere. Such awareness will greatly help when it comes to planning his day, scheduling his appointments and generally reducing pressure.

Also it will enable her to judge how much her boss needs, or wants, to 'be organised'. Some bosses welcome having the pressure taken from them a little in the knowledge that the secretary will always be there to remind them, but others may be methodical and well organised themselves and resent what they consider to be unnecessary intrusion. This is always a delicate area and secretaries need to exercise their judgement and try to strike a happy medium.

Putting it into practice

Recognising the sort of things which eat into time is one half of the equation; the other half is applying the skills and strategies to rectify matters. This requires a lot of self-analysis and positive thinking plus the ability to exercise sound judgement and establish what is and is not important and in which direction energy should be expended. This is really the crux of being a successful secretary. Efficiency is one essential criterion but in itself efficiency is not sufficient. It needs to be combined with effectiveness because whereas efficiency suggests doing the job right, effectiveness necessitates doing the right job!

Time sharing

The need for sound diary and time management will become even more necessary where a secretary is dividing her time between two or even more executives. This is a common feature of many secretarial roles. The one-to-one situation is somewhat of a luxury reserved largely for top management. This change has come about largely due to the impact of technology which has enhanced office support and relieved secretaries of much of the repetitive routine work previously associated with the role.

The interests of economy are also major justifications for adopting the sort of organisational structure whereby one secretary may provide support for several executives, given that sophisticated technology is costly to install but capable of reducing many of the time-consuming technical elements of the job.

This change has significant implications for secretaries in that the emphasis is now on a different range of skills and attributes, viz the attitudinal, human relations and organisational skills rather than the technical capabilities. Working for more than one person is much more demanding in terms of the need to display flexible and adaptable attitudes and secretaries need the right personal qualities and characteristics together with good communication skills if they are to ensure that each individual is treated fairly and that time is shared on an equitable basis.

Office psychology – wearing different hats

Many secretaries will find that they need to become something of an amateur psychologist in certain time-sharing situations. It certainly requires energy and imagination on the part of a secretary to accommodate the different personalities and styles of working which executives are likely to have.

Some will be formal while others will be informal; some will be highly organised while others will be disorganised; some will be very specific and positive in terms of the way in which they want something done, while others will leave it to the judgement of the secretary; some may use shorthand, others will prefer audio; some will delegate a lot of work, others will not. Such a list could go on and on and consequently it will be necessary for a secretary to be extremely flexible and able to wear a number of different hats in the course of a typical day.

It will be essential to establish some sort of routine which is acceptable to all concerned and to resolve any problems which are likely to occur due to the different demands which are made on the secretary's time at the earliest opportunity. A lot of co-operation, co-ordination and understanding is required by everyone and it is important that the secretary establishes a good working rapport with each superior and is able to modify her working style accordingly.

Conflicting loyalties

It is likely that there will be occasions when a secretary feels that conflicting loyalties arise. This will most probably be where secretarial support is being provided within a section or department where superior/subordinate relationships exist. For example, the secretary may work for a director and a deputy director or a deputy and his assistants.

Almost inevitably there will be times when the senior member of staff will expect to have priority over the secretary's time and this can prove to be a difficult problem to resolve. Nonetheless, it is one which will need to be tackled assertively by a secretary, otherwise she will find herself unable to cope with the demands made of her. This is where it is essential to establish a good working relationship with each person so that problems can be discussed openly in a co-operative way and suitable compromises reached.

Confidentiality and individuality

It may also be the case that one executive's work must be kept confidential from the others and the secretary will need to discourage any attempts to have her gossip or divulge confidences. Under no circumstances should one executive be played off against another, and no more should the secretary allow herself to become a pawn in some sort of office power game. The secretary needs to develop an interest in each executive's work while managing to keep the work separate and allocate a fair amount of time and energy to each.

Making travel arrangements

More and more people travel each year and while travelling may sound very glamorous, in reality it can prove to be a very different experience. This will be more significant when travel is undertaken for business purposes and when the traveller is expected to be on top form and able to cope with all the pressures of business deals, meetings and decision making in a foreign country, even after a long, stressful and tiring journey.

One of a secretary's duties will be to organise the necessary arrangements and with careful planning this can help greatly towards the success of any business travel whether it is a day trip within this country, three days attending a trade fair in Europe or an extended tour to the other side of the world.

Travel departments and travel agents

Large companies whose personnel travel frequently are likely to operate their own travel section or department which in turn will be likely to liaise with a travel agent – possibly one specialising in business travel.

Nonetheless a secretary will still play a crucial role and will be the person to make contact with the travel section, or, in the case of a smaller company, direct with the agent. It is important to establish a good rapport with a reputable agent (one who is a member of the Association of British Travel Agents (ABTA)), as this relationship can save valuable time and resolve many problems.

Travel preliminaries

Before making any firm travel arrangements it is essential to go through standard preliminaries and draw up a draft itinerary for any business trip in consultation with the boss or other person(s) whose arrangements are being drawn up. There are certain things which need to be borne in mind and these can be identified by answering three main questions:

1 **What is the purpose of the trip?** An awareness of the objectives is vital as it will have a bearing on literally everything else from the amount of time which can reasonably be allowed for the trip, to the costs that can be justified and the additional preparations which need to be made. For instance, a routine visit to a subsidiary company in this country will be very different from an exploratory trip to the Far East in an attempt to forge new business links, and the arrangements for the latter will be decidedly more complex and time-consuming.

2 **When is it feasible to make the trip?** This will depend on a number of things including:

- the fixed dates of any special event(s) to be attended;
- existing diary commitments; the co-ordination of dates where more than one person is scheduled to travel;
- the existence of contacts or whether there is a need to obtain the necessary contacts first (this could take time);
- the availability of contacts (there is no point in flying half way round the world if it is not possible to set up the desired meetings); the complexities of the arrangements which need to be made, eg visas, vaccinations, preparation of sales literature in a foreign language, transportation of samples;
- the availability of seats on a suitable flight;
- the availability of hotel accommodation (this can be problematic if the destination is popular and the trip is to be made in the holiday season);
- the time of year (climatic considerations);
- the need to be briefed by colleagues (arranging convenient and sufficient briefing sessions can take time);
- public or religious holidays in the country to be visited.

3 How long will it take to make the trip? Again existing diary commitments need to be taken into account together with:
- the type of journey, eg how long, how many transfers or stopovers;
- the need for recovery time, eg where the journey involves crossing the international dateline, there may be the problem of jetlag to consider if a series of important meetings is scheduled;
- the volume of business which needs to be transacted during the visit;
- whether there is additional local travel within the country of destination and the likely nature of that travel;
- whether any free time is to be included, eg it may be that a businessman wishes to do some sightseeing if he is visiting a country for the first time;
- the need to allow for contingencies, eg flight delays, industrial disputes, political unrest;
- the need for recovery time on the return to this country, as jetlag can be particularly bad where travel is in an easterly direction across time zones.

Once these issues have been clarified satisfactorily a draft itinerary can be drawn up by the secretary and once this is cleared by the boss she can begin to make the actual arrangements for the trip, in conjunction with the travel section or agent.

Personal travel files

One very useful thing that secretaries who are responsible for travel can do is set up confidential personal files for executives whose travel arrangements they undertake. This file should contain full details on everything that needs to be known in terms of personal data, documentation, preferences and previous travel arrangements, all of which greatly facilitate the ease and speed with which new arrangements are completed.

The type of information which should be included in an executive's personal travel file is as follows:

- personal data, ie name, address, date of birth, country of birth, etc.;
- passport details, including number and renewal dates;
- passport endorsements (these can be very important where a businessman may be travelling to countries which are, for example, politically opposed, in that one country may refuse entry to a passport holder whose passport contains a stamp from a recent visit to another country with which relations are hostile, so it is important to be aware in advance of any difficulties which might be encountered);
- visa information, including type and duration for which valid;
- details of vaccination certificates with dates;
- driving licence information including the validity of an international licence;
- details of all credit cards together with expiry dates;
- preferences in terms of air travel, eg airline, type of aircraft, class of travel, whether the executive is a BA Executive cardholder;
- preferences in respect of seat, eg smoking or non-smoking, window, centre or aisle seat, rear, middle or front of cabin;
- preferences in terms of flight services, eg meals, in-flight entertainment;
- attitude to day and night flights;
- preference in respect of Channel sea crossings, eg ferry, hovercraft;
- preference in terms of crossing routes and departure terminals;
- preferences in terms of types and class of hotel;
- reactions to previous hotels used in respect of location, service, accommodation and food;
- details of car hire firms used with reactions;
- preferences in terms of rail travel.

It is important that this file is treated as being strictly confidential and that it is updated as and when necessary, eg following each business trip when impressions are fresh in the traveller's mind. Where secretaries have collected this sort of information they will be able to go ahead with confidence and prepare travel arrangements without needing to ask for all sorts of standard information. This will not only save time in the working day but will enable the supply of detailed information which the travel section or agent will need and appreciate when making reservations.

Working within budget allocation

Another important thing which secretaries need to remember when making travel arrangements is the need to keep within the budget allocation. Even large organisations operate on a budget and sometimes this may seem quite tight, especially when attempting to make last-minute arrangements where the choices may be limited. For example, it may be technically possible to arrange a flight to a certain destination on a certain date but only at extra cost and it will be necessary to get clearance before confirming such a reservation.

Also where a strict budget is in operation it may be possible to offer a number of options to an executive in respect of both travel and accommodation and, of course, the more personal information which secretaries have at their disposal the more realistic these alternatives can be.

Air travel

Where vast distances are involved there will be little option but to fly, unless, of course, an executive has a phobia about flying, in which case, alternative arrangements would have to be made. However, this would represent a fairly exceptional set of circumstances.

Competition is fierce among airline operators and it will usually be advisable to rely on the advice of a specialist travel agent to come up with the best deal based on their knowledge of an executive's needs and preferences. This is where the secretary's personal travel files can prove useful.

Classes of flight

On long-haul flights there are generally three classes:

- **Economy**, ie tourist class;
- **Executive**, club or business class; and
- **First Class**.

Executive or first class seats are well worth considering where an executive has a long trip to make. Executive class offers roomier seating arrangements than the tourist class and enables business travellers to work more easily where they choose to do so, or simply to rest without the general disturbance, eg duty free sales and in-flight entertainment of economy travel. In addition to the standard service there is often a choice of menu and a selection of wines, and on the ground there are separate check-in arrangements and often executive lounges.

First class travel is even better, particularly in respect of the 'sleeper seats'. These are particularly welcomed during a long flight in that they enable the traveller to stretch out completely. Certain airlines have gone even further by converting the upper cabins of their Boeing 747 aircraft into first class sleeping accommodation by installing bunk beds.

Concorde

All seats on Concorde are first class, but the main advantage is Concorde's supersonic speed which means that for a little more than a normal first class fare, it is possible to cross the Atlantic in about four hours, ie approximately half the time of a normal flight. It also enjoys superior cabin service, special check-in and baggage handling facilities, all geared to maintain the time saved in the air. Additional services such as courtesy cars or helicopters can also be provided for passengers flying into John F Kennedy airport in New York to take them to downtown Manhattan or to one of New York's other airports (La Guardia or Newark) to continue their journey.

Flying considerations

As with any other mode of travel flying has its own peculiarities and it is advisable to take these into account when making flight reservations. The travel agent will be indispensable here. Some of the things to look out for are as follows.

Transfer difficulties Where it is necessary to change planes during a trip it is essential that sufficient time is allowed between flights, particularly where it may be necessary to move between airports.

Direct flights It is important to note the distinction between non-stop and direct flights, as the latter may involve a stopover en route either to refuel or to drop passengers.

Weather problems It is impossible to forecast good flying weather, regardless of the time of year.

Booking difficulties It can be particularly difficult to arrange flights to some countries as seats seem to be regularly fully booked. Where this happens the travel agent will place the traveller on a waitlist in the hope of securing a cancellation, as well as trying to arrange an alternative. It is advisable, therefore, to book as far in advance as possible.

Open tickets Even where someone is travelling on an open ticket this is no guarantee that a seat will be available on the return flight preferred, so again as much advance notice as possible is recommended.

Economy tickets While there may appear to be a number of good deals to be had by, for example, booking an economy ticket, say at least two weeks in advance, it should be remembered that with most of these deals it is impossible to change flight dates or times and in the event of a cancellation there is no recovery of the fare, even where insurance has been taken out, unless the cancellation falls within the bounds of the policy and often in the event of business travel it will not.

Seat preferences Travel agents can reserve particular seats according to a traveller's preferences, so full instructions should be given when making reservations.

Executive cards British Airways, for example, operate an Executive cardholder system whereby for an annual fee travellers can enjoy special services and facilities, eg they may use executive lounges, even when travelling economy class, they are guaranteed seats and they can benefit from good insurance offers. Regular business travellers will be justified in the extra expense which membership entails, given the facilities available.

Baggage allowances Care should always be taken to check the baggage allowance on particular flights. Many executives do, however, prefer to travel light, particularly where they may be operating to a tight schedule and where time can be saved by avoiding the need to check in baggage or wait for it at the collection point on reaching the destination. This can be done by using one of the popular folding traveller packs which are accepted as cabin luggage in addition to a briefcase. They can easily hold a spare suit/outfit, shoes and so on.

Shuttle services

Businessmen regularly avail themselves of the shuttle services which operate between major UK airports. They offer an efficient and frequent daily service on a 'walk-on/walk off' basis which does not require advance booking. Fares can be collected during the flight and where a flight is over-subscribed a second plane will automatically be added to the schedule. While flights are slightly more expensive than first class rail travel the time-saving can be considerable. However it is important to take into account the distance between the airports and city centres.

Timesaver tickets

A lot of domestic travel within the UK is undertaken at short notice so the 'Timesaver' ticket scheme introduced by the major domestic airlines (British Airways, British Caledonian and British Midland) can prove extremely useful.

Single flight tickets are issued, through a travel agent, in cheque book form and may be completed whenever required. Advance reservations may be made either via the travel agent or direct with the airline. Where a traveller wishes to use the shuttle service the booking may be made at the airport on departure. The tickets, which are simple to complete, are collected in by the airline and the flight cost is debited directly to the holder's account with his travel agent.

Rail travel

While air represents by far the greatest proportion of travel arrangements which secretaries are required to make, many executives do travel regularly by rail. Tickets may be booked at British Rail stations or via agencies and payment may be made by credit card. Where a company's personnel make frequent use of rail travel it is possible that they may choose to operate a British Rail account in which case personnel simply present a British Rail travel warrant at the booking office and the cost is charged to the company's account for payment at a later date. Alternatively a secretary may hold an emergency stock of pre-paid tickets for British Rail travel and these can be particularly useful where last minute arrangements are made.

As with air travel, bookings should take into account traveller preferences in respect of seats, and care should be taken to study the timetables as some trains are very much faster than others. Also different services are available in respect of food and drink and many business people prefer to use the InterCity Pullman services where meals are served directly to the first class seats. Additional services are also provided in the form of sleeper trains and Motorail (the transporting of cars by rail).

Road travel

Travel by road can have its advantages primarily in that journeys are made from door to door and there is no problem in respect of the amount of luggage that can easily be transported. However, driving can prove particularly tiring in that it requires intense concentration, particularly on today's busy, congested and over-taxed roads.

Taking a car on the continent

Where a car is being taken abroad ferry reservations need to be made (including cabin bookings where the crossing is a long one), sometimes well in advance if crossings are to be made at peak times or during holiday periods. It is also important to ensure that the car complies with all regulations in respect of driving on the continent. For example, British cars need to display a GB plate, tinted headlamps are required (removable covers may be fitted to existing headlights) and in some countries it is obligatory to carry a first-aid kit. An organisation like the Automobile Association (AA) or the Royal Automobile Club (RAC) will supply all the necessary advice and information as well as issuing an International Driving Licence required in some countries.

Whether driving in this country or abroad the driver should always carry his driving licence and insurance certificate, as well as his membership card for the AA, RAC or other rescue service, as this needs to be presented when services are called upon. Where someone is travelling by road in winter road conditions it is also advisable to carry a shovel and to have a flask with a hot drink, as well as some food and a warm travelling rug in case of emergency.

Essential documentation

The documents required vary according to the nature of the trip and the country to be visited but are likely to be principally passports, visas, vaccination certificates and insurance cover.

Full British passports are valid for 10 years and may be obtained (and renewed or amended) at one of the UK passport offices located in London, Belfast, Glasgow, Liverpool, Newport or Peterborough. Application forms are available from the Post Office for passports containing 30 or 94 pages. It is important to allow sufficient time to process a full passport application (about 4 weeks is the usual time) and extra time should be allowed during the peak summer period. Personal applications can be made direct to the Passport Offices although this does not necessarily ensure priority treatment.

British Visitors Passports, valid for one year only, are available direct from main post offices and are issued on production of two photographs, proof of identity and the appropriate fee. However, such passports are not valid worldwide and can only be used for holidays and unpaid business trips of up to 3 months' duration.

Whichever form of passport is used it is important to note the number in case it is lost or stolen. Certain countries are notorious for thefts of this nature and all precautions should be taken to safeguard passports.

Certain countries require visas or entry permits and it is important to check current requirements when arranging business travel as regulations are continually changing. Checks can be made direct with the appropriate embassy, via a travel agent or by consulting the monthly travel manual published by the International Air Transport Association (IATA). Visas are available from embassies, either direct or by postal application, and through travel agents. It is important to allow sufficient time to organise visas as some countries take a long time to issue them and issue may even be dependent on personal attendance at the embassy. Exit permits are also a requirement in certain countries and again it is important to check.

Likewise it is always prudent to check health regulations when arranging foreign travel. The main health risks are in respect of cholera, malaria, typhoid, polio and yellow fever and for some countries inoculations/vaccinations may be recommended or even compulsory. It is advisable to have any necessary inoculations/vaccinations well in advance to allow full recovery time. Current information on International Certificates of Vaccination is available from a travel agent or from the aforementioned Travel Information Manual (TIM).

When travel arrangements are made at short notice and immunisation is recommended, British Airways Medical Centres in London can get the necessary vaccine so that travellers can be quickly vaccinated. Appointments can be made by telephone.

Additionally travellers who are in receipt of any medical treatment should ensure that they have arranged medication to cover the duration of their trip and where necessary any documentary medical evidence should also be taken with them.

Insurance cover is another essential. Travelling can prove hazardous in a variety of ways and adequate cover is vital. This will normally be catered for by a company's own policy, but individual travellers need to carry the necessary documentation in case they need to make a claim. Cover should be available for all contingencies including death, personal accident, medical expenses, loss of money and property, including luggage. Individuals may wish to take out their own supplementary cover as they consider necessary.

One other form of insurance necessary when taking a car abroad is a Green Card, available from the the insurance company handling the car insurance. This covers the holder while driving in Europe.

Financial arrangements

It will be important to ensure that the necessary financial arrangements have been made for any business trip. Sometimes this will be purely the funds necessary to sustain the executive during the trip but on other occasions it may mean arranging currency for business deals, perhaps involving large sums of money, although in such instances this would be the responsibility of the Finance Department.

In any event, it is important to check currency regulations and restrictions in advance. Up-to-date information will be available from the National Bank of the country concerned but general details with regard to the import and export of currency are available in TIM.

Most business travellers will tend to rely largely on Eurocheques (issued by banks for use abroad, and accompanied by a Eurocheque card), traveller's cheques or credit cards. Additionally it will be essential to have some actual currency available in suitable denominations to cover early incidental expenses. For instance large bills can be difficult to exchange in an airport lounge where all the traveller wants is a cup of coffee, and equally, large denomination bills can prove an embarrassment likely to end up as an inflated tip, when used to pay for a short trip in a taxi. Where travel is in a country which operates in unusual currency, extra time should be allowed for a bank to place the necessary order.

Traveller's cheques may be bought from banks and certain travel agents in specified denominations either in sterling or foreign currency. Cheques are signed at the time of purchase and need to be countersigned when exchanged. Most experienced travellers recommend that cheques be purchased in the currency of the country to be visited as exchange is then very easy, the cheques operating virtually as currency. Sometimes it can be difficult to locate a bank or bureau de change to exchange sterling cheques and in the USA there is even decided reluctance to change sterling cheques for real money!

A record should be kept of all traveller's cheque numbers in case of loss or theft. Records should also be kept of all currency transactions with regard to the exchange rates prevailing during the trip including commission charges for the conversions, so that expenses may be worked out accurately on return.

Credit cards are now a regular feature of business travel being accepted readily in most countries, although acceptability should be checked in advance. Prior to trips abroad the validity of all cards should be checked as it could prove disastrous if a card expired during a trip. Also all numbers should be carefully recorded and any loss or theft should be reported to home base immediately so that the appropriate notification can be given to the credit card company.

Hotel accommodation

Where someone has travelled to a particular destination previously and used a particular hotel to his/her satisfaction it will usually be a matter of booking the same again, unless an alternative has been stipulated. However, where arrangements need to be made in respect of a new territory it will be necessary to rely either on personal recommendation, perhaps from the contact to be visited or another business firm who visit the area or the advice given in a hotel guide.

In any event, whenever hotel accommodation is to be booked either directly or via an agent the following need to be taken into account:

- **location**, ie how convenient for the businesss which has to be conducted?
- **ambiance**, ie if business meetings are to be held there is it suitable (eg is it quietly situated)?
- **cost**, ie does it come within the budget allocation?
- **facilities**, ie does it have any special facilities which might be required, eg secretarial support or fax or does it have sports and recreational facilities which the traveller may wish to use after a hard day?
- **food and service**, ie where business entertaining is required does the hotel enjoy a good reputation?

Making reservations

Reservations may be made direct by telephone or telex, ensuring that a written letter or telex confirmation is received afterwards, via the travel agent or through one of the central reservation offices which are operated by large hotel chains like Holiday Inn or Novotel who operate computerised reservation services which supply instant confirmation.

It is usual, when making and confirming reservations, to indicate the name of the traveller for whom the reservation is made, the company he/she represents, estimated time of arrival, duration of stay, method of payment and any special requirements, eg special diets or special facilities and services.

Other arrangements

While these are the main and obvious things requiring a secretary's attention in organising a business trip there are several other details which may require her attention and these are likely to include the following:

- confirming all meetings and appointments;
- arranging transport to and from the airport, certainly at the home base but perhaps also at the destination, if this is possible;
- arranging for the separate transportation of any trade samples required during the trip;
- arranging for a hire car for the duration of the visit (the travel agent will normally make all the necessary arrangements);
- obtaining necessary street maps and perhaps travel guides or good food guides and phrase books;
- booking meals in advance where an executive wishes to entertain clients at a popular local restaurant;
- booking theatre tickets (again the travel agent can do this);
- finding out about any customs regulations or restrictions in operation in the country to be visited;
- reading up on the business and investment conditions appertaining to the country and reporting back;
- carrying out any other advance research in relation to the business to be transacted, eg gathering import statistics;
- where the trip is for sales promotion purposes it is important that the literature should be prepared in the language of the country, taking care that translation is accurate and that the presentations and/or illustrations can in no way cause offence. (It should be borne in mind that this sort of provision cannot be achieved overnight so sufficient forward planning is needed);
- where electrical samples are to be used it is important that the voltage and plug types are correct for the country;
- business cards should be up-to-date with details given in the appropriate language on the reverse side;
- where the traveller does not have a working knowledge of the language, arrangements will have to be made for an interpreter;
- where cultural differences exist it will be important that the traveller is aware of protocol requirements and of any taboos;
- where an executive may wish to report back during the trip he may wish to take a pocket dictating machine and plenty of cassettes;
- pre-addressed envelopes should be prepared for sending material back to base.

Additional tips

Where someone is scheduled to travel for the first time in a strange country certain other measures can help ensure that the trip runs smoothly. The following are a few suggestions:

- it will be important to establish what the weather will be like during the visit in order that the traveller may take appropriate clothing;
- where there is a mixture of formal and informal occasions to be attended during a visit it is important to establish the type of dress that would be considered appropriate;
- where someone expects to be invited into someone's home during a visit it may be appropriate to take a gift, so enquiries should be made as to what sort of gift would be welcomed and appreciated, as it will be important not to cause embarrassment or offence;
- it is also important to try to find out about social behaviour and convention where travellers are entering private homes;
- where a business trip is to be combined with a vacation it may be advisable to check whether there are any regulations in respect of camera equipment;
- it will be useful to ensure that the traveller has the address and telephone number of the appropriate British Embassy or Consulate General;
- the traveller should also carry details of the following information, written in the language of the country:
  a the host company's address;
  b the hotel at which he/she is staying.

  This can prove very useful to provide for taxi drivers, police or other officials where the traveller is unable to communicate in the language.

Preparing the itinerary

When all the details are finalised and confirmed the final trip itinerary can be prepared. Basically an itinerary sets out the dates and appointments in connection with the trip, together with the modes of travel (including flight numbers), departure and arrival times, hotel accommodation, contact addresses and telephone numbers and any other information which might be considered useful to the traveller.

They may be prepared in a variety of ways and in varying degrees of detail, according to the complexities of the trip and individual preferences. Where it is a lengthy itinerary it is likely that a detailed document will be prepared, itemising all necessary information and this will be retained by the executive in his briefcase, but for convenience an abbreviated version will be carried in the pocket or handbag for easy reference.

When preparing itineraries it is customary to prepare several copies for issue as considered necessary. For example, copies may be given out as follows:

- the traveller;
- his/her home;
- immediate superior;
- deputy;
- the co-ordination secretary (if there is one) in the host country;

plus, of course, a copy for the office file and one for the secretary. An example of an itinerary is given as Fig. 12.1.

ITINERARY

Trip of Mr A B Carson to Paris
17–19 June inclusive

Tuesday, 17 June

1550 hrs	Company car at office to take to airport
1645 hrs	Arrive London Heathrow, Terminal 2
1730 hrs	dep Flight AF817
1930 hrs	arr Charles de Gaulle (1 hour ahead)
	Taxi to Hôtel Saint-Louis

(Dinner Le Monde des Chimères?
Tel 43.54.45.27)

Wednesday, 18 June

0800 hrs	Breakfast briefing meeting with M Gentil
0930 hrs	Car to collect to take to Terrail et Cie
1000 hrs	Meeting with Jean-Paul Terrail
	Early afternoon to be spent touring the factory
1530 hrs	Return to hotel
1600 hrs	Meeting in hotel with Henri Duval
2000 hrs	Dinner booked for self and six guests at Brasserie Balzar

Thursday, 19 June

1100 hrs	Meeting at The Sorbonne with Louis Castel
	Suggest lunch at Dodin-Bouffant, rue Frédèric-Sauton (43.25.25.14)
1830 hrs	dep Charles de Gaulle (Flight AF 818)
1830 hrs	arr London Heathrow Terminal 2
	(take off 1 hour)
	Company car will collect

Fig. 12.1 A specimen itinerary

Countdown calendar

Prior to any business trip the secretary should devise a countdown calendar to ensure that all necessary arrangements are made and confirmed where necessary. Some things may take considerable time to organise and co-ordinate and where months of advance notice are available for a trip it is important to begin the preparations well ahead of schedule. For example, where an executive may have been asked to present a paper at a conference, the date will be known many months ahead but there may be considerable research to undertake. Similarly if a promotional stand is being set up for a trade fair or exhibition it needs to be planned to ensure that it achieves the desired results.

Also, where a senior executive may be absent from the office for a period of time appointments and meetings will need to be rescheduled and others may need to be briefed to deputise as necessary. All these things have to be fitted into an existing diary which in all likelihood will be busy already.

A secretary will open a file or files for all matters related to the trip and will monitor progress on all the items concerned.

Sources of reference

A glance round the travel section in any good bookshop will give you some idea of the range of reference books which exist and you will know from the press and television how much attention is given to travel so there is no shortage of information. In fact, the problem is more likely to be the reverse and some of the information provision is of an extremely sophisticated nature. Take, for example, the automated systems and travel services which are now available to travel agents.

The Travicom system

Travel automation has been around since the late 1970s but it has improved substantially in recent years. The majority of airline bookings in the UK are made through a multi-access system called Travicom, which enables the agent to obtain immediate access via direct videotex link to the main computers of over 40 airlines. Agents specialising in large volume business travel can have 24-hour, high speed access to reservations and information facilities via a special leased line.

Travicom provides up-to-date information on flight and seat availability to any destination on any date, together with an instant booking option. Special requests in terms of seats and meals can be accommodated and precise fares provided at the touch of a button. As well as airline booking the system is used by agents for hire car, hotel and British Rail bookings. It is extremely versatile and easy to use and has the advantage of being able to print out all ticket and accounting documentation on the spot.

Reference books

As far as a secretary is concerned the following selection of reference books should satisfy most requirements.

The Travel Trade Directory, published annually by Morgan-Grampian, contains a valuable selection of useful and up-to-date information on all forms of travel, as well as providing details of all travel operators, addresses of passport and visa offices and all other specialist services. The publishers also produce the *Travel Trade Gazette*, which is a weekly newspaper of travel information.

The World Calendar of Holidays, published annually, details public holidays both chronologically and in alphabetical order of country.

Hints to Businessmen, produced by the DTI and obtainable from the Publicity Department of the British and Overseas Trade Board, is a free series of booklets covering many countries of the world and providing useful advice on travel, entry regulations, customs control, consular facilities, hotels, etc.

Hotels and Restaurants in Great Britain, published annually by the British Tourist Authority, lists hotels and restaurants which conform to certain minimum standards.

Travel Information Manual, a joint monthly publication of 14 IATA member airlines, contains the information which is automated and accessible by airline computer terminals. It provides data for all countries on governmental requirements in respect of passports, visas, health regulations, airport taxes, customs and currency.

The ABC World Airways Guide, published monthly, contains complete timetables for the airlines of the world. It gives details of fares, international travel requirements, passports, visas, and health regulations in operation.

The ABC Guide to International Travel, published quarterly contains similar information to the *World Airways Guide*, but includes journey times from country to country as well as more comprehensive information on a country-to-country basis.

ABC Air/Rail Europe, published monthly, provides fast and easy reference to air and InterCity rail timetables throughout Europe as well as through flights to the Middle East and North Africa.

ABC Rail Guide, published monthly, gives complete services, timetables and fare charges from all London main line stations. It also includes a provincial InterCity section and gives all rail services for London and Southern England.

Cook's International Timetable, published monthly, is a guide to the principal rail services of Europe, Africa, America, Asia and Australasia and also supplies local shipping services in the North Sea, the Baltic and the Mediterranean.

ABC Shipping Guide, published monthly, provides a worldwide guide to passenger shipping services and cruises.

AA or RAC Handbooks, both published annually, provide useful details of all major towns and cities in Britain, together with road maps and town plans, information on hotel accommodation, garage facilities, market days, early closing days and other details of use to any motor traveller.

Good Food Guide, published annually by the Consumers' Association, features eating establishments throughout the UK and Ireland. It has a large section for London.

Executive Travel, published monthly by Business Magazines International Ltd, for regular travellers, company travel managers and IATA travel agents in the UK, is carried aboard 20 international airlines and available to guests at key UK hotels.

Business Traveller, published monthly by Perry Publications Ltd, is a subscription magazine with an independent editorial policy and it carries a range of articles of interest to the business traveller.

In the boss's absence

When anyone who has a normally hectic routine is absent for any length of time this usually provides a splendid opportunity 'to catch up'. There are likely to be several things of a time-consuming nature which are difficult to accommodate amidst normal routine and the following are some examples:

- weeding out the filing system;
- modifying an existing filing system;
- getting up to date with general disk management and housekeeping;
- learning new software packages;
- setting up a 'clippings file' (it is all very well to cut out useful articles and references but a different matter to find the time to file them in a way that will be useful later);
- tidying drawers and cupboards.

Additionally there is the need to generally oversee the workings of the office, and in this respect the duties should have been clearly laid down prior to the boss's departure. It is important that a secretary knows precisely what authority she has personally to take action and make decisions, when she can instigate a holding operation until the boss returns, when she needs to refer matters to someone else, or when she needs to contact the boss (if this is possible and permissible).

Much will depend on the nature of the boss's work, eg how technical or how confidential it is. In some cases there may be very little that a secretary can do, where, for example the boss possesses some form of expertise which is beyond a secretary's sphere of competence or which clients will find only acceptable from him. On the other hand, where a secretary works very closely with her boss and where she has learned a lot about his job and the work of the organisation generally, she may be able to deputise very adequately and successfully. In any event it is important that the ground rules are established prior to the trip so that the secretary knows the score.

Keeping in contact

Some executives always wish to keep in touch with the office, even when they are on the other side of the world and, of course, with modern telecommunications facilities this is a relatively straightforward matter. Nonetheless, it will be important to be absolutely sure of the itinerary and to determine, in advance, how, where and when contact should be made. Sometimes it will be advisable to set aside a specific time each day when contact can be made or alternatively it may be a matter of checking telex messages on a regular basis.

Helping out elsewhere

Sometimes a secretary may be called upon to help out in another office during her boss's absence and this can be both an advantage and a disadvantage. It will be useful in that it provides an opportunity to learn the operation of another section or department and to compare systems and procedures but it can also restrict the time available to 'catch up' and generally get things organised for the boss's return.

Once again, this is something which, preferably, should have been arranged and agreed upon before the departure of the secretary's own boss, so that he is aware of the arrangement and appreciative of the fact that a lot of apparently free time has not been wasted.

Maintaining a log of events

One very useful thing which a secretary can do when her boss is away is to make a daily note of things which have happened and of the action which was taken, particularly when someone is absent from the office for a lengthy period. It is very easy to feel quite out of touch with things on return unless someone is able to fill in the gaps in sufficient detail.

Verbal accounts will prove sufficient for many things, but where something is more complex, and particularly if it is still ongoing, it will be necessary to set up a special file. Other relevant files concerning things which have happened in his absence should also be readily available.

Where there is a lot of 'catching up' to be done the secretary should also aim to keep the diary reasonably clear for a few days following a trip. That way the boss will quickly be able to get back in his stride and resume control.

CHECKLIST

1 The maintenance of office diaries is an important aspect of a secretary's role.

2 Electronic diaries can be particularly useful where it is necessary to co-ordinate plans for a number of people.

3 To get the most out of any working day it is vital to manage time effectively.

4 Certain things can be readily identified as habits or activities which eat into time.

5 Many secretaries have to learn to manage the art of working for more than one person.

6 An important organisational aspect of a secretary's work can be

arranging travel, in which case developing a good working relationship with a reputable travel agent will prove invaluable.

7   Some business travel can be extremely complex to arrange and it is important to discuss draft plans before attempting to confirm any arrangements.

8   A lot of executive travel is now undertaken by air and it is important that a secretary is familiar with the necessary procedures and aware of possible problems.

9   Many useful sources of information exist to help plan and organise successful business trips.

10 There are certain things which a secretary should do in the absence of her boss which will help the office run efficiently and generally smooth his return.

QUICK REVISION QUESTIONS

1   Why are there likely to be discrepancies between a boss's diary and the office diary?
2   What are the essentials of maintaining an effective office diary?
3   What are 10 things which might cause a secretary to waste valuable time?
4   Given that there is a certain psychology to working for more than one person what sorts of thing should a secretary be aware of?
5   What are the main questions which need to be addressed when planning a business trip?
6   What are the main items of information which a secretary needs to collect when setting up a confidential personal travel file?
7   What are the advantages to a business executive of flying to the USA by Concorde?
8   What points should be considered:
    a when making flight reservations and
    b when making hotel reservations?
9   When arrangements are being made for an initial business trip to the Far East, for example, in addition to the usual details, what are the other main arrangements which might need to be considered?
10 What things can a secretary do during the absence of her boss to ensure that he quickly resumes control on his return?

13 People skills

A secretary's role and function is to a large extent a communicating one as illustrated in Fig. 13.1. Irrespective of whether the skills involved are oral, aural or written, they will involve contact with other people and it will be essential to be aware of their perceptions, attitudes, emotions and opinions if situations are to be handled successfully employing the necessary tact, discretion and professionalism.

Also decisions are more easily reached and problems more readily solved when there is an appreciation of the human factors involved. Issues are rarely free from the human dimension and, while it may seem easy to suggest a solution on strictly procedural or operational grounds, once the people factors are introduced the situation will frequently take on a very different complexion.

This section examines the main areas in which a secretary will be called upon to exercise her 'people skills'.

At the end of this section you should be able to:

- appreciate the importance of reception duties;
- explain how to deal with visitors without appointments;
- explain what is meant by delegation;
- identify the essentials of effective delegation;
- appreciate the significance of human relations in the office;
- understand the advantages to be gained from team building;
- recognise the importance of solving problems;
- appreciate the significance of assertiveness to a secretary;
- suggest ways in which a secretary can be assertive;
- indicate ways in which a secretary can create a good impression.

Receiving visitors

How visitors are received will depend on the size and nature of a company. As was indicated in the previous unit security arrangements

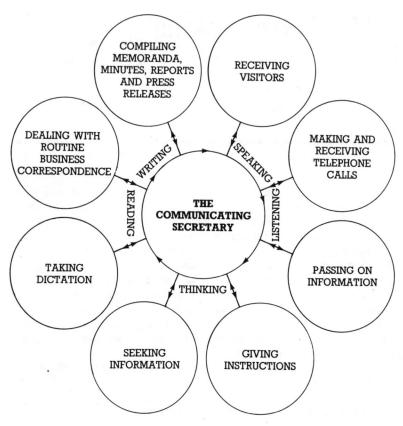

Fig. 13.1   The communicating secretary

may be particularly stringent within some companies and any visitor to a department or section may have to go through a fairly elaborate screening and reception process before reaching the person with whom he has an appointment. Sometimes a secretary will actually go to Reception to greet a visitor and escort him to the appropriate office, while on other occasions the visitor may be brought by a member of the Reception/Security team or simply given specific directions.

In any event visitors should always be received in a warm and courteous manner. Appropriate greetings are important as first impressions frequently last. Besides, a secretary will often welcome the diversion from routine which a visitor brings. It is always important to ensure that visitors are comfortable, particularly if they have to wait for any length of time. Where visitors may have travelled a distance they should always be advised where cloakroom facilities are to be found. The secretary should take the initiative here and not wait to be asked. It may also be appropriate to offer to take their coats, bags and cases. Although secretaries often object to the label of 'glorified coffee maker', part of a secretary's reception duties will often be to offer coffee or tea.

The waiting period

Dependent on the layout of the offices the secretary may find that she frequently has visitors waiting in her office or general work area. It is particularly important that the seating arrangements should be unobtrusive to her continuing with her normal work. Seats should be comfortable and there should be an up-to-date supply of newspapers, magazines and perhaps company literature, available. While the secretary can be expected to engage in some polite conversation with guests it will be appreciated that she has her own work to do and this will be easier for her where the waiting facilities are of a good standard.

It is also important that she does not allow herself to be drawn into conversation on topics which are of an unprofessional or confidential nature. It is always better to restrict such times to 'small talk'. Where a guest is having a long wait it is important to keep him informed about what is happening in order that he does not feel totally over-looked or forgotten.

Sometimes it may be possible, where the secretary is aware of the visitor's schedule, to assist in minor ways, so reducing any pressures caused by the delay. For example, it may be possible to advise the visitor's next appointment that his schedule is running late, or to order a taxi or notify a hotel or restaurant.

Visitors without appointments

Where there is not a really tight appointments procedure in operation within an organisation it is possible that there may be frequent callers without appointments. This is something which a secretary needs to clarify very precisely with her boss in order that some workable guide-lines may be established. It is very difficult to be cast iron about such things as there will inevitably be exceptions to any rule, but some advice from the boss should help. Then it will be largely up to the secretary to gauge the extent of the 'extenuating circumstances' or emergency which the caller claims and use her own initiative.

This will become easier the longer she is in the job and the better she gets to know her boss and his contacts. However, as a general rule it is typical company policy that visitors will not be seen without an appointment.

The 'gatekeeper' role

This function of the secretary is frequently referred to as the 'gate-keeper' role where she 'protects' her boss from unwanted intrusion. Secretaries can exercise particular power in using their discretion in these instances, both in terms of their handling of external visitors and those from within the company.

Some secretaries gain the unfortunate reputation of being 'dragons' by defending their boss's privacy to the extent that he becomes virtually inaccessible. Such zeal can, in fact, be detrimental to business and can result in missed opportunities and a feeling of isolation on the part of the boss who literally finds it difficult to learn what is going on outside his inner sanctum. Like anything else it will be a question of striking an effective balance and developing a sixth sense for what/who is and is not important.

Delegating and giving instructions

There will be instances in a secretary's daily routine when she needs to issue clear instructions to others. Sometimes this will be in the kind of situation where the success of overall arrangements will depend on the contribution of others, eg caterers, car hire firms, caretaking and cleaning staff. At other times it may be in respect of delegating duties to junior staff.

In either set of circumstances the instructions, whether they be verbal or written, must be clear yet sufficiently detailed and given in a manner which will not be considered as high-handed or unapproachable, should further clarification be required. Giving instructions emphasises the need for secretaries to possess yet another type of ability, viz that of supervising, as it will be important that the secretary accepts her responsibility of seeing that others have carried out her instructions satisfactorily.

Delegating duties

With changes in the secretarial role and often an increasing emphasis on the administrative and organisational aspects of the management support provided, many secretaries find themselves in the position of having to delegate work to junior members of staff.

Effective delegation is a key factor in making organisations work and yet delegating effectively can present problems for personnel at all levels. Delegation does not simply mean passing the responsibility for an aspect of work to someone else in a junior or subordinate position. That is only part of it. As well as the responsibility for the duty or task the junior must have the authority to match that responsibility and yet the delegator must be the person who is ultimately accountable for the success or failure of the work.

The importance of authority

Without authority true delegation has not taken place and the junior will possibly encounter difficulties in carrying out the task satisfactorily. For example, suppose a secretary has previously always carried out a particular checking job herself and that all the staff within the department associate the job with her and co-operate accordingly. The task may be relatively straightforward in terms of content and something which someone else could easily do. If, however, the secretary delegates the job to a junior member of the department and fails to make it known to the other staff that the junior now has the authority to ask for and collect the particular data so that the checks may be made, it is likely that problems will arise. While the junior has been given the responsibility for the task the necessary authority has not gone with it in that the others do not accept that the junior now has the authority to seek the information. In such an instance delegation would be ineffective.

The point the successful delegator must always appreciate is that delegation does not mean abdication or 'passing the buck'. At the end of the day the responsibility still rests with the delegator and the skill – in fact it is more of an art – is to select tasks which lend themselves to delegation and to identify individuals who are willing and capable of fulfilling the tasks satisfactorily.

Not all tasks can be delegated and it is important to select things which are appropriate and which fall within the capabilities of junior staff. The sorts of question a secretary needs to ask when considering what to delegate are:

- what minor tasks do I perform frequently?
- what things keep coming up in my job again and again?
- what things are junior staff as well equipped, or perhaps even better equipped, to deal with than I?
- which tasks do I enjoy doing just because I've always done them?
- which of my tasks would provide variety, challenge and experience in a junior's workload?

- which of my tasks are directly related to something a junior does already?
- what kind of experience would be useful to a junior in developing new skills and abilities?
- which tasks can be delegated which can be clearly explained and will require minimal control and supervision?

By posing such questions certain tasks should appear obvious candidates for delegation while others will clearly need to be retained.

Delegation should achieve two principal objectives, viz it should ease the secretary's personal workload so allowing more time to be spent supporting the manager and it should help develop junior staff by affording them new challenges and giving them opportunities to turn their hands to other things. Where these things are achieved not only will delegation improve the efficiency and performance of the department as a whole, but it will also help ensure a succession of suitably qualified staff when the secretary leaves or is promoted.

A secretary's procedure for delegating to juniors

Where a secretary is in a position to delegate some of her duties to junior staff it is useful for her to follow a procedure which will help isolate appropriate things for delegation, enable her to identify suitable staff and ensure that the tasks are adequately monitored. The following are possible steps for such a procedure:

- examine own job;
- list ALL tasks undertaken currently;
- add any tasks currently omitted through lack of time;
- extract tasks which cannot/should not be delegated;
- rearrange remaining tasks in descending order of importance;
- allocate an approximate time to each task;
- work down the list till the point is reached at which there are sufficient tasks to cope with in the time allowed;
- draw a line across the list at this point – all tasks below the line are possibilities for delegation;
- examine strengths and weaknesses of juniors;
- match the tasks to be delegated to the most appropriate junior, taking account of current workload and work content;
- fully brief junior on the task to be delegated;
- make sure that instructions are fully understood;
- inform junior of the support that will be given;
- indicate the amount of feedback expected;
- delegate the necessary authority;

- inform others who need to know about the delegation;
- check progress periodically;
- do not anticipate trouble, but keep a watchful eye out.

Relating to others

A large part of a secretary's communication role will be concerned with her ability to relate to other people, either face to face or over the telephone. Some people are natural communicators and find that this will come as second nature, while others will need to work at it.

Depending on the nature of the job, a secretary may find that she comes into contact with a wide range of people both within the organisation and from outside. One thing worth bearing in mind when looking for a secretarial position is the type and amount of contact that there will be. Some people enjoy meeting people and talking on the telephone; others prefer the sort of environment where they can adopt a lower profile. It is important to be honest with yourself in this respect rather than go for the sort of job which is not strictly in keeping with your personality.

Nonetheless, all jobs involve relationships with others and it is important that secretaries have positive attitudes to these relationships and possess the sort of qualities which are considered prerequisites of individuals holding secretarial positions.

Relationships with staff

Relationships develop from the first day in a new job and as the 'new girl' everyone's eyes will be on you – weighing you up and labelling you in one way or another. Your boss will be seeking reassurances that the qualities he saw and liked in you during your interview were not 'borrowed for the occasion' otherwise he will have made the wrong decision. Colleagues will observe your manner and general behaviour to estimate how you are going to fit in. Junior staff will wonder how strict you are and how approachable you seem to be. Coping with relationships is a very important aspect of any secretary's work and good relationships are well worth cultivating.

The secretary/boss relationship

A lot has been written about the secretary/boss relationship and it is often the object of criticism and asides about the so-called 'office wife' syndrome, particularly by strong feminist groups who choose to make much of minor aspects like making coffee.

Regardless of this side of things the secretary/boss relationship is a crucial one, and it is important that a suitable rapport is developed if two people are to work in harmony as a team and achieve results. The relationship should be based on mutual respect and co-operation but must be given time to mature. It is likely that a secretary will need to be in a job for about six months before she can exercise proper judgement on the success of the partnership. Of course, in some circumstances, there may be a personality clash where people simply cannot work together. However, it is hoped that such a possibility will emerge during the interview process and unhappiness and disappointment all round be avoided.

It takes time to adjust to one another's style and a new secretary can experience particular difficulties in this respect when taking over from someone whom the boss views as 'a hard act to follow'. In any event the following qualities and attitudes should help ensure an effective working relationship;

- commonsense;
- patience;
- tolerance;
- adaptability;
- a sense of humour;
- enthusiasm;
- tact;
- diplomacy;
- loyalty;
- discretion;
- initiative;
- versatility;
- flexibility;
- poise;
- professionalism;
- the ability to accept constructive criticism;
- the ability to work under pressure;
- the ability to anticipate problems;
- the ability to recognise when to take a back seat;
- the ability to know when to leave the boss alone;
- the ability to recognise when to 'jolly along';
- the ability to keep a confidence;
- the ability not to sulk;
- the ability to pass over 'bad days' without harbouring bad feelings;
- the confidence to bring problems into the open;

- the ability to accept a compliment;
- the grace to apologise;
- the ability to accept the boss's point of view;
- the ability to reconcile differences.

Relationships with superiors

Most secretaries will, in the course of their work, come into frequent contact with superiors, ie colleagues of their manager or his own superiors. It will be important for a secretary to demonstrate to superiors that she possesses the characteristics which are in keeping with her role. She should always be helpful and co-operative and never over-familiar.

Relationships with subordinates

Subordinates will include both staff who are junior in terms of age and experience and those who occupy positions of lower status. In terms of the former a good general rule is to relate to them in the way you expect your boss to relate to you. Provide clear instructions, have reasonable expectations, offer praise, be constructive in your criticism, tactful with any reprimand, appreciative that everyone makes mistakes sometimes, sympathetic where necessary and above all human.

As far as the latter are concerned it is important to remember that, although they do not hold a position of equal status to you, they perform functions which are vital to the organisation and often have had more actual work experience than you. You should attempt to establish a good rapport with support staff in all departments as it is more than likely that you will need to call on their help at some time. Where working relationships are cordial it will be a much easier matter to ask for help or favours when the need arises than would be the case if you were making the approach for the first time.

Relationships with colleagues

Human nature being what it is you cannot expect to get along equally well with everyone. None of us is the same but we all expect to be treated fairly and to be accepted for what we are – individuals. Your aim should be to try to avoid conflict and to get along with everyone in the interests of harmony. Where you may work closely with certain individuals it will be even more important to foster good relations. Not only does it make office survival very much easier, but it should enable you to approach a colleague for help or advice and likewise they should feel confident to approach you.

Relationships with outsiders

Whether you come into contact with clients, customers, members of the public, representatives from an external agency of some kind, eg a government department, an employment bureau, a professional body, hotel and restaurant staff, or whoever, face to face or on the telephone, it will be necessary for you to promote successfully the image of your organisation. Your communication and human relations skills will play a vital part in creating an impression – favourable or otherwise.

When contact is face to face it is important both to look and sound the part. Where you are meeting someone for the first time your greeting should be warm and friendly with a good handshake. Introductions should be meaningful and made according to recognised conventions. Men are introduced to women, eg 'Mrs Robinson, may I introduce Mr Fairhurst, our Managing Director? – Mr Fairhurst, Mrs Robinson' while with people of the same sex, juniors are introduced to seniors. Another important thing to practise is remembering names – it works wonders and people are always pleased and impressed. Also it is important to use titles and forms of address appropriately and certain jobs will necessitate a certain amount of research if gaffs in protocol are to be avoided. Useful reference books are available to help with such situations (see p 378).

How you look is also significant. Think of the attention that now goes into promoting the images of politicians and how much time they undoubtedly spend practising their self-presentation skills, eg cultivating a good voice, being a good listener, maximising eye contact, using positive body language and generally smiling. Know when to speak and when to keep quiet. Learn how to change the subject without causing offence and how to maintain confidentiality.

Contact over the telephone is less formidable to many people who feel more at ease when they cannot be seen. Here again, however, practice makes perfect and a good telephone manner can be an invaluable asset to any secretary.

Working as part of a team

Increasingly emphasis within organisations is placed on team building. This is partly to do with the fact that organisations have become more and more complex and it is appreciated that one person simply cannot do everything. Teams provide good opportunities for participation and help foster feelings of belonging among staff as well as creating an awareness of mutual dependence and the need for co-operation.

All kinds of teams will be formed each with specific objectives and comprising people with different skills, abilities and expertise. Secretaries will frequently find themselves members of such teams, providing secretarial, organisational and administrative support as well as contributing their own ideas where appropriate. Teamwork can be very rewarding and will certainly make staff feel more involved in an organisation's activities.

Being part of a team has the following advantages:

- it provides an opportunity to mix with others;
- it broadens outlooks;
- it develops confidence;
- it encourages the sharing and interchange of ideas;
- it boosts morale;
- it improves communication skills;
- it encourages collective approaches to decision-making and problem-solving;
- it enables team members to use their expertise and to benefit from that of others;
- it helps members develop different perspectives;
- it reduces anxiety;
- it develops commitment;
- it promotes healthy working relationships.

Handling problems

It would be a more than unusual job that posed no problems, and secretaries like any others find themselves in the position of dealing with problems, trouble-shooting, giving advice and making decisions to resolve situations. Like many other aspects of a secretary's role this will become easier with experience, but even the most inexperienced secretary will be called upon to use her initiative and exercise her judgement to resolve some difficulty or another.

Problems come in all shapes and sizes and can be general, work-related, personal in nature, to do with individuals and their relationships, or brought about by external events or pressures of some kind – to name but a few possibilities. Whatever their origin they need to be resolved. Sometimes solutions can be almost instantaneous, at other times they may be more difficult to identify.

For example a junior may have a problem with a piece of equipment or with the layout of some typing, either of which can be easily put right with a little time and help. Alternatively, a problem may be deep-rooted and far from obvious without knowledge of the facts and background in which case far more time, patience and energy will be required.

Effective listening

One quality which any problem-solver needs to possess is the ability to listen. You cannot expect to resolve a problem until you know what it is and you cannot know what it is until you ascertain the facts. Also in most instances there will be more than one side to the story and to get a balanced view you have to listen to both sides. It will be important not to prejudge an issue on the basis of past experience, personal opinion, prejudice or incomplete evidence. Such factors are typical barriers to effective communication (see also Section 7 p 132) and need to be broken down if there is to be a good chance of solving the problem.

Tactics

Problems need to be faced up to, and the sooner the better. They need to be considered in a matter of fact way rather than emotionally, and in the certain knowledge that all the necessary information is available. It is important not to reach a decision before you are fully aware of the ins and outs of a situation. While emotions should be kept in check, this is not meant to suggest that some problems will not require a sympathetic ear. In fact, where someone is simply given the opportunity to share their worries or anxieties with someone else, it may go a long way to resolving them. Likewise, the opportunity to get something off one's chest or use someone else as a sounding-board can often help resolve a difficult situation.

Seeking advice from superiors or experts

Where you feel that the problem you have encountered either personally or as a result of someone bringing it to you, is beyond your scope or perhaps outside your sphere of competence or experience, never be afraid to seek the advice of a superior or a specialist who is better equipped than you to handle such matters. Seeking help elsewhere is not necessarily an indication of weakness or failure but rather an ability to acknowledge that you cannot necessarily deal effectively with everything.

Sometimes it may even be dangerous to offer advice or suggest a certain course of action where you are not strictly qualified to do so. This will be particularly true of medical, legal or technical problems such as those to do with office safety, where you should always refer to an expert.

It comes with experience

Much that can be said about problem solving can be put down to common sense together with an awareness of the workings of your organisation, its policies, how it views issues, its codes of conduct and discipline, its client creed, public image and so on. Although no two problems will be identical there will be similarities, and precedents will have been set in terms of how problems were resolved. Problems should always be confronted and never swept under the carpet or ignored in the hope that they will go away – they rarely do and, in fact, often get worse.

Being assertive

We hear a lot of talk about assertiveness but what do we mean by 'assertion'? It is a mixture of standing up for one's own rights without treading on the rights of others and expressing wishes, opinions and feelings directly and honestly. Where we are not behaving in an assertive way we are likely to be either aggressive or non-assertive.

Aggression suggests that behaviour indicates a total disregard for the rights, feelings, needs and opinions of others and the belief that others have little or nothing to contribute. On the other hand non-assertion suggests an apologetic, diffident manner, where someone sells himself short and where others are likely to gain the upper hand.

Examples of assertive, non-assertive and aggressive behaviour in the same situation would be as follows. Suppose a typist produces a letter with a lot of uncorrected typographical errors. An assertive response from the person returning the letter to the typist might be, 'Diane, I'd like you to retype this letter as there are several mistakes in it.' A non-assertive response would be something along the lines of 'I'm sorry to bother you Diane, but when you have a minute do you think you could retype this letter as there seem to be a few things which need altering – it's probably my bad handwriting.' While an aggressive response would be, 'I don't know how you expect me to sign this – it's absolutely full of errors.'

The benefits of being assertive are numerous but basically it will mean a more effective performance in the job situation together with a greater degree of self-confidence and a saving of stress and energy. Where someone's behaviour is assertive issues will be resolved in the early stages before they develop and perhaps blow up out of all proportion.

In the office situation assertion will help in many ways and will solve a lot of minor problems. The following are some typical situations where being assertive will help:

- being constructive in making criticisms (see below);
- saying 'no' to an unreasonable request from someone;
- having a different opinion to others at a meeting;
- handling a difficult client;
- making telephone appointments with people who are difficult to pin down;
- having to disappoint a junior member of staff, eg telling them that you cannot support their application for promotion or for day release to attend a course at the local college.

Non-verbal signals

Assertiveness is shown in non-verbal ways as well as by what is said. For example, the voice and how it sounds is a strong indicator. A steady firm, middle-range, warm voice, which is neither too loud nor too quiet, will be an indication of assertion. Whereas a very low-pitched, quiet, monotone, sometimes shaking and frequently trailing off at the end, will be indicative of someone who is non-assertive and a harsh, strident, sarcastic, loud voice will belong to a person with an aggressive manner.

Likewise the actual speech pattern can convey a lot. The non-assertive person will be hesitant, with long pauses, often punctuated by the need to clear the throat, while the aggressive person will speak quickly and fluently often emphasising the blaming words. The happy medium, ie the assertive person, will be fluent and even-voiced, emphasising keypoints.

Other factors are facial expression and eye contact together with body movements. The non-assertive person's features will tend to change rapidly and he will raise his eyebrows and fane a smile between avoiding eye contact and dropping his eyes. He will also be likely to have nervous habits like shrugging his shoulders, moving from one foot to the other, covering his mouth with his hand, wringing his hands and moving back in a retreating manner. At the other extreme the aggressive person will be likely to have a firm, set jaw, with the chin thrust forward, to smile in a wry way and scowl when angry. He will try to dominate by staring. Posture-wise he will have a tendency to point or wag his finger, bang his fist on the table, lean forward in his seat, cross his arms in defiance or stride about. Assertive behaviour will produce an open expression, where the features are steady. There will be smiles of pleasure and frowns of displeasure and eye contact will be firm. Posture will be upright but relaxed and hand movement will be calm and open to encourage a response from the other party.

Making criticisms

Many people find it difficult to be assertive when making criticisms of, for example, other people's work. This is not an uncommon problem and it requires practice if you are to avoid damaging relationships by seeming to personalise the criticism or failing to make your point by being too general or too tentative in your remarks.

For example, supposing a junior member of staff handles the telephone badly and you need to raise the matter with the intention of bringing about improvements how do you go about it and what do you say?

The aim of the criticism is to improve performance and change the way the junior handles the telephone. Therefore it is important that the criticism is handled assertively rather than aggressively. It is your right to expect an improvement in the junior's performance but equally it will be your responsibility to offer constructive comment.

One way of doing this is to work the criticism through in your head first of all. Think what you are going to say and how you are going to say it. For instance, it will be a good idea to give some indication of what is coming by setting the scene first of all rather than pronouncing the criticism like a bolt from the blue. You could, for example, preface your remarks by saying something like, 'I've had several comments in the past few weeks about the way in which you answer the phone Diane . . .'. This establishes the contact between you and the junior and heralds what is likely to follow. Also the use of the word 'I' in prefacing your remarks is preferable to beginning with 'you' which is a much more aggressive opening.

Once you have elaborated on the content of your criticism it is important to get a response. If it is not immediately forthcoming you will need to probe a little. You may, for example, say something like, 'Do you agree with this?' or 'Have you felt at all awkward when answering the phone?'. Then proceed by asking for suggestions for improvement, eg 'How do you think you can improve the way you answer?' or 'How can you do it differently?' or 'What help can we give you with this?'.

Finally before you leave the matter you need to agree on the action you decided together, so you might conclude by saying something along the lines, 'So do you agree that the next time you answer you will try to . . .'. If there is any doubt expressed you may need to clarify matters still further and offer further constructive advice.

Receiving criticism

Just as you may have to make criticisms it is likely you will sometimes be on the receiving end and it is important that you are assertive then also. It is important, although not easy, to try to view criticism in a constructive way and to learn from it.

This will frequently mean dismissing any ideas of personal attack or deliberate attempts to destroy you and make you feel small. Where you are unclear about the criticism you should always seek clarification. Try to concentrate on using 'I' statements like 'I'd appreciate it if you could give me an example of what you mean' or 'I'd rather you made this issue less personal'.

Similarly, if you disagree, say so but try to take the initiative where you do agree and would wish to make changes for the future. In terms of the signals you transmit, try to keep your voice calm and quiet and retain eye contact. Don't be either constantly on the defensive or apparently deflated. Try to maintain a sense of balance as this will tend to bring out a better reaction from the other party.

Steps towards assertiveness

1 Be direct.
2 Don't be over-apologetic.
3 Be brief.
4 Don't feel you need to justify everything.
5 Be truthful.
6 Don't resort to unnecessary flattery.
7 Ask for clarification where you need it.
8 Ask for more time where you need it.
9 State disagreements clearly.
10 Be constructive where you express a doubt.
11 Use 'I' rather than 'you'.
12 Don't be afraid to change your views in the light of new information.
13 Be positive.
14 Don't understate yourself or your abilities.

Where individuals are able to implement some of these aspects into their working lives they will improve their self-confidence and hope-fully project themselves not as arrogant, over-confident, aggressive people but able and confident, skilled in interacting with others and in getting their points over in an effective and influential manner.

Creating a good impression

In a nutshell much of the business of 'people skills' is to do with image and creating and sustaining the right sort of impression. It is in this way that a secretary can act as an unpaid public relations officer for her organisation.

PR is all about marketing an organisation and its staff in such a way that it will enjoy a good reputation from its clientele. The people dimension is very important in that it is individuals who do the communicating and so serve to reflect company image.

What can a secretary do?

A secretary can play a very important part in helping to ensure that her organisation has the sort of image and enjoys the sort of reputation it desires and needs if it is to function effectively in a highly competitive world.

A lot can be achieved by being professional in everything she does. Professionalism will always take account of the other party to the communication and it encompasses a wide range of things including the following:

- presentation of work, ie no uncorrected errors, good layout, clear, concise, carefully worded correspondence;
- presentation of self, ie well turned out, always neat and tidy, with clean, well-groomed hair and well-manicured nails;
- setting a good example to junior staff, eg good time-keeping, a well-organised work area, an impeccable telephone technique;
- polite, helpful manner, ie taking time to listen to problems and hear complaints and making every effort to resolve issues and achieve results which help ensure satisfied clients or customers;
- maintaining a cool, calm and collected attitude despite the fact that others may be losing their tempers or letting off steam;
- resisting any temptation to indulge in office gossip;
- making a concentrated effort to remember names and faces;
- getting to know the likes and dislikes of regular visitors;
- being prepared to act in an ambassadorial role on behalf of the company, eg attending functions, giving talks, eg at a schools careers day, deputising for the boss.

These are only some suggestions and the list is not meant to be exhaustive. A secretary may quite unexpectedly find that she is in a position to enhance her company's image and demonstrate her skills and abilities in ways which can only add to her own standing in the eyes of others as well as increasing the prestige and esteem her company may already enjoy.

CHECKLIST

1 Much of any secretary's work will involve contact with other people.

2 Good communication skills are essential in dealing with any situation where human factors are involved.

3 One of a secretary's duties is to receive visitors, with and without appointments, so she operates a gatekeeper role on behalf of her boss.

4 Contact with other people will often be in the process of issuing instructions of some kind or in delegating work to junior staff.

5 It is essential that a secretary should attempt to develop good relationships with all those with whom she comes into contact in the course of her work and the relationship she has with her immediate superior is particularly significant.

6 People skills will often be developed as a result of working as part of a team.

7 Secretaries may sometimes find themselves faced with the need to handle problems of one kind or another which will involve the need to make judgements, reach decisions and resolve situations which often concern people.

8 One thing any secretary can usefully cultivate is assertiveness.

9 Being assertive does not mean being aggressive, but it does help individuals to give out or accept criticisms in a more positive manner.

10 Secretaries play strong public relations roles for their organisations and therefore it is important to create a good impression.

QUICK REVISION QUESTIONS

1 Suggest things which a secretary can do to ensure that visitors are received in a welcoming manner.

2 What might a secretary's procedure be in terms of a visitor without an appointment?

3 What do you understand by the term 'delegation'?

4 What sort of task might a secretary reasonably delegate to a junior member of staff?

5 What qualities and attitudes might a dynamic, ambitious marketing executive look for in a secretary/PA?

6 What sort of general advice would you give to anyone in respect of the relationships they have with subordinates?

7 If you were approached by a colleague for advice on a personal problem, what would you do if you felt unable to help?

8 List three indicators of non-assertive behaviour.

9 Suggest three situations in which assertiveness should prove helpful to a secretary.

10 In what ways can a secretary project a professional image which will help enhance her company's reputation?

14 Meetings and conferences

A large proportion of business time is spent attending meetings, seminars or conferences of one kind or another. These will range from impromptu sessions organised at short notice in response to some unexpected event or emergency, to informal business meetings, to meetings of a more social nature, eg retirement lunches, to presentation ceremonies, eg suggestion scheme awards, to routine committee meetings of a more formal nature, through to complex large scale conferences lasting for several days and catering for several hundreds of people.

Such events necessitate forward planning and preparation if they are to be purposeful and successful. Where high levels of expenditure can be incurred, it is reasonable to suppose that considerable attention is given to the arrangements surrounding events in order to ensure that they achieve their aims and objectives and produce results.

While there is a fast growth in what has become known as the 'meetings industry', with its large number of professional organisations established to make all the necessary arrangements and offer a wide range of specialist venues and facilities, secretaries, too, need to be well versed in the necessary procedures and attendant support entailed.

For secretaries the organisational aspects of meetings and conferences will call upon a range of skills and abilities. This section examines the types of arrangement that are involved, starting with straightforward informal meetings, moving on to the formal arrangements which are required where a secretary may set up and service regular committee meetings and concluding with the organisation involved in mounting a full-blown conference.

At the end of this section you should be able to:

- list the sort of arrangements entailed in organising informal meetings;
- appreciate the factors which would need to be taken into account in arranging a business lunch;
- suggest the factors which would contribute to a successful event of a social or semi-social nature;

- describe the duties a secretary would have in relation to setting up and servicing committee meetings;
- identify and explain the principal documents required in connection with meetings;
- appreciate the essentials of effective minute taking;
- understand basic meeting terminology;
- identify the principal features in organising a conference;
- explain the kinds of check which would be built into arrangements to ensure effectiveness;
- identify external support which is available.

Small informal meetings

In the course of a week an executive may arrange or attend a variety of less formal meetings. These may be in the form of briefing meetings or progress meetings or meetings called to deal with a sudden change of plan, a new development, a change in staff or procedure or some unexpected emergency or crisis. Sometimes meetings will be scheduled to take place regularly at a fixed time every week, provided there are items to discuss, and they will be attended by the same people on each occasion. As such their format will tend to be informal with little or no paperwork and often transacted in an individual manager's office rather than in a special meetings room. As far as the secretary is concerned her involvement will be likely to include:

- ensuring that the diary is kept free for the appointed time and duration of the meeting;
- liaising as necessary either directly with those staff attending or with their respective secretaries;
- ensuring that any essential paperwork is available;
- taking notes where required;
- dealing with all telephone calls and visitors during the meeting;

Checklist – well before meeting
- liaise with others over mutually convenient time;
- venue (book, or confirm block booking);
- prepare notice, agenda and previous minutes (where circulated);
- prepare other paperwork;
- arrange refreshments;
- book any andio/visual support materials needed;
- organise car parking where necessary.

- arranging refreshments;
- reminding the boss of the time if the meeting seems to be overrunning.

Business lunches

Another popular forum for the small informal meeting is the business lunch. Many successful meetings are transacted in this way and many important business deals are signed over the lunch table. It will frequently fall to the secretary to make the necessary booking.

Here it is not so much her organisational skills which are put to the test as her instinct for an appropriate venue. Sometimes, of course, her boss will have decided on the location and it will simply be a matter of making the necessary booking sufficiently in advance to ensure, for example, a preferred table or time. All that will be required later will be to check on the booking a few days beforehand and on the day of the meeting ensure that the boss leaves the office in good time and that he has any essential papers with him.

Where the choice of restaurant is left to the secretary she must be sure that she selects an appropriate one, taking account of location, convenience, style, atmosphere, type of food (bearing in mind differing tastes, ethnic or religious differences) and perhaps price range. A range of useful reference guides is available to help in this respect and it can also be useful to study the leisure sections of the press and keep a scrapbook of cuttings which provide useful suggestions on attractive venues to suit all types of occasion.

Where an organisation may have good catering facilities of its own it may fall to the secretary to discuss the arrangements and menu with the Catering Manager. This is always easier in that it is on the spot.

Meetings with a social flavour

As well as meetings held to transact business a secretary will occasionally have to organise certain office gatherings where the emphasis will be on the social side of things but where there will be some formal aspect to be incorporated, eg the presentation of a leaving present or some type of company award.

Here the location will also be important as will the notice given to all those entitled to attend. Venue is important in terms of size and atmosphere. It should be sufficiently large to accommodate all those wishing to attend, while not being so big as to make the occasion seem impersonal, being conducive to maximum guest interaction in a relaxed manner. This can sometimes be difficult to achieve within an organisation where there are a lot of gatherings of one kind or another, and so the importance of making arrangements as far in advance as possible is emphasised. The 'wrong' venue for such an occasion can totally spoil it while the 'right' one will ensure its success.

Checklist – just before the meeting
- draw up chairman's agenda;
- prepare minute book for signature;
- prepare attendance register;
- make up name plates or cards if necessary, eg where committee members are unknown to one another;
- confirm parking arrangements;
- check accommodation in terms of seating, heating, lighting and ventilation;
- check for water, glasses and ashtrays in meeting room;
- confirm refreshments and time for serving;
- notify reception;
- redirect incoming telephone calls where necessary;
- have spare agendas and other papers available;
- have scribbling pads, pens and pencils available;
- organise all necessary files and documents to take to the meeting;
- place 'Meeting in Progress' sign outside the door.

Likewise it is important that any refreshments and/or buffet are well planned. As with the business lunches this may mean liaison with outside caterers or it may be an internal affair. Either way, reasonably precise numbers need to be provided together with an idea of the type of food and drink required. Where a company wishes to hold a function 'in house' but has no catering department or facilities of its own 'instant' buffets and even full meals can be provided by many freelance catering agencies which have sprung up in recent years. The Yellow Pages will provide details, from delicatessen shops and sandwich bars to the type of organisation which supplies everything from general crockery and cutlery right down to ice buckets and silver salvers.

Sometimes social events have to be managed within certain budget limitations and it will be important not to exceed any stated amount.

Presentations

Where presentations form part of the occasion suitable arrangements may include:

- organising a collection;
- advising those who wish to attend of time and venue, sometimes retaining the element of surprise for the recipient;
- ensuring that the recipient turns up;
- ensuring that an appropriate person is able to make the presentation and that he/she has sufficient background information to make any necessary speech, eg where it is a retirement presentation and the person leaving is not personally known to the presenter it will be necessary to supply biographical details on which remarks may be based;
- selecting a gift and having it suitably gift-wrapped;
- ensuring that everyone who contributed signs any special card (where a very large number is involved it may be better to attach a few separate lists which have been independently circulated);
- making sure that any in-house magazine is made aware of the occasion so that suitable coverage, perhaps including a commemorative photograph, is arranged.

Arranging and servicing formal meetings

Given that the day-to-day activities of any manager will involve meetings of some kind this will mean that secretaries will find themselves involved in the repetitive cycles of many formal meetings and committees. There will be a significant amount of routine work to do in this connection. Committees need to be planned and co-ordinated if they are to fit into busy schedules. For example, it will usually fall to the secretary to book the venue, circulate the essential paperwork, organise refreshments and generally prepare for the meeting.

Checklist – during the meeting
- pass round the attendance register;
- sit where you can see and hear;
- generally assist the chairman;
- answer queries as required;
- remind chairman of time constraints as necessary;
- take minutes (unless special minute secretary in attendance);
- deal with any emergency, eg answer the telephone, leave the room to collect papers on behalf of chairman;
- serve refreshments (where the meeting may be discussing confidential matters and does not wish catering staff to be present).

Acting as committee secretary

While secretaries may undertake the arrangements referred to above they may also perform a more specific role where, for example, they are required to undertake all the duties and responsibilities in relation to the operation of specific committees. This will involve preparing and sending out all essential paperwork as well as arranging things like venue and refreshments, and will often necessitate taking minutes and ensuring that all the necessary follow-up procedures are dealt with. This role, although carrying no formal decision-making authority outside that vested in the position by the committee, is a powerful role in that anyone appointed as Committee Secretary will tend to possess a sound knowledge of the organisation and so will frequently be called upon to advise the committee. Consequently he/she is in a strong position to influence decisions reached as well as having a strong reliance placed on him/her by the chairman.

The paperwork of meetings

1 The notice Where a secretary is acting as committee secretary she will, having agreed a date with the chairman, or following the date determined at the close of the previous meeting, be responsible for sending out the notice convening the next meeting. This will be done as soon as the venue has been checked. Even where a fixed booking is made it is wise to check arrangements in case a change has had to be made.

A notice of meeting should always include details of the type of meeting, eg committee, special, public, AGM, together with the day, date, time and place and should have the name or designation of the convenor and the date on which the notice is sent out. This latter detail is particularly important where there is a statutory period of notice involved, eg according to the Companies Acts 21 clear days' notice is required for an annual general meeting of a company, which means 21 days between the date of sending out the notice and the date of the meeting itself.

2 The agenda Often the notice will be accompanied by a preliminary agenda, although there may also be a request for the submission of additional agenda items by a certain date. The final agenda which is simply a list of 'things to be done' at the meeting (in the order in which business is to be transacted) will be prepared by the secretary, usually in consultation with the chairman.

Agendas may take slightly different forms and be presented in different levels of detail but should set out clearly the items to be dealt

```
EXECUTIVE COMMITTEE MEETING

There will be a meeting of the Executive Committee
on Tuesday, 29 June 19.. at 1400 hours in the Board
Room of Foster Building.

S Davidson
Secretary

12 June 19..

AGENDA
1.  Apologies for absence
2.  Minutes of the previous meeting
3.  Matters arising from the minutes
4.  Report on the Saudi Arabia project (Paper 22.1)
5.  Arrangements for the Royal Visit
6.  Progress report on introduction of the new MIS
7.  Safety Report (to be tabled)
8.  Early retirements (Paper 22.2)
9.  Any other business
10. Date of next meeting
```

Fig. 14.1 Specimen notice and agenda

with and discussed. There is a fairly standard order for most agendas
in terms of the opening and closing items with variation in the middle
which represents 'the meat'. A typical agenda for an Executive
Committee is given as Fig. 14.1.

It is usual for committee members to receive their copies of the final
agenda together with any supporting documents (often referenced in
brackets following the agenda item) sufficiently in advance of a
meeting to provide them with the opportunity to study the material
carefully, do any necessary research, perhaps liaise with one another
over certain items and come to preliminary agreement over matters
to be discussed, even in advance of the meeting!

3 The Chairman's Agenda It is usual practice for the secretary to
prepare a special, more detailed agenda for use by the chairman. This
will contain the same running order as that in the agenda sent to
committee members but will be printed only on the left-hand side of
the paper, so leaving the right side free to add comments and key
words to assist the chairman in the effective conduct of the meeting.

The preparation of this agenda is usually held over until the last
possible moment so that details may be up-to-date, eg the latest apologies for absence or any last minute information which has come to
light. Such a device can be particularly helpful to a chairman who may

have been absent from the office and yet be required to chair a meeting on his return, as the secretary will have been able to supply the necessary information to enable the chairman to introduce agenda items with authority and clarity.

4 Minutes The principal supporting document which a committee secretary is responsible for preparing prior to a meeting is the minutes of the previous meeting. It is usual to circulate these in advance and it could be argued that the sooner this is done the better, otherwise committee members may find it difficult to recall what actually took place at the meeting, particularly if they attend many meetings in the course of their work. (Types of minute are detailed below.)

5 Other documents Committees may need to refer to a variety of other documents during the course of a meeting. These may be minutes of subcommittees or reports which are put before the committee for approval and acceptance, as well as discussion documents for consideration by the meeting, statistics which may have been requested at the previous meeting, copies of correspondence, eg copies of job applications and references in the case of an Appointments Committee and sets of final accounts at an AGM.

Sometimes where documents are not ready for circulation prior to a meeting the agenda will indicate that they will be presented at the meeting. The usual way of doing this is to add the words 'to be tabled' in brackets after the agenda item.

Additional duties of a committee secretary

It is also a committee secretary's responsibility to anticipate requirements prior to a meeting, eg the need for extra agendas, or additional information to support an agenda item.

While a committee secretary will help the chairman by providing formal rulings in keeping with the rules and regulations governing proceedings, drawing his attention to a committee member who is trying to catch his eye in order to speak, counting votes and reminding him of the time where necessary, it is not normal practice for her to enter into the discussion. However, she may be called upon to correct factual inaccuracies or misquotes of previous decisions reached by the committee.

Taking the minutes

Where a separate minute secretary is not appointed to a committee it will fall to the secretary to take notes during the proceedings.

Minute taking is something which takes practice and demands a high level of concentration. Obviously it will be more difficult where someone is new to an organisation or even a committee and it will pay dividends to do your homework beforehand.

This will include familiarising yourself with the back copies of recent meetings and noting the level of detail in which minutes are recorded. Accurate minute taking will also be helped by a good chairman who summarises the discussion and defines any decision, making sure that the secretary has made appropriate notes.

Types of minute

Basically there are four main types of minute, viz:

1 Narrative minutes, which as the name suggests provide a fairly detailed account of what took place, summarising the discussion and indicating who said what, prior to recording any decisions reached.

2 Resolution minutes, which simply provide a record of any resolutions passed in a succinct way, and sufficient to meet with any legal requirements.

3 Action minutes, which provide a very clear account of who has agreed to take responsibility for what. This format is particularly useful where a committee is part of a hierarchical committee network in that lines of authority are clearly demonstrated.

4 Verbatim minutes, which provide a 'word for word' account of what has taken place. Their use is very unlikely in a business context. For one thing accuracy would be virtually impossible to ensure and for another it would take too long to read them!

The current trend is toward briefer summary minutes certainly for distribution. Ironically the more detailed minutes are the more likely people are to feel that something has been omitted or underplayed.

Where minute taking can present problems is in instances where the chairman requires a lot of support from the secretary, eg where it is necessary to refer to rules and regulations of the committee or to locate an item in a previous set of minutes or to assist in the counting of hands in voting procedures. However, where it is felt that a lot of such support may be required at a particularly important meeting which is to be attended by a large number it will make sense to ensure that someone is 'In attendance' purely to take notes and so remove the pressure of attempting to do both.

Follow-up procedures

The committee secretary's duties do not finish with taking the minutes. Notes need to be transcribed as quickly as possible afterwards, usually in draft form for agreement with the chairman. Once the draft is agreed it should be accurately indexed and prepared in its final form for circulation to committee members.

Checklist – after the meeting
- remove the notice;
- clear the room of surplus papers;
- notify catering section to remove cups, etc.;
- return minute book and official documents to the safekeeping of the office;
- enter date of next meeting in diary;
- draft minutes;
- agree minutes with chairman and prepare final copy ready for duplication and circulation;
- write any necessary letters;
- take any follow-up action called for during the meeting;
- remind others to do likewise;
- open file for the next meeting.

Accurate indexing will greatly facilitate the ease with which committee members locate particular items which have been minuted. Various indexing sequences can be used (see also Section 11 p 293) but it can be useful to adopt a consecutive numbering system prefixed by the year in which the meeting takes place. For example, the first agenda item of the first meeting of a particular committee in the year 1989 could be indexed 89.1. Supposing there were fourteen items on that particular agenda, then the indexing reference for the first agenda item of the second meeting of the committee would be 89.15 and so on. This is a very simple system both to implement and follow.

A copy of the minutes will also be kept aside for insertion within the official Minute Book. Minute books used to be bound books and, of course, minutes were handwritten. However with modern forms of preparation it is usual to adopt a loose-leaf form, although the pages are numbered and the fastening will often carry a double locking device to ensure security and prevent anyone from tampering with or altering the minutes.

It will also be necessary to take any action on matters agreed by the committee during the course of the meeting or to remind others, including the chairman, of their undertakings to follow up particular matters for reporting back at the next meeting.

Between meetings the secretary should be on the lookout for information relevant to the committee, perhaps circulating any appropriate detail to committee members.

Meeting terminology

Formal meetings, in particular, have a terminology of their own and secretaries need to be aware of the main terms used if they are to feel comfortable at meetings.

A GLOSSARY OF MEETING TERMINOLOGY

ab initio   from the beginning

abstention   where a member refrains from casting a vote either in favour or against a motion

addendum   an amendment which **adds** words to a motion

address the Chair   where a member wishes to speak he must first address the chairman, ie 'Mr Chairman . . .' or 'Madam Chairman . . .'.

ad hoc   from the Latin meaning 'for the purpose of'. For example, an ad hoc committee, sometimes referred to as a 'special committee', is one set up for a special purpose and when that purpose is fulfilled the committee is disbanded

adjournment   the chairman, with the consent of those present, may adjourn a meeting and reconvene it at a later date to complete unfinished items on the agenda

advisory   offering advice or suggestion and making recommendations, but taking no direct action

agenda   schedule of items drawn up for discussion at a meeting

amendment   an alteration to a motion by the addition, deletion or modification of words

annual general meeting (AGM)   a statutory meeting held once a year which the organisation's entire membership is eligible to attend

apologies for absence   excuses given in advance for inability to attend a meeting

Articles of Association   the rules required by law which govern a company's internal organisation and activities.

ballot   a written secret vote conducted in accordance with the organisation's constitution.

by-laws   rules governing an organisation's activities

casting vote   In accordance with the rules and regulations a chairman may be granted a second vote when there is an equal number of votes for and against a motion

chairman   the person given authority to conduct a meeting

chairman's action   the right of the chairman to make a decision within his/her terms of reference without reference to the committee

chairman's agenda an elaborated form of the basic agenda with space left on the right for the chairman to make notes

collective responsibility a convention whereby all members agree to abide by a majority decision

consensus agreement by general consent without a formal vote being taken

convene to call a meeting

co-opt to invite an individual to serve on a committee as a result of a majority vote. A person is normally co-opted because of some specialist knowledge or expertise he/she can provide

ex officio one invited to attend 'by virtue of his office' but without voting rights

in attendance present on invitation to give expert help, advice or information but with no voting rights

in camera in private

lie on the table something is said to 'lie on the table' when the meeting decides that no action should be taken on it at the present time

lobbying the term given to the practice of seeking the support of others prior to a meeting

majority vote one where the greater number of members voting were either for or against a motion. Articles or rules will set out whether a majority is necessary for a motion to be carried or defeated

Memorandum of Association the statutory requirements which govern a company's objects and general relationship with the outside world

motion a formal proposal moved by a member that a certain topic be discussed at a meeting and certain action be taken upon it

nem con no one contradicting, ie no votes against the motion, but some members may have abstained

nem dis no one dissenting, as nem con above

no confidence a vote of 'no confidence' may be passed by members of a meeting if they are at variance with the chairman

opposer one who speaks against a motion

out of order the chairman can rule a member 'out of order' where the member is not keeping to the point under discussion or speaking improperly

point of order a query raised in respect of procedure or a possible infringement of the standing orders or constitution

postponement the action taken to transfer the holding of a meeting to a later date

proposer the member putting forward a motion for discussion at a meeting

proxy a member may be appointed to vote by proxy, ie on behalf of another member who is unable to attend a meeting, subject to the articles, standing orders or constitution

quorum the minimum number of persons that must be present at a meeting to make it valid

resolution once passed, a motion becomes a resolution

rider this is an addition to a resolution after it has been passed. It adds to a resolution rather than altering it. It must be proposed, seconded and put to the meeting in the usual way

right of reply   the proposer of a motion has the right of reply once the motion has been fully discussed but before it is put to the vote

seconder   one who supports the proposer of a motion

sine die   for an indefinite period

Standing Orders   the rules compiled by an organisation in respect of the way in which business must be transacted

status quo   as things stand at present

statutory meeting   a meeting (usually of the shareholders of a public company) which **must** be held in order to comply with the law

subcommittee   a group of members from the main/parent committee appointed to deal with a specific aspect of the main committee's work. The functions will be delegated by the main committee, to whom reports and recommendations will be submitted

tabled   the description applied to a document to be presented to a committee 'on the table' – not one which has been included with the agenda and supporting papers

terms of reference   a statement of the work to be carried out by a group or committee, providing guidelines as to how it should be done and expressing any limitations in respect of methods

ultra vires   outside the legal power of authority of the organisation or committee

unanimous   all being in favour

verbatim   word for word

Organising a conference

Another role a secretary may find herself adopting is that of Conference Organiser. The role has a lot in common with making arrangements for meetings, but involves a much greater timescale and frequently residential accommodation as well.

A conference can be any event from a one-day seminar activity for departmental staff to a full-blown residential programme arranged for several hundred people and lasting a few days. Conferences have become a very popular means of imparting or exchanging information and the conference industry is expanding rapidly with many hotels and other organisations offering their facilites for use in this respect.

Successful conferences need a lot of careful planning and the role of conference organiser is both demanding and challenging, calling on a range of abilities and expertise. Making the necessary arrangements can be a complex and time-consuming business, and any secretary undertaking the task needs to be clear in her own mind that she fully appreciates the aims and objectives of the conference to be organised as well as being sure that she has the authority from management to press ahead and take any decisions necessary to complete arrangements. She needs to be in on the discussions relating to the proposed conference from the beginning so that she knows:

1 what the organisation is looking for;
2 what it hopes to achieve from the event;
3 where and when it should be held;
4 who should attend; and
5 how much is being budgeted for the event.

Once these preliminary considerations are clear the organiser can then begin to get down to the actual detail.

The venue

An important consideration in holding any event will be the venue. The first decision will rest on whether the event is to take place on company premises or elsewhere. A large proportion of such events take place away from company premises and so it will be essential to choose a suitable venue. The main considerations will be as follows:

- the date(s) selected;
- the geographical location;
- the surrounding town/country;
- proximity to road and rail networks (possibly even airports if it has an international dimension);
- the time of year – how busy, eg summer season, how accessible, eg difficult weather conditions;
- the size of the hotel or other accommodation;
- the facilities needed;
- the amenities provided;
- the food;
- the service, eg how accustomed to catering for such events;
- other features considered, eg sports facilities on site;
- whether a specialist venue, eg an exhibition or conference centre is required;
- any novelty value sought, eg a public relations venture held somewhere different, eg a stately home, or a floating conference on a Sealink ferry or an Executive Boardroom on a British Rail express train, are some of the varied possibilities.

Any conference organiser will prefer to inspect a venue personally, wherever possible, rather than rely on glossy literature. Having sent for details of a range of possibilities it will be worth the time and effort to draw up a short list and visit those places to assess for yourself. It will be adyisable to stay overnight, sample the food and generally soak in the atmosphere (preferably unknown to the management!)

It will depend on the proposed content of the programme, together with the nature of the audience what type of venue is more appropriate. For example, where the event may be more of a public relations exercise, where delegates are encouraged to relax a little and enjoy themselves, socially as well, more comfortable and interesting accommodation will be called for. However, where delegates are attending particularly to learn and gain information and where they would benefit from a high level of technical and technological support, facilities such as those provided by universities or polytechnics are likely to be preferred.

The preparation of a venue checklist can be helpful in this respect to ensure that nothing is omitted. A specimen is given as Fig. 14.2.

A special word about accommodation and food

Although conferences are organised primarily for the programme content and the opportunity they provide to gain information, interchange ideas and discuss issues, considerable importance is attached, by delegates, to things like facilities and food. People's standards generally have risen in recent years and the quality of the accommodation and service can literally make or break an event. Pleasant, comfortable surroundings greatly add to the success of any programme, particularly where free time has been built in. Also the quality and variety of food is an important consideration, particularly now that so many people are more diet and health conscious.

The programme

Programme content needs to be decided at the earliest opportunity and plans will frequently be under way at the same time as information is being sought on possible venues. Conferences frequently have a theme and the aim will be to devise a well-balanced programme which consists of a selection of speakers, delegate activities and events which will develop the theme. The points which will need to be borne in mind are as follows:

- number of sessions to be filled;
- duration of sessions;
- logical order of presentation;
- material to be included – how difficult, how new, how serious;
- level of delegate involvement.

Venue Checklist
Event: Date:
Location: Date of visit:

Hotel/Centre:
Full postal address:
Tel. No.:   Telex No.:
Contact: Answer back code:
Position: Ext No.:

Nearest railway station: Distance:
Nearest airport: Distance:
Distance by road from London/wherever?

Accommodation
No. of bedrooms: Double   Twin
                                       Suites   Singles

Bathroom/shower
facilities: Private   Public

Dining/Lounge/Bar/Additional facilities:

Garaging/Car parking facilities:
Star rating:
Tariff details:

Other Facilities

Meeting room   Max. seating for
Acoustics?   Lighting?
Microphone?   Blackout?
Visual aids?   Cine projector
                         Video — VHS/BETA/U-Matic/Philips
                         OHP
                         CCTV
Screens?   Fixed/Portable   Size?
Lighting?   Dimmable?
Heating?   Ventilation?
Air conditioning?   Noise factor?
Syndicate rooms   No.   Size
Display area?   Size
Office support?   Audio/shorthand/typing/photocopying
Technical support?   Projectionist/Technician/Translator

General comments/observations
Recommendation:
Details of preliminary reservations made
Final confirmation date
Special rates negotiated
Signed   Date
Conference Organizer

Fig. 14.2   Venue checklist

Additionally there will usually be a social element to any programme which is residential and extends over a few days, and this, too, will need to be considered and planned.

The participants

Selecting good speakers can be difficult and it is preferable if they come recommended. Where it is hoped to engage well known presenters it must be appreciated that demand for their services can be high and other commitments may restrict their availability. For instance, in a 3-day conference there may be only one time when a particular speaker is available, and this may mean arranging the entire programme around this person if he is to make a key contribution and if his presence is vital. In selecting speakers it is important to strike a balance and have sufficient variety of presentation. It is also essential to remember cost, as some speakers charge a high fee and there will also be their expenses to consider.

Briefing speakers

Speakers need to be well briefed on what is expected of them, eg how long they are to speak, the likely numbers in the audience, whether they are expected to take questions and whether there will be press coverage. It is a good idea to have synopses of talks to be delivered well in advance and circulated amongst all speakers, otherwise there can be a lot of overlap and repetition. Where presentation papers are of a formal nature and for subsequent publication, speakers need to know the format that is required of their printed speech.

Conference sessions will often be chaired and it will be essential that individuals chairing particular sessions are well briefed in advance. They will need, for example, to have biographical details of the speakers in order that they may make suitable introductions and also be competent in handling the timing of sessions so that they do not overrun as well as dealing with any question and answer sessions which may be included.

Other contributions

As well as formal presentations a conference may include some sort of exhibition or display and locations, space allocations and timings will need to be worked out in respect of their contributions. There may also be the security of materials to arrange.

Support staff

Certain support staff will also need to be available, eg technicians, where audio-visual equipment is used, chauffeurs to collect speakers and drive them back to their accommodation or to catch trains, and staff to act as ushers where it is a large event. All such personnel need to be fully briefed on their duties and responsibilities, knowing precisely where they are expected to be at any given time.

The budget

Any major event will have a budget. Sometimes it will be allocated in advance and the organiser will be required to work within it. At other times the organiser will be expected to cost out the event in advance and specify the budget required. Either way certain fixed and variable costs will always be included.

Fixed costs
- use/hire of venue;
- speakers' fees and/or expenses;
- paperwork, including advertising and postage;
- art and printwork;
- transport costs;
- insurance;
- materials, eg hire of equipment;
- administrative costs;
- contingencies, ie unanticipated last-minute costs (usually estimated as a percentage of overall costs).

Variable costs
- accommodation (unless paid separately by delegates);
- food and refreshments;
- any special, additional function or event;
- special materials for issue to delegates, eg badges, folders or packs.

The paperwork

There will inevitably be a lot of paperwork and it will be important that all material sent out is accurate and reflects the style and image of the event. Most of the paperwork will be likely to be prepared in-house but where there is no reprographics department an organisation may have to rely on outside printers for the more complex artwork. Word processing is a great boon in preparing conference material as not only will the quality be high but delegates will all receive personalised information. The type of paperwork for any event will vary but it is likely to include:

- routine correspondence;
- registration documentation;
- supporting information;
- conference papers;
- programmes;
- lists of delegates attending;
- breakdowns of any syndicate or seminar groups;
- invitations to special or optional functions;
- menus;
- name badges;
- confirmation of all arrangements;
- press releases;
- evaluation questionnaires;
- thank you letters.

Security arrangements

All venues need to be safe and secure in respect of delegates and their belongings. Therefore a conference organiser would wish to be satisfied about fire exits, privacy afforded to delegates and general security arrangements. Certain types of conference will call for special security measures and the appointment of specialist personnel. This can come about because of the nature of the organisation, eg something which attracts adverse reaction from certain sections of the community or as a result of a theme which is very controversial, or due to the presence of a particular speaker, or because of the secrecy associated with the event, eg the type of information to be discussed or the value of the items to be displayed, either in terms of monetary value eg antiques or the value to competitors, eg dress designs or other items which could be copied.

Registration arrangements

These should always be efficient, well organised and dealt with as quickly as possible in order to create a good initial impression. How it is done will depend largely on the number of delegates and whether or not the conference is residential. Either way, delegates will normally be presented with some form of conference folder or delegate pack when they register and this will include:

- conference programme;
- list of delegates;

- site plan of the venue;
- details of the surrounding area and attractions, where appropriate;
- promotional materials from exhibitors, where in attendance;
- advanced circulation of speakers' papers or handout materials;
- writing paper and pen.

It is also important to make provision for queries, perhaps arising out of last minute substitutions or late arrivals.

Countdown Calendar	
5th Annual Conference of to be held at during the period of 3–6 May inclusive 1987	
19— June	Preliminary discussions Adoption of theme Provisional locations discussed Guest speakers nominated.
July	Course organiser to visit three possible venues and report back Invitations extended to guest speakers
August	Provisional assessment made of numbers likely to attend Provisional booking of venue
September– December	On-going preparations, initial printing, etc. Confirmations from speakers Advance notice to interested parties General publicity
19— January	Programme finalised Details sent out together with application forms and notification of closing date
February	Pre-conference meeting with speakers Contribution synopses co-ordinated
March	Attendance numbers finalised Places confirmed and additional details sent, including travel directions
April	Visit to venue to finalise menus and accommodation, including lecture facilities, technical support and security arrangements Administrative details finalised Staff briefing; delegation of duties
May	Final check of venue, accommodation and support facilities organised

Fig. 14.3 Conference countdown calendar

Organiser's checklists

Any conference organiser has a lot to remember and it can be useful to devise checklists to ensure that nothing is overlooked. The venue checklist referred to earlier is a typical example. Given that most events tend to be organised over an extended timescale, another device which can be useful in monitoring the programme arrangements generally is a Countdown Calendar. An example is provided as Fig. 14.3.

Follow-up arrangements

It will also fall to the organiser to ensure that all the loose ends are tied up, that all participants have been formally thanked, that all bills have been cleared for payment and, where an evaluation is required, that all delegates have been sent a questionnaire to complete and return. Although it is unlikely that all delegates will return these forms, they can provide useful information and highlight problems or particularly successful aspects of which an organiser will be alerted for next time.

External help

Given that conferences are now such big business many companies have sprung up which offer advice on the organisation of conferences. There is even a conference and exhibition in London for conference organisers! Also a growing number of useful books are available on the subject.

CHECKLIST

1 Meetings and conferences play an increasingly significant role in business communications.

2 Meetings range from short, informal encounters to full-scale meetings fulfilling a statutory requirement.

3 Sometimes meetings incorporate a social element like a business lunch.

4 Secretaries are frequently called upon to make all the necessary arrangements in connection with meetings from booking the meetings room to attending to all the necessary paperwork.

5 The paperwork associated with meetings includes notices, agendas, minutes and tabled papers or reports.

6 Where a secretary acts as committee secretary she needs to be familiar with meeting terminology and be well-versed in procedural matters governing the particular committee, so that she may be effective in assisting the chairman in the conduct of the meeting.

7 The conference industry is growing every year with all types of conferences and seminars being organised to serve a range of different purposes, some incorporating a social element, others being strictly confined to business.

8 The selection of a venue for any conference is extremely important and can make or break an event.

9 A conference organiser is responsible for the organisation and co-ordination of all elements including, venue, programme, budget, paperwork and security arrangements.

10 It is normal practice to monitor and attempt to evaluate the success of any conference and use the feedback obtained to tighten up on any weaknesses when planning the next one.

QUICK REVISION QUESTIONS

1 When booking a restaurant for a business lunch what are the main points which a secretary needs to bear in mind?

2 What essential information needs to appear on any notice of a meeting?

3 List the agenda items which you would expect to appear on agendas for most business meetings.

4 Briefly explain what you understand by 'Action Minutes'.

5 Summarise a secretary's duties after a meeting.

6 Explain the following terms:
a adjournment;
b collective responsibility;
c ex officio;
d nem. con.;
e rider.

7 Suggest six things you would consider in selecting the venue for a conference.

8 Where your programme consists of a number of presentations what steps can you, as conference organiser, take to ensure that the subject matter does not overlap between speakers?

9 What information would you be likely to include in a delegate pack issued when people register for a conference?

10 Distinguish between fixed and variable costs in budgeting for an event.

15 Information processing skills

Never before has information been available in such large quantities on so many subjects and never before have there been such exciting possibilities for its fast updating, retrieval and transmission.

As was indicated in Section 1 the functions of an office are substantially concerned with handling information and consequently a secretary needs to possess a range of skills in this respect.

This section deals with the ways in which information is needed, handled and presented while highlighting the vast array of information resources which exist, together with the possibilities for transmitting information to others in the most efficient and effective ways.

At the end of this section you should be able to:

- explain the importance of up-to-date information;
- appreciate the importance of sound follow-up systems;
- identify the various resources available to a secretary in researching information;
- highlight some of the specialist information sources available;
- list suitable reference books which a secretary might consult when carrying out research;
- describe effective ways of presenting information;
- devise appropriate ways of displaying information.

Passing on information

Another of the communicating skills which a secretary needs to use and develop is that of passing on information. This can involve a range of things from passing messages on to the boss either verbally or in writing, possibly as a result of something which has happened when he has been out of the office, to passing on information to colleagues, clients, members of the public and possibly the Press.

Several decisions will have to be made including the communication medium to be used according to the circumstances. Selection criteria will be based on such factors as the nature of the communication, the need for a written record, accuracy, legibility, credibility, cost, distance, convenience, speed, degree of urgency, the identity of the recipient, confidentiality or legal considerations and the options available in terms of facilities and equipment.

Exercising judgement and identifying priorities

In terms of transmitting information to your boss it will be important to exercise judgement in terms of what is and is not important as well as the level of detail required. Also where your boss may be absent from the office for lengthy periods of time it will be necessary to prioritise the items on his return. Some form of aide-mémoire and follow-up system will prove useful here. It is foolish to try to rely on your memory, regardless of how good it may be, as inevitably you will overlook or omit something which turns out to be important.

Making lists

Aide-mémoires can simply take the form of lists, and often a name or subject heading will be sufficient to jog your memory and ensure that you pass the information on. A useful, relatively recent arrival on the office stationery market is the 'Post-it' note which has an adhesive strip which sticks conveniently on practically any surface, including other paper, and yet is easily removed without trace.

Follow-up systems

Any secretary worth her salt will devise some form of follow-up or bring-forward system. These are necessary in that frequently the information to be passed on may be incomplete, or something you have initiated which demanded a response may need chasing. A simple system is to use an expanding file numbered 1 to 31. Within the pocket for the appropriate day of the month insert the aide-mémoire or a photocopy of the letter you sent requesting information. If, for example, a reply has not been received for the latter, it is time you started to chase up the information.

Where a secretary may work for more than one executive, all of whom may have busy schedules and a lot of appointments to keep track of, it may be prudent to set up a colour coded card index, numbered again from 1 to 31. This is sometimes referred to as a 'tickler file' and is useful to note meetings, appointments, business trips and invitations. This is not an alternative to the diary but rather a supplementary information source. This way nothing should be left to chance, all relevant information should be recorded for passing on and the general efficiency of the office should be ensured.

Dealing with the Press

Where your job may bring you into contact with representatives of the media, particular care needs to be exercised in giving out information. Newspaper reporters or other media personnel can be very persistent and where, for example, your company may be the subject of a lot of media interest or speculation, it will be vital to ensure that no harmful publicity is forthcomning as a result of careless talk from members of staff.

Very often companies have a policy whereby the only information given to the Press should come from an authorised source such as the Public Relations or Press Officer. Nonetheless, it is important that good relations are maintained with the media as sometimes it may be desirable to receive publicity, when, for example, promoting a new product or informing the public of some activity which raises the reputation and prestige of the organisation.

Seeking information

An increasing aspect of many secretaries' roles is that of seeking out information. Never before has so much current information been so readily available from so many different sources and where an organisation wishes to compete effectively it must have access to the fullest, most up-to-date information at its disposal.

Secretaries may be called upon to research into all sorts of things, and it is therefore vital to have a clear idea of the sources of information that can be tapped. Obviously, in terms of the research a secretary is called upon to do, a lot will depend on the type of organisation, the nature of its activities and the amount of technology that is available.

The human resource

Often a lot of valuable time can be saved by consulting someone else who may know the answer already. Experts exist in all fields and it pays to utilise their specialist knowledge. Sometimes they will be found within the organisation, perhaps in a different department, and this alone is one good reason for familiarising yourself as well as you can with the structure of your organisation and with the staff and their respective duties.

Company files and records

Information you need will often be held already in company files and it will be a matter of searching carefully through the files in your own office or knowing precisely what it is that you want and then approaching the individual with the authority to locate and release the required information. Company information can take many forms and will include correspondence files, reports, minutes and in-house publications of all kinds as well as data held on computer.

It may even be that the company has its own archives and reference library specialising in the preservation and maintenance of a resource bank of information which is of particular significance to the organisation.

General reference sources

The sort of general information providers which are used on a daily basis by both organisations and private individuals are newspapers and periodicals, radio and television, public libraries, travel agents, local council offices, government departments, information bureaux, post offices, tax offices and chambers of commerce. Such services are readily available and can often supply the sort of up-to-date information which is sought.

Newspapers and periodicals

Newspapers and periodicals will provide the most up-to-date coverage on a topic but it can sometimes be difficult to find the relevant one or the relevant article. You need to know exactly what you are looking for and it is important to be as accurate and specific as possible when trying to locate relevant material.

Where you do have good references it is a relatively straightforward matter to obtain a back copy either direct from the newspaper or by contacting the **Official Publication Library** at the British Library. It holds stocks of the preceding month's newspapers, eg *The Times*, *Financial Times* and *International Herald Tribune*.

Abstracts and indices

When your research is less specific and you wish general information on what has appeared in newspapers and journals you need to consult reference books at your local library. Two useful forms of abstracts of a general nature are *Keesing's Contemporary Archives* which is loose-leafed and regularly updated and provides a synopsis and index of current news and subjects and the *British Humanities Index* which is produced quarterly by the Library Association and provides an invaluable subject index on UK publications for the previous 3 months. Specialised subject areas also frequently produce their own abstracts, while many periodicals carry a running back numbers index in their back covers.

Once you have the relevant publication you can obtain the necessary back copy either from the publisher or direct from the Back Numbers Department of the British Library.

The Daily Telegraph Information Bureau

It is worth noting that *The Daily Telegraph* operates a free telephone information service. The bureau which has been in operation since 1948 and takes around 500 queries daily, provides information on a wide range of matters including current affairs, sport, etiquette, general matters, geography and history. Most queries are answered on the spot and those requiring more detailed research are telephoned back later. The service does not deal with legal, medical or technical queries of any kind.

Specialist resources

Many specialist resource services and facilities are available to the researcher and these can be categorised as:

- specialist libraries;
- government departments and publications;
- information about companies;
- professional bodies and associations;
- databanks;
- miscellaneous;
- reference books.

Specialist libraries

As far as specialist libraries are concerned it is important to appreciate that libraries exist throughout the UK which specialise in particular topics. It is, in fact, quite common practice for many public libraries to specialise in certain subject areas while holding details of other libraries' specialisms on microfilm in the ASLIB (Association of Special Libraries and Information Bureaux) Library Directory. As well as the British Library itself there are also National Libraries of Scotland and Wales located in Edinburgh and Aberystwyth respectively.

Another useful source is the ASLIB two-volume *Directory of Infor-*

mation Sources in the UK. Volume I details information sources on science, technology and commerce, while Volume II details sources on social sciences, medicine and the humanities. ASLIB has a subscription for member organisations, but where companies need to undertake a lot of research the services which the Association provides will pay dividends. It also operates training programmes for those involved in research activities and maintains a useful register of translators.

A particularly informative guidebook to specialist libraries is the *Guide to Government Departments and other Libraries* published bi-annually by the British Library.

Government departments and publications

Government departments hold vast quantities of information much of which is free or available for a nominal charge. Useful lists and catalogues are compiled frequently to advise on the information which is available. It can be worth contacting relevant departments, the addresses of which may be found in *Whitaker's Almanac*.

The Government itself is responsible for the official publication of a wide range of materials, mostly via Her Majesty's Stationery Office (HMSO) and available through HMSO bookshops in the major cities or through official agencies. Publications include:

- Acts of Parliament;
- White Papers – statements of policy intentions;
- Green Papers – consultative documents;
- *Hansard* – verbatim reports of Parliamentary debates in daily or weekly edition format;
- Votes and Proceedings of the House of Commons and Minutes and Proceedings of the House of Lords which provide concise accounts of daily business transacted;
- Command Papers, eg reports of Royal Commissions and other inquiries and statements of government policy;
- House of Commons Papers – largely annual reports from government departments and reports from special committees, eg the Expenditure Committee or Select Committees set up to investigate particular subjects or issues.

An annual trade catalogue is produced by HMSO. This contains details of all HMSO publications listed according to subject and is available free from HMSO, St Crispins, Duke Street, Norwich NR3 1PD.

Other government departments which produce useful sources of information are the Central Office of Information (COI) which is largely responsible for the preparation of publicity material, designed primarily for use overseas and the Central Statistical Office which publishes annually (free of charge) a useful booklet entitled *Government Statistics: a Brief Guide to Resources*. This provides information on how to find and use government statistics.

Company information

The Department of Trade and Industry (DTI) is responsible for the operation of the legal framework which ensures the means of accountability for all registered companies in the UK. All such companies, in accordance with their formation are required to lodge certain documents, viz the Memorandum of Association and the Articles of Association, with the Registrar of Companies, as well as submitting financial details on a regular basis to their particular registration authority (offices are located in London, Edinburgh and Cardiff). It is possible to institute company information searches from these offices which hold details of all live companies, together with those dissolved during the previous ten years. It should be noted that Northern Ireland operates its own independent Companies Act and records of company registrations are kept in Belfast. The DTI produces a number of useful leaflets which provide details of the search facilities which exist.

Extel Statistical Services Ltd of London produce, on an annual basis, Extel cards, stocked by many public libraries. These cards carry details of around 7000 quoted British companies in respect of directors, capitalisation, activities, subsidiaries, profit and loss accounts and balance sheets. The service is continually updated.

Professional bodies and associations

There are a large number of professional bodies, eg the British Institute of Management (BIM), the Chartered Institute of Public Finance and Accountancy (CIPFA), the Institute of Administrative Accounting (IAA), the Institute of Administrative Management (IAM), the Institute of Bankers, the Institute of Chartered Secretaries and Administrators (ICSA), the Institute of Personnel Management (IPM) and the Royal Institute of British Architects (RIBA), which offer a variety of useful services and facilities, frequently including the publication of their own journals. Some also set examinations to qualify for professional membership of their institutes and have the right to use their designatory letters.

Some associations are linked directly with particular trades, eg the Motor Agents Association and the British Independent Grocers Federation and the Institute of Purchasing and Supply. Addresses of all societies and institutions may be found in *Whitaker's Almanac*.

Databanks and databases

With such rapid recent developments in technology a lot of information is now held on computers and this is something which has great potential to develop much more in the future. Computer storage enables vast volumes of information to be stored in space that is virtually negligible while providing the facility to augment, manipulate, retrieve and update at very high speeds.

Many organisations have their own private databases, but facilities exist for organisations to access information held on a centralised facility. This can be done by using viewdata systems such as Prestel or Teletext as well as via the communication facilities of computer networks.

This increased capacity for storage, retrieval and update greatly enhances potential which organisations have to apply a wealth of current information to business problems, developments and opportunities, so improving the quality of management decision making.

Miscellaneous

Other organisations which provide a range of useful services include:

- **the British Institute of Management (BIM) Foundation** which operates what might be termed a clearing house for information on management matters;
- **the Industrial Society**, which is a leading UK advisory and training body in management and industrial relations;
- **the Stock Exchange**;
- **the British Standards Institution (BSI)** which, as well as providing technical help for exporters, gives detailed information on regulations and approval systems via their advisory and consultancy services and operates as *the* recognised body in the UK for the preparation and assurance of national standards. (Goods satisfying their criteria carry the familiar Kite mark);
- **the Commission of the European Communities** which circulates regular Background Report sheets to those on its mailing list on a wide range of topics of current interest concerning the European community. A periodic index is produced to facilitate easy reference;

- accommodation agencies;
- ticket agencies;
- advertising, publicity and public relations agencies.

Using reference books

Although there is a growing number of specialist resource services and sophisticated facilities available, secretaries still need to be conversant with the vast range of reference books that are available. It would be impossible even to begin to list them all. However, the following represents what can be considered as a basic selection of essential items:

Telephone Directories (British Telecom) including *Yellow Pages* classified versions
Whitaker's Almanac
The Statesman's Year Book – two sections, one providing information on a country by country basis, the other detailing international organisations, eg World Health Organisation (WHO) (Macmillan Ltd)
UK Telex Directory (British Telecom)
Annual Abstract of Statistics (HMSO)
Who's Who – short personal biographies of eminent people in the UK (A & C Black Ltd)
Titles and Forms of Address, a Guide to their Correct Use (A & C Black Ltd)
Oxford English Dictionary
Roget's Thesaurus of English Words and Phrases (many editions including one by Penguin)
The Stock Exchange Official Year Book – includes details of all officially listed securities and a classified list of companies and their registrars

Presenting information

Researching information represents only half the story. Once relevant and appropriate information has been located it must then be presented in a format which is in keeping with the purpose for which it is intended. This can be anything from a straightforward written report, to a speech, punctuated and supported by visual materials of some kind, to the making of a video for promotional purposes.

The range of options is considerable and secretaries may find themselves at the sharp end of the necessary preparatory work or perhaps even assisting their bosses during presentation sessions. Where a lot of information has been gathered it will have to be sifted through and analysed for its relevance in terms of how and where it has to be used or incorporated. This may include things like checking on copyright and requesting permissions to use material, or trying to locate a suitable photograph or graphic illustration to accompany the text.

Many secretaries particularly enjoy this sort of activity as it enables them to exercise a still different range of skills, including editorial ones, design abilities, layout artistry, decision making and problem solving. Presenting information is something of an art form and the range and variety of support materials which can be used is growing all the time.

Modern office equipment (see Unit 1) greatly facilitates the ease with which material can be drafted, updated, altered, blown-up or reduced in size and literally prepared to camera-ready copy standard by using word processing or even desk-top publishing software.

The importance of presentation standards should not be underestimated. People in general are accustomed to high standards of presentation in all areas of their lives, particularly via the media where things like newspaper layouts, photographs and print have been greatly improved while the calibre of high resolution graphics used by television in news and documentary-type programmes is of a particularly high standard.

The use of OHPs

As a result of such improvements people are less favourably disposed to having to struggle to read bad copy handouts or poorly presented overhead projector (OHP) transparencies during even the most basic of business presentations. Hastily scribbled OHPs are no longer acceptable and there are a variety of means of simple, yet effective, preparation now available.

For example, the use of lettering machines to prepare adhesive strips, using various letter sizes and styles is. simple but effective. Once prepared the strips are stuck on plain paper which is then run through a photocopier and the headings transferred onto acetate sheets for projection. (A less expensive alternative is to use press-on adhesive letters – again available in different sizes, styles and colours.) The introduction of colour to the transparencies can add a totally new dimension to presentations. It can be done either by using coloured adhesive strips or letters directly with clear acetates or by using different coloured acetates. Alternatively it may be possible to generate the material on computer and print out the acetate using coloured pens on a graphics plotter.

379

When talking about OHPs it is also worth while mentioning that high quality, portable OHPs are available for a relatively modest outlay, and many managers who may make a lot of presentations in all sorts of venues may prefer the reassurance of having their own machine rather than having to rely on one which is perhaps noisy and difficult to focus. A poor OHP can absolutely ruin a presentation which has been prepared around even the best set of transparencies. Something else which will often be helpful is to take time to mount the transparencies as handling will be easier and they will also be less likely to get damaged and so can be used over and over again.

Slides

Sometimes a presenter may prefer to have his material transferred onto 35-mm slides. This may lead to a mixture of photographs, printed text and diagrams, carefully sequenced and set up in a remote-controlled carousel. The presenter can then give a very slick and polished performance moving through the slides at the press of a button.

Flip pads and white boards

Flip charts offer yet another simple but flexible alternative when making a presentation or leading a briefing session. Pads are available in a variety of sizes and can be conveniently mounted on an easel or come as part of a presentation portfolio which can be easily transported as required.

Whiteboards, too may be freestanding or wall-mounted and come in a wide range of sizes. This type of support is useful where a presenter wishes to ad-lib or where additional ideas are being taken from the group or audience. They are also particularly suitable for planning meetings or brainstorming sessions where ideas are coming thick and fast. They are used in conjunction with coloured marker pens and it is easy to write or draw on a scale which is easy to read and follow. One point worthy of note with white boards is that the pens used are of the dry, non-permanent variety to ensure easy erasing!

Copyboards

A rather more recent product to appear among the visual presentation range of equipment and ideas is the copyboard. This is really a sophisticated additive to the plain white board referred to above. The idea is that once material has been placed on the screen (think of the writing surface as a screen rather than a board) images can be copied electronically to produce hard, black and white copies, produced more or less instantaneously at the press of a button. The original image is either erased from the screen altogether or retained while the copyboard moves to another screen.

Such a facility is particularly useful where a flow of sometimes complex ideas is coming and where it is preferred to concentrate on the creative, thinking processes rather than having the distraction of needing to make notes, sometimes at high speed (with the consequent possible loss of accuracy) before the material is removed from the board. Copies of what has been written on the screen are made using a fax-type technique rather than standard photocopy technology and the copies appear in a tray beneath the unit.

Different manufacturers of copyboards have produced models with either two or five screens and at the press of a button it is possible

Fig. 15.1 A copyboard

to move from one screen to another. The surface of the screens is very similar to that of an ordinary white board and is just as easy to write on and to erase. The two-screen models have a smaller overall surface dimension and are usually portrait shaped whereas the five-screen boards are large and have a landscape display format.

Various options, including side-by-side copies of materials featured on two screens, or reduction A4 to A5 size copies, are possible with certain of the machines currently on the market. Some also have a remote control facility while others allow copies of material, prepared in advance of a meeting, to be attached to the screen and copied. This option can be useful where more accurate graphical representations need to be incorporated as a presentation progresses. An example of a copyboard is given as Fig. 15.1.

Displaying information

Information may also need to be displayed on a more permanent basis or incorporated into some form of written report and it is here that charts and graphs of one kind or another come into their own. Most people have come across charts and graphs during their school careers and are familiar with their use in the press and on television and it will be a matter of selecting the type most appropriate for the sort of information you need to convey.

Often the information will be of a statistical nature and the criteria for selection will be whether fine detail or general impression is called for. The scale of the chart will be important as will the labelling and the provision of a key. Basically in terms of charts and graphs the options are as follows:

- **line graphs** which may be single or multi-line;
- **bar charts** which may be single, compound or multiple bar and may be presented vertically or horizontally;
- **histograms** which are a type of bar chart where the bars will not be of equal width, but permitted to touch one another in graphic representations of frequency distributions;
- **Gantt charts** which are used to compare and contrast estimated figures or projections with actual ones;
- **pie charts** which are used to illustrate parts in relation to a whole;
- **pictograms** which rely on pictorial or symbolic methods of representing statistics, eg a complete house representing 1000 people, half a house representing 500 and so on;
- **flow charts** (see also pp. 25) which illustrate the progress and

process by which a system or procedure is followed through from beginning to end.

In addition, diagrams, maps and models are other familiar ways of displaying information. Three-dimensional models can be a particularly effective way of illustrating something like a housing development or an office complex, the added dimension being helpful to the non-specialist in particular in developing spatial awareness.

Visual planning and control boards

These boards have tended to become a common feature of many offices and, as the term suggests, are designed to provide quick and easy reference to all sorts of information. They can be set up for virtually any purpose, eg to plot sales progress, to identify different staff holiday periods, to highlight important dates and deadlines.

While many planning boards are made-up laminated boards drawn out in some sort of grid formation with adhesive strips and symbols added to represent the progress or data, others may operate like basic white boards with dry markers, while yet others are made of high quality metal with a range of coloured magnetic strips, symbols, labels, numbers and letters available to set up the board.

Another board commonly found in many business offices, as well as banks and other venues, is the black background, perforated board onto which white letters may be fixed. The setting up of such a board may well be one of a secretary's daily tasks where, for example, information is posted regarding room allocations for the day or special events. Such information would be displayed prominently, eg in a foyer or reception area.

One very important thing to remember in relation to the use of planning boards of any kind is the need for them to be kept up to date, otherwise they are a hindrance rather than a help. Also they need to be located in positions where they can be used with ease. Boards need to be set at the correct height and positioned at a distance which is in keeping with the eyesight of the user. Where they are well positioned and set up they do provide a very flexible and useful aid to quick, easy and comprehensive reference.

CHECKLIST

1   Information is an important corporate resource.

2   Information is only useful when fully up to date, easily located and capable of being efficiently processed.

3 An important aspect of many secretaries' work is to research information.

4 Information always needs to be categorised and prioritised and this is part of a secretary's daily routine.

5 One particularly useful source of information is the human resource, ie other people, and another is a company's own files and record systems.

6 A range of specialist facilities exist which provide valuable sources of information.

7 Reference books still prove useful and there are publications (many produced annually) on a wide range of subjects and specialisms.

8 Once it is located information needs to be checked for accuracy and presented effectively if it is to achieve its true potential.

9 Many support materials and facilities are available which enable a presenter to give impact to the information he wishes to put over, as well as making an audience more receptive to what may be complex detail which can be difficult to absorb.

10 Information may also be displayed on a temporary or permanent basis in ways which make it more readily accessible and easily updated.

QUICK REVISION QUESTIONS

1 In what circumstances might a secretary set up a follow-up system?
2 When required to research information suggest different resources which are available to a secretary:
  a within her company;
  b outside.
3 List four classes of government publication which a secretary may consult.
4 What type of information is lodged with the Registrar of Companies?
5 In what circumstances might it be useful to consult a database?
6 Name two independent bodies which provide a useful information resource for the business world.
7 Suggest six general reference books which a secretary might consult.
8 What information would you expect to get from the following reference books?
  a Black's *Titles and Forms of Address*

b *Who's Who*
c *The Stock Exchange Official Year Book*
d *The Statesman's Year Book*
9 Describe one way in which a set of overhead transparencies could be prepared for a marketing presentation.
10 Explain how a copyboard operates.

APPENDIX 1
Health and Safety at Work, etc Act, 1974

When this Act came into force in April 1975 it provided a new, integrated and comprehensive system of law to deal with problems relating to health and safety in the working environment. It is what is termed an 'enabling Act' in that it confers powers on organisations to produce regulations which must be implemented in the interests of health and safety. The Act itself, therefore, deals with generalities which need to be interpreted by different bodies according to their own needs and circumstances. However, where properly formulated they carry the force of the law.

In accordance with the HASAWACT every employer must ensure 'as far as is reasonably practicable' (a phrase used frequently throughout the legislation) the health, safety and welfare at work of all his employees. This means that employers must carefully weigh up any risks which might conceivably be involved for their employees against the costs they would incur in attempting to minimise the risk by installing and implementing such safety measures as are considered necessary. Such measures would be likely to include the following:

- exit routes in the event of an emergency, eg fire;
- safe working environment;
- safe and well-maintained equipment;
- necessary protective clothing;
- necessary safe storage facilities;
- adequate safety information, including the provision of codes of safe working practice;
- appropriate training and supervision.

Employers also have two other important duties towards employees:

1 To issue a written statement of general policy with respect to health and safety matters in their organisation, and arrangements for the implementation and revision within the organisation. (Employees have a legal right to demand such a policy from employers and it is common practice in large organisations for staff to receive individual copies which they may add to their Staff Handbooks.)
2 To provide for the appointment of safety representatives from

among employees by trade unions 'recognised' by employers in any negotiation procedures.

The requirements of every employer will differ in preparing a safety policy according to the nature of the organisation's activities. For example, a chemical company handling toxic substances will need to have different regulations from those of a firm of chartered accountants. Nonetheless, both are required to produce a statement in keeping with their individual requirements. In any event a basic policy is reflected in the specimen provided here.

Specimen Basic Safety Policy

1 The policy of this company is as follows:
   a to take all practical steps to safeguard the health, safety and welfare of all employees and of all customers and visitors to our premises;
   b to provide adequate working conditions for our employees with proper facilities to safeguard their health and safety and to ensure that any work which is undertaken produces no risks to health or safety;
   c to encourage employees to co-operate with the company in all safety matters; to identify hazards which may exist and to report any condition which may appear dangerous or unsatisfactory; and to ensure that each member of the staff accepts his own responsibility not to endanger himself or others and actively to assist in fulfilling the requirements and spirit of the Act.
2 While the final responsibility for matters of health and safety rests with the company, it is important that all employees, as part of their duty, involve themselves in matters of health and safety, reporting back to their departmental manager any condition which appears dangerous or unsatisfactory and making suggestions for the improvement of existing facilities and arrangements.
3 All injuries, however slight, must be reported to the employee's departmental manager/supervisor and must be entered in the Accident Book immediately.
4 The Accident Book can be located in _____
5 The First Aid Box is situated _____
6 Any person discovering a fire shall immediately press the fire alarm and notify the telephonist. If it is possible for that person to extinguish the fire, without danger to him/herself, he/she shall immediately do so: if not, he/she must evacuate the building.

7 Upon hearing the fire alarm all employees must immediately vacate the premises by the nearest exit and gather in _____

8 The executive responsible for fulfilling this policy is _____

Employees' duties and responsibilities

For the first time this legislation places a duty on employees as well as employers. According to the Act, one of the duties of every employee (including those working part time) is:

'to take reasonable care for his own health and safety and that of other persons who may be affected by what he does or what he omits to do at work.'

Also an employee has a duty:

'to co-operate with an employer or any other person who has duties to carry out under the Act or related legislation.'

Failure to comply with the duties outlined in the Act is a criminal offence and both employers and employees could be liable to prosecution. It is important to appreciate that ignorance of the law is no defence. Both parties need to know the extent of their responsibilities and to ensure that they perform them to the letter.

Health and Safety Commission

A single authority in the shape of the Commission for Health and Safety at Work, made up of an independent chairman, and between six and nine members it is independent of any government department and is responsible for:

- developing strategy in connection with health and safety at work;
- preparing proposals for updating and extending existing provisions;
- suggesting non-statutory standards and codes of practice;
- making arrangements for carrying out research, publicising results and providing training and information;
- giving advice to government departments;
- promoting safety education and training;
- providing facilities for carrying out essential testing;
- appointing individuals or committees to assist and advise as necessary;
- directing the Executive to investigate accidents and occurrences;
- organising the Employment Advisory Service.

The Executive is a three-man body charged with implementing the Act. The Director is appointed by the Commission and approved by the Secretary of State for Employment and two other persons are appointed by the Commission with the approval of the Director. Under the Commission the Executive has the power to enforce statutory requirements and to appoint inspectors to carry out its enforcement functions.

The inspectors, in addition to possessing the right of prosecution, have many useful powers of enforcement. For example, they may issue:

- **Improvement notices** which will specify faults and advise remedial action within a specified time;
- **Prohibition notices** which specify that the operation or practice must cease immediately until the cause of risk is removed.

The former represents a deferred notice while the latter is immediate. Rights of appeal against improvement of prohibition notices must be lodged with an industrial tribunal within seven days. Failure to comply with a Notice may lead to prosecution which may, in turn, result in a fine or even imprisonment.

APPENDIX 2
Data Protection Act 1984

The main purpose of this legislation is to safeguard the interests of individuals where information about them is stored on computer. It has far-reaching effects on many aspects of business including, in particular, the maintenance of employee records and credit control procedures.

Under the Act, employers holding computerised data need to register as data users (manual records are not covered by the Act provided any reference to the records is for purely factual information). The registration of data users and computer bureaux is supervised by the Data Protection Registrar, a post created by the Act. Users are required to disclose the nature of the data held, why it is held, how and from where it has been obtained and to whom it will be disclosed. Employees have a statutory right to access all computerised information held on them and may claim compensation for damage and distress if the information is found to be inaccurate.

The terminology

Two important terms used in the Act are 'data subject' and 'data user'. The 'data subject' is the individual who is the subject of the personal data, ie the person about whom the data is stored. The 'data user' is the person who holds the personal data. This is a more complex term in that to be classed as a data user the person or persons must do more than simply access the data, he/they must control the contents and use of the data held.

The eight data protection principles

There are eight principles, which together form a standard against which the Registrar will seek to ensure compliance and these are as follows:

1 The information to be contained in personal data shall be obtained and processed fairly and lawfully.
2 Personal data shall be held only for one or more specified and lawful purposes.
3 Disclosure of personal data held shall not be in a manner

incompatible with the purpose or pruposes for which it is held.

4 Personal data held shall be adequate, relevant and not excessive to the purpose or purposes.

5 Personal data held shall be accurate, and where necessary kept up to date.

6 Personal data shall not be kept for longer than necessary.

7 An individual shall be entitled:
   a at reasonable intervals and without due delay or expense:
   i to be informed by any data user that information is held on him;
   ii to access any data held;
   b where appropriate, to have data corrected or erased.

8 Appropriate security measures shall be taken against unauthorised access to, or alteration, disclosure or destruction of personal data and against accidental loss or destruction.

Over and above those eight principles the Secretary of State has the right to modify or supplement them to provide additional safeguards in respect of personal data concerning:

a racial origin of the data subject;
b political opinions, religious or other beliefs of the data subject;
c physical or mental health, or the sexual life of the data subject;
d criminal convictions of the data subject.

Those principles form an operational guideline for data users, rather like the Highway Code, in that while advisory and subject to certain modification and interpretation, they may be forgotten in practice. However, where the principles or provisions are ignored or diverged from, the Act is legally enforceable.

Exemptions

Part IV of the Act deals with exemptions and the following are examples of instances in which data is exempt:

- where data is held for the purposes of national security;
- where data is held for the detection or prevention of crime;
- where data is held for the assessment or collection of taxes or duties;
- information held for calculating payroll or for keeping accounts;
- information held for household affairs or recreational purposes, eg lists of names and addresses;
- information held for the subsequent preparation of text, eg documents held on a word processor.

Duties of the Registrar

Under the Act the Registrar is expected to:

- promote the observance of the principles by data users and those carrying on computer bureaux services (easier to say than to enforce, although the Act does provide the necessary powers of investigation);
- consider any complaints and follow up as considered appropriate;
- disseminate information in respect of the legislation;
- encourage those bodies who represent data users, to prepare and disseminate guidelines and codes of practice;
- report annually before both Houses of Parliament.

The Act came into force in stages but was fully enforceable in November 1987.

APPENDIX 3
LCCI Private Secretary's Certificate Office Organisation and Secretarial Procedures

Following this advice section are the two complete papers set for the 1986 examinations, together with the Background Notes.

Advice to candidates

Success in any examination depends on the overall study pattern and revision techniques adopted by candidates throughout a course of study. One thing to be sure that you have at the very beginning of your course, is a copy of the **current syllabus**. Remember that syllabuses do change and that it is important that you are aware of the precise contents. You should also have studied and worked through **past examination papers**, making sure to time yourself carefully. This way you really begin to get a feel for the requirements of the examination and become familiar with the type of questions set.

Examiners' Reports

One thing that students are often unaware of is the existence of examiners' reports. These are prepared by the examiners after each series of examinations and provide very useful information in respect of the major areas of weakness, common errors and omissions and points which may have been misinterpreted in the questions set. It is particularly helpful to study a few of these reports carefully in conjunction with the appropriate examination papers. The suggestions made may prevent you from making similar mistakes when you sit your examination. Examination Reports are available from the LCCI Examinations Board, Marlowe House, Station Road, Sidcup, Kent, DA15 7BJ.

Before the examination

As well as a consistent study technique and the acquisition of the relevant supporting materials there are certain points which can prove useful to remember in the immediate run up to an examination and the following represents advice for those preparing to sit the Office Organisation and Secretarial Procedures paper in particular.

Making the best use of Background Notes

To get the most out of these notes which are issued six weeks prior to the actual date of examinations comprising the Private Secretary's Certificate it is essential to study them very carefully and to thoroughly familiarise yourself with the contents, bearing in mind that they apply to **all** the examinations which you are scheduled to take in a particular series.

The idea behind the Background Notes is to help provide realism and enable you to answer the questions set in the context you are given. You will need to be fairly flexible, however, as you will be adopting a different role for each of the papers set and it is important that you are clear in your mind about each one and that you know which hat you are wearing for which examination.

While it is not possible to glean any detailed information from the notes they do, when taken in conjunction with the company organisation chart, provide a useful overview. Background notes should also serve as a prompt for your revision. You should certainly concentrate on developing a feel for the type of organisation the questions are to be set around and the roles of the various members of staff.

It is important that you assume an appropriate level of responsibility, neither overstepping the authority which would be vested in the position, nor failing to use sufficient initiative. It will be a question of striking a suitable balance. For instance, where you are asked to assume the role of someone providing secretarial support for two senior executives (as in the December 1986 paper) it will be important for you to bear this fact in mind and respond accordingly in your examination answers.

The organisation chart

You should study the organisation chart carefully in order to gauge the relationships and work out the lines of communication which are likely to exist. You should make yourself totally familiar with the names of the different people represented as well as having a good idea of the type of work you would expect them to undertake. You will not have time to spend working this out during the examination, so valuable time can be saved where you are well briefed beforehand.

Spotting likely question areas

Spotting questions, even where you have been given Background Notes, always sounds easier than it is. However, there is certainly no harm in trying, and certain features of the notes should provide useful clues. For example, where reference is made to other locations such as branch offices abroad, it is reasonable to suppose that there might be a question involving travel arrangements or long distance communications. One point to make sure of is that you know the geographical location of any places specifically mentioned in the notes. There is no excuse, for instance, in concentrating on rail and sea travel when the only feasible route would have been by air! (see December 1986).

Where specific items of equipment, or types of system are mentioned in the notes it will also be worth while spending some revision time brushing up on those areas. Reference to something like 'regular meetings' should also provide a useful clue, as should something like 'In-house training' (see also December 1986).

In fact, study the Background Notes for the December 1986 paper and see how many likely topic areas you can spot. Then compare your ideas with the actual paper set.

Observing the rules

Remember that although you may have access to the Background Notes as much as six weeks prior to the examination you may only make limited 'unabbreviated notes in ink' on the actual Background Notes form for use in the examination. It is important that you observe these rules to the letter. Therefore, the bulk of your research and revision will have been done at home and you should only make key references to points you feel you might forget, in the space provided on the paper.

Tackling the actual examination

When you go into the examination room and receive your copy of the examination paper read the Instructions to Candidates very carefully. Do not assume that the rubric will always be exactly the same – even though it usually is. It is up to you to make sure that you know **precisely** what is required and permitted in the examination.

In this examination you will need to answer FIVE questions from a choice of TEN. This is a very reasonable degree of choice so be sure that you choose wisely. You will also see from the rubric that 'All questions carry equal marks'. However, some questions consist of several parts and it is usual for the paper to indicate the marks allocated to each part. Where you select a question which is split into parts you should be careful to answer in accordance with the marks awarded, ie spend more time and write more where there are more marks given.

The types of question set are varied so enabling you a good degree of scope and the opportunity to convince the examiner that you have a sound knowledge of the subject matter. Remember that this type of examination is not set simply to assess textbook recall but to test your ability to apply your knowledge and understanding to the situation, so you need to interpret the questions and adapt your answers accordingly.

Answering the questions

One vital thing to do when tackling any examination, if you want to achieve success, is to ensure that you *answer the question*. This may seem to be stating the obvious but any examiner will tell you that students fail examinations because they do not answer the questions set, choosing to write about what they know of the topic area in general, or what they wish the question had asked!

Therefore, if the question asks you to 'describe' be sure that this is what you do. If, on the other hand, you are asked to 'briefly outline', your explanation can be much less detailed, relying on points rather than more lengthy descriptions.

Where you are asked for three ways or for a specific number of advantages and disadvantages, be sure that you supply the precise number requested. Extra marks will not be given for offering more – all you will be doing is wasting valuable time. Conversely, where you are asked for a 'checklist' or to give 'a number of points' it will not be sufficient to mention only one or two things. This is where you need to expand and mention as many relevant points as you can so that the examiner will appreciate that you possess in-depth rather than superficial knowledge.

The marks awarded to a question may prove helpful to you in gauging how many points to look for or how much to write generally. If, for example, in question 2(b) of the December 1986 paper you can think of eight precautions you could take then cover them all, but where you can perhaps think of only four specific things, be prepared to elaborate a little more on each one.

Right and wrong answers

An examiner will tend to expect certain types of answer and will look for reference to essential points. Sometimes a question will automatically lend itself to your producing a number of things which seem appropriate and worthy of inclusion and that way it is likely that you will gain marks for the different points you introduce in your answer, provided, of course, that they are relevant. Where providing a number of points is less easy, guard against repeating yourself by saying the same thing but in different ways. Remember that quantity is no substitute for quality in an examination answer.

However, many questions can be answered in a variety of ways, so technically there may be no right or wrong answer. What will be important is that your answer is sensible and competently put together, taking into account the context of the paper and your adopted role. Where you may perhaps be making certain recommendations they may not be the ones the examiner necessarily expected but where they are reasonable and where you have justified them appropriately they will be perfectly acceptable.

While some questions require factual answers others rely more on opinion or point of view and provided the reasoning is well-considered and the content of the answer appropriate there is no reason why it should not receive due recognition. After all, regardless of what you may think, examinations are not set to trick students but to test their skills and abilities.

Following the requested format

It is also important to follow the instructions in respect of the format requested. For example, where you are asked to 'Write a memo' be sure that you do just that. This means that you need to head it up appropriately, state who it is from, to whom it is going, the date and the subject. In other words it should look like a memo. After all you are hoping to achieve the Private Secretary's Certificate so you will be expected to know the right format.

Similarly where you are asked for a list, provide a list and where you are asked to make notes, make notes. By doing this you are following the ground rules and will be off to a good start.

Apportioning your time

Time is the enemy in every type of examination and it is all too easy to run out of time. You have $2\frac{1}{2}$ hours to complete the 5 questions in the Office Organisation and Secretarial Procedures paper, so allocate it wisely.

In round terms this means half an hour per question, but given that you need to read the paper through, decide on your 5 questions and plan your answers, you obviously have less than half an hour for each in terms of actually writing your answers. It will be better to estimate between 20 and 25 minutes, assuming that you will wish to make a few preliminary rough notes prior to committing your final answers to paper. It is always advisable to gather your thoughts and jot down ideas, rather than start writing before you have had an opportunity to explore possibilities in your mind and structure your thinking a little. Nonetheless, you need to be careful that you do not spend so much time planning that you run out of production time!

Also be sure to attempt all 5 questions. The examination asks for 5 and the examiner wants to see that you have tackled 5 – not 3 or 4 or even 6! So even where you feel that you could write more than your timescale allows for a question, resist the temptation and proceed to your next question.

Attention to detail

Finally it is important to remember that this examination is part of a Private Secretary's Certificate so it is reasonable that a good standard of English (ie spelling, grammar and punctuation), together with clear and neat presentation is expected. Therefore, you can expect to be penalised for poor layout and English errors, so take care.

All in all an examination of this kind gives you an opportunity to demonstrate your knowledge, understanding and appreciation of the subject areas reflected by the syllabus, as well as to express yourself in a clear, competent manner. Provided that you follow instructions, direct your answers towards the situation set out in the question and use your common sense, you should not go far wrong, so good luck!

THE LONDON CHAMBER OF COMMERCE AND INDUSTRY EXAMINATIONS BOARD

GROUP SECRETARIAL EXAMINATIONS

JUNE 1986

PRIVATE SECRETARY'S CERTIFICATE

BACKGROUND NOTES

These Background Notes may be given to Tutors and Candidates in the Private Secretary's Certificate examination on or after Friday 25 April 1986.

Candidates may make longhand unabbreviated notes in the margins as indicated on pages 3 and 4. Candidates may have only **one** copy of the Background Notes for use throughout the examination.

THESE BACKGROUND NOTES MAY NOT BE COPIED.

COMLON INTERNATIONAL plc

Comlon International plc is a company providing Office Equipment and Stationery. The Head Office is in Central London where the Directors of the Divisions have offices.

The Office Equipment Division is responsible for the making and production of office furniture.

The Office Design Division undertakes consultancy work where the layout and decor of the office together with the provision and installation of the necessary equipment is provided as a full service.

The Stationery Division designs stationery as required by clients.

The Printing Division produces and delivers stationery ordered by customers.

The Production Departments of both the Printing Division and the Office Equipment Division are sited in High Wycombe.

The company is expanding and has branches in 4 major cities approximately 80-100 km away from the Head Office, 2 branches overseas (one in Germany and one in France), and agencies in Australia, Hong Kong, Japan and the United States of America.

The Southern Regional Office is in Bargate, Southampton, where new showrooms have been opened recently.

Comlon metal office furniture has offered 3 successful ranges for the past 20 years. The demand for office furniture made from wood has been increasing and in order to keep abreast of this trend the company wishes to market their Ministerial range shortly.

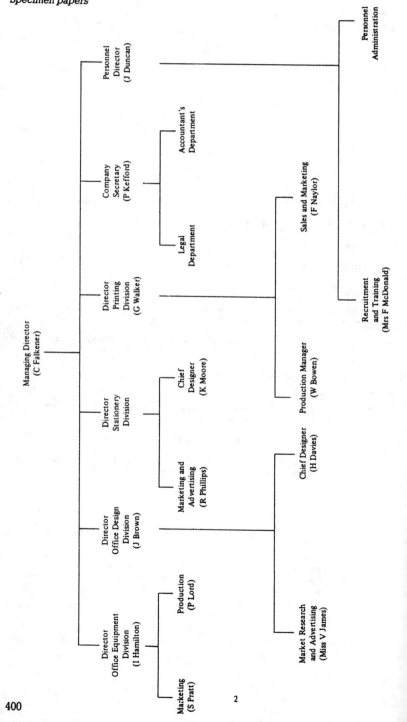

COMLON INTERNATIONAL plc

Managing Director
(C Falkener)

Director Office Equipment Division
(I Hamilton)

Marketing
(S Pratt)

Production
(P Lord)

Director Office Design Division
(J Brown)

Market Research and Advertising
(Miss V James)

Chief Designer
(H Davies)

Director Stationery Division

Marketing and Advertising
(R Phillips)

Chief Designer
(K Moore)

Production Manager
(W Bowen)

Director Printing Division
(G Walker)

Sales and Marketing
(F Naylor)

Company Secretary
(P Kefford)

Legal Department

Accountant's Department

Personnel Director
(J Duncan)

Recruitment and Training
(Mrs F McDonald)

Personnel Administration

2

9 JUNE 1986

Unabbreviated longhand
notes may be written
in this margin **only**

STRUCTURE OF BUSINESS

The paper is a general one and the candidate is not to be
regarded as working in one particular division.

10 JUNE 1986

COMMUNICATION – USE OF ENGLISH

The candidate works for Mr Christopher Falkener, the
Managing Director.

Since the move to new business premises a year ago,
Mr Falkener has become concerned about general
untidiness and the growing incidence of minor accidents
in the new head office office.

11 JUNE 1986

SECRETARIAL TRANSCRIPTION – SHORTHAND

PAPER A

The candidate is secretary to Mr John Duncan's Personal
Assistant, Mrs S Caldwell.

PAPER B

The candidate works for Mrs Fiona McDonald who is
Manager of Recruitment and Training.

–3–

12 JUNE 1986

OFFICE ORGANISATION AND SECRETARIAL
PROCEDURES

The candidate works for Mr John Brown, Director of
Office Design Division. The Chief Designer, Mr Henry
Davies, works in the Head Office in London with 10
designers. He also has additional design staff in the
branches in the United Kingdom and overseas.

13 JUNE 1986

SECRETARIAL TRANSCRIPTION – AUDIO

PAPER A

The candidate is Secretary to Miss T Yates, who is
Personal Assistant to Mr Ian Hamilton, Director of Office
Equipment Division. Miss Yates has left a tape for you to
transcribe ready for Mr Hamilton's signature when he
returns later today.

PAPER B

The candidate is Secretary to Miss H Norris who is
Personal Assistant to Mr Greg Walker, Director of Printing
Division. Today's tape has been given to you by
Miss H Norris. The work has to be typed for Mr Walker's
signature.

–4–

THE LONDON CHAMBER OF COMMERCE AND INDUSTRY

PRIVATE SECRETARY'S CERTIFICATE EXAMINATION 1986

OFFICE ORGANISATION AND SECRETARIAL PROCEDURES

THURSDAY 12 JUNE 1986 — 0930 - 1200

INSTRUCTIONS TO CANDIDATES

Answer 5 questions.

All questions carry equal marks.

Put a line through any rough work

WRITE LEGIBLY AND PAY PARTICULAR ATTENTION TO CLARITY OF EXPRESSION, SPELLING, PUNCTUATION AND LAYOUT, FOR WHICH DISCRETIONARY MARKS ARE AVAILABLE

The candidate works for Mr John Brown, Director of Office Design Division.

1   Communication is vital within any organisation. Explain briefly how each of the following systems works and state how each could be used most effectively:

(a) Facsimile

(b) Telex

(c) Telemessage service.

OVER

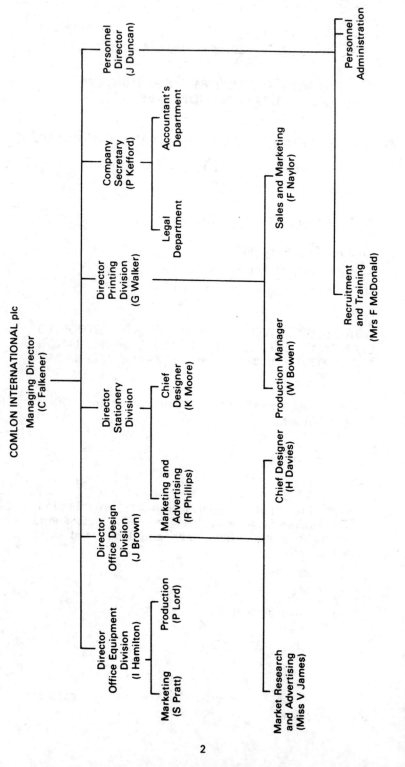

COMLON INTERNATIONAL plc
Managing Director
(C Falkener)

Director Office Equipment Division (I Hamilton)
- Marketing (S Pratt)
- Production (P Lord)
  - Market Research and Advertising (Miss V James)

Director Office Design Division (J Brown)
- Marketing and Advertising (R Phillips)
- Chief Designer (H Davies)

Director Stationery Division
- Chief Designer (K Moore)
- Production Manager (W Bowen)

Director Printing Division (G Walker)
- Sales and Marketing (F Naylor)

Company Secretary (P Kefford)
- Legal Department
- Accountant's Department

Personnel Director (J Duncan)
- Personnel Administration
- Recruitment and Training (Mrs F McDonald)

2   As the Company's work has increased it has been agreed to invest in additional computer software for the furniture designers. You are asked to arrange a one-day training session at a local hotel for 20 designers, 10 of whom work at Head Office in the UK, 5 in Germany and 5 in France. List and explain the arrangements which need to be undertaken to ensure a successful day.

3   The Company has decided to centralise its reprographics facilities at Head Office and offer a variety of machines, although any large amounts of printing will be carried out by the Printing Division.

   (a) What are the advantages and disadvantages of such centralisation?

(12 marks)

   (b) Describe how modern photocopiers could help the Company.

(6 marks)

4   The new post of Word Processing Supervisor has been created. The Supervisor will be responsible for setting up a small word processing pool. When drawing up a short list from internal applicants what should Mrs McDonald be looking for?

(14 marks)

   Why would a present employee be better suited to fill this position?

(4 marks)

5   There has been an increase in the need for overtime to be worked by secretaries and Mr Brown has asked you for your views before discussing the matter with Mrs McDonald.

   (a) Give reasons why the need to work late may arise.

(6 marks)

   (b) Suggest means of diminishing the amount of overtime required.

(12 marks)

OVER

6   Write notes for your new junior on how to handle the opening and sorting of incoming mail.

(11 marks)

List the items of equipment which would improve the efficiency of this task.

(7 marks)

7   Choose **3** of the following cards and explain how they are used. Suggest an occasion when John Brown could make use of **each** card.

(a) charge card

(b) cheque card

(c) service card

(d) business card

(e) phone card

8   Explain the different methods of storing information on microform and whether it could be of use to your organisation, bearing in mind that the Company is thinking of buying a series of microcomputers. Give your reply in the form of a memorandum to Mr Brown.

9   Mr Brown frequently goes on tour seeking potential markets. He uses a car for travelling within the country he is visiting.

(a) Which books of reference would you need to consult?

(b) List the arrangements to be made before he leaves.

(c) State the items Mr Brown should take with him in his briefcase.

10 As secretary to the Social Committee you have been asked to arrange a Christmas staff outing for 50 people to a theatre. Explain fully how you and the Committee would undertake to organise such a trip.

THE LONDON CHAMBER OF COMMERCE AND INDUSTRY
EXAMINATIONS BOARD

GROUP SECRETARIAL EXAMINATIONS

DECEMBER 1986

PRIVATE SECRETARY'S CERTIFICATE

BACKGROUND NOTES

These Background Notes may be given to Tutors and Candidates in the
Private Secretary's Certificate examination on or after Friday 24 October
1986.

Candidates may make longhand unabbreviated notes using **ink** in the
margins as indicated on pages 3 and 4. Candidates may have only **one**
copy of the Background Notes for use throughout the examination.

THESE BACKGROUND NOTES MAY NOT BE COPIED.

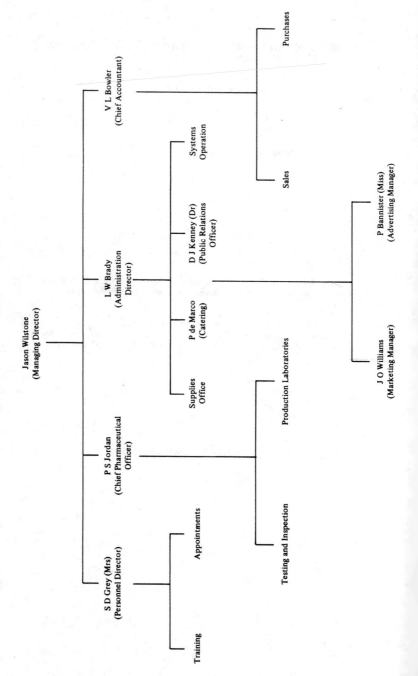

COMLON INTERNATIONAL plc

Jason Wilstone (Managing Director)

- S D Grey (Mrs) (Personnel Director)
  - Training
  - Appointments
- P S Jordan (Chief Pharmaceutical Officer)
  - Testing and Inspection
  - Production Laboratories
- L W Brady (Administration Director)
  - Supplies Office
  - P de Marco (Catering)
  - D J Kenney (Dr) (Public Relations Officer)
  - Systems Operation
  - J O Williams (Marketing Manager)
  - P Bannister (Miss) (Advertising Manager)
- V L Bowler (Chief Accountant)
  - Sales
  - Purchases

COMLON INTERNATIONAL plc

Comlon International plc is a large pharmaceutical company with its Head Office in Comlon House in London. In this office there is a centralised word-processing system and an electronic switchboard with over 1500 extensions. Computers are used and there is also a FAX machine.

There are UK Research and Production Laboratories in Manchester. The Chief Pharmaceutical Officer, Mr Jordan, has an office in the Manchester complex; he frequently travels all over the world and often visits staff based in the Research Laboratory in Geneva. When he is in London, he has an office in the Directors' suite in which the candidate works. When he is abroad he keeps in touch by telex and sometimes FAX.

Comlon International plc has recently developed a new formula for a decongestant for relief from the common cold virus. This is soon to be launched, the target population being the socio-economic groups A, B and C1.

The Advertising Section is engaged in promoting the new product by a special offer of jars. Miss Bannister is arranging for the necessary meetings between the Marketing Manager, copywriters and visualisers.

The Administration Department has regular meetings with other departments to ensure that staff are kept fully informed about projects undertaken.

NCR forms are being introduced in order to reduce the amount of written work required from customers.

The company employs a number of people who have never been in full-time employment before — often young people straight from college. In-house training is provided and staff are able to attend a wide range of courses if they wish.

As an international company, Comlon International plc jealously guards its good name and reputation and has a policy of responding quickly to all items in the media on the pharmaceutical industry.

> Unabbreviated longhand notes may be written in **ink** within this margin **only**

Monday 8 December 1986

STRUCTURE OF BUSINESS

The candidate works for Mrs S D Grey, Personnel Director.

3

Unabbreviated longhand notes may be
written in **ink** within this margin only

Tuesday 9 December 1986

COMMUNICATION – USE OF ENGLISH

The candidate works as secretary to Dr D J Kenney,
Public Relations Officer.

Wednesday 10 December 1986

SECRETARIAL TRANSCRIPTION – SHORTHAND

The candidate is secretary to Mr V L Bowler, Chief
Accountant of Comlon International plc.

Thursday 11 December 1986

OFFICE ORGANISATION AND SECRETARIAL
PROCEDURES

The candidate is secretary to **both** Mr L W Brady,
Administration Director and Mr P S Jordan, Chief
Pharmaceutical Officer.

Friday 12 December 1986

SECRETARIAL TRANSCRIPTION – AUDIO

The candidate is secretary to Miss Patricia Bannister,
Advertising Manager.

4

410

The London Chamber of Commerce and Industry
—————— EXAMINATIONS BOARD ——————

MARLOWE HOUSE, STATION ROAD, SIDCUP, KENT, DA15 7BJ

When Replying
Please Quote **MAE/AB**

Telephones: 01-302 0261 All Departments
01-309 0440 Secretarial Studies
Telex: 888941 LCCIG ATTN EXAMS BOARD

Telegraphic Address:
Exams Sidcup

Erratum

PRIVATE SECRETARY'S CERTIFICATE EXAMINATION

OFFICE ORGANISATION AND SECRETARIAL PROCEDURES

THURSDAY 11 DECEMBER 1986

Question 5 Paragraph 2 should read
'Write a memo to Mrs S D Grey from Mr Brady,
setting out in detail the points you would
expect to be included in the course'.

When giving instructions, the Invigilator
should read the question to the candidates,
drawing their attention to the alteration.
The correction should be displayed prominently
on the board for the duration of the
examination.

LC/PSC/DEC/86

Director: R W CATTELL, MA, FESB, FBIM

THE LONDON CHAMBER OF COMMERCE AND INDUSTRY

PRIVATE SECRETARY'S CERTIFICATE
EXAMINATION 1986

OFFICE ORGANISATION AND SECRETARIAL
PROCEDURES

THURSDAY 11 DECEMBER 1986 – 0930 - 1200

INSTRUCTIONS TO CANDIDATES

Answer 5 questions

All questions carry equal marks

Put a line through any rough work

The use of **standard English dictionaries** and **cordless non-programmable calculators** is permitted

WRITE LEGIBLY AND PAY PARTICULAR ATTENTION TO CLARITY OF EXPRESSION, SPELLING, PUNCTUATION AND LAYOUT, FOR WHICH DISCRETIONARY MARKS ARE AVAILABLE

The candidate works for Mr L W Brady the Administration Director **and** Mr P S Jordan the Chief Pharmaceutical Officer.

An organisation chart is given on page 2

OVER

COMLON INTERNATIONAL plc

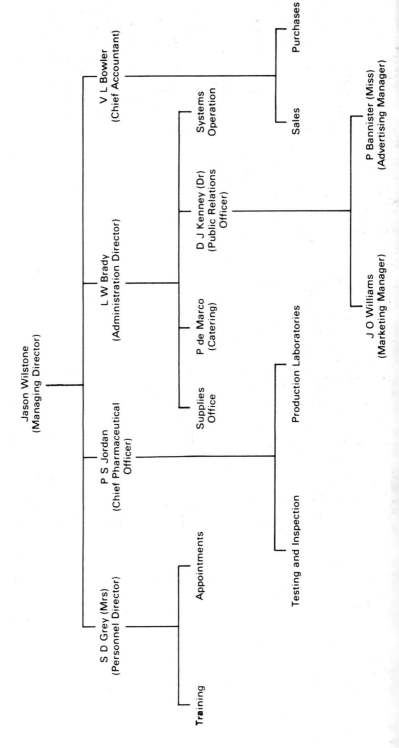

1   One morning Mr Brady is taken seriously ill and rushed to hospital. He is likely to be away from the office for some weeks. What must be done in his absence to ensure that the work of the department proceeds as smoothly as possible?

2   There has recently been a spate of thefts (personal belongings and company equipment) from the Head Office building and in Manchester. The UK Comlon Research Laboratory is in a central position, making it particularly vulnerable to intruders.

    (a) What steps might the company take to reduce the risk of intruders into the company premises?

                                                            (10 marks)

    (b) What precautions should be taken to ensure the safety of personal belongings and of equipment?

                                                             (8 marks)

3   Mr P S Jordan frequently travels from the Manchester office of Comlon International plc to the Research Laboratory in Geneva at very short notice. All bookings are made direct rather than through a travel agent. Prepare a checklist of arrangements to be made for any visit.

4   Comlon International plc has an in-house training facility which runs courses for staff on a wide range of subjects. You attend a course on 'Effective Speaking' to deal with any problems which may arise during the course of the programme. Explain briefly how you would deal with the following:

    (a) a delegate fails to arrive

                                                             (5 marks)

    (b) on arrival, a delegate informs you of a specific dietary requirement – the centre was not notified at the time of the booking

                                                             (4 marks)

    (c) an outside speaker complains about the standard of overnight accommodation – the room allocated is small, cold and noisy

                                                             (5 marks)

    (d) a speaker informs you that an expensive item of centre equipment has been accidently broken during a lecture.

                                                             (4 marks)

5   Mr Brady suggested that, as part of the internal training programme for secretarial and clerical staff, a half-day course on the correct and most efficient use of the telephone should be provided. The Board approved Mr Brady's suggestion and Mrs Grey has asked Mr Brady to work on the programme with her.

Write a memo to Mrs S D Grey from Mr Brady, setting out in detail the parts you would expect to be included in the course.

6   Comlon International plc uses computers for a wide variety of applications in its offices, the major ones being –

Ledger work
Personnel records
Payroll calculations
Stock records.

(a) Give **3** advantages and **3** disadvantages of using computerised systems in a company of this size

(b) Give **3** ways in which computers can be used for the maintenance of personnel records

(c) What information would be required by the computer to process payroll calculations?

7   You are responsible for the paperwork of the monthly departmental liaison meeting.

Describe your follow-up procedures between meetings.

8   (a) With reference to the organisation chart of Comlon International plc, identify which documents will be dealt with by the Marketing and the Sales Departments.

(8 marks)

(b) Briefly outline the procedure which should be followed when payment is received from a customer.

(10 marks)

OVER

The Personnel Director has decided to present an Induction Course in September specifically tailored to the needs of people obtaining full-time employment for the first time. Participants will be drawn from all departments across the organisation.

It is anticipated that the programme will be on general employment matters and company organisation and business.

Detail the points you would expect to be covered in each part of the programme. (The parts need not necessarily be equal).

10 The following advertisement has been placed in several national daily papers:

"The Marketing Director of this well-known International Company requires a Secretary/PA. Good shorthand/typing speeds (100/50), and the ability to work on own initiative essential. Please apply with cv and accompanying letter to the Personnel Director, Comlon International plc."

(a) What items should be included in a curriculum vitae?

(b) Briefly explain what you would expect to see in an accompanying letter.

(c) What criteria would the Personnel Department use to select suitable candidates for interview?

INDEX